Evidence-Based
Public Management

Evidence-Based Public Management

Practices, Issues, and Prospects

Edited by

Anna Shillabeer

Terry F. Buss

Denise M. Rousseau

Routledge
Taylor & Francis Group

LONDON AND NEW YORK

Anna Shillabeer dedicates this book to her three sons, Callan, Declan, and Aydan.

Terry Buss dedicates this book to Thuy, Dan and Janet, Steve and Mary Ann,
Sandy and Bill, Anna and Bronte, and Gwyneth and Laura.

First published 2011 by M.E. Sharpe

Published 2015 by Routledge
2 Park Square, Milton Park, Abingdon, Oxon OX14 4RN
711 Third Avenue, New York, NY 10017, USA

Routledge is an imprint of the Taylor & Francis Group, an informa business

Library of Congress Cataloging-in-Publication Data

Evidence-based public management : practices, issues, and prospects / edited by
Anna Shillabeer, Terry F. Buss, and Denise M. Rousseau.
    p. cm.
  Includes bibliographical references and index.
  ISBN 978–0-7656–2420–8 (hardcover : alk. paper)—ISBN 978–0-7656–2422–2 (pbk. : alk. paper)
1. Public administration—Decision making. I. Shillabeer, Anna, 1970– II. Buss, Terry F.
III. Rousseau, Denise M.

JF1525.D4E94 2011
352.3′3—dc22   2010040047

ISBN 13: 9780765624222 (pbk)
ISBN 13: 9780765624208 (hbk)

Contents

Part II. Evidence-Based Public Management

Part III. Applications and Research

Part IV. Future Directions

Foreword

Geoff Mulgan

This is a good moment to publish a collection on evidence-based management. In the United States, federal government is returning to a much greater interest in what works. In China, policy makers are looking for hard data in a system where it has been largely absent, and many other national governments are becoming more interested in formal evaluations. The World Bank has programs such as the Global Partnership on Output-Based Aid to tie money to evidence, while the World Health Organization promotes evidence-based health care and, beyond it, programs to promote "health in all policies," drawing on the evidence showing just how much health comes from factors beyond the control of health services. Meanwhile, among the public, one effect of growing numbers passing through higher education is that there is an extraordinary hunger for explanation, whether to make sense of what worked and what did not work in economic policy or in relation to public health.

These all explain the burgeoning interest in the different forms of evidence-based activity, from evidence-based practice (which is generally associated with the professions), to evidence-based policy (generally meaning governments) and evidence-based management (which could potentially cover much of the daily work of guiding organizations to achieve better results).

But as this book adroitly demonstrates, these different activities are rarely straightforward. Many of the dilemmas posed by different kinds of knowledge are not in themselves new. Decision makers, at least some of them, have throughout history wanted to base their decisions on knowledge and evidence. Builders of irrigation systems and city walls, monetary systems and public health, have always wanted to rely on more than guesswork or anecdote. Yet all have struggled with the ambiguities of knowledge, the risks of relying on authoritative experts whose knowledge might turn out to be obsolete or the peril of finding that what works in one place may not in another. Although the sheer volume of formal evidence available to governments puts us in a quite different context, dilemmas set out in this book are not so different.

For all that, however, we probably have a clearer ideal of evidence-based activity than did any previous generation. First there is the accumulation of insight and evidence from social scientists, studying patterns, correlations, and causes. Then a policy or practice is designed, and piloted, with a randomized control trial to judge whether it really works. Then over time the policy or program is extended, with continuous improvement and testing on the margins, with managers and decision makers scrupulously supporting whatever has the strongest evidence behind it.

This ideal, derived in part from medicine, is inherently appealing for many. It appears to dissolve away the confusions of ideology and assumption, turning the blunt incompetence of much government into something more like surgical precision. Fortunately, too, there are indeed examples of this kind of evidence-based policy, including some labor-market policies and some policies for research and development and for supporting children or managing environments.

But each of the words *evidence* and *based* turns out to be somewhat less reliable than might be assumed. President Obama's former economic adviser, Larry Summers, once said that the laws of economics are universal. But in fact all social knowledge, including economics, turns out to be contextual, or at least limited in its applicability across time and space. Indeed it is hard to think of a single "law" in social science (even such apparently firm laws as the one that says demand falls when prices rise turns out to have counterexamples). Part of the reason is of course that all human knowledge is reflexive: any new knowledge becomes part of the environment it is trying to understand. So even the most perfectly judged intervention, which works well for a time, may before long become obsolete.

Then there is the question of what counts as evidence. Randomized control trials are generally seen as the gold standard for evidence. They certainly bring rigor and clarity, and they have helped to solidify knowledge on issues ranging from lung cancer to food and life expectancy to parenting programs and mental health. But they are not a panacea. Some randomized control trials have subsequently been overturned, including some that have been very influential in policy making. A recent survey from the medical field looking at what counts as evidence provided a useful warning to people working in other fields who look to medicine as the pinnacle of certainty. It showed many examples of apparently solid evidence that had been subsequently challenged or overturned, and its main conclusion was that it is wise to say that x causes y only when research findings coming from very different angles and using very different methods all point in the same direction.[1]

This question also opens up what kinds of evidence matter to making policy. If you sit within a government, it is striking how many different kinds of knowledge are in contention. There is policy knowledge, for example, on what works in reducing re-offending. There is statistical knowledge, for example, on migration flows; scientific knowledge, for example, on genetically modified crops; but there is also professional knowledge, for example, what is believed by doctors or teachers; knowledge about public opinion, for example, from quantitative and qualitative polling; practitioner views, for example, what the police think about organized crime, or what senior managers have to come to believe about how to make services more efficient. There is political knowledge, for example, a balance of opinion in a ruling party; economic knowledge, for example, about which sectors will grow or contract; classic intelligence, for example, on the intentions of terrorists' networks; and performance knowledge on operations, for example, survival rates in hospitals.

What is striking about this list is that there is no obvious hierarchy, in terms of reliability or authority. We might like to believe that meta-analyses must obviously trump any other kind of knowledge. But this is not always the case. Indeed there are few if any fields where meta-analyses can be definitive. They will often provide invaluable insights (for example, meta-reviews of education practice by John Hattie, at the University of Auckland, show that class size rarely matters, or that two computers per child is better for learning than one). But it would be a very brave politician or official who based their policies solely on these findings.

Another striking feature of the daily practice of evidence is that in many governments, each type of knowledge has its own experts, interpreters, and professionals with quite different conceptions of what counts as evidence. Some are better than others at making their knowledge usable (an issue explored by Roberto Cavazos and David Cavazos in Chapter 3, and by Alan Lyles in Chapter 5). But several decades of research on how knowledge comes to be used in governments shows that the power of evidence and force of logic are not enough to overcome cognitive barriers that make some professions or groups simply see the world in a different way from others. Managers working with strong professions learn this early, and learn too how to translate findings and ideas into the very different languages that function in the different parts of, for example, a health system or infrastructure.

There is now a much greater supply of evidence, even if the arguments about its quality are unlikely to be resolved soon. But what of demand? There are some background conditions that are probably essential for evidence to be wanted and then used. They may include the dominance of political leaders who care or understand about evidence. Creationist leaders, or for that matter leaders who are convinced of their own powers of intuition, are unlikely to promote an evidence-based culture. Pragmatism probably helps too, and the relative power within the system of people who are concerned about real results as opposed to appearance. Any government that is dominated by a figure like Karl Rove (George Bush's very influential political adviser) will see issues through a highly partisan lens; usually it will be hard for evidence to fight its way through.

Governments can of course design devices to strengthen demand as well as supply. The U.S. Program Assessment Rating Tool should have institutionalized greater rigor. But as several chapters here point out, it wasn't sufficiently tied in to budget allocations. Regular strategic audits can bring out into the open benchmarks and performance data, as can periodic reviews by international bodies such as the Organization for Economic Cooperation and Development (for example, through the Program for International Student Assessment studies on education) or the European Union's open coordination of economic policy. Budget allocation processes that overtly draw on evidence about what is and is not working (of the kind Nancy J. Kingsbury, Nancy Donovan, Judith A. Droitcour, and Stephanie L.

Shipman describe for the GAO in Chapter 10) should help to instill a different climate of decision making.

But all of these methods will compete with other pressures and with other powerful interests who will work hard to obscure or counter evidence, from talk radio to lobbying by powerful professions.

Other measures can also help in normalizing the use of evidence, including fairly basic principles of knowledge management, like having lessons-learned reviews at the end of projects, directories of individuals with useful experience, and directories of knowledge, which you might think would exist in any government. Unfortunately these are generally lacking within governments, with the result that governments rarely know what they need to know, and even if they do know what they need to know, they don't know that they know it. The more sophisticated models (such as the one in South Australia described by Denise de Vries in Chapter 14) are even rarer.

If we did have them in place, new issues would then come into sharper relief. One is that it would then be necessary to address more systematically the epistemological state of the fields being discussed. Not all fields are equal when it comes to evidence. First, there are some fields where knowledge is quite settled, where the theoretical foundations are strong, governments roughly know what works, there is a strong evidence base, and most new knowledge is incremental. In these cases, pilots can be designed to fill in the gaps, and the field is closer to a normal science. Some of macroeconomics, labor-market policy, and perhaps curative and some preventive health are in that category, and the professional bodies and leading experts can be relied on to give good advice. Benchmarking is straightforward.

A second category of fields is very different. In these fields, knowledge is in flux. There are arguments about what is known, about what categories or theories are relevant. There may be islands of consensus, but they are surrounded by seas of contention. I fear much of education falls in this space, as does environmental policy, crime, or the organization of public services, where the evidence is patchy, better at showing things not working than being able to provide the basis for deductively designing policy. In some cases, the professions in these fields can be as much part of the problem as the solution. Expert views may be consistently wrong. Therefore, any government needs to be open to the heterodox, to the critics as well as to the orthodoxies.

Third, there are inherently novel fields, in which the very newness means almost by definition that there cannot be a strong evidence base. These fields would include the regulation of biotechnology, e-government, privacy on the Internet, new forms of governance whether European or global, and to a degree climate change. Amazing work has been done by the Intergovernmental Panel on Climate Change and I think good work by the UK government's stern review on the economic dimensions of climate change. But no one can possibly know how reliable these forecasts are. In these sorts of virgin territories (and we might also include widespread obesity here), it is inevitable that the pioneers will make many mistakes and that one requires a speed of reaction to new knowledge, which is quite different from the practice in the settled fields. As organizational theorist Karl Weick once wrote, in the truly novel situation the only thing one can do is act, and it is only through acting that you create new knowledge, a point that also comes through in the chapters by Joshua Earl (Chapter 6), and Aaron Osterby and Robert Hanson (Chapter 7).

All of us live and swim now in a world of easily accessible global data. Google and its equivalents have done as much for evidence-based practice and evidence-based management as any other single factor. But the question of what actually does allow a policy or practice to be replicable becomes even more acute in this context of easy information. Things like airport design or information technology systems management clearly are quite easily spread from country to country, but the closer you come to the fine grain of family life, the world of civil society and culture, the less easy it is to replicate. Indeed adoption of ideas is more likely to be a version of cutting and grafting than to be one of replicating or copying. This point often gets lost, not least when advocates point to a single pilot for an idea in a single country and conclude that the idea has been proven (at the moment the development field may be most at risk of this, having swung from an excessive emphasis on context to an equally excessive faith that solutions can be universal).

There may also be fields where practical knowledge is ahead of formal, codified knowledge. Keynesianism is sometimes presented as issuing from the theories of John Maynard Keynes, but in fact practical Keynesianism was put into effect in Scandinavia and New Zealand independently of Keynesianism as a theory, and ahead of Keynes's writing of the general theory. There are many fields where the knowledge and the heads of practitioners may be superior to the formal knowledge of evidence, and in these cases the responsibility of the researchers and academics is to learn rather than to teach.

All of these types of knowledge contend with one another, it is hoped with smarter clients (and smarter managers) to judge their competing claims. Ironically, the rise of evidence-based policy making has coincided with the emergence of an environment in which many more people and voices can claim authority and build up reputations, particularly on the Web, sometimes without the backing of the formal academic hierarchies. They may be newspaper columnists who act as the de facto gatekeepers for the use of scientific knowledge in government. They may have influential blogs. But it is their interaction with formal knowledge that in fact drives knowledge forward.

This has become very visible in monetary policy. In the United Kingdom, making transparent the deliberations of the monetary policy committee of the Bank of England was an important shift toward a much more open government. The committee's arguments are now made public, but also contested by columnists and bloggers, in the often feverish contest to make sense of a shifting economy. The net result is probably a better informed economic system, but the formal structures work better because they are being scrutinized and challenged by informal ones, in what is at root a contest for authority as well as understanding.

Here we come to another set of limits. In a democracy, the people and the politicians who represent them have every right to ignore the evidence and won't always be wrong to do so. You don't need much knowledge of the history of the last century to know how often highly authoritative expert opinion was wrong on really important issues (and not just in monetary policy). Nor is the public always wrong to question the apparent facts. One example is police on the beat. For as long as I can remember, criminologists have said that the worst thing you could do with public money to cut crime is to spend it on police officers walking the streets. But any conversation with members of the public, certainly around Britain or the United States, confirmed that that is what they wanted to make them feel safe. Should politicians in that environment ignore the public and listen to the experts? I do not think it is obvious they should, and in recent years crime policy has started to take seriously the idea that fear of crime might be as important a policy goal as crime itself, in part a response to the tension between public and expert views of what matters.

Another example is climate change. In my job in the UK government, I had to oversee three successive attempts to design strategies for carbon reduction, the first in the late 1990s. Each had to show how to achieve a 60 percent carbon reduction target by 2050, and each used admirably sophisticated analytic methods, simulations, and scenario building. But each ultimately stumbled against the fact that the public, and the politicians, were not yet convinced that climate change warranted substantial sacrifices, and at that point it seemed that no amount of evidence would convince them.

All evidence is by its nature about the past, whereas all action is about the future. This is why knowledge can only ever guide us: it can't command us. Managers and decision makers cannot do their jobs well without evidence, and ultimately they are let down if they make do with policy-based evidence (or for that matter management-based evidence). But those providing the evidence need to be humble too, and to acknowledge its limitations. This very useful and timely book helps to define the preconditions for a constructive partnership in which public institutions show more capacity to be intelligent and less to be stupid. Let us hope so.

Note

1. "Identifying the environmental causes of disease: how should we decide what to believe and when to take action" (working group report chaired by Sir Michael Rutter CBE FRS FBA FmedSci, Academy of Medical Sciences, London, November 2007). Available at http://www.acmedsci.ac.uk/p99puid115.html.

Acknowledgments

The editors would like to thank Tim Zak, former director of the Heinz College of Carnegie Mellon University, Adelaide, Australia, for his steadfast support and funding of this project, without which this book would not have been possible. Alan Lyles deserves special accolades for his insightful comments on and review of the chapters submitted for publication. We also benefited greatly from discussions with Steve Redburn, Robert Shea, and Morgan Kinghorn, leading experts in evidence-based policy and management in the United States. Last but certainly not least, we owe a continuing debt of gratitude to Harry Briggs, executive editor at M.E. Sharpe, for his support and encouragement over the years, and to Elizabeth Granda, also at M.E. Sharpe, for keeping us up and running and on track.

Part I

Background on Evidence-Based Public Management

1

The Emerging Field of Evidence-Based Public Management

Terry F. Buss and Anna Shillabeer

> *There is nothing a politician likes so little as to be well informed;*
> *it makes decision-making so complex and difficult.*
> —John Maynard Keynes

What Is Evidence-Based Management or Public Management?

It is a simple question to ask, but a complicated one to answer. Let us start with the purpose of evidence-based approaches: to improve public management and policy making by grounding decision making in evidence. This in turn leads to three contentious questions: What is evidence; how is evidence used in practice, policy, programs, and management; and what is new (or "emerging") about the field?

Evidence

The first point of contention and confusion concerns the issue of what constitutes evidence. On one extreme are those who believe that evidence for decision making can, and in many cases should, come from any of a variety of sources—from experience and expert opinion through case studies to sophisticated experimental research—subject to some caveats, over which there is further disagreement: that evidence is of high quality, the best available, good enough, the only available, or compliant with widely accepted standards in a research, policy, or management field. At the other extreme are those who hold that only evaluations based on rigorous social science experimental research designs—either random control trials or, for some, quasi-experimental designs—can be evidence. In the middle ground between these polar opposites are those who try to classify evidentiary methods in either hierarchies or matrices, suggesting that some methods are better suited than others for answering certain questions. Finally, there are those who try to reconcile these divergent positions by suggesting that no evidentiary method is without serious flaws, and, therefore, evidence must be marshaled using a variety of methods and sources in an effort at triangulation: if multiple methods and sources point to the same conclusion, then managers and policy makers will have increased confidence in its veridicality. In the real world of management and policy making, most practitioners treat evidence as only one of several factors taken into account in decision making, the others being experience, feasibility, strategy, and politics. For practitioners, then, the question is not so much what is the best evidence, but rather what weight to give that evidence in their decision calculus. Chapter 2 lays out the controversies involving these issues.

How one views evidence is entirely a question of values and, in our view, is just as unresolvable as trying to decide which is best; chocolate or vanilla ice cream. What is clear is that disagreements about evidence trace their origins to decades-old debates in the philosophy of social sciences and about public management and policy methods. As such, it is unlikely that issues surrounding evidence-based management approaches will be resolved anytime soon. It is also likely the case that these long-standing issues raise questions in the minds of managers and decision makers who are not too keen about grounding decisions in such uncertainty.

Practice, Policy, Programs, and Management

Concerns about practice, policy, programs, and management create a second point of contention and confusion about evidence-based approaches. If one conducts a search on Amazon.com and Google, one finds that literature from all four approaches appears in the same search even after narrowing the search criteria: so the terms in use are ambiguous, overlapping, and inconsistent. Consider evidence-based practice (EBP). Much of the literature in EBP resides in the helping professions. How do social workers get the best outcomes for clients? Which treatment modalities work best for patients with chronic disease? In these contexts, practice is typically associated with management. Physicians, for example, use the phrase *patient management strategy* to lay out a treatment plan. But the concept of *practice* is also prevalent in public management. What is the best way to manage "talent" in the federal service? What steps should be taken to identify management and policy risk in public agencies? Evidence in this context means management (or practice) that complies or comports with widely accepted standards, guidance, lessons (irritating referred to as "learnings"), or best practices. Generally, they are a priori assumptions about what managers should do (Hewison 2004). They are nearly always prescriptive. These standards, and so forth, themselves are not necessarily (and likely not) derived from evidence-based studies. Chapter 8 sorts out the meaning and application of good management practice in government.

With respect to evidence-based policy (EBP)—which shares its acronym with evidence-based practice—one sees the application of every evidentiary method imaginable. Why? By *public policy* we mean a vision, goal, plan, or direction articulated by the executive, legislature, or courts that translates into *programs,* services, actions, or activities; attempts to solve a problem, make an improvement, or change a course of action; and tries to realize desired outcomes or impacts in the political arena. Public policy takes the form of legislation, regulation, executive orders, directives, and pronouncements. So, as a first cut, public policy is so broad that it legitimately employs every method in the social or policy sciences, and even the medical or hard sciences, often through metaphors and analysis.

But it is whether the focus ought to be on program performance that causes issues. Much of what government does involves assessing program performance, variously known as performance-based management and budgeting, results-based or results-oriented management, or management for results or outcomes (see Chapter 8 for a review and assessment of performance-based management and management reform in government and Chapter 16 for a modest proposal to the Obama administration to improve the federal performance management system). Evidence of good management, then, concerns the attainment of program goals against a set of quantifiable performance measures or indicators. So, a program's performance is prima facie evidence of good or bad management.

Assessing program performance is not viewed as research, and hence many would exclude it from evidence-based management or evidence-based policy approaches, preferring to reserve "evidence" to refer to rigorous program evaluation, especially that grounded in experimental or quasi-experimental research design. So, some would exclude qualitative research as evidence or even science. While a compelling case can be made for experimental research designs, that approach does not apply to much of what public managers actually do. Some critics believe that a focus on experimentation is an attempt to elevate program evaluation to the same status as that enjoyed in medical research. What is interesting about this is that the *New England Journal of Medicine*, perhaps the most prestigious journal in the world, regularly publishes case studies as evidence.

To complicate matters, some include program evaluation and performance in the same management system, requiring that both be accomplished to demonstrate program effectiveness. If this were not enough, many believe that one cannot (or should not) separate management from policy. For them, evidence-based policy and management can be used interchangeably. So, for example, discussions of evidence in public management often use EBP and even medicine to make their points. We have done so in Chapter 2! In any case, Chapter 8 attempts to sort out these conundrums.

This leaves evidence-based management (EBMgt). Evidence in management, whether in the public or private sector, concerns the need to support management decision making with sound research. The impetus for EBMgt comes from the fact that much of what constitutes good management practice is likely based on *faddism*—personal memoirs, limited case studies, rank speculation, and many textbooks and the like that purport to be the latest in good management (Watson 2009; Moss and Francis 2007; Pfeffer and Sutton 2006; Brindle and Stearns 2001). Unfortunately, when examining these resources, one soon finds they have no scientific basis in fact, most are contradictory when examined side by side, a lot have led to organizational failure, and over time advice for managers dramatically changes as one fad replaces another.

So, the field is cluttered with terms of art that really do not represent a body of knowledge where there is much consensus. The field has no common view about what management is, what good management is, what evidence is, what good evidence is, what methods ought to be used, and perhaps what it all means. Every chapter in this volume touches on these issues in one way or another. This makes EBMgt a very interesting enterprise in which to work! We believe the work is well worth doing.

Origins

A third point of contention and confusion concerns whether evidence-based approaches, especially in management, are new, emerging, or long established. Most of the commentary on evidence-based approaches suggests that use of evidence in medical research and practice is the antecedent of and the inspiration for the approach. For our purposes, modern evidence-based medicine (EBM) emerged as a field in the 1970s with the work of Archie Cochrane (1992). Cochrane advocated for and convinced the medical research community they needed to demonstrate through experimental research that their practices and treatments were efficacious: patients have a way of getting well regardless of the treatment or lack thereof. Cochrane, who passed away in 1988, was honored when his colleagues launched the Cochrane Collaboration in 1993 with this rationale: "Evidence-based medicine is the conscientious, explicit and judicious use of current best evidence in making decisions about the care of individual patients. The practice of evidence-based medicine means integrating individual clinical expertise with the best available external clinical evidence from systematic research" (http://www.cochrane.org/docs/ebm.htm).

In *Communicating Social Science Research to Policymakers* (1998), Vaughan and Buss decried the fact that policy analysts lacked a knowledge base about what works and what does not comparable to their counterparts in medical research and practice.

One irony of this fascination with EBM is that health care organizations, both public and private, have been unable to import advances in medical practice into the management of the organizations where medicine is practiced (e.g., see Chapter 13). Additionally, there is considerable disagreement about EBM as an approach in and of itself.

Although we think commentators on EBMgt are right to link its inspiration to medical practice, it is ironic that few seem to have recalled the long tradition of evidence-based activity (as broadly defined) in government. Consider just two. Aristotle, in the third century BC, served as a political adviser to Alexander the Great. Some scholars believe that Aristotle's advice helped Alexander model his empire after the Greek city-state. Where did Aristotle's knowledge come from? He conducted studies of different governance structures in various city-states, including their constitutions, to determine which features would lead to desirable political consequences. He published this in the *Politics,* perhaps the most famous policy book of all time. Machiavelli, in the fifteenth century, provided management and policy advice in the second-most famous policy book, *The Prince*, to Renaissance rulers in Florence. His methodology was to study policy decisions drawn from ancient Rome and Greece to derive lessons for his political masters. The list of contributions over time is legion and continues uninterrupted to the present.

A final point concerns whether public management needs its own acronym, perhaps EBPMgt, to be included among evidence-based medicine (EBM), practice (EBP), policy (EBP), and management (EBMgt). We vote no. As this set of acronyms illustrates, we are running out of options, and as the chapters in this book suggest, there is much commonality across these fields to suggest that EBMgt will do just fine (see especially Chapter 3).

What Are the Methods in Evidence-Based Approaches?

Contrary to what many believe, EBMgt as a method does not produce original research, but rather looks at the findings and methods of studies already completed or promulgates methodological standards to guide studies in the future (Pawson 2002). As observed, the evidence in public management comes in all shapes, sizes, and colors—case studies, expert opinion, experience, best practices, and evaluation. Strictly speaking, however, evidence-based methods concern research synthesis—looking at a body of literature or empirical studies, or both, about a particular management problem or issue to determine whether they collectively provide credible, valid, and useful information for public manager or policy maker decision making. The two research synthesis approaches are systematic review and meta-analysis (see also Chapter 10).

Systematic Review

Systematic reviews apply a rigorous methodology in assessing the literature on a policy issue (Chapters 6 and 7 offer examples of the approach, as does Chapter 10). Systematic review lends itself to assessment of any and all public management and public policy issues, from social science research through management studies and policy analysis to program performance. Analysts clearly define a management or policy problem they wish to research. Then they construct a search methodology to locate and assemble documents, publications, and data, not only from the Internet, but also in physical searches in libraries, government offices, and repositories. Studies using meta-analysis can also be included in a review. Analysts take each document (including other literature reviews) and evaluate methods and analysis used, assessing their generalizability, validity, and reliability. The most sophisticated approaches employ a panel of expert or informed reviewers who individually rate each article, then come together to reconcile their ratings. In a final step, analysts attempt to reconcile inconsistencies and contradictions in findings. Systematic reviews are then published to inform the policy process. In addition to its more rigorous, comprehensive methodologies over traditional or narrative literature reviews, the systematic review is intended to be totally transparent in how it was conducted.

Controversy swirls around systematic reviews, even though the method seems superior to other traditional assessments of the management and policy literature (see Chapter 2). Critics question whether the search strategy can ever produce global coverage of the documents and data on any given policy issues. Some government documents containing valuable policy information may not be known or searchable, for example. Other critics disagree about what kinds of studies ought to be permissible in a systematic review. These disagreements parallel those concerning evidence discussed earlier. Should qualitative and non–social science research be included in a review, or should only quantitative studies find their way into the assessment? Still others contend that because analysts control what gets included and excluded from a systematic review, the approach is value laden and potentially biased. Notwithstanding these criticisms, systematic review is infinitely to be preferred over traditional literature reviews prepared for and by government. Why? If these criticisms of systematic review are valid, then they also apply to traditional or narrative reviews, only much more so.

Meta-analysis

Meta-analysis is a sophisticated statistical technique in which data from two or more studies are combined to produce a better estimate of "treatment effect" or "effect size." In simple terms, do several program evaluations all lead to the same policy conclusion, from a statistical perspective? For example, researchers analyzed eighty-four quantitative studies to determine the impact of democracy on economic growth (Doucouliagos and Ulubasoglu 2008). This book does not include an example of meta-analysis: the approach is much too complicated to explain even in a chapter, and there are relatively few meta-analysis management studies (see Cooper 2010 for an overview of this approach; see also Kristof-Brown et al. 2005 for an example).

Because meta-analysis has such stringent analytic requirements, its application in public management studies is limited because there are relatively few studies that can meet these statistical and methodological requirements (see Bouckaert and Halligan 2007). Most work that has been done usually concerns programs from a policy perspective, not from a management one. There are so few studies because quantitative research that can be used in meta-analysis (especially experimental design) is expensive to conduct and therefore undertaken sparingly by government; moreover, researchers do not like to replicate studies that have already been completed: incentives and rewards in their field are not forthcoming for replication. Clearly, if EBMgt is to succeed in the public arena, the field needs to stimulate more rigorous management studies that can be subjected to meta-analysis.

Critics have roundly criticized meta-analysis, both because the studies that researchers analyze are problematic as social science and because meta-analysis has been found to be poorly executed, even in medical research. For example, meta-analysis, in an effort to place all studies under review in a common framework, tends to minimize or ignore contextual effects. If a program is evaluated in fifty states, but each state is different, then it will be difficult to derive policy conclusions. But if the fifty state differences are explained away or ignored, then, in principle, the policy implications will become clear. Studies of meta-analysis research, especially in evidence-based medicine, where they abound, are frequently found to be methodologically flawed and hence not useful to inform policy making. A takeaway from this is there is nothing likely wrong with meta-analysis in theory, but much more needs to be done to correct it in practice.

Some critics and researchers, concerned about either the quality of EBMgt research or its ability to actually stand as strong evidence in decision making, prefer to use the phrase *evidence-informed* or *fact-based* management or policy (this could add yet another set of acronyms to the ever-growing list). This convention takes nothing away from the evidence-based approach so far as we can see. Chapter 15 offers an example of a fact-based approach.

Is Evidence-Based Management Used in Government?

Use of Evidence

The answer in brief is, sometimes. Research shows mixed results. In 2004, the United Kingdom's King's Fund—a charitable foundation reviewed social programs created since 1997 to determine whether they were evidence based, as the Tony Blair government claimed (Coote, Allen, and Woodhead 2004). They found that in spite of government claims, the programs were not evidence based. Rather, programs were "designed through informed guesswork and expert hunches, enriched by some evidence and driven by political and other imperatives" (p. 3).

By contrast, some governments produce a lot of evidence but do not use it extensively in decision making. The Bush administration's Program Assessment Rating Tool (PART), used to assess the performance of more than one thousand federal programs, was perhaps the most evidence-based performance management system yet devised (see Chapters 2, 8, and 17 for an analysis and discussion of PART). Yet the evidence produced was not extensively used in budget decisions or to terminate unnecessary or poorly performing programs (Redburn, Shea, and Buss 2008).

Some agencies, however, produce a lot of evidence and use it in decision making. The Department of Education once had a bad reputation for producing studies of very poor quality, which were in effect useless. In the past ten years, after coming under intense scrutiny by Congress, the National Research Council, and other research organizations, the department has turned around its studies program and is now using it to inform policy and to some extent management (see Chapter 2).

Those interested in exploring the use of evidence-based research in decision making might consult "utilization" and "diffusion" studies (e.g., Johnson et al. 2009;

Fleischer and Christie 2009; Ginsburg and Rhett 2003; Nutley and Davies 2000). Utilization studies of evaluation research in decision making have themselves come under fire. Brandon and Singh (2009) in their study concluded that these studies had methodological issues that limited their usefulness.

Regardless of the facts about utilization of evidence to inform management and policy decision making, perceptions are quite strongly held among stakeholders in EBMgt. Many researchers complain that a lot of money is spent conducting studies that public managers and policy makers do not read or act upon. Many practitioners complain that research does not address their needs in either a management or policy context and is therefore irrelevant to them. Some researchers do not care and may even be loath to make their research accessible to practitioners, while some practitioners weigh political concerns much more strongly than evidence in decision making. The gulf between the two is wide but not endemic. Chapters 2 and 3 explore the gap between practitioners and researchers, while Chapter 12 looks at where state agencies obtain evidence. Chapter 9 reports on the extensive use of evidence at the Department of Veterans Affairs.

Most observers would likely agree that there are numerous barriers prohibiting the use of evidence in decision making, as described in the following sections.

Barriers to Use

Three factors—management, organizations, and research capacity—pose barriers for those who would like to incorporate an EBMgt function in an organization, whether in government or in academe.[1]

Management

Many perceive public managers to be barriers in EBMgt implementation, for four reasons: (1) EBMgt may threaten their autonomy and power and increase accountability, perhaps in unwanted ways; (2) depending on their training, they may have difficulty accessing and understanding evidence; (3) they face time and resource constraints—it is infeasible for policy makers to keep abreast of the latest evidence; and (4) managers are rightly suspicious of the validity of EBMgt research, and many are loath to adopt it.

Organizations

Organizations sometimes adopt EBMgt approaches without providing the support for management necessary to effectively use the evidence produced. EBMgt requires sophisticated research support to conduct studies, gather data or information, or assemble and analyze literature. This can be expensive or resource intensive. Because many organizational cultures militate against EBMgt, managers must invest heavily in organizational change initiatives to bring along recalcitrant policy makers. This also can be expensive. Finally, there are few incentives for engaging in EBMgt, while there are huge incentives in most organizations for making good decisions. So, why would effective managers undertake EBMgt if they are already being rewarded in practice?

Research Capacity

A common perception is that a great deal of academic research is theoretical, impractical, speculative, or experiential; it focuses on what not to do, rarely offering solutions, making it difficult to translate research findings into practice; and, as with any scientific evidence, there are always errors or imperfections in data. Chapter 5 offers an agenda for training graduate students in public management and policy so that they are better able to produce and utilize EBMgt studies. Additionally, there are holes in the research base, and insufficient evidence exits to inform all areas of management and policy. Some believe that EBMgt research is doomed to be a spotty patchwork of studies undertaken with differing contexts, differing methodologies, and differing quality.

Chapters 10 and 11 suggest a model to improve the capacity of government agencies to produce and utilize EBMgt.

Whither the Field?

It is much too early to tell whether EBMgt will survive in business, let alone in public management. Evidence-based policy, however, seems well established, at least in the evaluation field (as broadly defined). We believe that two relatively recent developments—knowledge management and collaboration—may further EBMgt in public management, depending on how these fare.

Knowledge Management

Knowledge management is becoming a pressing issue as more and more management and policy research is produced (see Chapters 14 and 17 for an overview of the issues). Government is awash with information, so much so that even the narrowest of topics could yield thousands of documents. How is information to be stored, maintained, updated, and retrieved? Although much has been made of knowledge management advancements in information technology, more needs to be accomplished before it adequately serves the needs of evidence-based policy. Much of the information produced is simply not accessible on the Web or elsewhere. Information that is accessible requires deviously complicated search strategies to extract it. Moreover, there is an overwhelming amount of information to sift through, much of which in the end turns out to be irrelevant or useless.

The key to effective knowledge management starts in the development stages of producing evidence, not at the dissemination stage. Much of the problem with government information is that no one thought in advance what to do with documents, so they are randomly loaded on Web sites, relegated to file cabinets, or simply lost on an analyst's hard drive. There is little or no "corporate memory" or organizational "learning." Unless government finds a way to manage knowledge better, our evidence base will be incomplete and therefore potentially biased. Chapter 17 lays out a knowledge management agenda for EBMgt, and Chapter 13 provides an example in the social services arena.

Collaborative Technology

Over the past few years, policy makers and scholars have tried to garner greater citizen input into and support of policy making, in short, citizen-centric government (Buss and Redburn 2006). The rise of collaborative technology—everything from blogging and tweeting through social networking to wiki sites—has created an explosion in the ways citizens can affect policy. Rather than fighting technology, this book argues that policy makers should embrace it as a way to improve the evidence they use to inform policy. For example, it is becoming more common for managers to post requests on a Web site for citizen input on a policy. Rather than eliciting comments, some are allowing citizens to edit documents in a wiki site. Citizens post changes to a policy document, offering new evidence or criticizing existing evidence on a policy. Then other citizens edit these comments in an iterative process until the document has several powerful variations for consideration. Following this process, citizens vote on which policy they prefer. The Obama White House has been using this technique to test out some of its policy proposals. In Chapter 6, this book makes explicit the connection between EBMgt and collaborative technology.

Road Map for the Book

Because it is widely considered to be an emerging field in public management, the book presents six chapters, in Part I, that provide background for understanding the EBMgt field. Chapter 2, by Terry Buss and Nathaniel Buss, presents four controversies in the use of the social sciences for EBMgt. The controversies show why an evidence-based approach is necessary if public managers and policy makers are to be assured that the social sciences are in fact offering the best evidence possible for decision making. At the same time, the chapter reveals why public managers and policy makers do not tend to rely very heavily on social science. In spite of the advances in EBMgt, though, the method itself is fraught with problems that must be addressed if it is to inform management and policy. The chapter offers some modest suggestions for improving the social sciences.

Chapter 3, contributed by David Cavazos and Roberto Cavazos, explores the reasons for the rift between practitioners and researchers arising out of the use, or lack thereof, of social science in decision making. Cavazos and Cavazos explain why practitioners have little use for social science and why researchers do not address practitioner research needs. They then draw on perspectives from both the public and private sectors to offer an agenda for bringing practitioners and researchers closer together in their use of research.

Chapter 4, presented by Ruth Zaplin and Don Blohowiak, ask two fundamental questions of the field: (1) What is EBMgt from a practicing manager's perspective, and is implementing it possible in today's public institutions? and (2) Assuming there is a clearly determined process for implementing a best practice or most effective action as indicated by the evidence, will such a protocol be followed? Zaplin and Blohowiak present a preferred method for managing public organizations, including a description of the conditions necessary for EBMgt practices to have the greatest potential for successful implementation.

EBMgt relies heavily on statistics and analysis in either producing or evaluating evidence to inform public management. Alan Lyles, in Chapter 5, points out that statistics and analysis are taught as a mathematical skill rather than as a management tool. As a result, many students come away able to calculate formulas but unable to translate these into decision making. Because many students tend to shy away from mathematical approaches, they are ill equipped to evaluate evidence available to inform management decisions. Lyles offers a much-needed alternative to the formula-driven approach to learning, offering instead one that focuses on learning core concepts through narrative grounded in practical applications. Lyles's chapter contributes to the debate about how to get public managers and policy makers to use evidence, and about how to get researchers to produce the kind of evidence decision makers need.

The literature review is a major tool for gathering, analyzing, and informing public managers and policy makers. In Chapter 6, Joshua Earl employs the systematic review, looking at the literature on the "management of virtual e-learning teams." Earl shows how the problem guiding the literature search is defined and lays out a literature search algorithm. Earl's chapter illustrates not only systematic review as an EBMgt approach, but also the major difficulty for most researchers in conducting a review—for the vast majority of management issues in public management, there is not a lot of good information on which to base an analysis, let alone decision making. Aaron Osterby and Robert Hanson, in Chapter 7, look at the EBMgt literature undergirding the use of information and communication technology (ICT) in organizations to illuminate reasons for ICT failure or unmet expectations. Osterby and Hanson, unlike Earl in Chapter 6, employ a more traditional literature review methodology, looking closely at the use of evidence in ICT. Both chapters, then, show how evidence is marshaled for EBMgt.

In Part II, contributors explore the meaning and uses of EBMgt in government. Buss, Buss, and Hill, in Chapter 8, present an overview of EBMgt initiatives in five countries—the United Kingdom, Australia, Canada, New Zealand, and the United States. The authors show that in government, EBMgt revolves around three separate but related approaches: performance-based management—evidence of effective management as attaining good performance against a set of goals and performance measures; good management practices—evidence of good management as compliance with standards and guidelines for management; and performance, management, and budgeting integration—evidence drawn from performance and management and integrated with budget decision making. They show that rather than being a new approach, evidence-based performance and management systems have been in use for nearly a hundred years. The authors argue that these systems should focus on performance rather than on management and strategic management. The chapter sets the stage for the next two chapters, which show how policy makers apply EBMgt in the Department of Veterans Affairs and in the Government Accountability Office, two forward-thinking organizations in the field.

Chapter 9, prepared by the National Academy of Public Administration (NAPA), presents a study done at the Department of Veterans Affairs (VA) in two of its branches—Veterans Benefit Administration (VBA) and Veterans Health Administration (VHA). The VA is arguably a department where EBMgt is pervasive and is credited with contributing to the VA's performance. The VA case study presents a balanced scorecard and strategy-map approaches not only as important tools for EBMgt, but also as ways to drive organizational transformation with evidence.

Nancy Kingbury, Nancy Donovan, Judith Droitcour, and Stephanie L. Shipman, in Chapter 10, report on efforts at the Government Accountability Office to build evaluation capacity in government. They argue that, often, managers lack good-quality, relevant evidence on the size and significance of a pressing problem or promising opportunity—as well as on program outcomes or the effectiveness of alternate strategies. New problems may spring up, and agencies may have difficulty developing evidence quickly, or long-standing problems may be very difficult to study. Because of a lack of good-quality evidence, a manager's consideration of what evidence exists might need to be supplemented with, for example, a risk-based approach to decision making, as well as a continuing effort to encourage or work toward evidence development.

Part III presents four chapters that analyze EBMgt in a variety of applications in public management. In Chapter 11, Kenneth Meier and Laurence O'Toole employ a grounded theory of management that generates precise predictions about what managerial techniques should affect organizations, answering the question, What works, and what does not? Meier and O'Toole apply their approach in the area of managerial capacity and program performance, drawing on their own work and that of others, as they have done in several areas of public management. Their conclusion: management matters, and matters a lot.

In Chapter 12, Edward Jennings and Jeremy Hall present the results of research on six hundred state government agencies in an effort to determine where and how they obtain and use information to guide decisions and improve program operations. Results of this research are critically important in informing the debate on the use of evidence in decision making by practitioners. Agencies differed in their use of information, but there was more use of evidence-based information than the conventional wisdom (or criticism) in EBMgt discourse would suggest.

Paul Kearns, in Chapter 13, develops the concepts of "value creation" and "common sense" as fundamental to EBMgt, then looks at their application in management at the National Health Service in the United Kingdom. Kearns concludes that EBMgt is really not new, but simply a repackaging of older ideas in management. EBMgt needs to develop a single, coherent combination of management philosophy, business strategy, and management practice if it is to succeed.

Denise de Vries, in Chapter 14, offers an example of the use of a sophisticated software tool as a way to bring together data and metadata in an EBMgt approach to improve social and health services delivery to marginalized populations in South Australia. The software allows decision makers to store, retrieve, and analyze complex data and information so that they can be converted into knowledge. Specifically, the system allows for case management functions, highlights what works and why, and allows allocation and scheduling of resources.

Part IV looks at EBMgt as it might evolve in the future in three very different public management fields: presidential fact-based decision making, reengineered performance-based management, and development of knowledge management systems. John Kamensky, in Chapter 15, points out that much of the performance-based management undertaken in government is at the program level, but many problems go well beyond the capacity of programs to address them. In short, there are national issues that must be attended to. Neither the Barack Obama administration, nor the George Bush administration, is or was equipped to deal with these broader challenges. Kamensky proposes a model that might address this void, employing a system designed to identify and monitor challenges in a fact-based, evidentiary approach.

Kathryn Newcomer and Steve Redburn, in Chapter 16, look closely at the Bush administration's performance, management, and budget system to extract lessons learned there that might be of interest to the Obama administration. The authors conclude that a successful system must: (1) be a high priority, (2) involve leadership by the Office of Management and Budget and department heads, (3) focus on programs of high priority, (4) promote transparency and high standards, and (5) reduce analytical and data-gathering burdens on agencies.

Anna Shillabeer, in Chapter 17, addresses the emerging issue of knowledge management (KM) in EBMgt, asking two questions: How can KM facilitate the provision of evidence to augment management and policy making? and, What is the state of play for KM implementation within public management? Shillabeer answers these in a discussion of knowledge as evidence, providing in the process an overview of the advantages and issues in implementing KM in public management.

Note

1. This section was abstracted from Durst, Dodd, and Buss (2009).

References

Bouckaert, G., and J. Halligan. 2007. *Managing Performance.* London: Routledge.
Bovaird, Tony, and Ken, Russel. 2007. "Civil service reform in the UK, 1999–2005: Revolutionary failure or evolutionary success?" *Public Administration* 85 (2): 301–328.

Brandon, Paul R., and J. Malkeet Singh. 2009. "The Strength of the Methodological War-rants for the Findings of Research on Program Evaluation Use." *American Journal of Evaluation* 30 (3): 123–157.

Brindle, Margaret C., and Peter N. Stearns. 2001. *Facing Up to Management Faddism.* New York: Praeger.

Buss, Terry F., and F. Stevens Redburn. 2006. *Modernizing Democracy: Innovations in Citizen Participation.* Armonk, NY: M.E. Sharpe.

Cochrane, Archie. 1992. *Effectiveness and Efficiency.* London: Nuffield Provincial Hospitals Trust. www.cochrane.org/docs/archieco.htm (accessed November 1, 2009).

Cooper, Harris. 2010. *Research Synthesis and Meta-Analysis.* 4th Edition. Thousand Oaks, CA: Sage.

Coote, Anna, Jessica Allen, and David Woodhead. 2004. *Finding Out What Works.* London: King's Fund.

Doucouliagos, Hristos, and Mehmet Ali Ulubasoglu. 2008. "Democracy and Economic Growth: A Meta-Analysis." *American Journal of Political Science* 52 (1): 61–83.

Durst, Adam, Tracy Dodd, and Terry Buss. 2009. "Evidence-Based Management." *Ency-clopedia of Public Administration and Policy.* New York: Marcel Dekker.

Fleischer, Dreolin, and Christina Christie. 2009. "Evaluation Use: Results from a Survey of U.S. American Evaluation Association Members." *American Journal of Evaluation* 30 (3): 158–175.

Ginsburg, Alan, and Nancy Rhett. 2003. "Building a Better Body of Evidence: New Op-portunities to Strengthen Evaluation Utilization." *American Journal of Evaluation* 24 (4): 489–498.

Hewison, Alitstair. 2004. "EBMgt in the NHS: Is It Possible?" *Journal of Health Organiza-tion and Management* 18 (5): 336–348.

Johnson, Kelli, et al. 2009. "Research on Evaluation Use: A Review of the Empirical Lit-erature from 1986 to 2005." *American Journal of Evaluation* 30 (3): 377–410.

Kristof-Brown, A.L., et al. 2005. "Job Demands Abilities Preferred over Public Service Dedication." *Personnel Psychology* 58 (2): 281–320.

Moss, Simon, and Ronald Francis. 2007. *The Science of Management: Fighting Fads and Fallacies with Evidence-Based Practice.* Queensland: Australia Academic Press.

Nutley, Sandra, and Huw T.O. Davies. 2000. "Making a Reality of Evidence-Based Prac-tice: Some Lessons from the Diffusion of Innovations." *Public Money and Management* (October–December): 35–42.

Pawson, Ray. 2002. "Evidence-Based Policy: In Search of a Method." *Evaluation* 8 (2): 157–181.

Pfeffer, Jeffrey, and Robert Sutton. 2006. *Hard Facts, Dangerous Half Truths and Total Nonsense: Profiting from Evidence-Based Management.* Cambridge, MA: Harvard Business School Press.

Redburn, F. Stevens, Robert Shea, and Terry F. Buss, eds. 2008. *Performance Management and Budgeting: How Governments Can Learn from Experience.* Armonk, NY: M.E. Sharpe.

Vaughan, Roger J., and Terry F. Buss. 1998. *Communicating Social Science Research to Policymakers.* Thousand Oaks, CA: Sage.

Watson, Don. 2009. *Bendable Learnings: The Wisdom of Modern Management.* Sydney, Australia: Random House.

2

Four Controversies in Evidence-Based Public Management

Terry F. Buss and Nathaniel J. Buss

There seems to be no study too fragmented, no hypothesis too trivial, no literature citation too biased or too egotistical, no design too warped, no methodology too bungled, no presentation of results too inaccurate, too obscure and too contradictory, no analysis too self-serving, no argument too circular, no conclusions too trifling or too unjustified, and no grammar and syntax too offensive for a paper to end up in print.
—Drummond Rennie, deputy editor,
Journal of the American Medical Association (1996)

Methodological issues undergirding the social sciences (and hard sciences for that matter) are one key factor explaining why public managers do not in many cases use this research in decision or policy making; if they do rely on it, critics believe they do so at their own peril. Methods of evidence-based management (EBMgt), and its cousin evidence-based policy (EBP), attempt to eliminate from consideration poorly done research and focus on the implications of the remaining high-quality research to improve public decision making. However, because it relies so heavily on problematic social science studies, EBMgt is subject not only to the criticisms leveled against these studies, but also to attacks on its own methodological underpinnings (Hansen and Rieper 2009). Before public managers and researchers place too much credence in EBMgt approaches as the silver bullet in improving public decision making, they must understand some basic issues in the social sciences that these approaches, at least in principle, attempt to solve.[1]

There is much more than a cottage industry dedicated to analysis, commentary, and criticism about the philosophy and methods of the social sciences, especially in the fields of public management and policy (Root 1993; Winch 2007).[2] We have selected four controversies plaguing the field:

- Experimental design as the gold standard of evaluation research
- Qualitative research as inferior to quantitative research methods
- Social science journals as a problematic source of policy evidence
- Unpublished studies as inferior to published studies

As observed in Chapter 1, because EBMgt is an emerging field, it has yet to amass a substantial body of research for assessment, in contrast to public policy, the hard sciences, and medicine. We have no reason to suspect that as it emerges, EBMgt will be markedly different from these three fields. So, we have looked at social science studies, and to a certain extent medicine, to identify issues that will likely plague EBMgt as it evolves. Because the approach is emerging, there is an opportunity to avoid some of the mistakes of other methods.

Controversy 1. Experimental Design as the Gold Standard

A canon of the social sciences is that researchers are obligated to employ the most appropriate and rigorous scientific methods available to address a policy question—or any research question—and in turn utilize them in practice (Kaplan 1998). This canon imposes a hierarchy wherein some evaluation methods are more or less preferred than others, at least to answer some policy questions. What constitutes the best evidence to inform public management is at the center of controversies about and prospects for EBMgt approaches as management tools.

The Methodological Hierarchy

Quantitative methods traditionally have been arrayed in this (or a similar) hierarchy (Concato, Shah, and Horwits 2000; Hansen and Rieper 2009), ranging from most to least preferred:

Randomized Controlled Trials

The randomized controlled trial (RCT) is an evaluation research design that measures a treatment's (program's, intervention's, test's, etc.) effect by randomly assigning cases (people, clients, patients, groups, units, organizations, etc.) to a group that will receive the treatment (*treatment* group) and to another that will not (*control* group). The simplest RCT design is reflected in Table 2.1 using standard notation (Ryan 2007). An example: the Manpower Demonstration Research Corporation researchers, interested in determining whether a training program (intended to improve the chances participants will obtain a job) succeeded, randomly assigned low-income people to a group that was to be trained and another that was not to be trained. At the completion of the program, researchers observed whether those in the training program performed better in the job market than those who had not received training (Hamilton 2002; Center for Education Policy 2009).

Direct Controlled Trials

The direct controlled trial is an evaluation design wherein external factors that may influence results of an evaluation are controlled (eliminated, removed, canceled

Table 2.1

Classic Experimental Design

Study group	Measurement before program	Exposure to program	Measurement after program
Treatment (R)	O_1	X	O_3
Control (R)	O_2		O_4

Note: R, random assignment to groups; O, difference observations for each group at different times; X, participation in a program (or receiving a treatment).

out, or accounted for) so that the impact of the factors—including interactions—under study can be observed. Researchers can experimentally manipulate these factors prospectively. Such trials are most commonly found in technology fields. For example, when the Environmental Protection Agency (EPA) wants to learn how best to plan for a response to a chemical spill, it will create a series of spills that are identical except for key factors expected to impact a spill. By controlling these factors, the EPA can determine what procedures work best in response. The EPA then applies chemical analysis and statistics to determine probabilities for successful management of the problem.

Quasi-Experimental Design

Quasi-experimental designs are similar to RCTs except that cases are not randomly assigned to treatment and control groups and often entail retrospective analysis. For example, Abt Associates looked at the recidivism rates for criminal offenders processed through drug courts in local jurisdictions in Florida and Missouri. In one group, the control, were offenders who were processed before the advent of the drug court option; two other groups were processed in drug courts: one that received treatment and another that had not. The three groups were then compared (Abt Associates 2002).

Nonexperimental Direct Analysis

Nonexperimental direct analysis is an evaluation design in which researchers examine cases in a group that have received a treatment but do not create a control group for comparison. For example, in one study, the Urban Institute employed a longitudinal study to determine the effects of high school employment on future employment of high school graduates over a twelve-year period (Chaplin and Hannaway 1996).

Nonexperimental Indirect Analysis

When only scant or preliminary data or information exist, a scientific study is not possible. Nonetheless, policy decisions often need to be informed even if only through examining preliminary data or information. For example, the Department of Homeland Security's Assistance to Firefighters Grant Program lacked the time and resources to conduct a scientific study of the factors that would impact local communities receiving funding. As an alternative, Homeland Security asked the National Academy of Public Administration (NAPA) to create a panel of experts drawn from professional associations in the firefighting community and employed a formal group process to elicit their opinions on how to reconfigure the fire grants program (NAPA 2008) (see section on panel studies later in this chapter). Qualitative methods, discussed later in this chapter, dominate this design.

Methodological Controversies

> The test of all knowledge is experiment. Experiment is the sole judge of scientific truth.—Richard Feynman, *Lectures in Physics*[3]

Many researchers and public managers consider RCTs to be the gold standard in evaluation research (Office of Management and Budget 2004; Treasury Board of Canada Secretariat 1998). Still others would add quasi-experimental designs along with RCTs as a preferred source of evidence. RCT research is controversial in evidence-based research. The controversy epitomized by standards or policies reflecting the methodological hierarchy revolves around at least four issues (for purposes here):

- Is RCT even applicable to large numbers of federal programs?
- Can other research designs serve as substitutes or alternatives to RCT? If they can, are there standards that these designs must attain to be acceptable?
- Is RCT appropriate for much of evaluation research?
- Are RCTs themselves rigorous enough to inform the policy process?

RCT Is Limited in Application in the Policy Arena

Some researchers reject any evaluation design except RCT because each of the other design alternatives has, in their view, the potential to produce misleading or biased findings as a result of design features.[4] There is a strong *philosophical* or methodological case to be made for employing RCTs in only some forms of evaluation, especially concerning programs (Campbell and Stanley 1963). Unfortunately, even if we stipulate that RCT is the only suitable design (National Research Council 2008), the trials are difficult to execute and not considered especially viable for the following reasons:[5]

- *Timing.* They take too long to design and execute, thus, RCTs may be of little use in the policy process, which tends to move at a different and much faster pace.

- *Funding.* Although public programs themselves can be well funded, RCT experiments are generally perceived by many as cost prohibitive.
- *Obtrusiveness.* RCTs tend to be too disruptive of programs and their clients, eliciting resistance from program managers.
- *Ethics.* RCTs, by definition, deny some people services or benefits (control group) but reward others (treatment group), making them politically controversial.
- *Design.* Study designs are often overlooked when a program is mandated or scheduled for evaluation; then it is too late to incorporate RCTs into the evaluation design.
- *Access.* Even when an evaluation has been approved and funded, program managers may be difficult to work with because of time constraints, availability, or resistance.

Perhaps the most crucial implication of RCT is that the research gets funded and completed based on policy priorities of an administration or Congress. This means there are evaluations undertaken for public programs, but these may not be of much interest for evaluation researchers who would like to study something else.

In any case, lacking the possibility of undertaking high-end evaluations, some researchers and critics bemoan the need to use nonexperimental, qualitative methods and nonscientific methods. For some, this attitude only perpetuates contention among researchers (Yin 2002) and raises doubts in public managers' minds about the utility of social science research.

Many Research Designs Can Produce Policy-Relevant Information

Some believe that a better stance on the RCT gold-standard issue was articulated by Judith Gueron, one of the leading evaluation experts in the country, as follows: "I do not think that random assignment is a panacea or that it can address all the critical policy questions, or substitute for other types of analysis, or is always appropriate" (Gueron 2000). Many researchers likely agree (Patton 2004). The Institute of Medicine questioned whether, with the limited circumstances under which RCT could be employed, the method should be abandoned as the gold standard in evaluation research (Olsen, Aisner, and McGinnis 2007).

The real issue with research design selection is how much potential uncertainty, bias, and ambiguity are tolerable in studies informing public management if the best design cannot be executed or if several designs are possibilities. Consider President George W. Bush's PART program, arguably the most advanced performance-based management system in any government (Redburn, Shea, and Buss 2008), though some might disagree (Radin 2006, 2008). It indirectly makes the case for flexibility in choosing methods for evaluation. PART, as discussed in Chapter 8, required all federal government programs to provide evidence of their effectiveness by undertaking and reporting evaluations. The RCT was the preferred method in guidance provided to agencies (Office of Management and Budget 2004). After six years in practice, few programs were able to undertake such an evaluation: their program designs were inappropriate, their resources and funding inadequate, their time horizons insufficient, and their political will lacking. The Bush administration backed off the gold-standard requirement and allowed much "softer" forms of evidence to serve as indicators of program effectiveness (Heinrich 2007).

The Diversity of Policy Problems Requires a Diversity of Methods

Some of the controversy about RCTs is based on a general discussion about their desirability rather than on their appropriateness. Evaluation research in government is multifaceted, not focused just on RCT designs, and most has nothing to do with RCTs, which, as noted, usually are executed in a limited way on public programs (Brass, Nunez-Neto, and Williams 2006): performance management, results management; customer satisfaction; cost-benefit analysis, cost estimates; business process reengineering; feasibility studies; implementation; policy analysis and evaluation; management studies; and impact studies (see also Chapter 8). The chief social science researcher in the British government opines, "Social experiments are never, or should never, be used as the sole source of evidence in evaluating a program or policy. Experiments need to be conducted alongside a thorough process study, which explicitly seeks to understand the context and causal processes being evaluated" (Government Social Research Unit 2007).

Some evaluation researchers see these studies as inferior, at least as compared to having opportunities to undertake RCT research. Many would like to elevate evaluation research to the same status as experimental research in the hard sciences and medicine (Kushner 2005). However, many evaluation researchers understand that most evaluation is done outside an experimental context and is thus legitimate in its own right.

RCT Has Its Own Methodological Problems

When speaking about the gold standard, some think research produced from it must be of high quality. This unfortunately is not the case (Staley 2008; Clark 2004; Steinberg and Luce 2005; Trochim 2001). Two issues—sample size and outcome measures—are especially problematic and plague the approach; there are numerous others. According to Chatterji (2007), "small sample sizes constrain confident use of particular statistical tests and raise issues about sample representativeness and generalizability of results." This is also referred to as *size effects* and *power analysis*. Also, "to be sensitive to the intervention, the selected outcome measures must have substantive links to it, as well as other relevant psychometric properties, such as reliability" (p. 248; see also Hansen and Rieper 2009). Outcome measures frequently do not do this. The size effects issue is being slowly (and painfully) addressed by professional journals trying to require researchers to include size-effects analyses in their articles as a condition for submission and publication. Some journals, especially in psychology, now require size-analysis reports in the articles they publish (Kline 2004; Charles 2009).

One startling conclusion from Charles's analysis is that a very high percentage of studies published before the advent of the widespread use of power analysis are likely invalid. They do not have sufficient sample size and sample characteristics to support their conclusions. This becomes a major problem for evidence-based medicine (EBM) approaches, which rely on statistical power. It is unlikely that this assertion could ever be tested in the literature, because the necessary statistical information is not reported in most publications.

Controversy 2. The Quality of Qualitative Methods

Qualitative methods are many and varied.[6] We have chosen three that are commonly employed in the social sciences and that are perhaps among the most controversial and interesting: expert opinion or expert panels, policy academies, and case studies.

Few would disagree with this proposition: by definition, qualitative research designs and methods are unable to control the assignment (random or otherwise) of cases into treatment and control groups and cannot control for external factors that confound results. Qualitative research is unable to sort out cause and effect, is not generalizable, and is heavily context dependent. So, the question is not whether qualitative methods can compete with quantitative ones, but rather how they can be used to inform the policy process and other quantitative research. Alternatively, can they be of value in and of themselves (see Gerring 2001; Cressell 2008; Ragin 1989)? Also, is poor quality to blame for the bad reputation these methods have?

Qualitative Methods Are Important in Informing Policy

Again, as was the case with RCTs, at one extreme are those critics who believe that qualitative methods are not worth employing in the policy arena—they are too problematic as evidence for public managers (Greene and Henry 2005). The U.S. Department of Education, for example, suggests that "RCTs generate strong evidence of what works; *all other designs yield meaningless or largely untrustworthy data on impact questions*" (Chatterji 2007, p. 240; emphasis added). The Department of Education goes on to assert that RCT designs are to be given priority over other research designs for program evaluation (U.S. Department of Education 2005; Brass, Nunez-Neto, and Williams 2006). The Coalition for Evidence-Based Policy echoes this view (2002).

For many, this narrow view overlooks the positive contributions qualitative methods can make, and denies public managers an entire body of informative evidence. Solid qualitative research can

- suggest alternative interpretations of data,
- offer new hypotheses for testing,
- supplement quantitative data with greater richness, especially about people, or
- provide interesting insights.

Again, the intent here is not to make a case for qualitative methods, but rather to show that many researchers find them useful and appropriate. For example, World Bank researchers suggest that

> Much of the early work on poverty was highly quantitative: . . . It became increasingly clear, however, that while numbers are essential for policy and monitoring purposes, it is also important to understand people's perception of poverty and their mechanisms for coping with poverty and other situations of extreme economic and social stress. Researchers have recognized over the past few years that quantitative analysis of the incidence and trends in poverty, while essential for national economic development planning, must be complemented by qualitative methods that help planners and managers understand the cultural, social, political, and institutional context within which projects are designed and implemented. (World Bank 2000; see also Gardenhire and Nelson 2003)

Qualitative Methods Can Contribute to Public Management in Their Own Right

Below are three widely used qualitative methods (Gardenhire and Nelson 2003).

Expert Opinion and Expert Panels

A great deal of evaluation work employs the use of experts or expert panels. The National Academies of Science (NAS) and NAPA are exemplars in the field in utilizing panels (Government Accountability Office 2008, 1988). Congress, a federal agency policy maker, or an organization asks either academy to assist an agency in improving a policy or a management function or process. The academies solicit expressions of interest from their fellows, and experts are selected to serve on a panel based on their expertise and experience. Panels vary in size from three to fifteen members. Panels direct a team of professional, seasoned social science or policy researchers, who gather information that will help the panel deliberate on solutions to the policy or management problem. The panel then issues a public report on its findings and recommendations. Panel reports are reviewed by internal assessors and often by outside, independent reviewers as an additional check on quality.

A major criticism of panels is that even experts get it wrong, and some experts continually get it wrong. Witness the poor track record of many expert commentators on "news" and commentary programs that broadcast 24/7 on cable television. Philip Tetford studied the accuracy of expert forecasts, finding that experts were often wrong, and interestingly, that the higher their credentials, the greater their reputations, and presumably the more extensive their knowledge, the more likely they were to be wrong (Tetford 2005). Panels typically work to build consensus, which generally facilitates groupthink. In attaining consensus, often the least controversial and most mundane policies are produced, rather than the best. Having said this, it is possible for groups of experts to give biased or politicized advice, sometimes to the detriment of the process (Bimber 1996). None of this serves public managers particularly well.

Policy Academies

Policy academies are a method employed most frequently and expertly by the National Governors Association (NGA) to take advantage of the collective wisdom of state governments and policy experts to solve problems of interest to most states. State governors or NGA staff identify an issue—developing the workforce in the next generation or coordinating housing and economic development, for example.[7] NGA then sends out a solicitation to governors announcing a *competition* to participate in a multistate, year-long policy project. States desiring to participate must assemble a team of high-level state officials and decision makers—including those from state agencies, the governor's office, and the state legislature—who meet at a central location over a year with their counterparts to address the policy issue. States must agree as a condition of participation to produce legislation or policy to solve the problem. Only five to seven states are chosen to participate. NGA supplements the meetings with technical assistance offered by nationally recognized experts and researchers in a field. Periodically throughout the year, states meet to define or refine the problem, develop policy options, and select a policy solution. In working on a policy problem, states consult with experts and other states to iron out details. At the conclusion of the project, states either emerge with their own unique policy solution (Osborne 1990)[8] or in some cases develop consensus on a common solution. State solutions are then disseminated to all fifty states.

Policy academies are light-years ahead of panels and expert advice methodologies because they draw policy information from a wide variety of sources, which is then carefully vetted and analyzed. They incorporate desirable evidence-based methodologies but do not produce research—as direct evidence—to inform public management.

Case Studies

Case studies are likely the most common methodology used in the social sciences. Although some critics reject the method as mere *description,* case studies can also be used for *exploration* or *explanation,* or for just about any other purpose that applies to quantitative analysis. The Government Accountability Office, an agency charged with conducting evaluations of federal programs at the behest of Congress, employs case studies as one of its leading evaluation methods, if not the one most frequently used in its work—evaluations of the Three Mile Island nuclear power plant and *Challenger* disasters, for example (Government Accountability Office 1990).

Case studies reflect every shortcoming imaginable in the qualitative research arena. Few would strongly defend this method, but public managers frequently use them, especially in speech making to make a rhetorical point. Virtually every presidential State of the Union address includes some case study reference to a person in need or a person who succeeded because of some public policy or other. Academic research is filled with examples that are the core in some policy or management studies curricula. A huge issue in EBM is whether to include case studies.

The Poor-Quality Stigma

We believe the real controversy is not directly qualitative methods, but their reputation for producing inferior-quality research. Torrance (2008) sums up this criticism well in education research, largely evidence based, policy relevant, much evaluated, and strongly criticized: "The argument has been that educational research—and in some respects social science research more generally—is too often conceived and conducted as a cottage industry, producing too many small-scale, disconnected, non-cumulative studies that do not provide convincing explanations of educational phenomena or how best to develop teaching and learning. There is not a cumulative or informative knowledge base in the field and it is characterized as being of both poor quality and limited utility" (p. 508).

Standards for Improving Quality

In the past few years, researchers have been trying to improve qualitative studies. The National Academy of Sciences offers workshops on the issue, for example. The Institute for Qualitative and Mixed Methods Research at the University of Syracuse, supported by the National Science Foundation, offers training and guidance on qualitative methods.[9] One of the most widely known is the United Kingdom's *Spenser Guidelines* (see Figure 2.1; Spenser, Ritchie, Lewis, and Dillon 2003). Liz Spenser is the chief social scientist in the British government. She conducted a comprehensive study of qualitative research methods and published a set of guidelines to be used by researchers working to inform public policy. She recognized the poor quality of the research available to public managers and sought to do something about it.

Controversy 3. Social Science Journals as a Source of Evidence

Social science research, notwithstanding its wide availability in professional journals in a variety of fields, is perceived by many critics to be little used by public managers in informing the policy process (McGinty 1999). Why are public man-

---

Figure 2.1

Guidelines

- *Contributory.* Advancing wider knowledge or understanding of policy, practice, or theory.
- *Defensible.* Providing a research strategy that can address the evaluation questions posed.
- *Rigorous.* Using systematic and transparent collection, analysis, and interpretation of qualitative data.
- *Credible.* Offering well-founded and plausible arguments about the significance of the evaluation produced.

---

agers loath to draw on social science publications in their work, even when these journals are the lifeblood of knowledge dissemination (Bolton and Stolcis 2003)? We focus on journal articles as reflective of the problems with social science, not only because they explain why social science is underutilized, but also because for many researchers and analysts they are the source of research that informs EBM approaches. EBM tries to correct for some of the problems recounted here in the development of their methodologies.

Social Science Journals

Journal articles are the equivalent of *laboratory reports* and, with few exceptions, share the same structure: a literature review summarizing why the research is important and where it fits into a field of inquiry; a hypothesis section laying out what will be tested empirically; methods showing how the research was performed; findings arguing whether the hypotheses were confirmed or rejected; and a conclusion that often takes the form of a summary or speculation. How do the contents of these journal article sections contribute to knowledge and evidence?

The Audience

The purpose of publication in social science journals is to convey study results primarily to other researchers, rather than to inform the policy process (Streib, Slotkin, and Rivera 2002). As it stands, journals do not address the needs of public managers or they impose too much work on the part of the reader to make the linkage between research and public management. Public managers tend to read short documents that are to the point: what the policy problem is and why, what the options are for addressing it, and what the implications of those options are (Vaughan and Buss 1998). Researchers do not write in the same language as public managers (Kelemen and Bansal 2002). From a researcher perspective: too much work, too little return. Let us look more closely at the sections of an article. In the social sciences, there are numerous paradigms based on "schools" or "movements" and "fields" or "disciplines" that publish mostly within their own circles (Spenser, Ritchie, Lewis, and Dillon 2003). Public managers typically do not find this useful.

Journal Literature Reviews

Every social science journal article begins with a one- to three-page literature review, generally reflecting one of three categories that place the research in context:

- *Extension.* Literature reviews that take a research problem that has been studied in the past and add to or round it out.
- *Refutation.* Literature reviews that are highly critical of past research and set the stage to refute it.
- *Innovation.* Literature reviews that support a new idea that does not fit in an existing paradigm or that combines different paradigms in new and interesting ways.

One consequence of research fragmentation across the social sciences is that researchers do not communicate with others outside their own narrow fields of expertise. Many policy-relevant studies remain untapped because they reside outside a paradigm. Some have referred to this as the *guild mentality* in the social sciences. On the other hand, Herbert Simon, Nobel laureate, made major contributions not only in economics, but also in public management and artificial intelligence. Scholars who are willing to "think outside the box" may become more successful in academe, but this may apply more to senior researchers than to those just starting their careers.

Methodology Sections

Methodology sections of journal articles pose major problems for analysts assessing them. They are presented in what Karl Popper called the "logic of justification" or the "context of explanation," as opposed to the "logic of discovery" (Popper 2002). The logic of discovery refers, in part, to how a researcher actually went about performing the research reported in a publication. Discovery rarely, if ever, gets published, except perhaps in personal memoirs (e.g., Crick 1990). Discovery tends to be very messy, an analogy being watching how sausages are actually made. The logic of justification systematically builds a case justifying the findings and conclusions of a study in the context of explanation. It is a description, in a sense, of the sausage as a finished product. The problem with this social science convention is that there generally is not enough material in a methodology section to determine whether the research was undertaken at a high enough standard to inform public policy. In an assessment of six public administration journals over a three-year period, Wright, Manigault, and Black (2004) concluded that "researchers often failed to report information that would allow their readers to appropriately judge the accuracy of reported research findings, interpret these findings with the context of other research, and learn from the research methods used" (p. 747). In fact, most methodologies are so terse that it is impossible to actually conduct the research guided only by what is in the methods section (McCullough, McGeary, and Harrison 2006).

Data Analysis and Findings

Data analysis and findings are as problematic, or more so, for analysts conducting assessments. Data are not generally offered up to other researchers to verify that the analysis as published was actually completed (Cardiff and Goodman 2009). First, many researchers guard their data because they do not want the ridicule that might attach to them if they have done an analysis improperly. Second, researchers do not like to tip off competitors about future publications that might be forthcoming from their databases. Third, most data sets are inadequately documented—researchers creating them have no need to completely document them because they know what they contain. If they were to make them available to "outsiders," documentation costs would be enormous. The same is true with data-analysis computer runs. There could be thousands of runs even on small studies. Few researchers save these following their analysis. Finally, there is little incentive to share, and every disincentive not to.

There is some movement in the social sciences to force researchers to make data available for analysis. Since 2003, the National Institutes of Health, the leading funder of health science research in the world, has required researchers receiving grants of more than $500,000 to have a plan to release data to the public for analysis, or to say why this is not possible (Towne, Wise, and Winters 2004).[10] The *American Economics Review* also requires that researchers make available data and software code so that replication can occur (Anderson, Greene, McCullough, and Vinod 2005). For the most part, this is not common practice across the social sciences. A major implication of this for EBM approaches is that much published research from the past is likely suspect because it was not subject to replication (Rennie and Luft 2000).

Findings sections of social science journal articles tend to focus on statistical significance (McCloskey and Ziliak 2008) rather than policy significance (Birks 2008), and they do so in language that is not useful to public managers (see also Marusic 2006). Many social scientists gain fame, but perhaps not fortune, discovering statistically significant relationships among variables. The relationships, although significant, in many cases are weak and unconvincing. When they fail to find statistical significance, either the research is not published or the research is thought to imply that there is no policy significance. The latter is incorrect. When using large databases—the decennial census, for example—it is not uncommon to compare two groups in an analysis and find that they do not differ significantly. Even so, one group or another may be so large that it poses policy problems for public managers, even though it does not significantly different from another.

Language used to convey research findings tends to be overly qualified and conditional (Vaughan and Buss 1998). Such phrases as "this might mean" or "this suggests" constitute the backbone of the journal article but do nothing to bolster the confidence of a policy maker who may risk his or her career using social science to support policy. Much social science research is complicated with a variety of assumptions—explicit and implicit—which so narrow the application of the research that it lacks generalizability. If this were not enough, it is difficult to find an article that does not end in one way or another with the phrase "more research is needed before. . . ." For some critics, sometimes this is a plea for more research monies, but for other critics, more likely it reflects a researcher's lack of confidence in his or her findings.

Article Conclusions

An article's conclusion poses yet more problems. Many conclusions are simply summaries of an article's contents. It is likely that many avoid reading the article and go directly to the summary: a dangerous practice indeed. Very often, journal articles conclude with speculation that extends considerably beyond the data analysis as presented, making it just another unfounded opinion. This does not count as evidence. It is equally likely that researchers do not make recommendations that might be of use to public managers. Some believe that this is not their role in the policy process, while others may not really know what the implications truly are.[11] Consider this quote (Nye 2009): "Scholars are paying less attention to questions about how their work relates to the policy world, and in many (academic) departments a focus on policy can hurt one's career. Advancement comes faster for those who develop mathematical models, new methodologies or theories expressed in jargon that is unintelligible to policymakers."

Even more evidence abounds for this trend: Lee Sigelman, longtime editor of the *American Political Science Review,* in an article on the evolution of political science and the *American Political Science Review* observes that one in five articles published before 1967 had policy prescriptions and criticisms, while few articles since then concern policy: "If speaking truth to power and contributing directly to public dialogue about merits and demerits of courses of action were still numbered among the functions of the profession, one would not have known it from leafing through its leading journal" ("The Coevolution of American Political Science and *APSR*" 2006).

Journal Content

The content of social science journals, for many critics, contributes only narrowly to the policy process. To get published in a top-tier journal (see next section), research must make a major contribution to the field, be of much higher quality than other articles submitted for publication, and be of wide interest to readers of the journal (Rennie, Lee, and Weber 2009). Even though a paper may be excellent, if it does not meet these standards, then it will be relegated to publication in a lower-tier journal or may not see publication at all. The self-publication of papers to the Web may change this. These days, an article like this could appear somewhere on the Web as a fugitive or gray paper. This is a problem in two ways: some good research fails to be published—referred to as *publication bias*—and its results are never widely known or taken into account in public management, while other articles are "shopped around" until a journal eventually accepts them, making one wonder about the validity of the *peer-review* process.[12] Social science journals are biased against publication of articles that are not consistent with the prevailing paradigm represented by the journal. Journals do not typically publish replication studies that would really add to the knowledge, and evidence, in a field (Towne, Wise, and Winters 2004; MacCoon 1998). There is not much interest in publishing pieces that support what is "already known." A paper refuting previous research will be more publishable. Editors want to publish new research. This has an unintended consequence for the social sciences: some researchers repackage or relabel models, concepts, and frameworks to make research look innovative, when the work basically is the same as that of the past. Additionally, journals with policy relevancy tend to be highly focused on methodological innovations, using analysis of programs as an application of a technique. Program evaluation becomes a secondary purpose.

Journal Quality

Social science journals are not all created equal. So, although the number of journals relevant to public policy continues to grow annually, most are not necessarily taken seriously either by researchers or by public managers. One-half of all peer-reviewed journals, for example, are not indexed by Thompson Scientific ISI, a company whose journal lists are the most widely used for assessing journal quality. Depending on one's notion of what a professional social science journal is and whether foreign-language journals are included, there are twenty-seven main public administration and public policy journals.[13] These tend to be published quarterly, yielding about two hundred articles, or eight hundred annually. Researchers have tried to rank journals against a set of quality indicators (Brennan, West, and Tempest 2009). One indicator is the existence of a strong peer-review process for assessing articles submitted for publication. The prestige of the journal's editor and editorial board are important as well. Another indicator is the rejection rate for articles submitted for publication. The higher the rejection rate, the higher the quality of the journal. High-quality journals may publish only one in twenty articles submitted. Still another indicator is citations in the literature (Thomson Reuters n.d.). The more a journal is cited in other professional journals, the higher its quality. Sadly, a vast number of articles written are not cited by anyone. The journal *impact factor* is a measure based on the number of times articles in a social science journal are cited in any other journal over a two- or three-year period.[14] According to Seligman, "In any scholarly field, some works are widely acknowledged as classics, whereas the rest—indeed, the great majority—are little noted nor long remembered. Indeed, according to the 'Iron Law of Important Articles,' the number of significant articles increases only to the extent of the square root of the number of published articles. It follows that as a research literature grows, important articles constitute an ever-decreasing proportion of the total output."[15]

The impact factor for the flagship journal, *Public Administration Review,* is 1.3. A final indicator is the prestige of the journal in the field. Many academic departments generally rank journals according to quality and influence and then require faculty and researchers to publish only in the best if they expect to be awarded tenure or promotion.[16] High-powered policy researchers may eschew publication in anything but the best journals, with the result that there is relatively little good policy research if only journals are consulted.

The issue of journal quality has not gone unnoticed by public managers. John Howard, prime minister of Australia, became so frustrated with the quality of publications produced by Australia's public universities that he directed the government to set up a scheme wherein US$500 million in research funds would be awarded to only those universities that could demonstrate that their research was of the highest quality (Maslen 2007). Universities were instructed to assemble "evidence portfolios" that were submitted to a panel of twelve experts who passed judgment on whether they were worthy of receiving government funding. Universities spent millions on self-audits in preparation. The newly elected Labour government quashed the program, arguing that it was too expensive to implement. More than any bit of evidence presented here thus far, having a national government take note of the poor quality of its university researchers adds much creditability to the assertion that research is widely substandard.

Peer Review

As noted, peer review is a major indicator of journal quality and hence should be an attractive feature for anyone looking to build an evidentiary case for decision making (Rocha e Silva, Marusic, and Stanley 2009). Ironically, peer review carries with it its own set of issues. Every year at the annual meeting of the Council of Science Editors, many of the paper presentations concern the "failure of the peer-review and editorial process" (Marusic 2006). Here are some major problems. Peer review can be highly political and hence unscientific. Peer review, by its very nature, stifles innovation (Tashakkori and Teddlie 1998). Only those articles that fit a journal's predominant paradigm, as observed above, tend to get published (Moran 1998).

Peer reviewers often have less expertise than authors. Campanaris examined the 205 *most cited* articles in the field of information science, finding that 22, or about 10 percent, had been rejected by a top-tier journal before they were eventually published (Campanaris 1998). One explanation for poor quality is inadequate preparation of public administration doctoral students to conduct policy or management studies of the highest quality. Rethemeyer and Helbig (2004), in their study of forty-four leading public affairs doctoral programs, found "that public affairs students may leave their programs only partially prepared to interact with the emerging public affairs literature and with less grounding in quantitative methods than some model curricula have prescribed" (p. 179). The National Research Council, in its comprehensive review of education research, found much the same lack of capacity among education doctoral students (Towne, Wise, and Winters 2004).

Peer review can be dishonest. Leading experts in a field are frequently asked to review papers for possible publication. These experts are often too busy to conduct the review but do not want to appear uncooperative in their discipline. Some resolve this dilemma by turning the review over to a graduate research assistant, who sends the review back on the expert's behalf.

As an indicator of how problematic peer review can be, consider this statement from a journal editor at the Council of Science Editors concerning the issue of whether peer reviewers should be allowed to know the names of the paper's authors when conducting the review:[17] "The strongest criticism of the partially masked peer-review process has to do with the fact that, even when all precautions are taken, the process remains highly subjective and relies on reviewers who may take advantage of ideas they find in yet-unpublished manuscripts; show bias in favor or against a researcher, an institution, or an idea; be insufficiently qualified to provide an authoritative review; or abuse their position because they do not feel accountable."

Some commentators are beginning to report that leading researchers appear to be abandoning peer-reviewed journals in favor of Web-based publication, possibly because of these issues (Ellison 2007).

Research Bias

There appears to be increasingly more bias in all kinds of research. Some of it, as illustrated in the following quote, seems to some to be unethical and perhaps criminal (House 2008).

> Drug studies are often cited as the best exemplars of evaluation design. However, many of these studies are seriously biased in favor of positive findings for the drugs evaluated, even to the point where dangerous effects are hidden. In spite of using randomized designs and double blinding, drug companies have found ways of producing the results they want, including manipulation of treatment, selection of sample, control of data, and calculated publication. Regulatory agencies have been neutralized. We have entered an era when evaluations are controlled by sponsors to produce the findings they want. Evaluations have become too important to be left to the evaluators. Such deceptive practices threaten the integrity of the evaluation field, perhaps its existence. There is no doubt these practices will spread into educational and social evaluation.

But we believe that evaluation research is not so much biased because it presents falsehoods. These practices are nearly always exposed under intense scrutiny, and most researchers do not engage in them. Bias occurs, first and foremost, because research is never really "objective," as postmodernists assert. Rather, everyone who conducts research imposes his or her own reality, which makes it different. Where bias may occur, though, is in the intentional omission of data, information, alternatives, or findings, which if known would change how study results would be interpreted (Hofstetter and Buss 1978, p. 518).

Controversy 4. Unpublished Research as Evidence

Because, according to many critics, social science journals have all but taken themselves out of the running in the policy arena, it is only natural that others would fill the vacuum: enter consulting firms, partisan and nonpartisan think tanks, and university research centers (all of whose research is referred to as *consulting work*), not to mention government policy analysts. Some of the most sophisticated, yet useful, policy research is conducted by those not interested in social science publication. These researchers survive and thrive on government, or in some cases foundation- and private enterprise–funded projects that specifically address the needs of policy makers. NAS and NAPA received funding from the MacArthur Foundation to analyze the burgeoning national debt and rolling budget deficits of the U.S. government.[18]

These research enterprises are incorrectly perceived—in our view—as posing problems for those who would use their studies in EBM approaches, including the following.

Hired Guns

Critics often suggest that consultants are nothing but hired guns who say what public managers (their clients) want to hear, rather than what is the truth. "Speaking truth to power," in Aaron Wildavsky's (1987) words, does not lead to further contract work. We believe this criticism is greatly exaggerated. Assuming the role of hired gun is a very shortsighted and short-term strategy. Once an administration or policy maker changes over, their replacements are unlikely to want to work with another's hired gun. Additionally, once a researcher acquires a reputation as a hired gun, he or she likely cannot go back to "objective work." Many researchers do not want to risk this, although many are tempted when research funding becomes scarce. Additionally, in the political environment of public management, research that is not "objective" is generally attacked by opponents or antagonists: it is risky to produce biased research that can and will be refuted. Finally, there is a presumption here that social science journal publications are unbiased. As we've seen above, this is not the case.

Journal Publication

As observed, many contract researchers are not motivated by publication in scientific journals. Those who work in drug research may be exceptions, as they seek validation of their work in the field. Critics reject unpublished work as having not gone through the rigors of the editorial and peer-review process. As such, unpublished work may be substandard. The peer-review process does not guarantee that a publication is of high quality, as we have seen. But, more important, critics forget that unpublished contract work is heavily reviewed in many cases before it is ever released. Government has its own highly qualified researchers and outside experts who typically review contract reports before they see the light of day. In some cases, as with the NAS and NAPA, reviews are much more comprehensive and detailed than journal peer review. Additionally, contract researchers know that their work will be scrutinized by opposition groups after it is released, so most will ensure that their work is of high quality. Nevertheless, critics typically forget that some, but certainly not all, contractors—Manpower Demonstration Research Corporation, Abt, Rand, and Mathematica, for example—are actually pioneers in the development and application of evaluation methods.

Inaccessibility of Reports

Another criticism of contract work is that much of it is inaccessible other than to those who funded it. Much contract work, depending on the agency and the issue, likely is not posted on the Web, especially if study results do not support the funder's policy position. As a result, evidence that would be useful may go unaccounted for (Hutchinson 2008). Even when outside researchers discover that contract research exists, it can prove difficult to acquire. Using Freedom of Information Act requests can be expensive, time-consuming, and self-defeating. Some organizations, such as NAS and NAPA, are required by statute to post reports on their Web sites and make them available to anyone who requests them. The real problem is that those hunting down publications do not know where to look.

Sole Source of Evaluation

Contractors thrive because they compete for government evaluation work and periodically win it. It is difficult for new contractors to enter that arena—start-up costs can be high, and government often limits access through procurement processes. Many contractors build a critical mass of researchers who are among the most qualified in a field. Many are former or future university research professors. Contract work may be the only high-quality source of evaluation research available. So eliminating it because it is "just" contract work is not appropriate. Because of the way government funds evaluation, it is unlikely that individual researchers, especially university-based ones, will ever get to work on a massive evaluation study.

As an aside on these issues, think tanks that are highly partisan pose an interesting case in EBM (Rich 2005). They tend to have the ear of administrations with whom they identify ideologically, and therefore greatly influence public policy throughout the process. The question becomes, Should their materials be included in the search for evidence?

As another aside, there is relatively little research conducted by government policy analysts, at least compared to contract researchers, in spite of the fact that government policy analysts are highly qualified and experienced in the research enterprise. For example, logical places where one would expect to see social science research performed in government—the Office of Management and Budget, Congressional Research Service, Congressional Budget Office, to name a few—do not have research budgets of any size, if at all. Much of their work is based on reviews of the work of others or on computer models usually related to the budget or the economy. The Government Accountability Office does have a large research budget, but it generally has insufficient funds to do "gold-standard" evaluations and avoids doing studies that take many months to complete. So ironically, government researchers rarely get to add to the evidence through direct research. For those few who do engage in research, their work generally must be approved by public managers, who may meddle in it. Additionally, government researchers trying to publish their work likely must seek approval to do so. Receiving this approval is certainly not automatic. Finally, there is very little incentive to publish government-based research, so many see it as a burden for which they will not see rewards.

Improving Social Science Evaluation Research

Below are a few thoughts on reforming the social sciences in ways that might improve it as input into EBM. These might make a modest contribution to that end, but that is highly unlikely: there have been decades of abuse, and relatively little progress in resolving issues. We offer these more as a way to help researchers and public managers better understand the foundations of EBM approaches.

Target Research to Public Managers

Evaluation advocates bemoan lack of interest of public managers in the work of the field and of the social sciences generally. Yet analysis and publications are not addressed to public managers. Rather, the audience is other researchers. What policy maker, for instance, would be interested in exploring research based on this description of a methodological approach (Noyes 2006):

> Meta ethnography is a method used to synthesise qualitative research findings. It involves induction and interpretation, and thus follows a similar approach to the methods

of qualitative data analysis used in the studies being synthesised. Through extracting concepts, metaphors and themes arising from different studies (first order analysis); subjecting these first order concepts to interpretive analysis to generate second order concepts; and synthesising these second order concepts through developing a "line or argument," meta-ethnography enables the reviewer to understand and synthesise the findings of two or more qualitative studies concerning a similar research question or topic.

In targeting their work to other researchers, social scientists seem much more interested either in touting their own methods and analysis as superior to those of others or in adding to the corpus of work in their field, while mostly ignoring public managers. Paradigm wars are good for those researchers—especially in academe—seeking to build reputations and gain tenure, and they may even be good for the enterprise over the longer term as it sorts itself out, but they do nothing but discredit the enterprise in the minds of public managers. Consulting firms and government policy analysts are more than capable of providing public managers with the evidence they need to inform the policy process.

So, rather than complain that evaluation work is not informing policy, researchers might want to actually try communicating with public managers (Vaughan and Buss 1998). One thing that might help is for journal editors and book publishers to stop publishing articles about how public managers do not listen to researchers. After all, this complaint has been around since there were public managers and researchers.

Promote Mixed Evaluation Methods

Some researchers try to reconcile the quantitative-qualitative method issue by calling for the use of *mixed methods* research designs (Tashakkori and Teddlie 1998). In this way the strengths of both approaches are exploited and their weaknesses minimized (Rao and Woolcock n.d.). Consider an example. Buss (2001) and colleagues conducted a mixed-method study of urban trauma in a small city emergency department to improve patient management while in the hospital system and to prevent urban violence on release from the hospital. Urban trauma was defined as cases in which victims had been bludgeoned, beaten, stabbed, or shot and presented at the emergency department for treatment. Researchers drew a random sample of medical files—the gold standard of medical research—from past urban trauma cases and content analyzed these (*retrospective* study). Medical records were linked to "claims" data files to identify treatment costs. Researchers then conducted telephone surveys with past victims, matching and supplementing the medical file with interview data. Researchers also conducted personal interviews with consecutive cases presenting at the emergency department and analyzed their medical records (*prospective* study). Researchers matched criminal record data to individual victim case records. Finally, a geographical location analysis was conducted, identifying the victim's home address and the address where the crime occurred.

Promote Triangulation in Evaluation

It is likely that there is no research methodology that offers definitive, incontrovert-ible, valid evidence in support of policy. Each methodology has its shortcomings or idiosyncrasies. As a consequence, better evidence derives from the *triangulation* of different methodologies (Cook 1985; Jick 1979).[19] If disparate study results all point to the same conclusions or implications for policy, then public managers likely will be more confident in applying the results in their work. By contrast, if disparate studies diverge, then public managers will be better able to understand why some approaches might work and others might not.

Triangulation will not be easy: incorporating the findings from other method-ological approaches into an analysis is tantamount to admitting that one's method might be problematic.

Promote Consensus Conferences on Big-Ticket Research

Public managers frequently face mega-policy issues—the global financial crisis and government interventions into the banking system in unprecedented ways, or the response of the international community to swine flu, bird flu, and SARS—where there may be some research available, but not enough. Public managers may need help in figuring out the best course of action. One mechanism for resolving conflicting interpretations of policy research is to hold *consensus conferences* on the issues, an approach common in medical practice but much less so in social science (Buss 2009).

Even consensus conferences can produce invalid information, or their original conclusions might change with access to newer information, but in general, it is a good idea to have researchers, public managers, and consumers look at evidence.

Reform Peer Review

Based on the critique of the peer-review process presented earlier, many researchers would like to get rid of it. That likely will not happen.[20] However, there are some things that might be done to shake the process up some. Journals, as a condition for publication, could force researchers to make their data public, or report why they choose not to do so. Some journals already do this, but the practice needs to be more widely adopted. As an alternative, rather than making everyone submit their data for public scrutiny, journals could create an independent board and force some researchers—chosen at random—to submit their data for reanalysis and evaluation. If this were widely practiced, researchers would have a great incentive to improve the quality of research. There could be an appeals process and other restrictions to prevent abuse by the review board. As social science publishing now stands, much information on methodologies and findings is omitted from publications because of space limitations. Editors could require authors to publish additional information to the journal's Web site, so that those interested in replication or review would have the information they need. Finally, papers could be posted on collaborative technology Web sites—like wikis—so that the public and other researchers could comment on them. The so-called wisdom of crowds (Surowiecki 2005) is a powerful tool for ferreting out problems with research. Several journals experimented with this but abandoned the process as being too unwieldly.

Increase Transparency in the Process

Researchers should continue to improve the quality of research by promoting transparency in all aspects of the research process, especially in publication in professional journals, but even more importantly in Web-based publication. This will not be easy. In a recent case, Australian researchers completed a report commissioned by the government on publishing research funded in public health so that researchers could see who got what funding to do what research. The government suppressed the report, causing the scientists working on it to go public, a rare breach of protocol for scientists who depend on public grant money (Sweet 2009).

Another way to encourage transparency is to ask researchers to sign conflict-of-interest statements about their research and post them on the Web. Researchers would have to indicate whether they have worked on a program in the past, advocated for it especially on behalf of political interests, and/or benefited from the program, and would have to address numerous other issues. This is not unreasonable. NAS and NAPA publically ask panelists to certify this information when they begin working on a project, then post it on the Web for public comment. Few panelists complain.

As noted, publication bias is a problem for social science researchers. One possible solution would be to develop a registry wherein researchers would report studies they conduct to test hypotheses even though the studies are not published (Sherman 2003). In so doing, researchers looking at the evidence can contact others to see what they found. The National Science Foundation, NAS, and NAPA might take on this effort. It could be funded either by government or by foundations.

Conclusion

Although the discussion of the social sciences as a source of evidence is sobering, it should not be taken to mean that the social sciences and EBM or policy are foolhardy enterprises. One way to look at social science (and evidence-based approaches) is that it engages in self-study and there is much information on what is good, bad, and ugly. The issue is how to sort through the research and settle on the very best for public managers to use in decision making. The bottom line is that each study, regardless of who produces it, must be judged on its merits, not on blanket condemnations or acceptance. What we mean by this is that just because a study appears in a prominent journal does not mean that it is actually good. Likewise, just because a study employs qualitative methods does not mean that it is bad. The double bottom line is that for all research used in public management, caveat emptor applies. EBMgt approaches are intended to overcome the issues, problems, and limitations of the social sciences. None of this will be easy: the costs of producing and evaluating evidence are often prohibitive.

Notes

Unless otherise noted, all Web sites reported in these notes were accessed on November 1, 2009.

1. In addition to assessing the literature on methods in the social sciences, we looked at the hard sciences and medicine as well. The latter have done a great deal more work on their methods and have long served as a standard against which the social sciences measure their progress as a field. So, if the hard sciences and medicine have methodological issues, then the social sciences are likely to have the same ones as well.

2. We did a search on Amazon.com on "social science methods" and received twelve thousand hits. Although some of these are duplications, there is a massive literature available in books. There are legions more in journals. Those interested in the issues might start with Root (1993).

3. Feynman goes on to add that he doubts whether there is such a thing as a social *science.*

4. It goes without saying that if research is well designed, it could still be biased or misleading if it was poorly executed. See the section later in this chapter on social science journal articles.

5. From the Mathematica Web page at: http://www.mathematica-mpr.com/about%20us/evaldemdesign.asp; see also Government Social Research Unit (2007). A February 2009 letter from the American Evaluation Association to Peter Orszag, director of the Office of Management and Budget, laid out many of these issues and suggested ways for the federal government to address them (see the letter at http://www.eval.org/aea09.eptf.eval.roadmapF. pdf); Olsen, Aisner, and McGinnis (2007).

6. A review of these methods is beyond the scope of this work, but those interested in exploring qualitative methodological approaches might explore papers of the National Science Foundation–supported Institute for Qualitative and Mixed Methods Research, University of Syracuse, at www.maxwell.syr.edu/moynahan/programs/cqrm/iqrm2009.html.

7. See http://www.nga.org/Files/pdf/WorkforceAcademyReport04.pdf and http://www.nga.org/Files/pdf/0701HOUSINGACADEMY.PDF, respectively (accessed October 26, 2010).

8. NGA is well aware of the advantage it has to experiment with a variety of state solutions to policy problems. States, as observed by David Osborne, are "laboratories of democracy." See Osborne (1990).

9. See www.maxwell.syr.edu/moynahan/programs/cqrm/iqrm2009.html.

10. For the National Institutes of Health policy statement, #NOT-OD-)#-032, February 26, 2003 see, http://grants.nih.gov/grants/guide/notice-files/NOT-OD-03–032.html.

11. Many social scientists are trained to believe that if they make policy recommendations, then they become part of the policy process and as a consequence are no longer objective or independent. An example of this issue is raging in the field of defense studies. The Obama administration appropriated $700 billion for defense research to universities, yet critics are trying to get academic researchers not to participate. Similar issues apply to drug research sponsored by pharmaceutical companies.

12. The National Institutes of Health, funder of a lot of health care research, and some publishers are trying to make more transparent how much revision on articles submitted for

publication occurred in the peer review process. "Wiley-Blackwell will support our authors by posting the accepted version of articles by NIH grant-holders to PubMed Central upon acceptance by the journal. The accepted version is the version that incorporates all amendments made during peer review, but prior to the publisher's copy-editing and typesetting. This accepted version will be made publicly available 12 months after publication. The NIH mandate applies to all articles based on research that has been wholly or partially funded by the NIH and that are accepted for publication on or after April 7, 2008." Wiley-Blackwell Publishers, http://www.wiley.com/bw/journal.asp?ref=0033–3352.

13. This seems an odd statement, but many indexes of social science journals do not list all the journals. The creators of these indexes do not believe that certain publications are of high enough quality to be considered professional journals.

14. See this site for an explanation: http://www.sciencegateway.org/impact/ (accessed October 26, 2010).

15. See Lee Sigelman in *American Political Science Review* at: http://journals.cambridge.org/action/displayAbstract?fromPage=online&aid=560896 (accessed October 26, 2010).

16. See, for example, the list for the School of Management, University of Melbourne: "Journal Quality List," available at www.harzing.com/jql.htm (accessed October 26, 2010).

17. Council of Science Editors (CSE). 2010. *CSE's White Paper on Promoting Integrity in Scientific Journal Publications.* Wheat Ridge, CO: CSE. http://www.councilscienceeditors.org/editorial_policies/whitepaper/2–3_reviewer.cfm#2.3.4.

18. See MacArthur Foundation, Chicago, IL: http://www.macfound.org/site/c.lkLXJ8MQKrH/b.4979973/k.8E29/Recent_Grants.htm (accessed October 26, 2010).

19. In the philosophy of social science literature, this is referred to as *critical multiplism.* See Cook (1985).

20. See National Institute of Health. 2007. *Peer Review Self Study.* Washington, DC: NIH. http://enhancing-peer-review.nih.gov/index.html and http://enhancing-peer-review.nih.gov/meetings/NIHPeerReviewReportFINALDRAFT.pdf (accessed October 26, 2010).

References

Abt Associates. March 2002. *Evaluating Drug Treatment Courts in Kansas City, Missouri and Pensacola, Florida.* Washington, DC: Abt Associates. http://www.abtassociates.com/reports/es-eval_treatment.pdf.

Anderson, Richard, William Greene, Bruce McCullough, and H.D. Vinod. 2005. "The Role of Data and Program Code Archives in the Future of Economic Research." Working paper, 2005–014C, Federal Reserve Bank, St. Louis, MO.

Bimber, Bruce. 1996. *The Politics of Expertise in Congress.* Albany: State University of New York Press.

Birks, Stuart. 2008. "Statistical Significance and Policy Significance." Posted on Social Science Research Network website at http://papers.ssrn.com/s013/papers.cfm?abstract_id=1156166 (accessed October 26, 2010).

Bolton, Michael, and Gregory B. Stolcis. 2003. "Ties that Do Not Bind: Musings on the Specious Relevance of Academic Research." *Public Administration Review* 63 (5): 626–630.

Brass, Clinton, Blas Nunez-Neto, and Erin Williams. 2006. *Congress and Program Evaluation: An Overview of Randomized Controlled Trials and Related Issues.* Report RL 3330. Washington, DC: Congressional Research Service.

Brennan, Patricia, Jevin D. West, and David Tempest. 2009. "Modes of Quantitative Analysis for Scientific Papers." http://www.councilscienceeditors.org/events/2009_presentations.cfm (accessed October 26, 2010).

Buss, T.F. 2001. "Managing Urban Violence Cases in Hospital Emergency Departments."
In *Handbook of Crisis and Emergency Management*, ed. A. Farazmand, 267–281. New
York: Marcel Dekker.
———. 2009. *Governance Challenges and the Financial Crisis: Seven Key Questions*.
Washington, DC: IBM Center for Business of Government.
Campanaris, Juan. 1998. "Have Referees Rejected Some of the Most-Cited Articles of All
Times?" *Journal of American Society of Information Science and Technology* 47 (4):
302–310.
Campbell, Donald, and J. Stanley. 1963. *Experimental and Quasi-Experimental Designs
for Research*. Chicago: Rand-McNally.
Cardiff, Robert D., and Steven Goodman. 2009. "How to Ensure the Integrity of Research
Data in Published Papers: Images, Statistics, and the Editors' Role." Council of Science
Editors, Wheat Ridge, CO: at http://www.councilscienceeditors.org/events/2009_pre-
sentations.cfm (accessed October 26, 2010).
Center for Education Policy. 2009. *National Evaluation of Writing Program Professional
Development*. Washington, DC: Stanford Research Institute. http://policyweb.sri.com/
cep/publications/WPD_reportY2final.pdf.
Chaplin, Duncan, and Jane Hannaway. 1996. *High School Employment*. Washington,
DC: Urban Institute. http://www.urbaninstitute.org/toolkit/data-methods/instrumental.
cfm.
Charles, Pierre. 2009. "Reporting of Sample Size Calculations in RCTs: A Review." *British
Medical Journal* 338:1723. http://www.bmj.com/cgi/content/full/338/may12_1/b1732?
maxtoshow=&HITS=10&hits=10&RESULTFORMAT=&fulltext=charles&searchid=1
&FIRSTINDEX=0&sortspec=date&resourcetype=HWCIT.
Chatterji, Madhabi. 2007. "Grades of Evidence." *American Journal of Evaluation* 28 (3):
239–255.
Clark, Mike. 2004. "Systematic Reviews and the Cochrane Collaboration." The Cochrane
Collaboration, Oxford, England. April 22. http://www.cochrane.org/docs/whycc.htm
(accessed November 1, 2009).
Coalition for Evidence-Based Policy. 2002. *Bringing Evidence-Based Progress to Education*.
Council for Excellence in Government, Washington, DC: http://coexgov.securesites.net/
admin/FormManager/fileuploading/coalitonFinRpt.pdf (accessed November 1, 2009).
Concato, John, Nirav Shah, and Ralph Horwits. 2000. "Randomized Controlled Trials,
Observational Studies and the Hierarchy of Research Designs." *New England Journal
of Medicine,* June 22.
Cook, T.D. 1985. "Postpositivist Critical Multiplisms." In *Social Science and Public Policy,*
ed. R.L. Shotland and M.M. Mark, 21–62. Beverly Hills: Sage.
Cressell, John. 2008. *Research Design*. Thousand Oaks, CA: Sage.
Crick, Francis. 1990. *What Mad Pursuit: A Personal View of Scientific Discovery*. New
York: Basic Books.
Ellison, Glenn. 2007. *Is Peer Review in Decline?* NBER Working Paper No. 13272. Cam-
bridge, MA: National Bureau of Economic Research.
Gardenhire, Alissa, and Laura Nelson. 2003. *Intensive Qualitative Research*. New York:
Manpower Demonstration Research Corporation.
Gerring, John. 2001. *Social Science Methodology*. Cambridge: Cambridge University Press.
Government Accountability Office. 1988. *Welfare: Expert Panel's Insights in Reform*. Report
HRD-88–59. Washington, DC: Government Accountability Office.
———. 1990. *Case Study Evaluations*. Report 10.1.9. Washington, DC: Government Ac-
countability Office. http://archive.gao.gov/f0202/143145.pdf.
———. 2008. *Climate Change*. Report 08–605. Washington, DC: Government Accountability Office. http://www.gao.gov/new.items/d08605.pdf.
Government Social Research Unit. 2007. *Why Do Social Experiments?* Chapter 7. London:

HM Treasury. http://www.civilservice.gov.uk/my-civil-service/networks/professional/gsr/resources/magenta-book-main-page.aspx (accessed October 26, 2010).

Greene, Jennifer, and Gary Henry. 2005. "Qualitative-Quantitative Debate in Evaluation." In *Encyclopedia of Evaluation,* ed. Sandra Mathison, 345–350. Thousand Oaks: Sage.

Gueron, Judith. 2000. *The Politics of Random Assignment.* New York: Manpower Demonstration Research Corporation. http://www.mdrc.org/publications/45/workpaper.html.

Hamilton, Gayle. 2002. *Moving People from Welfare to Work: Lessons from the National Evaluation of Welfare to Work Strategies.* New York: Manpower Demonstration Research Corporation (MDRC). http://www.mdrc.org/publications/52/print.html.

Hansen, Hanne, and Olaf Rieper. 2009. "The Evidence Movement." *Evaluation* 15 (2): 141–163.

Heinrich, Carolyn J. 2007. "Evidence-Based Policy and Performance Management." *American Review of Public Administration* 37 (3): 255–277.

Hofstetter, C. Richard, and Terry F. Buss. 1978. "Bias in the Television Coverage of Political Events: A Methodological Analysis." *Journal of Broadcasting* 22 (Fall): 517–530.

House, Ernest R. 2008. "Blowback: Consequences of Evaluation for Evaluation." *American Journal of Evaluation* 29 (4): 416–426.

Hutchinson, Brian. 2008. "Sequestered Evidence: Inaccessible Findings from Health Services and Policy Research." *Health Policy* 3 (3): 10–13. http://www.pubmedcentral.nih.gov/articlerender.fcgi?artid=2645149.

Jick, T.D. 1979. "Mixing Qualitative and Quantitative Methods: Triangulation in Action." *Administrative Science Quarterly* 24 (4): 602–611.

Kaplan, Abraham. 1998. *The Conduct of Inquiry.* New York: Transaction Publishers.

Kelemen, M., and P. Bansal. 2002. "The Conventions of Management Research and Their Relevance to Management Practice." *British Journal of Management* 13:97–108.

Kline, Rex. 2004. *Beyond Significance Testing.* New York: American Psychological Association.

Kushner, Saville. 2005. "Qualitative Control." *Evaluation* 11 (1): 111–122.

MacCoon, Robert J. 1998. "Biases in the Interpretation and Use of Research Results." *Annual Review of Psychology* 49:259–287.

Marusic, Ana. 2006. "Evidence-Based Review." *Science Editor* 29 (2): 42–43.

Maslen, Geoff. 2007. "Australia: Research Quality Scheme Scrapped." *University World News.* http://universityworldnews.com/article.php?story=20071130100220387&mode=print.

McCloskey, Deidre, and Steve Ziliak. 2008. *The Cult of Statistical Significance.* Ann Arbor: University of Michigan Press.

McCullough, Bruce, Kerry McGeary, and Teresa Harrison. 2006. "Do Economic Journal Archives Promote Replicable Research?" Social Science Research Network Web site http://ssrn.com/abstract=931231 (accessed November 1, 2009).

McGinty, Stephen. 1999. *Gatekeepers of Knowledge.* Westport, CT: Greenwood.

Moran, G. 1998. *Silencing Scientists and Scholars in Other Fields: Power, Paradigm Controls and Peer Review.* Greenwich, CT: Ablex Publishing.

National Academy of Public Administration. 2008. *Fire Grants.* Washington, DC: NAPA. www.napawash.org/pc_management_studies/firegrants_assessingperformance.html.

National Research Council. 2008. *Improving Democracy Assistance: Building Knowledge through Evaluation.* Washington, DC: National Research Council.

Noyes, Jane. 2006. "Use of Meta-Ethnography in Synthesizing Qualitative Research Findings." Presented at the Systematic Review of Qualitative Findings Conference, Sigma Theta Tau International Online Abstract Service System (STTI), July 20, London, UK. http://stti.confex.com/stti/cpngrs06/techprogram/session_7039.htm (accessed November 1, 2009).

Nye, Joe. 2009. "The Decline of Public Intellectuals." *Washington Post,* April 13, as commented on in a blog by Chris Blattman. http://chrisblattman.blogspot.com.

Office of Management and Budget (OMB). 2004. *What Constitutes Strong Evidence of Program Effectiveness.* Washington, DC: OMB. www.excelgov.org/admin/FormManager/ filesuploading/OMB_memo_on_strong_evidence.pdf.

Olsen, LeighAnne, Dara Aisner, and Michael J. McGinnis. 2007. *Institute of Medicine Roundtable on Evidence-Based Medicine.* Washington, DC: National Academy Press.

Osborne, David. 1990. *Laboratories of Democracy.* Cambridge, MA: Harvard University Press.

Patton, Michael Quinn. 2004. "The Debate about Randomized Controls in Evaluation: The Gold Standard Question." Paper delivered at the National Institutes of Health, National Cancer Institute, Bethesda, MD, September 14. http://videocast.nih.gov/ram/nci091404. ram.

Popper, Karl. 2002. *The Logic of Scientific Discovery.* London: Routledge.

Radin, Beryl. 2006. *Challenging the Performance Movement.* Washington, DC: Georgetown University Press.

———. 2008. "The Legacy of Federal Management Change." In *Performance-Based Management and Budgeting: How Governments Can Learn from Experience,* ed. Steve Redburn, Robert Shea, and Terry F. Buss. Armonk, NY: M.E. Sharpe.

Ragin, Charles. 1989. *The Comparative Method.* Berkeley: University of California Press.

Rao, Vijayendra, and Michael Woolcock. N.d. "Integrating Qualitative and Quantitative Approaches in Program Evaluation." In *Evaluating the Poverty and Distributional Impact of Economic Policies.* Washington, DC: World Bank, unpublished paper. http://siteresources. worldbank.org/INTPSIA/Resources/490023–1121114603600/12930_Chapter8.pdf (accessed November 1, 2009).

Redburn, F. Stevens, Robert Shea, and Terry F. Buss. 2008. *Performance Management and Budgeting.* Armonk, NY: M.E. Sharpe.

Rennie, Drummond. 1996. "Guarding the Guardians: A Conference on Editorial Peer Review." *Journal of the American Medical Association* 256 (27): 2391–2392.

Rennie, Drummond, and H. Luft. 2000. "Pharmacoeconomic Analysis." *Journal of the American Medical Association* 283:2156–2160.

Rennie, Drummond, Kirby Lee, and Ellen Weber. 2009. "What Do We Know about Editorial Decision Making?" Wheat Ridge, CO: Council of Science Editors. www.councilscienceeditors.org/events/2009_presentations.cfm (accessed November 1, 2009).

Rethemeyer, R. Karl, and Natalie C. Helbig. 2004. "By the Numbers." *Journal of Policy Analysis and Management* 24 (1): 179–191.

Rich, Andrew. 2005. *Think Tanks, Public Policy and the Politics of Expertise.* Cambridge: Cambridge University Press.

Rocha e Silva, Mauricio, Ana Marusic, and Adrian Stanley. 2009. "Editors' View of Evaluating and Rating Scientific Papers." Wheat Ridge, CO: Council of Science Editors. www.councilscienceeditors.org/events/2009_presentations.cfm (accessed November 1, 2009).

Root, Michael. 1993. *Philosophy of Social Science.* Cambridge: Wiley-Blackwell.

Ryan, Thomas R. 2007. *Modern Experimental Design.* Hoboken, NJ: Wiley.

Sherman, Lawrence W. 2003. "Misleading Evidence and Evidence-Led Policy." *Annuals* 589:6–19.

Sigelman, Lee. 2006. "The Coevolution of American Political Science and *APSR.*" *American Review of Political Science* 100:463–478.

Spenser, Liz, Jane Ritchie, Jane Lewis, and Lucy Dillon. 2003. *Quality in Quality Evaluation.* London, UK: UK Cabinet Office, National Center for Social Research.

Staley, Louise. 2008. *Evidence-Based Policy and Public Sector Innovation.* Victoria, Australia: Institute of Public Affairs. www.ipa.org.au/library/publication/1226382181_document_staley_vic_gov_innovation.pdf (accessed November 1, 2009).

Steinberg, Earl P., and Bryan R. Luce. 2005. "Evidence-Based? Caveat Emptor." *Health Affairs* (January–February): 82–84.

Streib, Gregory, Bert Slotkin, and Mark Rivera. 2002. "Public Administration Research from a Practitioner Perspective." *Public Administration Review* 61 (5): 515–525.

Surowiecki, James. 2005. *The Wisdom of Crowds.* New York: Anchor.

Sweet, Melissa. 2009. "Australian Report Urging More Transparency in Public Health Research Is Kept Unpublished." *British Medical Journal* 338:2238.

Tashakkori, Abbas, and Charles Teddlie. 1998. *Mixed Methods.* Thousand Oaks, CA: Sage.

Tetford, Philip. 2005. *Expert Political Judgment.* Princeton, NJ: Princeton University Press.

Thomson Reuters. N.d. "Journal Citation Reports." www.afxnews.com/products_services/scientific/Journal_Citation_Reports.

Torrance, Harry. 2008. "Building Confidence in Qualitative Research." *Qualitative Inquiry* 14 (4): 507–527.

Towne, Lisa, Lauress Wise, and Tina Winters. 2004. *Advancing Scientific Research in Education.* Washington, DC: National Research Council.

Treasury Board of Canada Secretariat. 1998. *Program Evaluation Methods: Measurement and Attribution of Program Results. Ottowa, Canada: Treasury Board of Canada Secretariat.* www.tbs-sct.gc.ca/eval/pubs/meth/pem-mep_e.pdf (accessed October 26, 2010).

Trochim, William. 2001. *The Research Methods Knowledge Base.* 2d ed. Cincinnati, OH: Atomic Dog Publishing.

U.S. Department of Education. 2005. "Scientifically Based Evaluation Methods." *Federal Register,* vol. 70, 3586, January 25.

Vaughan, Roger J., and Terry Buss. 1998. *Communicating Social Science Research to Policy-makers.* Thousand Oaks, CA: Sage.

Wildavsky, Aaron. 1987. *Speaking Truth to Power.* New York: Transaction Publishers.

Winch, Peter. 2007. *The Idea of a Social Science.* London: Routledge.

World Bank. 2000. *Integrating Quantitative and Qualitative Research in Development Projects.* Washington, DC: World Bank. www-wds.worldbank.org/external/default/main?pagePK=64193027&piPK=64187937&theSitePK=523679&menuPK=64187510&searchMenuPK=64187283&theSitePK=523679&entityID=000094946_0212310400155&searchMenuPK=64187283&theSitePK=523679.

Wright, Bradley, Lepora Manigault, and Tamika Black. 2004. "Quantitative Research Measurement in Public Administration." *Administration and Society* 35 (6): 747–764.

Yin, Robert. 2002. *Case Study Research.* Thousand Oaks, CA: Sage.

3

Evidence-Based Management and the Scholar/Practitioner Rift in the Private and Public Sectors

David E. Cavazos and Roberto J. Cavazos

In this chapter, we examine issues surrounding evidence-based management (EBMgt) and the existence of a practitioner/scholar rift in the public and private sectors. We explore the existence of underlying causes of the rift in the two sectors stemming in part from differences in the purposes and incentive structures between the public and private sectors. We then explore steps to ameliorate the rift.

There is an abundance of fads, trends, theories, and movements in management, geared toward understanding or improving the performance and effectiveness of private sector, public sector, and nonprofit organizations. New ideas developed by management school scholars migrate either attenuated or improved in a modified form to other sectors of management inquiry but rarely to practitioners. Currently, the wide recognition and appeal of the EBMgt approach as articulated and popularized by Pfeffer and Sutton (2006) has highlighted not only dissent among management scholars and practitioners as to its usefulness but also, and more important, the lack of communication of management research to practitioners. The origins of EBMgt in medicine provide the approach with a basis in objectivity. Despite this, there is disagreement among some scholars about whether this translates into applicability in sectors outside of medicine and if in fact objective evidence even exists.

Evidence-Based Management Defined

EBMgt as defined in the introduction has several permutations and nuances subject to the various EBMgt perspectives. While definitions of EBMgt differ in subtle ways, it is essentially about translating core principles based on best evidence into organizational practice (Rousseau and McCarthy 2007). The Evidence Based Management Collaborative at the Carnegie Mellon Tepper School of Business states as its credo: "Evidence-Based Management (EBMgt) enhances the overall quality of organizational decisions and practices through reflective use of relevant and best available scientific evidence. EBMgt combines conscientious, judicious use of best evidence with individual expertise; ethics; valid, reliable facts; and consideration of impact on stakeholders. Its success is enhanced by quality connections among practitioners, management educators, and scholars."

The definition and concept of EBMgt do not differ significantly between private sector and public sector organizations. While similar in core concept, the rationale, motivation, and ostensible benefits of EBMgt in the two principal sectors differ significantly.

The aspect of organizational functioning to which EBMgt is applied can be a source of misunderstanding. In some cases EBMgt is understood as an internal organizational tool to gain insights into processes, functions, and increasingly performance. Similarly, EBMgt is also used as a means to understand the context, market, or constituency of an organization.

The Private Sector View

EBMgt, based on the principles of evidence-based practice (as discussed in Chapter 1), involves achieving a critical informed analysis of management practice (Learmonth 2008). In health care, where evidence-based practice was derived, it has included using the best evidence available to make decisions regarding patient care (Pfeffer and Sutton 2006). In medicine, researchers and practitioners, who are many times embodied in the same people, have relied largely on universally accepted forms of evidence, which include randomized controlled trials, meta-analyses, and critical reviews of trials (Sackett and Mullen 1993). Examples of practices in health care derived from critical analysis include allowing staff members to call on rapid-response teams to treat patients showing signs of decline; developing steps to prevent bloodstream infections related to the use of particular types of catheters; and keeping records of medications taken by patients (Rao and Sutton 2008).

The application of evidence in EBMgt is designed to help managers make informed decisions (Sackett and Mullen 1993). EBMgt has additionally been hailed as a way to reach an informed analysis of management issues and to reach more definite conclusions regarding the uncertain nature of many management constructs and measures (Learmonth 2008). It has additionally been described as a way to get past the "strategic snake oil, discredited nostrums, partial remedies and untested management miracle cures" (Pfeffer and Sutton 2006, p. 14). Beyond such issues are the cognitive biases that influence the perceptions and thus decisions and performance of all managers, leaders, and human beings. EBMgt is thus viewed as a means to obtain objectivity.

A number of practitioner and academic publications apply EBMgt to topics ranging from business and management ethics (Miceli, Near, and Dworkin 2009) to innovation (Rao and Sutton 2008). Despite such applications, evidence-based management has not taken hold in either management practice or academe as it has in medical research and practice (Learmonth 2008). There are many reasons for the lack of diffusion; among them are the nature and status of management as a profession and the differences in nature between management researchers and practitioners.

The Scholar/Practitioner Rift

Some scholars argue that EBMgt highlights the rift between management researchers and practitioners. This rift has been explained as the result of paradigm proliferation in management science (Pfeffer 1993), management's philosophical grounding and epistemological orientation (Learmonth 2008), and the lack of scientific training and application among management practitioners (Rynes, Giluk, and Brown 2007). For instance, there are scholars who assert that, unlike medicine, management has not developed into a true profession (Trank and Rynes 2003). Thus, there are no requirements regarding scientific knowledge, certification exams, or continuing education (Rynes, Giluk, and Brown 2007). Moreover, few managers read academic journals (Rynes, Colbert, and Brown 2002).

Critical, informed analysis in management research has been accomplished with an emphasis on epistemological orientation and philosophical grounding (Learmonth 2008). However, the precise epistemological orientation that management should embrace remains in question (Azevedo 2002). There are also debates regarding whether the epistemological attributions made in management are accurate (Moldoveanu and Baum 2002). As a result of such debate and uncertainty, numerous theoretical explanations have arisen seeking to explain similar phenomena. Hence, management has been characterized by some as suffering from paradigm and theory proliferation (Pfeffer 1993). This diversity in theoretical frameworks, empirical approaches, and outcomes has been hailed as both a strength and a weakness of management (Azevedo 2002).

A seemingly contradictory phenomenon occurs in management when applying a core premise of EBMgt. Quantitative inquiry in management leads to multiple measures and explanations regarding fundamental constructs such as motivation, firm performance, and firm change. Furthermore, there remains debate regarding the extent to which standardized quantitative measures can be used to explain the complex phenomena that organization studies examine (Azevedo 2002). Causal explanation of intra-organizational behavior and phenomena may be difficult because of the inherently murky nature of organizations. As a result, the quantitative approaches relied upon by EBMgt may call into question certain established, yet empirically underdeveloped, pillars of management theory such as first-mover advantage and resource advantage (Pfeffer and Sutton 2006). Finally, because of the unresolved nature of management epistemology, as well as the complex nature of organizations, there are no universal criteria for how to determine the quality of evidence in management. Moreover, there is not an agreed-upon means to developing a common evidence base (Dopson 2006).

Proceeding without the Scholars

Despite the argument that practitioners lack the ability to comprehend complex EBMgt approaches, there appears to be a burgeoning analytics and data industry. Practitioners of analytics are found both in consulting and specialty analytics firms and in organizations. Increasingly, large organizations are relying on complex statistical software and technically trained professionals to inform organization management and strategy.

Examples of firms using rigorous analytic and evidence-based approaches and tools to improve performance and increase profitability or market share are extensive. Well-received popular books such as *Super Crunchers* (Ayers 2006), *Competing on Analytics: The New Science of Winning* (Davenport and Harris 2007), and *Money Ball* (Lewis 2004) detail the adoption of data- and evidence-intensive management approaches and tools in industries as varied as gambling, baseball, wine production, insurance, car rental, and many others. It is difficult to believe the contention that practitioners are having difficulty understanding or grasping the complexity of EBMgt. The prominent examples of Harrah's chief executive officer, Gary Loveman, formerly of Harvard Business School, or of Google's senior adviser, Hal Varian, a distinguished economist and onetime dean at the University of California, Berkeley, demonstrate that first-rate analytic and methodological talent exists among practitioners. Similarly, there are accounts of well-trained statisticians and other rigorously trained quantitative professionals working in analytic and evidence-gathering and analysis roles in business and other organizations. In brief, large and niche leading firms do not lack well-qualified methodologically sophisticated talent.

However, despite the proliferation of analytics-, data-, and evidence-based decision support systems, there does not appear to be a consistent approach to collecting, evaluating, and using evidence.

The Public Sector

Widely cited EBMgt benefits as well as its basis in objectivity have resulted in calls for its use in government and other organizations not subject to a market test. Despite its increasing appeal among public managers and some scholars, there remain doubts among management scholars as to EBMgt's efficacy and usefulness. When applied to public sector organizations, EBMgt faces many additional complexities. Lack of a market test, no clear consensus as to what constitutes evidence, and no consensus on the appropriate methodological approach to obtain evidence are but a few of these complexities. Further complicating matters are multiple disciplines, including political science, economics, public administration, social work, law, and others that form the core of public management research. There are influential postmodern and structuralist approaches doubting whether objective evidence exists. In the public sphere, practitioners and scholars must also inevitably deal with the issue of politics. While many scholars in public and traditional management express doubts about EBMgt, organizations in the public, private, and nonprofit sectors remain undeterred and widely rely on data and evidence to support decisions. It is unclear if the reservations held by some scholars are due to EBMgt being difficult to implement or to its departure from disciplinary orthodoxy and paradigms. Similarly, it is unclear if the doubts expressed by some scholars are based on the concern of practitioners about being unable to test managerial theories within organizations. Are their efforts to gain greater understanding and thus improve performance or to use evidence-based approaches to understand the organization's environment.

In an era characterized by organizations, increasingly dependent on powerful information systems and technologies for understanding the nature of evidence and its uses to support decisions, the gap between scholars and practitioners must be bridged (Moldoveanu and Baum 2002).

Use of EBMgt is not limited to Internet marketing and national security agencies. Examples of innovative and effective use of data and other forms of evidence to improve market share or effectiveness by private and public sector organizations abound. Similarly, public management scholars and social scientists have been proceeding apace researching EBMgt and evidence-based policy in a number of settings, including criminal justice, education, national security, and social services.

Among scholars of public management and administration, it has been a tenet of the "new public management" that public sector organizations should adopt techniques and advances from private sector organizations (see Chapter 8 for a discussion of this movement). Similarly, public management and administration scholars have adapted the approaches, techniques, and advances from management scholars in schools of business and enriched them with tools and insights from the social sciences.

While some claim that public sector organizations can benefit from adopting private sector approaches, some authors have questioned the veracity of this belief. It has been stated that private sector and public sector organizations are similar in all unimportant ways. Indeed, authors deploying postmodern and structural approaches have argued against EBMgt. Others have found more fundamental issues with EBMgt. Even if the premise is assumed to be useful, pragmatic constraints and room for error, fraud, and incompetence suggest a skeptical view of the use of EBMgt in public management and, more worryingly for many, in public policy formation and advocacy.

Public Sector Practice

While there are differences in the extent to which various commentators and scholars agree on the adoption of EBMgt approaches as formally articulated by Pfeffer and Sutton (2006), there has been a steady adoption of many evidence-reliant management and administrative techniques in the public sector.

The movement toward rigorous performance measurement gathered momentum with the widespread adoption of privatization beginning in the United Kingdom in the late 1960s. As the movement gathered political and popular support, cost measures were supplemented with various effectiveness and performance measures to enable comparisons between public and private sector service providers. Use of performance measurement in public organizations has become increasingly widespread in the United States (see Chapter 8 for an overview of these approaches). High-profile efforts such as the state and local innovations generated by the "reinventing government" and "laboratories of democracy" movements spawned many EBMgt approaches. At the national level, reinventing government as well as the Government Performance and Results Act of 1993 (GPRA), followed by the Program Assessment Rating Tool initiative, led to improvements in performance measurement and, in turn, in performance that relied on rigorous measurement and data collection—evidence.

Public organizations are distinct from their private sector counterparts in several ways. In government there is the issue of "complexity." Public organizations face multiple stakeholders and must frequently attend to competing requests and priorities. Conflicting stakeholders such as recipients of services and nonservice-consuming taxpayers are a complexity that public managers must frequently address. There is also permeability. Most public organizations are open systems and are, therefore, permeable. These organizations are readily influenced by external factors and often caught up in the fad of the day. They face instability, as the political cycle often forces changes, which in turn alters an organization's priorities. The change in priorities can fundamentally alter the mission and thus performance benchmarks. This in turn undermines extant performance measurement and other evidence-gathering and decision support systems. The most frequently cited difference between private and public sector organizations is the absence of competitive pressures faced by the latter. Frequently, the lack of competitive pressure leads to the absence of "market" discipline signals, guiding managers toward more optimal—based on efficiency, effectiveness, and economics—decisions. There is also the issue that the objectives of public organizations frequently tend to be vague and occasionally contradictory and incomprehensible due to the nature of the political process.

The Public Sector Scholar/Practitioner Rift

Despite cited limitations in the application of EBMgt by researchers, applied researchers and policy organizations have been actively using EBMgt principles and deploying them in the public sector and in applied policy settings.

The (medical) Cochrane Database of Systematic Reviews and Cochrane Collaboration have served as a template for the (social) Campbell Collaboration's register of Systematic Reviews of Interventions and Policy Evaluation and the Campbell Collaboration itself. The Campbell Collaboration is an international coalition of scholars whose aim is to "bring about positive social change, and to improve the quality of public and private services across the world, by preparing, maintaining and disseminating systematic reviews of existing social science evidence" (Campbell Collaboration 2007). The organization is affiliated with the American Institute for Research, "one of the largest behavioral and social science research organizations in the world [whose] overriding goal is to use the best science available to bring the most effective ideas and approaches to enhancing everyday life" (Campbell Collaboration 2007).

One of the issues that arise and distinguish private and some public sector approaches toward EBMgt can be found in the quote in the previous paragraph about the American Institute for Research. A distinguishing characteristic of some public sector EBMgt approaches is that of using existing social science data rather than firm or organizational data, as is taken to be the case in other research approaches. The point is that large-scale data are used to advocate for policy and evaluate public sector organizations, regardless of whether the relationship of the organizations' role to large-scale social indicators is firmly established.

An important consideration in deploying EBMgt in the public sector is the reality of the intersection of politics and interests in public sector organizations. It has been found that some of the findings and approaches advocated by the Cochrane Collaboration in clinical settings are not always appropriate. Moreover, EBMgt approaches are adopted as rules rather than guiding principles and are sometimes forced on managers and clinicians despite being inappropriate for the task at hand. Such forceful and compelled adoption lacking clear benefits or clinician/manager buy-in can undermine the appeal of the approach. It is also straightforward to conceive that if difficulties arise in medical clinical settings, the challenges and inappropriate use are likely to increase in more subjective or less-well-defined activities.

Similarly, a fundamental issue of true EBMgt is that it is deductive rather than inductive. A deductive-based system takes evidence and constructs theories or responses to the underlying phenomenon identified by examining the evidence. However, much of public management is based on induction. Theories of history, politics, social problems, and job creation form the foundation of many of the efforts and missions of public organizations.

Simultaneously, public sector organizations must address multiple and often conflicting goals, stakeholders, and functions, and public management scholars apply multiple research perspectives and traditions to public organizations.

Despite the presence of constraints inherent to public sector organizations, many principles of EBMgt are practiced under the guise of performance measurement. In recent years, there has been an increasing movement toward greater accountability of public sector organization performance. Traditionally, accountability for funds and meeting legal and other administrative requirements were the focus of much of public management.

Performance measure is reliant upon the development of measures and indicators, a process that requires judgment to select those that provide information useful to managers. There are many evidence-based and oriented practices in public sector organizations. There have been a good number of evidence-based techniques in some of the program evaluation literature. Still, some techniques in program evaluation consist of little more than descriptive program narratives or justifications; others are rigorously evidence based.

Disciplinary Considerations in Public Management

Beyond the practical issues of politics and constraints faced by public managers, there are the issues associated with the various academic disciplines deployed to examine issues of public management and policy. While the public management counterparts in schools of business have some disciplinary diversity with management departments, the range of disciplines and traditions conducting public management and administration is very broad. In some cases, postmodern and structural approaches question the very notions of evidence, preferring to focus instead on the preferences of citizens. There are cases of disciplines that are action oriented and others such as traditional public administration that are more concerned with compliance than with performance.

Government Also Proceeds without the Scholars

Much of the literature in both public and general management has noted the difficulties encountered in determining what constitutes evidence and the unproven ability of practitioners to grasp complex methods. Alternatively, the tendency of scholars to pursue sometimes esoteric lines of inquiry confirms the old adage, 'Those who can—do; those who can't—teach."

Despite what is conjectured in the management literature, managers in both the private and public sectors are deploying vast and sophisticated evidence-gathering and analytic systems to support managerial, policy, and strategic decisions.

Academic critiques of EBMgt warrant examination in light of the fact that several disciplines and tools have arisen to provide evidence-based decision support. It is paradoxical that while scholars in public and general management have cited the limits of EBMgt, most large organizations have moved to embrace data mining and analytics to support decisions (e.g., Davenport and Harris 2007). In fact, the increasing creation and availability of data provide an increasingly valuable storehouse of evidence. The growth of analytics and EBMgt seems to have exploded despite the reservations of management scholars.

Public management scholars have raised important and substantive questions with respect to EBMgt. Many of these methodological, philosophical, and epistemological concerns, while well founded, do little to assuage the realities of public managers who must comply with greater accountability and constituent demand all while facing resource constraints.

Examples of public sector organizations deploying rigorous EBMgt techniques abound. The New York City Police Department Compstat and Baltimore City Citystat programs alone have contributed to data-driven management and policy for law enforcement agencies around the United States and elsewhere. The school district of Philadelphia launched its School Stats program in 2006 and with it a comprehensive data- and evidence-based management of resources and instruction (Patusky, Botwinik, and Shelley 2007).

Beyond availing themselves of the tools of data management and data analysis, all brought about by improvements in information technology, public sector organizations are working in the framework followed by several U.S. federal government agencies resulting from a fundamental philosophical shift in management philosophy. The change in government management philosophy has transitioned from appraisal of performance to management of performance. It has moved from backward looking to real time. This shift has required more robust decision support systems and better understanding of measures and the basis upon which these measures are created (Government Accountability Office 2004).

Several deployments of quantitative and other rigorous EBMgt and related approaches have garnered attention and even brought popular fame to public sector leaders responsible for their adoption and implementation. Despite the positive press, there have been some obvious flaws in many of these approaches. For most scholars and scientists, finding a replicable and repeatable phenomenon is what constitutes scientific knowledge and discovery. For all of the attention, relatively few of the much-touted public sector EBMgt initiatives have yielded repeatable findings or discovery of a general principle.

Understanding Methodology: A Step toward Closing the Practitioner/Scholar Gap

Much of the controversy surrounding EBMgt centers around the nature of knowledge and inquiry and the different approaches used by scholars and practitioners (Kelemen and Bansal 2002; see also Chapter 2). Scholars are testing hypotheses and confirming earlier research. In fact, the bulk of academic disciplines, especially those steeped in the social science tradition, are built around testing hypotheses to confirm an a priori hypothesis. Often, some of these hypotheses have built-in biases and seek to confirm or find evidence of some disciplinary tenet. The notable exception is the case study approach, but according to some that is a pedagogical tool rather than a research methodology. In contrast, practitioners are seeking to understand their firms, their markets, their constituents, their customers.

The inductive approach deployed by analytical and other evidence-based organizations is widespread and discomfiting to the deductive approach dominant among some management academics and, generally, social scientists. This in part is due to the differing approaches of data gathering and analysis. The manner in which management academics and social scientists collect data and other forms of evidence is via transparent and structured data gathering. Typically, to be considered unbiased, data must be broadly aggregated and statistically reliable and preferably obtained by random sampling. The data and the methodology should enable scholars to deduce general findings and conclusions useful to gaining insights into a sector, industry, or region.

A practitioner in an organizational setting has somewhat different priorities and approaches toward data gathering and use of evidence-based findings. Frequently, the practitioner's approach is ad hoc. Evidence and the analysis supporting its use for decision making are often not part of a research program for knowledge's sake but for solving immediate and pressing problems or for evaluating performance and effectiveness in challenging environments in short time frames. The risk is that while the approach used by the practitioner may be expedient and timely, it may not be the most robust and reliable approach.

A common explanation for the disconnect between scholars and practitioners is the lack of training on the part of practitioners. As discussed, there is much capable talent being deployed on solving practical problems through EBMgt; however, much of that talent is concentrated in large or niche organizations. An additional issue is that some management scholars and social scientists are not well versed in evidence and the scientific method (Westen and Bradley 2005). This combination of differing approaches and limitations on both sides provides fertile ground for misunderstanding and perhaps even mutual suspicion; alternatively, the two sides may simply ignore each other.

Knowledge Diffusion and Feedback

Since the early 1990s (Willmott 1994), there has been a body of work demonstrating that the mechanisms and processes of diffusion of management research to so-called practitioners and functional managers are flawed. The very structures through which research knowledge is transmitted outside of academe are an impediment to the dissemination of new and potentially useful findings. While this is the case for management research generally, we have no basis to suspect that this is any different for a subset of management research—EBMgt. Most management scholars do not write for practitioners but rather for other researchers. Practitioners often take ad hoc and unconventional approaches to assembling and processing evidence to guide managerial decision making.

Similarly, many management findings and innovations by practitioners are not effectively made known to scholars. Even when practitioner findings are promulgated in practitioner trade journals and even popular business and general interest publications, they frequently fail to be acknowledged by scholars. In fact, given its history, it can be argued that EBMgt was developed outside of academic management and succeeded in obtaining academic attention when it became well known and widespread, contrary to the experience in the field of medicine.

Kelemen and Bansal (2002) advance the case that differences in communication

Table 3.1

Stylistic Differences Between Research Targeted to Academics and Research Targeted to Practitioners

	Academic	Practitioner
Orientation of research	Descriptive/predictive	Descriptive/prescriptive
Focus of research	Process	Outcomes
Attitude	Reflexive	Projective
Data collection/analysis	Thorough	Ad hoc, ambiguous
Data aggregation	High	Low
Referential system	Theory	Practice
Rhetorical devices	Narrow and institutionalized	Wide and eclectic
Criteria of goodness	Methods rigor	Practical appeal

and approach between academics and practitioners are a source of the rift between the two and of the limited diffusion of academic findings—and vice versa (see Table 3.1).

Besides the stylistic differences listed, there are some reservations among academics with respect to the basic integrity of much academic research. Some have noted that many academic fields do not have replication policies for quantitative research. In other words, often academics will not provide data from surveys or generated from other sources. The increasing importance of institutional research boards and privacy protections may reinforce and even extend the opacity. Hard science and some economic journals have replication requirements, but management and public management journals do not have replication or data warehouse requirements (McCullough and McKitrick 2009)

Conclusion: Bridging the Gap

> *Then I realized that there has to be a problem with education—any form of formal education. I collected enough evidence that once you get a theory in your head, you can no longer understand how people can operate without it. And you look at practitioners, lecture them on how to do their business, and live under the illusion that they owe you their lives. Without your theories and your learning they will never go anywhere.*
> —Nassim Taleb, *History Written by the Losers*,
> Foreword to Pablo Triana's *Lecturing Birds How to Fly* (2009)

Despite the limitations of EBMgt, both general and public management scholars agree that the movement toward EBMgt has been progressing apace for a number of years. Ideally, research findings by scholars would be very useful to practitioners and vice versa, yet a communication gap between researchers and practitioners exists. The explanations provided for this gap have ranged from sociological explanations to misunderstandings and differences on the nature of inquiry, and, most salient to EBMgt, what constitutes evidence. The gap is evidenced by many practitioners eschewing research and many researchers eschewing research benefiting practitioners. Obviously, both groups can benefit from sharing information, findings, and perspectives and from enriching each other's efforts. How should the gap be bridged?

Several solutions to closing the gap have been proposed. One suggested solution is to craft academic research in response to or in collaboration with applied researchers. Some of the approaches based on changing knowledge diffusion through some form of journal versioning—or abstracting—can make significant inroads into bridging the scholar/practitioner gap in EBMgt. The social sciences have some versioning in their best-known professional journals. The American Economics Association, publisher of the very rigorous academic journal *The American Economic Review,* publishes several journals targeted to both practitioners and interested lay readers. In one of these journals, cutting-edge complex research is distilled to its implications for practitioners and policy makers. While such an approach has been discussed for the management literature, it has yet to be undertaken.

In public management and administration, a prominent scholar and practitioner once noted that public management and public administration journals were nowhere to be seen on the shelves of top public managers' offices or homes.[1] To these authors it is evident that the rift between management scholars and practitioners is fundamental and cannot be entirely rectified via a few workshops, outreach efforts, and new journals. There is a fundamental knowledge issue at work in this rift. Events in financial, economic, and other sectors have shown a disconnect between theoretical knowledge and practical knowledge. The core issue is whether theory informs practice and vice versa. That EBMgt arose in an applied setting is instructive. It has followed a progression from know-how, bottom-up tinkering rather than ideas developed in an ivory tower and promulgated to practitioners. No hypotheses were being tested and no top-down demonstration programs were started. It was shop-floor, front-line tinkering that brought EBMgt to the fore. Here knowledge went from the practitioner to the academic. The rift can best be bridged by examination of the assumptions of knowledge present for millennia. How does knowledge flow in all areas of human endeavor, and is management in general, and EBMgt specifically, any different?

Note

1. Comment by Terry Buss on the use of academic publications by practitioners.

References

Ayers, I. 2006. *Super Crunchers: Why Thinking by Numbers Is the New Way to Be Smart.* New York: Random House.
Azevedo, J. 2002. "Updating Organizational Epistemology." In *The Blackwell Companion to Organizations,* ed. J.C. Baum, chapter 31. Oxford: Blackwell.

Campbell Collaboration. 2007. *Steps in Proposing, Preparing, Submitting, and Editing of Campbell Collaboration Systematic Reviews.* London: Campbell Collaboration.

Davenport, Thomas H., and Jeanne Harris. 2007. *Competing on Analytics: The New Science of Winning.* Boston: Harvard Business School Press.

Dopson, S. 2006. "Why Does Knowledge Stick? What We Can Learn from the Case of Evidence-Based Health Care." *Public Money and Management* 26:85–86.

Government Accountability Office. 2004. *High Performing Organizations: Metrics, Means, and Mechanisms for Achieving High Performance in the 21st Century Public Management Environment.* GAO-04–343SP. Washington, DC: Government Accountability Office.

Kelemen, M., and P. Bansal. 2002. "The Conventions of Management Research and Their Relevance to Management Practice." *British Journal of Management* 13:97–108.

Learmonth, M. 2008. "Speaking Out: Evidence-Based Management: A Backlash against Pluralism in Organizational Studies?" *Organization* 15:283–291.

Lewis, Michael. 2004. *Money Ball.* New York: W.W. Norton.

McCullough, Bruce D., and Ross R. McKitrick. 2009. *Check the Numbers: The Case for Due Diligence in Policy Formation.* Calgary, Canada: Fraser Institute.

Miceli, M.P., J.P. Near, and T.M. Dworkin. 2009. "A Word to the Wise: How Managers and Policy-makers Can Encourage Employees to Report Wrongdoing." *Journal of Business Ethics* 86:379–396.

Moldoveanu, M.C., and J.C. Baum. 2002. "Contemporary Debates in Organizational Epistemology." In *The Blackwell Companion to Organizations,* ed. J.C. Baum, chapter 33. Oxford: Blackwell.

Patusky, Christopher, Leigh Botwinik, and Mary Shelley. 2007. *IBM Center on the Business of Government: The Philadelphia SchoolStat Model.* Washington, DC: IBM Center for the Business of Government.

Pfeffer, J. 1993. "Barriers to the Advance of Organization Science: Paradigm Development as an Independent Variable." *Academy of Management Review* 18:599–620.

Pfeffer, J., and R. Sutton. 2006. *Hard Facts, Dangerous Half-Truths and Total Nonsense: Profiting from Evidence-Based Management.* Boston: Harvard Business School Press.

Rao, H., and D. Sutton. 2008. "The Ergonomics of Innovation." *McKinsey Quarterly* 4:131–141.

Rousseau, D.M., and S. McCarthy. 2007. "Educating Managers from an Evidence Based Perspective." *Academy of Management Learning and Education* 6:8–101.

Rynes, S.L., A.E. Colbert, and K.G. Brown. 2002. "HR Professionals' Beliefs about Effective Human Resource Practices: Correspondence between Research and Practice." *Human Resource Management* 41:149–174.

Rynes, S.L., T.L. Giluk, and K.G. Brown. 2007. "The Very Separate Worlds of Academic and Practitioner Periodicals in Human Resource Management: Implications for Evidence-Based Management." *Academy of Management Journal* 50:987–1008.

Sackett, P.R., and E.J. Mullen. 1993. "Beyond Formal Experimental Design: Towards an Expanded View of the Training Evaluation Process." *Personnel Psychology* 46:613–627.

Trank, C.Q., and S.L. Rynes. 2003. "Who Moved Our Cheese? Reclaiming Professionalism in Business Education." *Academy of Management Learning and Education* 2:119–122.

Triana, Pablo. 2009. *Lecturing Birds How to Fly. Can Mathematical Theories Destroy the Financial Market?* New York: John Wiley and Sons.

Westen, D., and R. Bradley. 2005. "Empirically Supported Complexity: Rethinking Evidence-Based Practice in Psychotherapy." *Psychological Science* 14:266–271.

Willmott, H. 1994. "Management Education: Provocations to a Debate." *Management Learning* 25 (1): 105–136.

4

Believing Is Seeing

The Impact of Beliefs on Evidence-Based Management Practices

Ruth T. Zaplin and Don Blohowiak

Managing in today's public institutions can be a very complex affair. In this complex environment, it is a conceit, we believe, to expect that by simply considering more data and obtaining more information about evidence-based management (EBMgt) practices, including allegedly *best* practices, managers will effect wiser or more successful management practices. Here we consider EBMgt from the perspective of scholar-practitioners and outline concerns from both the theoretical and practical domains. Additionally, we detail a practical approach that managers can take to pursue the worthy aims of EBMgt that takes a holistic, and we believe realistic, view of the complexity and challenges of managing in modern public organizations.

The first question we explore is: What is EBMgt from a practicing manager's perspective and is implementing it possible in today's public institutions? Even if adopting EBMgt were a practical goal, we have deep concerns that at the heart of EBMgt is a critical, and terribly flawed, assumption—that the EBMgt practitioner is a rational actor who responds favorably to the premise that *knowing better yields doing better.* This assumption leads us to pose a second question: Assuming a clearly determined process for implementing a best practice or most effective action as indicated by the evidence, will such a protocol be followed? In our consideration of these two questions, we present a preferred method for managing public institutions, including a description of the conditions we believe necessary for EBMgt practices to have the greatest potential for successful implementation.

Question 1: What Is EBMgt from a Practicing Manager's Perspective and Is Implementing It Possible in Today's Public Institutions?

EBMgt practices have been influenced strongly by the developments, roughly over the past decade, by the practice of evidence-based medicine. Evidence-based medicine originated in the United Kingdom in the early 1970s as part of an agenda first propounded by Cochrane (as cited in Hamlin 2002) for improving the effectiveness and efficiency of medical practice in Britain. This agenda was taken up by the Mc-Master Medical School (as cited in Hamlin 2002) in Ontario, Canada, which coined the term *evidence-based medicine*. Its Evidence-Based Medicine Group (as cited in Hamlin 2002) defined evidence-based medicine as "the collection, interpretation, and integration of valid important and applicable patient-reported, clinician-observed, and research-derived evidence . . . to improve the quality of clinical judgments and facilitate cost-effective health care" (Tanner 1999, as cited in Hamlin 2002).

EBMgt enthusiasts err, we suggest, when implying that an evidence-based orientation for managerial practice is comparable to the scientific method used in the practice of medicine; this applies to managing complex institutions. We conclude this for two reasons: (1) despite the body of qualitative research on managerial work in the literature, we argue that managing a public institution, with multiple constituencies of humans in dynamic relationships, numerous pressure points resulting from conflicts in priorities, policies, and resource allocations, and numerous other sources of complexity, is not as consistent or predictable as phenomena subject to the laws of physics or biology, and (2) effective management practices, no matter how well documented, cannot be expected to be replicated the way physical science phenomena are. In plain English, managing effectively in today's public institutions is not a matter of *insert tab A into slot B* or *push on X to cause Y* or other protocol (or, in the vernacular, *cookbook*) solutions.

In regard to our first point about the flawed analog between evidence-based medicine practices and managerial practices, organizations do not share characteristics as predictable or consistent as the human body. Every human being comes into the world with a virtually identical skeletal structure (as the familiar song instructs, "the leg bone's connected to the thigh bone"). Organizations, conversely, organize in hugely diverse ways. There may be a human resources department or not, or policy research or not, or three layers of management or thirteen or more. While every human body the world over is basically structured and functionally operates the same as all others, the same cannot be said for organizations. Even if one were to accept the desirability of EBMgt in public institutions, a very formidable practical challenge looms, threatening to thwart its potential implementation as a preferred method for managing public institutions.

Thus, while evidence-based medicine rests on the foundation of the scientific method—rigorous testing amid stringent controls, copious data gathering amid defined documentary procedures, reproducible results, predictable consistency in generalized outcomes, and so on—establishing the primacy of evidence for the complexities of organizational decision making, which takes place among myriad open systems, arguably makes it considerably different from the evidentiary base for establishing medical or other physical phenomena protocols.

Rousseau (2006b) notes that "arriving at consensus in social science takes different forms than it does in medicine and other fields, because cause-effect connections in organizational research are not as readily subject to controlled experiments" (p. 1091).

In the words of Nobel laureate Friedrich August von Hayek, aspiring to have social science imitate physical science processes constitutes the "pretense of knowledge" (von Hayek 1989). Economist von Hayek argued that there was a danger in social sciences' attempting to model themselves after the methods of the physical sciences, whereby they adopt a "'scientific' attitude . . . since it involves a mechanical and uncritical application of habits of thought to fields different from those in which they have been formed" (p. 3).

Sumantra Ghoshal echoed the sentiment and injected the critical element of human intentionality as a distinction between the physical and social sciences: "We have adopted the 'scientific approach' of trying to discover patterns and laws, and have replaced all notions of human intentionality with a firm belief in causal determinism for explaining all aspects of corporate performance. In effect, we have professed that business is reducible to a kind of physics in which even if individual managers do play a role, it can safely be taken as determined by the economic, social, and psychological laws that inevitably shape people's actions" (2005, p. 77).

What is measurable and measured may not be meaningful in guiding effective practice toward successfully delivering desired outcomes. Albert Einstein was said to have a sign hanging in his office reading, *Not everything that counts can be counted, and not everything that can be counted counts.* In the same spirit, von Hayek notes, "While in the physical sciences it is generally assumed, probably with good reason, that any important factor which determines the observed events will itself be directly observable and measurable; in the study of such complex phenomena as the market, which depends on the actions of many individuals, all the circumstances which will determine the outcome of a process . . . will hardly ever be fully known or measurable" (p. 3). What ends up being measured in complex environments may not be what is important but rather that which is easily measurable.

Just as bad, turning to so-called expert advice as a proxy for meaningful measures may place managerial judgment teetering on the flimsiest of foundations. In her 2005 address as president of the Academy of Management, Denise Rousseau lamented, "Research findings don't appear to have transferred well to the workplace. Instead of a scientific understanding of human behavior and organizations, managers, including those with MBAs, continue to rely largely on personal experience, to the exclusion of more systematic knowledge. Alternatively, managers follow bad advice from business books or consultants based on weak evidence" (2006a, p. 257).

Regarding our objection concerning the reproducibility of so-called best practices, that is, taking some "proven processes" from Organization A and transplanting them to Organization Z, we think it is important to think of organizational practices with a *systems* orientation. Every manager operates in a large context that involves the policies and practices not only of his or her area of responsibility but that interact and influence other departments within the organization and multiple constituencies beyond the institution. Such complex relationships, which can vary widely from public agency to public agency, will impact the efficacy of any evidence-based practice that one attempts to implement. Borrowing an analogy from management theorist Russell Ackoff, implementing an amalgam of "best practices" in an organization is akin to trying to build a car with the best car parts in the world collected from different makes. Because those parts, even those demonstrated as best by clear and compelling evidence, were not designed to fit together, you would have nothing more than a heap of shiny but disjointed—and therefore useless—parts. As leadership expert Michael Maccoby, who worked with Ackoff on client change projects and shared the auto parts example with us, puts it, "Improving one part of a system does not necessarily make that system better and may make it worse" (2010).

An additional concern worth noting here is that even if EBMgt could be implemented in an organization, it is ripe for practice in a fashion that is reductionist, formulaic, and risk averse. In other words, favoring EBMgt's "proven" techniques inherently discourages innovation and risk. Once managers believe they are using the best techniques, they may conclude they have *the answer* and are doing it *right,* and stop seeking improvements or, arguably, more appropriate approaches to their challenges and opportunities. This, as Karl Popper (1985) argued, is the mistake of attributing authority to empirical evidence.

All that said, we believe EBMgt seems far more appealing than seat-of-the-pants management. Yet, ironically, unlike the case of evidence-based medicine, the efficacy of EBMgt is far from empirically established by evidence (Arndt and Bigelow 2009). It is therefore not surprising, as works in this volume demonstrate, that the case for EBMgt is far from definitive.

This takes us back to our concern over how one defines EBMgt in the first place. In Britain, for example, the type of evidence used in the practice of EBMgt can vary in strength ranging typically from "a systematic review of multiple, well-designed randomized controlled trials" to "the opinions of respected authorities based on clinical evidence, descriptive studies or reports of expert committees" (Sackett 1997, as cited in Hamlin 2002). To Stewart (1998, as cited in Hamlin 2002), EBMgt is simply an attitude of mind that:

- thinks in terms of evidence for decisions and about the nature of the evidence;
- asks questions such as, What is happening? How is it happening? Why? What are the consequences?
- is aware of the potential limitations of the different answers; and
- is interested in research to try to find the answers or at least to reduce the ignorance.

In theory, we conclude that EBMgt, as an attitude of mind, is certainly possible within public institutions. And, while we accept the fact that EBMgt cannot match the research, clinical trials, and patient preferences of evidence-based medicine,

EBMgt should consist of good-quality research; a consensus of recognized professional experts and/or affirmed professional experience that substantiates practice; quality improvement; operational or evaluative data; and the systematic feedback of opinions or preferences of client managers (Hamlin 2002). An ideal was suggested crisply by Rousseau (2006a, p. 267): "Evidence-based practice is not one-size-fits all; it's the best current evidence coupled with informed judgment."

In practice, though, as scholar-practitioners, we suggest that actual implementation of EBMgt is another matter. Our fear is that EBMgt once popularized will manifest itself as merely a more sophisticated version of prevailing practices that might be described as "techniques of the month." Significantly, however, under EBMgt's rubric such hodgepodge approaches to so-called best practices will appear to have the imprimatur of "legitimate authority." When patchwork implementations fail to show efficacy, EBMgt will be tossed like another worn-out fad of the month. "We tried that it and it didn't work; EBMgt is overrated" will be the common refrain.

Any serious attempt to import the principles of EBMgt into real organizational environments must answer a key question for any "hot" or "proven" practice: *Why* does this method or approach work? In other words, what are the general underlying theories or principles giving rise to a specific practice's effectiveness? Without identifying that principle-based foundation, one cannot predict the applicability of a technique that is apparently successful in Environment A to the differing particulars in Environment Z. As Cavazos and Cavazos write hauntingly in Chapter 3, "For all of the attention, relatively few of the much-touted public sector EBMgt initiatives have yielded repeatable findings or discovery of a general principle." While repeatable findings may or may not equate to valid evidence of best practice, as noted, the idea of discovering and stating a general principle to guide additional implementations is vital. As Kurt Lewin, the social psychologist, wrote more than a half century ago, "Nothing is as practical as a good theory" (Lewin 1945, p. 129). Without establishing the underlying theoretical bases for the "evidence base," EBMgt risks becoming a mishmash of practices available wholesale from Tactics R Us.

Question 2: Assuming a Clearly Determined Process for Implementing a Best Practice or Most Effective Action as Indicated by the Evidence, Will It Be Followed?

Implicit in the EBMgt proposition is the assumption that a practitioner is a rational actor. In practical terms—*give the manager enough good data, and he or she will take prudent and effective action.* This sounds both appealing and reasonable in the abstract. However, this same rational-actor assumption that undergirds much traditional economic theory has been discredited because of its glaring deficiencies. Any theory, framework, or practice model largely predicated on rational actors fails to explain and predict how real people make real decisions regarding their own economic interests—with their hearts and guts, hopes and fears, prides and prejudices.

Opposition from the Depths

Human behavior is largely driven by influences that are neither rational nor often even in the actor's conscious awareness. Consider that *manager* is but a role occupied by individuals subject to all the predilections and foibles facing other humans. As with the general population, it is not difficult to locate overweight managers with poor eating habits, or managers who smoke, drink too much, or sleep too little. As should be obvious to even the most casual observer, information about best practices, even those for one's own well-being, do not effectively and consistently influence behavior. Well-educated and savvy individuals who make poor lifestyle choices live in a media-saturated society. While they certainly have been exposed to ample evidence that they are making choices in opposition to best practices for good health and longevity, they often make choices contrary to their own interests.

Dramatic testimony to the failure of information to trump other motivations can be found in the medico-psychological literature (for example, Gordon and Haskell 1997; Linden, Stossel, and Maurice 1996; Nordmann et al. 2001) covering the challenges of prompting sustained lifestyle changes in patients who suffered a heart attack. When a cardiologist tells a patient who has already suffered a heart attack, "Change your lifestyle to healthier habits or you will *die,*" that, it sadly turns out, is not sufficiently motivating evidence to provoke behavioral change. Much more elaborate interventions, such as a twelve-month counseling program including a four-week residential stay, are required to effect "everyday habitual behavioral changes" (Lisspers et al. 2005, p. 43).

Is it reasonable to expect that managers exposed to EBMgt will be more conscientiously rational stewards of their organizations than so many appear to be of themselves? We contend that implementing EBMgt, or any practice that necessitates modifying behavior, requires more than a persuasive or even compelling list of reasons why this makes sense. We argue that it requires a rational actor exercising what Chalmers Brothers (2005) calls the "big eye"—the increased ability to see and notice ourselves and our actions, which, in turn, requires, according to Brothers, "taking a look at how we look at things" (p. 3).

Many of the inputs to behavior, even for the most rational of managers, lie outside the rational, intellectual mind. Every mind holds many conceptions of the world and beliefs about it that shape one's perceptions, judgments, and actions. Consider, for example, why a large percentage of organizational change initiatives go nowhere. It is not, we suggest, because they lack grand visions, noble intentions, and sound business cases but because people cannot see or appreciate the "real" reality they face. Likewise, in the words of Senge et al. (2004), "Studies of corporate mortality show that most Fortune 500 companies fail to outlast a few generations of management, not because of resource constraints, but because they are unable to 'see' the real threats they face and the imperative to change" (p. 29). They quote Arie de Geus: "The signals of threat are always abundant and recognized by many. Yet somehow they fail to penetrate the corporate immune system response to reject the unfamiliar" (p. 29). In short, behavior can be thought of as the visible output of many complex inputs, most of which are invisible and some of which are largely elusive or inaccessible within the recesses of the mind.

In a variation on the familiar phrase from the U.S. Declaration of Independence, we all hold certain truths to be self-evident. In the diverse world at large, and even in an organization with clearly declared, self-avowed "core values," people do not all hold the same truths, no matter what they profess. Even one's most deeply held truths may be evident to everyone except the person holding them, and this has fueled psychotherapy for a century and a half.

Truths and beliefs are essentially synonymous (Dewey 1910; Newberg and Waldman 2006; O'Connor and McDermott 1997). A belief is a conception and conviction about how things are or should be (Koltko-Rivera 2004). We each hold our own distinct beliefs about the nature of the world, the nature of humanity, morality and justice, our own capabilities and worth, the appropriate role of our institution in society, and the capability and potential of the people we work with. We believe that the world is ordered and rational or not; that justice tends to prevail or not; that people are basically good or not, and trustworthy or not; that the future is secure or not. A person may believe that she has free will or not; that she is autonomous or not; that she is worthy of loving or not, that she is competent or not; and so much more (Beck 1995; Koltko-Rivera 2004; McMullin 2000; Rokeach 1960).

Beliefs influence actions. This simple, albeit powerful, hypothesis was graphically depicted in the Ladder of Inference, Figure 4.1, initially developed by Chris Argyris and subsequently presented in Peter Senge's *The Fifth Discipline* (1990).

As explained by Bellinger (2004), what the diagram shows is that we begin with *real data and experience,* the kind that would be captured by a movie camera, that did not lie. We then choose a set of *selected data and experience* that we pay attention to. To this selected data and experience we *affix meaning,* develop *assumptions,* come to *conclusions,* and finally develop *beliefs.* Beliefs then form the basis of our *actions,* which create additional real data and experience. It is our beliefs that influence the selected data and experience we pay attention to—they essentially establish an internal reinforcing loop that short-circuits reality. The tendency is to select data to pay attention to that which supports our beliefs. Bellinger suggests that as our beliefs become more rigid, the selected data and experience we are willing to pay attention to will become a smaller and smaller portion of reality and poses a relevant question: How do we stop short-circuiting reality and begin to see reality for what it really is?

Again, beliefs influence actions. Thus, if one believes that life is a zero-sum game and that rewards tend to flow to those who are the most fortunate no matter how earnest their work effort, one is going to be a very different kind of boss

Figure 4.1 **The Ladder of Inference**

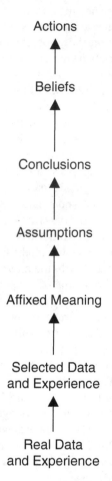

Actions

Beliefs

Conclusions

Assumptions

Affixed Meaning

Selected Data
and Experience

Real Data
and Experience

(or parent) from one who believes that life is boundless in its abundance and that rewards should be shared equally among team members.

Mark Koltko-Rivera won an award from the American Psychological Association for his article on beliefs, or *worldviews,* as he calls them. "Worldviews," he wrote, "exercise a pervasive influence on many different kinds of behavior throughout many levels of social abstraction, from the individual and the dyad to the collective and the society" (Koltko-Rivera 2004, pp. 11–12).

Beliefs, more than objective evidence, color judgment and action. As Albert Bandura (1995) contends, "People's level of motivation, affective states, and actions are based more on what they believe than on what is objectively the case" (p. 2), or on what the evidence suggests, one might say. In turn, what people believe is often bolstered by evidence, but only such evidence as selected consciously or not, to confirm what they already believe. Psychologist Martin Seligman (1993) explains, "It is perilously easy to live our lives noticing only evidence in favor of our deep beliefs and to shun testing whether those beliefs are false" (p. 246).

A book chronicling many examples of "the irresistible pull of irrational behavior" recently made it onto the best-seller lists of both the *New York Times* and the *Wall Street Journal* (Brafman and Brafman 2008). Evidence of humans' irrationality and apparent immunity to information born of rational thought abounds (see some notable examples in the next section).

EBMgt is positioned as a counterbalance to these proclivities. In Chapter 3, Cavazos and Cavazos write that "cognitive biases . . . influence the perceptions and thus decisions and performance of all managers, leaders, and human beings. EBMgt is thus viewed as a means to obtain objectivity." Likewise, Lyles, in Chapter 5 suggests, "Optimally, EBMgt should counterbalance bias, overcome individuals' limited personal experiences, develop judgment, and challenge groupthink."

While we agree that would be optimal, by what mechanism will EBMgt somehow trump humans' pervasive propensities to eschew objectivity? People, after all, are renowned for their capacity to ignore the evidence.

Three Examples of Truly Irrational Decision Making

Here is a disturbing cautionary tale of nonrational decision making overruling the other kind, as documented by PBS's *NOVA* (NOVA 2006). KLM airlines pilot and aviation safety expert Jacob Van Zanten, with more than eleven thousand hours in the cockpit, is frustrated after being routed for an unscheduled stop in the Canary Islands. About to come up on his mandatory rest time, a practice designed to minimize human error caused by fatigue, during which the pilot could not fly under penalty of imprisonment, Van Zanten grows impatient at the small airport, which is crowded by other planes also diverted there.

Apparently Captain Van Zanten believes that takeoff is paramount to avoid the inconvenience of an unscheduled overnight in a tropical backwater requiring accommodations for 234 passengers, 52 of them children. Compounding the impact, an unscheduled overnight stay for KLM 4805 would mean the delay of returning fourteen crew to their home base in Amsterdam. Furthermore, that implies the ripple effect of disrupting flights elsewhere in the KLM system, because a large plane and more than a dozen crew will not be where they are expected to be.

While waiting for clearance to depart the Tenerife airport, Van Zanten seizes the opportunity to refuel his plane. He fills up—fifty-five tons, not just enough to get to the scheduled next destination, but enough to take the plane all the way back to Amsterdam, adding significant weight to the plane's takeoff from the small airport with its short runways. With weather worsening, and many diverted planes jockeying for takeoff position, Van Zanten, KLM's chief pilot, whose main job at the Dutch airline was to train other pilots in safe flying procedures, orders his crew to do the unthinkable. He initiates takeoff of his 747 on a heavily fog-shrouded runway, without clearance from the tower.

Klaas Meurs, the first officer in Van Zanten's cockpit, speaks up. "Wait a minute, we don't have an ATC clearance," he says, according to the cockpit voice recorder. The captain, caught in a potentially embarrassing lapse of safety protocol, tells his copilot to ask for clearance from the tower. The tower responds with permission to fly the planned route once airborne, but, critically, not permission to take off, which is given in a distinct communication protocol.

Nonetheless, the impatient-to-fly captain orders, "Let's go," and thrusts the plane's engines. Thirteen seconds later, as the KLM crew begins taking off, it sees through the fog a wayward 747 on its runway. That Pan Am jet, also unexpectedly diverted to Tenerife airport, took a wrong turn at the unfamiliar airport. It lay immediately in the path of the prematurely accelerating KLM plane.

Captain Van Zanten catches sight of the obstructing jet in front of him and implores his fuel-ladened craft to rise faster than aerodynamics will allow. "Damn! Come on! Come on! Come on! Come on!" Finally, he implores, "Please!"

The force of his impatient will and all of his formidable experience and skill were insufficient to overcome the physics of the situation. The bottom of the KLM jet strikes the top of the Pan Am jet. The KLM plane plummets and explodes into a massive fireball, killing everyone onboard and taking the lives of many Pan Am passengers. This collision between two 747s, in 1977, became the worst accident in aviation history, taking the lives of 583 people.

From an evidence-based perspective, ample evidence, knowledge, training, and experience were tragically trumped in this situation by other factors, very human factors that lie outside the rational domain. This highly dramatic example of a professional overruling what he knows in service to other needs or commitments (in this case, maintaining a schedule, preserving customer service by avoiding inconvenience, upholding a reputation for reliability) might be dismissed as a glaring aberration, a rarity that proves the general rule that people yield to their knowledge and act rationally and responsibly. That hopeful interpretation is not supported by the evidence.

For example, Senge et al. (2004) describe how in the early 1980s, executives from U.S. auto companies started making regular trips to Japan to find out why the Japanese automakers were outperforming their U.S. counterparts. Speaking with one Detroit executive after such a trip, Senge could see that the executive had not been impressed by the competition. "They didn't show us real plants," the Detroit executive said.

"Why do you say that?" Senge asked.

"Because there were no inventories. I've seen plenty of assembly facilities in my life, and these were not real plants. They'd been staged for our tour."

Within a few years, it became painfully obvious how wrong this assessment was. According to Senge et al. (2004), "These managers had been exposed to a radically different type of 'just-in-time' production system, and they were not prepared to see what they were being exposed to. They were unprepared for an assembly facility that didn't have huge piles of inventory. What they saw was bounded by what they already knew. In short, they hadn't developed the capacity for seeing with fresh eyes" (p. 28). Not only is human perception selective; people commonly overrule the evidence they do perceive. This is further demonstrated in our third example.

It is generally accepted that it was Al-Qaeda terrorists from several different nations and not the Iraqi government that executed the destruction of the World Trade Center buildings in New York City and crashed commercial airliners into the Pentagon and a Pennsylvania farm field on September 11, 2001. From an evidentiary standpoint, the nation of Iraq was no more culpable than Ireland. And yet, during the 2004 U.S. presidential campaign, several polls showed that majorities of those surveyed believed that Saddam Hussein was either partly or largely responsible for the 9/11 attacks (University at Buffalo 2009). Even when confronted during "challenge interviews" with what researchers described as overwhelming evidence that there was no link to Iraq, voters who reported believing in a link between Saddam and 9/11 continued to believe their own arguments in support of the discredited link (with one lone exception). So common is this tendency to freely dismiss evidence, our vernacular offers a sardonic shorthand to describe the situation: "Don't confuse me with facts; my mind is already made up."

Such an attitude can be found in abundance. Drive down most any freeway and notice the well-dressed, apparently smart and successful professionals and managers who are reading and texting while driving—this, despite ubiquitous and incessant news reports presenting compelling evidence that such practices can be fatally dangerous. In 2008, nearly six thousand people died in crashes involving a distracted or inattentive driver, and more than half a million were injured; driver distraction accounted for about one in five crashes (National Highway Traffic Safety Administration 2009). A study by Virginia Tech showed that texting while driving increased one's risk of a crash more than twentyfold (Box 2009). It is not a lack of evidence or awareness of the facts that contributes to the problem, which is growing, not shrinking, despite the publicity of the dangers.

Becoming aware of information or best practices does not necessarily change behavior—in the workplace or life at large. Rynes, Brown, and Colbert (2002) surveyed experienced managers of the human resources function and found that a majority of them labored under mistaken assumptions about effective human resources practices according to the research literature. In the executive commentary following the article in the Academy of Management's *Executive* journal, Richard A. Hansen, both a human resources practitioner for more than a quarter century and a former professor at the City College of New York, with a PhD from Columbia, wrote a most candid and revealing rejoinder to the indictment of practitioners' professional ignorance. "For most [human resources] officers, belief follows practice. We tend to believe in those things we do and are able to implement." Then, in an astonishingly candid challenge to the very premise of EBMgt, Hansen, the practitioner with scholarly roots, concluded with, "Unfortunately, I don't think that greater exposure to the literature will have much impact on us" (Hansen 2002, p. 103). Need we translate? "Don't confuse me with facts, my mind is already made up."

A manager who neither is open to considering the value of evidence nor appreciates how she uniquely processes and assesses data cannot derive the benefit of EBMgt, we posit, no matter how deeply steeped she becomes in its intricacies.

The challenge might be thought of as managers becoming aware of and balancing their personal beliefs (personal creed or dogma) with evidence. As scholar-practitioners who coach managers and executives in the public, private, and not-for-profit sectors, we recognize that the opportunity to improve management of public institutions (and others) includes an orientation to evidence—the attitude of mind we suggested earlier. The approach we advocate is broader, however. It entails helping managers learn to think more holistically about themselves, the people they lead, and the environment in which they operate. Thinking more holistically about themselves entails increasing their awareness of their unique mind-set and its attendant beliefs and worldviews, including their preferred ways of knowing, their taken-for-granted processes for drawing conclusions and making judgments, their core beliefs, and the like. Thinking more holistically about the people they lead entails the ability to exercise what Maccoby (2007, p. xviii) calls personality intelligence—the ability to understand people, including different kinds of personalities. Thinking more holistically about and acting skillfully in the context they are working in entails developing what Maccoby calls strategic intelligence—an interactive mix of analytic, practical, and creative elements (p. 186). Not only does Maccoby's model, described in the next section, encompass the critical capabilities today's leaders need; we believe it rises to fulfill the *intent* of EBMgt.

The Leaders We Need

In his book *The Leaders We Need, and What Makes Us Follow* (2007), leadership expert Michael Maccoby concludes that managers who are effective leaders of change take a systems view of themselves and their organizations. Maccoby terms this managerial competence, *strategic intelligence.* This capacity includes *foresight,* the ability to see patterns and trends that are likely to impact the organization; *partnering,* the ability to work with others who complement the manager's skills, to develop an effective leadership team; *visioning,* the ability to think systemically and design the holistic system that fits the organization's purpose; and *motivating,* the ability to empower and motivate followers and collaborators to implement programs and processes that realize the vision. Such abilities are further strengthened, in truly effective managers, by *personality intelligence,* the understanding of self and others, which requires both intellectual and emotional development.

In leadership workshops based on his book, Maccoby added that leaders gain the trust of followers by communicating and practicing a defined, personally relevant leadership philosophy. The most effective philosophies, he suggests, include a

Figure 4.2 **Strategic Intelligence**

Copyright © The Maccoby Group, PC.

statement of the organization's purpose, the core values necessary to achieve that purpose, and specific definitions of how results will be evaluated. By articulating a leadership philosophy, Maccoby argues, managers clarify what people can expect from them, and it becomes the basis for open dialogue about decisions. These elements are graphically represented in Figure 4.2.

This model, like so many others offered by countless management theorists and consultants, might be assailed as overly idealistic. It is, we admit, comprehensive—and that is exactly why we find it appealing. Managing today means doing more than solving problems; it means, as Harvard's Ronald Heifetz put it, adapting to complexity (Heifetz 1998). The energy behind interest in EBMgt in public institutions, we suggest, is really a call for better—meaning more thoughtful and effective—management. Steeping public sector managers and leaders in models such as Maccoby's—and helping them move past their biases, blind spots, and limiting worldviews—is what we believe public institutions need to do. While it may seem self-serving for us to say so, our experience as executive coaches leads us to conclude that intensive, candid, dialogue-based management development serves as an excellent antidote to managerial mental myopia. Mentoring, peer groups, and other dialogue-based methods may also be effective in helping managers to *think* more effectively—and this, we contend, really is the challenge.

As executive coaches who work with managers, we strive to help them overcome common lapses and distortions in thinking about evidence. These include the following:

- "Will the boss buy it?" (an idea's attraction to power is not a test of its efficacy)
- "I know this works because it has in the past." (trend bias error)
- "Obviously this works—everybody does it." (popularity as efficacy error)
- "This must work. Organization X uses it. They're successful. So this method must be an effective 'best practice.'" (attribution error)
- "You may have those figures, but . . ." (dismissal/preemptory negation error)
- The error of overprivileging particular data or ignoring a dimension of salient value, for example, tracking efficiency measures such as units per whatever, without also measuring—or valuing—quality, customer satisfaction, or retention of competent employees. Additionally, this error could manifest itself by not seeking relevant data such as employee input on or assessment of key programs (see Mykalovskiy et al. 2008).
- Overvaluing irrelevant data. A couple of familiar examples: (1) "Smile sheet" evaluations in training courses. Liking a course, an instructor, or a venue may have no correlation to either actual learning or whether any learning ends up being applied in new action or sustained performance improvement. (2) Customer satisfaction scores. "Satisfied customers" are not necessarily loyal or well-served ones.
- Relying exclusively either on experiential *or* objective data. (data-selection error)
- Ignoring what one knows in order to meet a psychological need (such as to be liked, to be perceived as a team player, to appear bold or conservative, to not draw attention to oneself or to be the center of attention, and so on).
- Confirmation bias, seeking or valuing only data that confirm one's current opinion or judgment.
- Diagnostic prejudice, staying ardently committed to one's first impression or initial judgment.

This is an incomplete list of how thinking about—and emotionally reacting to—even otherwise compelling facts or evidence can quickly go wayward. For EBMgt to take successful hold in organizations, managers will need to understand not only its rudiments, but also their own personal pitfalls in trying to apply the discipline effectively. Furthermore, since we subscribe to Michael Maccoby's model and definition of a leader—a leader is *someone people follow* (to which we add, *willingly*)—we advocate not just the importance of EBMgt, but also integrating its ideals into public institutions via a more comprehensive conception about, and systemic approach to create, the leaders we need.

Conclusion

The trick for EBMgt, and indeed for all management methods, is to identify effective and practical means for integrating humans' unique capacity to be both rational and intuitive. If managers truly could manage by the evidence, by the data alone, they quickly would be replaced by devices optimized for rational computation—computers.

As actors inextricably linked to their humanity, the social character of their culture, and the specific situations they find themselves in, managers set priorities, solve problems, and make decisions with their inherent intuition, emotion, and judgment born of both experience and moral sensibilities. In our opinion, an effective implementation of EBMgt will, therefore, place greater emphasis on cultivating effective managerial judgment—inclusive of personality and strategic intelligence—and less reliance on adhering to allegedly best practices. In this regard, instead of asking, What is the best demonstrated practice?, managers will apply strategic intelligence, and from the EBMgt mind-set advocated by Stewart, ask a question such as, Based on what we know about our specific situation and the best available information, what is the most appropriate practice to achieve our aims? And how can we test that? This is a subtle but critical shift. If public institutions can get their managers to think and act this way, and *that* is what one means by EBMgt, we're all for it.

We return to von Hayek and Ghoshal for perspective here. "If man is not to do more harm than good in his efforts to improve the social good," von Hayek argued, "he will have to learn that in all fields where essential complexity of an organized kind prevails, he cannot acquire the full knowledge which would make mastery of the events possible" (1989, p. 7). Ghoshal wasn't writing about EBMgt when he penned these words, but they couldn't be more appropriate: "Excessive truth-claims based on extreme assumptions and partial analysis of complex phenomena can be bad even when they are not altogether wrong. In essence, social scientists carry an even greater social and moral responsibility than those who work in the physical sciences because, if they hide ideology in the pretense of science, they can cause more harm than good" (2005, p. 87).

Committing to gathering good-quality data and fully considering and weighing the evidence appropriately, coupled with the capacity to exercise personality and strategic intelligence as presented in Maccoby's model of leadership, are worthy objectives for humans engaged in the craft of management—and, we expect, will cause more good.

Acknowledgment

The authors gratefully acknowledge the assistance of Michael Maccoby, whose suggestions and contribution to the chapter were invaluable. Mistakes, errors, and poor judgment are the authors' alone.

References

Arndt, Margarete, and Barbara Bigelow. 2009. "Evidence-Based Management in Health Care Organizations: A Cautionary Note." *Health Care Management Review* 34 (3): 206–213.

Bandura, Albert. 1995. "Exercise of Personal and Collective Efficacy in Changing Societies." In *Self-Efficacy in Changing Societies,* ed. Albert Bandura, 1–45. Cambridge: Cambridge University Press.

Beck, Judith S. 1995. *Cognitive Therapy: Basics and Beyond.* New York: Guilford Press.

Bellinger, Gene. 2004. "The Ladder of Inference." Systems Thinking. www.systems-thinking. org/loi/loi.htm (accessed December 5, 2009).

Box, Sheri. 2009. "New Data from Virginia Tech Transportation Institute Provides Insight into Cell Phone Use and Driving Distraction." Virginia Tech News, July 29. www.vtnews. vt.edu/story.php?relyear=2009&itemno=571 (accessed November 29, 2009).

Brafman, Ori, and Rom Brafman. 2008. *Sway: The Irresistible Pull of Irrational Behavior.* New York: Doubleday.

Brothers, Chalmers. 2005. *Language and the Pursuit of Happiness.* Naples, FL: New Possibilities Press.

Dewey, John. 1910. *How We Think.* Boston: D.C. Heath.

Ghoshal, Sumantra. 2005. "Bad Management Theories Are Destroying Good Management Practices." *Academy of Management Learning and Education* 4 (1): 75–91.

Gordon, Neil F., and William L. Haskell. 1997. "Comprehensive Cardiovascular Disease Risk Reduction in a Cardiac Rehabilitation Setting." *American Journal of Cardiology* 80 (8): 69H–73H.

Hamlin, Bob. 2002. "Towards Evidence-Based HRD Practice." In *Understanding Human Resource Development: A Research-Based Approach,* ed. Jim McGoldrick, Jim Stewart, and Sandra Watson, 93–121. London: Routledge.

Hansen, Richard A. 2002. "Executive Commentary." *Academy of Management Executive* 16 (3): 103.

Heifetz, Ronald. 1994. *Leadership without Easy Answers.* Cambridge, MA: Belknap Press of Harvard University Press.

Koltko-Rivera, Mark E. 2004. "The Psychology of Worldviews." *Review of General Psychology* 8 (1): 3–58.

Lewin, Kurt. 1945. "The Research Center for Group Dynamics at Massachusetts Institute of Technology." *Sociometry* 8 (2): 126–136.

Linden, Wolfgang, Carmen Stossel, and Jeffrey Maurice. 1996. "Psychosocial Interventions for Patients with Coronary Artery Disease: A Meta-analysis." *Archives of Internal Medicine* 156 (7): 745–752.

Lisspers, Jan, et al. 2005. "Long-Term Effects of Lifestyle Behavior Change in Coronary Artery Disease." *Health Psychology* 24 (1): 41–48.

Maccoby, Michael. 2007. *The Leaders We Need, and What Makes Us Follow.* Boston: Harvard Business School Press.

———. 2010. "Learning from Two Great Teachers of Change Leadership." *Research/Technology Management* 53 (2): 68–69.

McMullin, Rian E. 2000. *The New Handbook of Cognitive Therapy Techniques.* New York: Norton.

Mykhalovskiy, E., et al. 2008. "Qualitative Research and the Politics of Knowledge in an Age of Evidence." *Social Science and Medicine* 67 (1): 195–203.

National Highway Traffic Safety Administration. 2009. *An Examination of Driver Distraction as Recorded in NHTSA Databases.* Washington, DC: National Center for Statistics and Analysis.

Newberg, Andrew, and Mark Robert Waldman. 2006. *Why We Believe What We Believe: Uncovering Our Biological Need for Meaning, Spirituality, and Truth.* New York: Free Press.

Nordmann, Alain, et al. 2001. "A Case-Management Program of Medium Intensity Does Not Improve Cardiovascular Risk Factor Control in Coronary Artery Disease Patients: The Heartcare I Trial." *American Journal of Medicine* 110 (7): 543–550.

NOVA. 2006. "The Deadliest Plane Crash." Public Broadcast Service. www.pbs.org/wgbh/nova/planecrash/. Detailed cockpit transcript available at www.pbs.org/wgbh/nova/planecrash/minutes.html (both accessed October 11, 2009).

O'Connor, Joseph, and Ian McDermott. 1997. *The Art of Systems Thinking: Essential Skills for Creativity and Problem Solving.* San Francisco: Thorsons.

Popper, Karl. 1985. *Popper Selections.* Princeton, NJ: Princeton University Press.

Rokeach, Milton. 1960. *The Open and Closed Mind: Investigations into the Nature of Belief Systems and Personality Systems.* New York: Basic Books.

Rousseau, Denise M. 2006a. "Is There Such a Thing as 'Evidence-Based Management'"? *Academy of Management Review* 31 (2): 256–269.

———. 2006b. "Keeping an Open Mind about Evidence-Based Management." *Academy of Management Review* 31 (4): 1091–1093.

Rynes, Sara L., Kenneth G. Brown, and Amy E. Colbert. 2002. "Seven Common Misconceptions about Human Resource Practices." *Academy of Management Executive* 16 (3): 92–102.

Seligman, Martin E.P. 1993. *What You Can Change and What You Can't.* New York: Fawcett Books.

Senge, Peter. 1990. *The Fifth Discipline.* New York: Random House.

Senge, Peter C., Otto Scharmer, Joseph Jaworski, and Betty Sue Flowers. 2004. *Presence.* New York: Society for Organizational Learning.

University at Buffalo. 2009. "How We Support Our False Beliefs," *ScienceDaily,* August 23. http://www.sciencedaily.com/releases/2009/08/090821135020.htm# (accessed October 4, 2009).

von Hayek, Friedrich August. 1989. "The Pretence of Knowledge: Nobel Memorial Lecture, December 11, 1974." *American Economic Review* 79 (6): 3–7.

5

Analytic Reasoning for Evidence-Based Public Management

Adapting Education to Practice Realities

Alan Lyles

Faced with the choice between changing one's mind and proving that there is no need to do so, almost everyone gets busy with the proof.
—John Kenneth Galbraith[1]

Evidence-based public management (EBMgt) requires analytic reasoning; however, statistics and analytic technique courses are typically taught as mathematical rather than management skills. In "Be Data Literate—Know What to Know," Peter Drucker observed that few executives "are information literate . . . they know how to get data. But most still have to learn how to use data."[2] All too readily, quantitative courses become the nemesis of intelligent but math-anxious adults and a career terminator for the truly phobic. Public administrators and professionals-in-training require a different educational approach. The private sector is sensitive to this gap. STATA, a leading producer of statistical analysis software, stressed in a recent announcement that "STATA is used extensively throughout the text, making it possible to introduce computationally complex methods with little or no higher-level mathematics. As a result . . . [the text] focuses on concepts and model assumptions, rather than on the underlying mathematics."[3]

This chapter proposes an alternative to calculation and algorithm-based instructional methods (Table 5.1). It adapts features from an innovative approach to economic education: learning objectives focused on a carefully selected list of core concepts, which are then mastered through narrative and reinforced with numerous applications throughout the semester. Robert Frank and Ben Bernanke, who pioneered narrative learning for economics education, organized *Principles of Microeconomics* around seven concepts and their applications.[4] The framework proposed in this chapter incorporates advances in quantitative pedagogy (peer instruction[5]), general systems theory,[6] software capabilities that bypass symbolic mathematical language, and simulation. Simulation in this educational framework has two different roles. In a first course, simulation and visualization rather than

Table 5.1

The Framework for Analytic Reasoning Mastery (FARM)

1. Identify a limited set of the most critical concepts
2. Pedagogical strategies
   a. Narrative learning
   b. Peer instruction
3. Frequent reinforcement of the concepts through application to professional practice
4. Simulation and visualization to develop understanding of the quantitative concepts
5. General systems theory as a generic model for quantitative analyses
6. Describe the model in block outline using words and narratives for factors and relationships
7. Translate the model description of the systems model into its quantitative spreadsheet application using spreadsheet cell- and range-naming capabilities, and perform deterministic sensitivity analyses
8. Use spreadsheet add-in capabilities to add simulation software that supports probabilistic scenario testing and sensitivity analyses
9. Develop oral and written skills for communicating the results of a quantitative analysis to a nontechnical audience

mathematics alone are used to communicate critical insights that support statistical concepts. In a second course, modeling and simulation build on a systems approach to develop the students' skills in examining decision and policy alternatives. EBMgt also requires a portfolio of additional competencies: qualitative methods, integration of theory- and practice-based frameworks, as well as effective public and interpersonal written and oral communications. These are, however, a secondary concern in this chapter.

Managing analytic modeling projects for EBMgt and using their results are structurally no different from other managerial responsibilities: expectations and goals are set, resources are managed, and team members, including technical experts, are held accountable for results. To accomplish this, professional education must develop a "philosophy of practice" that includes a conceptual framework and its mastery, an emphasis on quantitative reasoning, and cultivation of informed skepticism of what can and what cannot be achieved through quantitative techniques. Public administrators must understand the limits of null hypothesis testing, the meaning of effect size, and the very real consequence(s) of type II errors. Effective pedagogy assists the professional-in-training to develop a systems framework for evidence-based practice and understand the core concepts that can be applied within this framework. It requires independent acts of judgment as the legitimate professional education outcome from quantitative assignments, rather than tedious repetition of numeric solutions to equations. How many public administrators can explain what a p-value means in terms that are meaningful for their work? If there is minimal understanding or no recall of the concept of statistical power, how can public administrators adequately appraise an evaluation that reports no impact? This reflects as much on *what* is being stressed in course work as it does on *how* it is being presented. Both must change.

Optimally, EBMgt should counterbalance bias, overcome individuals' limited personal experiences, develop judgment, and challenge groupthink.[7] This requires making decisions systematically and transparently, employing data to the extent feasible, and clearly communicating decision rationale(s) and results. Advanced in 1990 as the basis for medicine,[8] evidence-based practices have become the standard for clinical medicine,[9] integral to the process for setting public policy,[10] and, despite conflicting views,[11] the clear future of public administration. However, methodologically flawed evidence-based medicine relegates large and possibly practically important effects that do not achieve conventional levels of statistical significance to obscurity.[12] Inappropriate professional training for public administrators poses a similar risk—the diffusion of EBMgt will require objective external standards, similar to those for accounting, that all agree constitute the standard for sufficient evidence.

The National Association of Schools of Public Affairs and Administration and Professional Competencies

Dean Jay O. Light of the Harvard Business School observed that an era of extended financial growth had led "people [to become] less focused on risks and risk management and more focused on making money."[13] Global financial crises have refocused attention on risk and the understanding and management of systemic risk, particularly within public and private sector fiduciary responsibilities. Testifying before the House Financial Services Committee, Treasury Secretary Timothy Geithner said, "We need strong and uniform supervision for all financial products marketed to consumers and investors, and tough enforcement of the rules to ensure full accountability for those who might violate the public trust . . . [accomplishing this] will require comprehensive reform—not modest repairs at the margin."[14] Who will do this work? What skills will be required by the work, and what skills will those who perform it actually have?

The National Association of Schools of Public Affairs and Administration's (NASPAA's) 2008 standards, section 4.21 ("Common Curriculum Components") address the application of quantitative and qualitative analytic techniques. These applications include (1) policy and program formulation, implementation, and evaluation and (2) decision making and problem solving. NASPAA requirements "do not prescribe specific courses or imply that equal time should be spent on each area or that courses must all be offered by the public affairs, public policy or public administration programs."[15] The requirements accommodate each school of public administration's determination of its concentration(s) and methods.

The standards were updated in 2009 as *Standards 6.1: Universal Required Competencies.* "As the basis for its curriculum, the Program will adopt a set of required competencies related to its mission and public values . . . the required competencies will include . . . the ability to analyze, synthesize, think critically, solve problems and make decisions."[16] These are commendable goals, but do current instructional methods accomplish these ends?

As written, the competencies are incomplete for EBMgt: quantitative analytic reasoning based on a Neyman-Pearson null hypothesis statistical testing (NHST) world that ignores results other than $p < 0.05$ is a practice failure. In the typical approach to quantitative analysis, mastery of the NHST framework is emphasized. Under that approach for introductory and intermediate courses, outliers may be interpreted either as a threat to the logic of the test or as without interest with respect to the tails of the distribution, rather than being a potentially important source of information. For these reasons, outliers may be discarded after perfunctory review or ignored to make empirical data fit distributional assumptions for hypothesis testing, modeling central tendencies, and variance. But in practice, outliers and tails may contain important evidence about risk—the low-probability but high-impact circumstances Nassim Taleb calls "black swans,"[17] which have such impact precisely because they are unexpected.

Consider the financial crises of this decade—according to the risk-management models, these events should not have occurred. There were warnings that portfolio theory relied on strong, untenable distributional assumptions, but how many public administrators are statistically adept enough and confident enough to participate in the discussion?[18,19] Arbitrary significance levels are a useful intermediate educational device, but the ultimate goal is for a fully trained professional to think using quantitative concepts, not to apply recipes. A public administrator should have sufficient understanding of probability distributions and risk, for example, to make informed demands regarding mathematical models of risk and statistical null findings. Every public administrator should be able to distinguish and act on the practical distinction between p-value and effect size.

Business schools also educate public administrators. The Association to Advance Collegiate Schools of Business's standards for accreditation[20] do not require specific statistics or analytic technique courses, or, in general management programs, the methods for teaching the material. Rather, the report on revised standards (effective July 2009) notes, "Normally, the curriculum management process will result in undergraduate and master's level general management degree programs that will include learning experiences in such management-specific knowledge and skill areas as . . . statistical data analysis and management science as they support decision-making processes throughout an organization." Most business schools require a minimum of two statistics courses, and many also require a third, management science course, but practices vary. At the determination of an individual school of business, quantitative management science is included in the curriculum or not based on that school's mission. These revised standards are similar to NASPAA's accreditation requirements in that an introductory course in quantitative modeling for management is not mandatory for all students. Where the course is required, the didactic approach is unlikely to use narrative learning and a framework comparable to that proposed in this chapter. Here, as earlier, the goal should be for students to have a philosophy of practice in which they are able to distance themselves from an analytic model and ask basic questions about the risks, costs, and benefits that may be outside of the models.

Core Concepts and Didactic Approaches

Thirty concepts for practitioners (Table 5.2), divided into a two-course sequence, are proposed as an integrated curriculum for quantitative critical reasoning, analytic modeling, and evidence-based decisions. The five main pedagogical elements for mastering these concepts and applications are narrative learning, peer instruction, general systems theory, software, and simulation.

Narrative Learning

A survey that assessed understanding of "opportunity cost," arguably one of the most fundamental concepts in economics, revealed that having had an economics course did not improve performance in identifying the correct answer (7.4 percent) over those who had not had an economics course (17.2 percent).[21] The survey concluded that results for "undergraduates with no prior exposure to economics" did not differ from those of economists with doctoral training. Is there any reason to expect quantitative reasoning in general to be any better?

In the list-of-topics and equation-focused approach, visualization of data and relationships receive limited coverage. Exploratory data analysis, an essential step in an analytic strategy, begins with descriptive statistics. Though its purpose is to understand the location, dispersion, and shape of the data, possible relationships among variables, or pathologies of data collection, the tools for doing so are unnecessarily constrained in conventional statistics approaches. The course time allotted for exploratory data analysis generally limits coverage to histograms, box plots, scatter plots, and perhaps stem-and-leaf diagrams. The professional-in-training is then propelled into correlation and NHST statistics so that, perhaps, adequate time will remain to cover multivariate statistics before the term ends. Yet, the effective visual display of quantitative information[22] or the discerning rejection of charts that contain distortions may be their most frequent applications of quantitative reasoning. There have been important advances both with static[23] and with dynamic displays,[24] but these are not yet routinely included in academic course work.

Contrary to the lack of recall of unused chemistry or mathematics, there often is recall of a play, a movie, or a work of literature decades later. The narrative form is consistent with how we learn and construct sense in the world. Consequently, when learning objectives and didactic material are organized at the intuitive and conceptual level of narrative in the first quantitative course, there is a greater likeli-

Table 5.2

Core Analytic Reasoning Concepts: An Integrated Two-Course Sequence

First Course

1. Bias
2. Central Tendency
3. Data Types
4. Description vs. Inference
5. Distribution
6. Errors: Type I and Type II
7. Evidence-Based Management
8. Exploratory Data Analysis and the Visual Display of Quantitative Information (1)
9. Multivariate
10. Outlier
11. Parametric vs. Nonparametric
12. Probability: Independence, Joint, Conditional, Bayesian
13. Risk, Relative Risk, and Absolute Risk
14. Samples and Generalizability
15. Statistical vs. Practical Significance
16. Statistical Power
17. Variability

Second Course

18. Communicating the Results of a Quantitative Analysis to a Nontechnical Audience
19. Cost Benefit Analysis, Including Distributional Impacts
20. Decision Tree
21. Effect Size
22. Forecasting
23. General Systems Theory Model
24. Limitations
25. Modeling vs. the Model
26. Nonlinear
27. Sensitivity Analysis
28. Simulation
29. Time Series
30. Visual Display of Quantitative Information (2)

hood that students can do more than pass the course—they can own the material. This enhances the prospect that they will use it subsequently.

Recent neuroscience research supports a biological basis for narrative in learning and comprehension.[25] Narrative learning uses the main ideas behind economics or statistics in story. It has a plot, demonstrates an action that is consistent with the idea being examined, invites active student participation, and explores the concept's implications. Robert Frank's "economic naturalist" class assignment requires students to identify an interesting question and then use the core course ideas to answer it in five hundred words or less.[26] The book based on these student assignments, *The Economic Naturalist*,[27] was a *Sunday Times* (London) best seller in 2008.[28]

Peer Instruction

Peer instruction is Professor Eric Mazur's method developed from teaching the required introductory physics course at Harvard University. Its aim is "to focus attention on the underlying concepts without sacrificing the students' ability to solve problems . . . [which it pursues by] exploit[ing] student interaction during lectures and focus[ing] students' attention on underlying concepts."[6] The text, preclass reading assignments, and lecture notes provide the details prior to class. Lectures then focus on the concepts, with a brief in-class ConcepTest following each unit.

The ConcepTest is a process more than a question. It is used to guide student attention and interaction—including discussions that require the students to "convince your neighbor" that an answer is correct. After brief discussions among the students, there is a class vote on a multiple-choice list. The results provide an immediate assessment of comprehension, but a low percentage of correct votes (less than 90 percent, according to Dr. Mazur) leads to review of the concept in greater detail. In this way the students' learning needs are the primary calibration for the actual rather than the planned lecture. After covering the concept at a slower pace and more completely, Professor Mazur gives a second ConcepTest before continuing to the next topic.

Dr. Mazur's data on quantitative scores before and after the introduction of his peer instruction method demonstrate improved problem-solving skills following its introduction. He reports, "The convince-your-neighbor discussions systematically increase both the percentage of correct answers and the confidence of the students." This approach to teaching physics directly transfers to mastering quantitative reasoning.

General Systems Theory

When analytic models are developed applying statistical concepts, the modeling process is more than the quantitative model that results from it. Modeling is a process. That idea needs to be emphasized repeatedly to counteract the misunderstanding that the purpose is solely to get a number. It begins with a judgment of whether or not a decision is a suitable candidate for a quantitative model and, if it is, the results that will be required from it. Analytic modeling uses statistics, the logic of quantitative reasoning, and the modeler's experience, formal training, and creativity to identify the essential issues—not just its symptoms. It is the public administrator's responsibility to identify the relevant factors, how they influence one another, the outcome(s) of interest, and what is not known or may not even be quantifiable. This function should not be outsourced to a technical analyst.

General systems theory provides a framework for organizing this complexity. An understanding of systems, hierarchies of systems, and their dependencies strengthens the results from quantitative reasoning for management. It sets boundaries on a system, structures its components, and includes the relevant features from the external environment, boundary-spanning activities, and feedback loops.[7]

Simulation (An Example)

When the central limit theorem is introduced, it does not have to be as an esoteric abstraction—an approach that might provide insights to only a select few. The power, significance, and even drama of this result can be demonstrated through simulation, and students can see the results as they unfold.[29]

Starting with a population that has a Gaussian distribution for the value of interest, subjects are randomly selected and the means of samples of the same size are plotted. This process is then repeated with various skewed distributions and, ultimately, a uniform distribution as the source for the samples. Because of visualization, students are more likely to remember the counterintuitive result that the distribution of sample means from independently and randomly selected samples of the same size has a normal distribution regardless of the distribution of the original population from which the samples were taken. This is particularly poignant as they see the population distribution and watch the accumulation of data on the distribution of sample means. Replication using different sample sizes and numbers of samples can reinforce their understanding that larger samples provide more stable estimates and using more samples gives more precise estimates. After the central tendencies are examined, it is useful to explore the tails of some specific skewed distributions, such as income or medical expenditures, and discuss what is gained or lost if only the central tendencies are used in setting or evaluating policy and regulations.

At this point there could be a discussion of the rationale behind the selection of a specific central tendency measure. In the compressed quantitative course schedule, coverage of central tendency, variability, basic probability, and distributions can be rushed to get to more substantial material. Students memorize the definitions of mean, median, and mode, but do they see them as useful tools? Assume that a government agency had been identified by the legislature as taking years too long, on average, for regulatory reviews, and would receive additional funds contingent upon reporting improvements. The mode is obviously not useful for this purpose. What measure would they report in their testimony and why? Review times likely follow a right skew distribution, so on reflection the student should also see that the arithmetic mean is not practical for the application. In addition, waiting to have complete data to calculate the mean could substantially delay its being available when needed. The median, however, does suit annual reporting and indexing progress since only half of the reviews for each year or batch must be complete to determine the metric.

From the simulation results, it will also be clear that the mean of the sample means converges to the population mean and that using the means of samples as estimates produces a distribution around this value. The visible results support an intuitive understanding of the distinction between the variability within the sample data (standard deviation) and variability in using the sample means as estimates of the population mean (standard error). Distinctions can be seen and, when linked with an appropriate empirical question, support a coherent narrative with quantitative information. Too often the approach is the opposite—statistical results are calculated, and then there is a search to convey to the student what they mean. Short of memorization, how do nonmathematician public administration students currently achieve these insights? And, if they do not, how durable are these fundamental concepts for descriptive and inferential statistics, hypothesis testing and modeling? What is their postgraduation understanding of risk and probabilities, expected value and cost-benefit analysis? Will they remember not just the normal curve and the central limit theorem, but the cautions of the risk in the tails of the distribution(s)?

Software developments and the ease of adding applications to a spreadsheet mean that if the student-practitioner can reason clearly and systematically, then in the second course they can communicate that thinking in an analytic model to produce useful results.

Spreadsheet Software Add-Ins

Basic relationships that are conceptually clear and can be stated in words may lose clarity when implemented using a spreadsheet's default alphanumeric naming convention(s). It is obvious that the following simplistic statements produce point estimates of the number of graduates in a given period from different programs to train junior military officers. Is it as clear for the equivalent alphanumeric formulas? Note the ease of transition by starting with prose (a) and transferring that to named cells using the spreadsheet cell naming function (b), compared to the not immediately clear alphanumeric formula (c). The example is trivial, but the benefits of a conceptual approach increase as the complexity of the analysis or model grows.

(a) Prose Total graduates in the period = (Senior Year Graduation Rate, Academy × Senior Class Population, Academy) + (Senior Year Graduation Rate, Civilian × Senior Class Enrolled Population, Civilian) + (Graduation Rate, Officer Candidate School × Population, Officer Candidate School)

(b) Formulas with Cell Names Total graduates in the period = (Population_Academy*Graduation_Pct_Academy) + (Population_Civilian*Graduation_Pct_Civilian) + (Population_OCS*Graduation_Pct_OCS)

(c) Formulas with Alphanumeric Names (omitting absolute reference indicator) = (C6*G6) + (D6*H6) + (E6*I6)

From this basic approach, it is quite easy to develop a model and demonstrate deterministic sensitivity analyses. Addition of a simulation add-in to the spreadsheet permits the students to apply the ideas of central tendency and distribution(s) to the cell contents. With this change, probabilistic sensitivity analysis with confidence intervals and not just point estimates is within the students' grasp.

Using cell and range names in spreadsheets improves clarity, facilitates error detection, and contributes to a self-documenting spreadsheet. Albright, Winston, and Zappe have identified good spreadsheet-modeling practices[30] that promote quantitative reasoning by focusing on standardization, clarity, transparency, natural language formulas, and documentation.

Communication, an Essential Link to Action

Communication is essential to gaining acceptance of an analysis or analytic model's results. The assumption that a good communicator is equally facile with any material is incorrect when it comes to communicating the quantitative aspects of a decision. It is a distinct professional competence to organize the quantitative and qualitative considerations, and oral presentations require discipline, as the time constraints are generally quite severe—perhaps twenty minutes or less. Scaling the presentation to the time available and the technical capabilities of the audience is critical.[31]

Lessons from Evidence-Based Medical Practice

As public administration begins the transition to evidence-based practice, the medical field's experience offers lessons. The scientific curriculum for medicine began in earnest following the Flexner Report (1910),[32] which used the Johns Hopkins University School of Medicine's curriculum of scientific theory and clinical case practice as its model. However, changing medical practice faced substantial hurdles, from disbelief that it was either necessary or possible, to doubts about the competence of practitioners to apply scientific criteria. As Feinstein noted, "In medical science, almost every plausible concept that has been held throughout the centuries about the causes, mechanisms, and treatment of diseases has been either wholly wrong or so deficient that it was later overthrown and supplanted by other concepts."[33] Evidence-based medicine—"the systematic identification, appraisal and synthesis of clinical studies, particularly randomized clinical trials"—was advanced to replace the art of medicine and physician practices based on personal journeys of discovery but contradicted by scientific evidence.[34]

Variations in medical practice are not solely attributable to patient differences, but include their physicians' practice style. Examples of such variations are reported regularly in the medical literature and in the Dartmouth Atlas of Health Care.[35] The procedures involved, such as coronary artery bypass grafting surgery, are not trivial. Continuing clinical epidemiologic evidence of unsupportable practice variations motivated renewed changes in medical education and, especially, pressure to move these changes from academic institutions to practice. A notable example is the revised recommendations for use of human replacement hormones in women.[36]

Defining Evidence

Research rarely establishes the evidence base with a single study or report. For evidence-based practice to develop, valid criteria for weighting individual reports were needed for medicine and will be needed for public administration. The lowest evidence rating is given to uncontrolled studies, expert opinion, and case reports ("I had this patient . . ."), leading to the medical gold standard of randomized clinical trials (see also Chapter 2 on this issue). For ethical and economic reasons, randomized studies are uncommon if not rare in public administration. Although public administrators will often be limited to quasi-experimental designs, their results must be as rigorous as feasible, and those who use the results must be intelligent consumers concerning conclusions, implications, and limitations to generalizability. Similarly, the cumulative meaning of individual reports of varying strength also requires a systematic taxonomy: at what point does accumulating evidence rise to the level of recommendation for or against an approach, or remain merely suggestive, or indeterminate? Recently, Meier and O'Toole consolidated some of their work assessing the evidence for generally accepted public administration principles, what has been called "Proverbs,"[37,38] and the support is not very strong.

Assessing the Influence of Evidence on Actual Medical Practice

Even with the highest level of evidence and the strongest recommendations, there will always be a gap between research and usual practice. The outcomes from a given therapy in usual community practice (effectiveness) may be less than that observed under the optimal circumstances of clinical research (efficacy) because of stringent research protocols that cannot be satisfied outside of the research setting. This efficacy-effectiveness gap is a caution when moving from research evidence to applications. Evidence-based medicine's results have been particularly underwhelming, demonstrating the limits to change in the short term and the need to withhold evaluations until a realistic time for achievement has passed. Even with evidence—strong evidence—change to make daily practice consistent with that evidence is slow and incomplete. Examining common services provided to adults in community medical care, McGlynn et al. reported that about 55 percent of evidence-based services were actually received in 2000.[39] This is only slightly better than a coin toss. This finding held whether the services were for screening, prevention, or treatment, and whether the treatment was for chronic or acute care. Some barriers to using evidence-based guidelines in medicine will also apply to public administration: lack of awareness, lack of familiarity, lack of agreement, lack of self-efficacy, lack of outcome expectancy, inertia of previous practice, and environmental barriers[40] (which can include management of conflicts of interest).

Access to Evidence

Evidence does not self-organize, nor does aggregated evidence spontaneously disseminate and change practice—especially when individual financial incentives may reinforce continuing the current practice. Each stage in the development and promulgation of evidence requires concerted effort and resources. The accumulating but fragmented medical literature grows faster than medical practitioners can assimilate. Many potential benefits are obscured by the sheer volume of information generated every week. To cope with this situation, the National Guidelines Clearinghouse was created and is maintained by the Agency for Healthcare Research and Quality.[41]

How will access to evidence be facilitated for EBMgt? As individual evidence reports are published, what entity will provide funding to integrate the published results based on objective, unbiased evaluation? The Department of Veterans Affairs' Center for Organization, Leadership, and Management Research is an example of an agency-specific approach to generating evidence for management practices (see also Chapter 9 on the Department of Veterans Affairs).[42] As units such as these promulgate, the next challenge will be to share results across entities.

Discussion

The intentional and unintentional risk taking demonstrated in recent market and regulatory failures reveals deficiencies in professional education as it is transferred to the realities of practice. Correcting these deficits must include redefining the expectations for public (and private) administrators' analytic reasoning capabilities and minimal competencies. There will be increasingly direct opportunities for application. For example, the goal of WolframAlpha is to make all of the information available on the Internet computable at the desktop. The Wolfram Research Company describes this application not as an Internet browser but as a "computational knowledge engine."[43] Having this capability will be meaningful only if the user has been trained to think analytically, in quantitative concepts and relationships.

It is tempting to overload students with courses and expect mastery of an encyclopedic set of quantitative techniques, yet it is a mistake to do so. The gains from an integrated framework of narrative learning, reinforcement of a limited number of key concepts, and instruction that incorporates simulation yield significant gains. It prepares students for a lifelong practice of competent quantitative and analytical reasoning. Instead of viewing quantitative models as determinative, graduates will have a more realistic view—that both the process of modeling and the resulting model are vital inputs to EBMgt. Effective public administrators must become comfortable asking questions, providing guidance, judging relevance, and assessing the risks posed by the results of quantitative models. It must be second nature to know that quantitative models do not solve problems, only equations,[44] and that the administrator is responsible for judging how best to translate model results into action.

Does this alternative educational approach mean that substance and rigor are being sacrificed for fluff and entertainment? Not at all. Instead of allowing quantitative courses to remain a rite of passage that, for too many students, is disconnected to actual use, narrative learning, peer instruction, and simulation can reinforce these core concepts throughout the curriculum. Quantitative reasoning and its mastery can become a satisfying, empowering experience. Those who aspire to more technical roles will have a good background for subsequent courses and conventional mathematical approaches.

Not every public administrator will be fully capable of performing quantitative analyses or creating analytic models. But all must be competent in using their outputs—conversant in interpreting their meaning and sensitive to their limitations. An update to Mr. Drucker's maxim might read, "Be Numerate—Know What the Data Mean."

Notes

Dr. Alison Snow Jones's encouragement, thoughtful review, and insightful suggestions are gratefully appreciated. Mr. Kyle James provided bibliographic services for this work.

Some of the ideas in this chapter were introduced in Alan Lyles, "Taking Quantitative Reasoning Seriously" (e-commentary), *Public Administration Review* 68, no. 3 (2008): 61–67. They are augmented and developed more fully here.

1. Galbraith, John. 1971. *A Contemporary Guide to Economics, Peace, and Laughter.* Boston: Houghton Mifflin.

2. Drucker, Peter. 1992. "Be Data Literate—Know What to Know." *Wall Street Journal,* December 1.

3. STATA Corporation. 2009. Description of Dupont, William D. 2009. *Statistical Modeling for Biomedical Researchers: A Simple Introduction to the Analysis of Complex Data.* 2d ed. Cambridge: Cambridge University Press. www.stata.com/bookstore/smbr.html#contents (accessed November 1, 2009).

4. Frank, Robert, and Bernanke, Ben. 2001. *Principles of Microeconomics.* New York: McGraw-Hill/Irwin.

5. Mazur, Eric. 1997. *Peer Instruction: A User's Manual.* Upper Saddle River, NJ: Prentice Hall.

6. Athey, Thomas. 1982. *Systematic Systems Approach: An Integrated Method for Solving Systems Problems.* Upper Saddle River, NJ: Prentice Hall.

7. Hart, Paul. 1994. *Groupthink in Government: A Study of Small Groups and Policy Failure.* Baltimore: Johns Hopkins University Press.

8. Eddy, David. 1990. "Practice Policies: Where Do They Come From?" *Journal of the American Medical Association* 263 (9): 1265, 1269, 1272 passim.

9. Eisenberg, John. 2001. "Evidence-Based Medicine." *Expert Voices* 1:1–2. http://www.nihcm.org/~nihcmor/pdf/ExpertV1.pdf.

10. Urban Institute. 2003. *Beyond Ideology, Politics and Guesswork: The Case for Evidence-Based Policy.* Washington, DC: Urban Institute. www.urban.org/Uploaded-PDF/901189_evidencebased.pdf (accessed November 1, 2009).

11. Pilkey-Jarvis, Linda, and Pilkey, Orrin. 2008. "Useless Arithmetic: Ten Points to Ponder When Using Mathematical Models in Environmental Decision Making." *Public Administration Review* 68 (3): 470–479.

12. McCloskey, Deirdre, and Ziliak, Steve. 2008. *The Cult of Statistical Significance: How the Standard Error Costs Us Jobs, Justice, and Lives.* Ann Arbor: University of Michigan Press.

13. Holland, Kelley. 2009. "Is It Time to Retrain B-Schools?" *New York Times,* March 14. www.nytimes.com/2009/03/15/business/15school.html?_r=1&scp=1&sq=retrain%20business%20schools&st=cse (accessed November 1, 2009).

14. Paletta, Damian; Randall, Maya; and Crittenden, Michael. 2009. "Geithner Calls for Tougher Standards on Risk." *Wall Street Journal,* March 26. http://online.wsj.com/article/SB123807231255147603.html (accessed November 1, 2009).

15. National Association of Schools of Public Affairs and Administration. January 2008. "Standards: 2008. General Information and Standards for Professional Masters Degree Programs. www.naspaa.org/accreditation/seeking/reference/standards.asp (accessed November 1, 2009).

16. National Association of Schools of Public Affairs and Administration. 2009. NASPAA Standards Review. Proposed Accreditation Standards 9/12/08 [Draft]. www.naspaa.org/accreditation/standard2009/docs/Standards2009Draft9.12.08.pdf (accessed November 1, 2009).

17. Taleb, Nassim. 2007. *The Black Swan: The Impact of the Highly Improbable.* London: Random House.

18. Mandelbrot, Benoît. 1999. "A Multifractal Walk Down Wall Street." *Scientific American* 280 (2): 70–73.

19. Mandelbrot, Benoît, and Taleb, Nassim. 2006. "A Focus on the Exceptions That Prove the Rule." *Financial Times,* March 23. www.ft.com/cms/s/2/5372968a-ba82–11da-980d-0000779e2340.html (accessed November 1, 2009).

20. The Association to Advance Collegiate Schools of Business. Accreditation Standards, January 31, 2008, and 2009 Revisions to the Standards and Interpretative Materials. www.aacsb.edu/accreditation/process/documents/AACSB_STANDARDS_Revised_Jan08.pdf; www.aacsb.edu/accreditation/StandardsReport-Revised23Jan09.pdf (accessed November 1, 2009).

21. Ferraro, Paul J., and Taylor, Laura O. 2005. "Do Economists Recognize an Opportunity Cost When They See One? A Dismal Performance from the Dismal Science," *Contributions to Economic Analysis and Policy* 4 (1): Article 7. www.bepress.com/bejeap/contributions/v0l4/iss1/art7 (accessed November 1, 2009).

22. Tufte, Edward. 2001. *The Visual Display of Quantitative Information.* 2d ed. Cheshire, CT: Graphic Press

23. Few, Stephen. 2004. *Show Me the Numbers: Designing Tables and Graphs to Enlighten.* Oakland, CA: Analytics Press.

24. Watts, Geoff. 2009. "Hans Rosling: Animated about Statistics." *British Medical Journal* 339:b2801.

25. Yarkoni, Tal; Speer, Nicole; and Zacks, Jefferey. 2008. "Neural Substrates of Narrative Comprehension and Memory." *Neuroimage* 41 (4): 1408–1425.

26. Inside Higher Ed. 2007. Economics Education 101. June 1. www.insidehighered.com/news/2007/06/01/frank (accessed November 1, 2009).

27. Robert, Frank. 2007. *The Economic Naturalist: In Search of Explanations for Everyday Enigmas.* New York: Basic Books.

28. Virgin Companies. 2009. "The Bestselling Economic Naturalist Makes a Return." April 30. http://www.virgin.com/money/news/the-bestselling-economic-naturalist-makes-a-return (accessed October 30, 2010).

29. Rice Virtual Lab in Statistics. 2008. "Simulations/Demonstrations." http://onlinestatbook.com/stat_sim/index.html (accessed November 1, 2009).

30. Albright, Christian; Winston, Wayne; and Zappe, Christopher. 1999. *Data Analysis and Decision-Making with Microsoft Excel.* Mason, OH: South-Western Cengage Learning.

31. Redelmeier, Donald A.; Detsky, Allan S.; Krahn, Murray D.; Naimark, David; and Naglie, Gary. 1997. [Technical Note] "Guidelines for Verbal Presentations of Medical Decision Analyses." *Medical Decision Making* 17 (2): 228–230.

32. Flexner, Abraham. 1910. *Medical Education in the United States and Canada.* New York: Carnegie Foundation for the Advancement of Teaching. www.carnegiefoundation.org/publications/pub.asp?key=43&subkey=977 (accessed November 1, 2009).

33. Feinstein, Alvan. 1985. *Clinical Epidemiology: The Architecture of Clinical Research.* Philadelphia: W.B. Saunders.

34. Elbrodt, Gary; Cook, Deborah; Lee, Jean; Cho, Michaela; Hunt, Dereck; and Weingarten, Scott. 1997. "Evidence-Based Disease Management." *Journal of the American Medical Association* 278 (20): 1687–1692.

35. Dartmouth Atlas of Health Care. N.d. http://www.dartmouthatlas.org/ (accessed November 1, 2009).

36. Naughton, Michelle; Snow, Alison; and Shumaker, Sally. 2005. "When Practices, Promises, Profits and Policies Outpace Hard Evidence: The Post-Menopausal Hormone Debate." *Journal of Social Issues* 61 (1): 159–179.

37. Waldo, Dwight. 1946. "The Proverbs of Administration." *Public Administration Review* 6:53–67.

38. Meier, Kenneth, and O'Toole, Laurence, Jr. 2009. "The Proverbs of New Public Management: Lessons from an Evidence-Based Research Agenda." *American Review of Public Administration* 39 (1): 4–22.

39. McGlynn, Elizabeth; Asch, Steven; Adams, John; Keesey, Joan; Hicks, Jennifer; DeCristofaro, Alison; and Kerr, Eve A. 2003. "The Quality of Health Care Delivered to Adults in the United States." *New England Journal of Medicine* 348 (26): 2635–2645.

40. Cabana, Michael; Rand, Cynthia; Powe, Neil; Wu, Albert; Wilson, Modena; Abboud, Paul-André; and Rubin, Haya. 1999. "Why Don't Clinicians Follow Clinical Practice Guidelines? A Framework for Improvement." *Journal of the American Medical Association* 282 (15): 1458–1465.

41. Agency for Healthcare Research and Quality. 2009. "National Guidelines Clearinghouse." http://www.guideline.gov/ (accessed November 1, 2009).

42. U.S. Department of Veterans Affairs. 2006. "A Framework for Management." Center for Organization, Leadership, and Management Research. www.colmr.research.va.gov/mgmt_research_in_va/ (accessed November 1, 2009).

43. Wolfram Research Company. WolframAlpha. http://www.wolframalpha.com/ (accessed November 1, 2009).

44. Ashley, Garland. 1964. "A Declaration of Independence from the Statistical Method." *Air University Review* (March–April): 83–84.

6

Toward Evidence-Based Public Management of Virtual E-Learning Teams

A Systematic Review Application

Joshua Earl

Evidence-based management isn't just a list of techniques that you can memorize, mimic and install. It is a perspective for traveling through organizational life, a way of thinking about what you and your company know and what you don't know, what is working and isn't and what to try next. It isn't a one-time fix that will magically solve all your problems. But there are effective steps that you can take every day to sustain the right mind-set—to keep facing the hard facts, avoid falling prey to dangerous half-truths and spot and reject total nonsense. We call these implementation principles for practicing evidence-based management.
—Jeffrey Pfeffer (2006)

This chapter explores the application of evidence-based management (EBMgt) principles in the e-learning context. It establishes a conceptual foundation that involves positioning EBMgt in relation to other management perspectives, defining virtual e-learning teams, and establishing the importance of investigating best practice management methodologies in this context. I conduct a systematic review of the relevant literature. The systematic review reveals both the potential contribution and limitation of the technique for EBMgt. Finally, I offer suggestions for further research.

Background

Positioning EBMgt: A Potential Bridge between Research and Practice

EBMgt is a methodology based on scientific principles. Like those in similar movements such as evidence-based medicine and evidence-based policy, the central principle in EBMgt is that decision making should be informed by knowledge of relevant and robust scientific insight into best practice, and implementation planning and evaluation should also be scrutinized in a similarly scientific fashion (Rousseau and McCarthy 2007).

A relatively recent movement, EBMgt provides managers with a means to assess the credibility of management concepts and their applicability to a given context. EBMgt also provides the means for practicing managers to contribute generalizable findings in a wider academic context. At this time, there is a wide gap between theoretical understandings of management and the practice of managers. Rynes et al. (cited in Rousseau 2006) suggest that less than 1 percent of management practitioners regularly read academic literature in this area, and this could be part of the reason for the wide variety of management practices observed within and between organizations, and the perceived gap between management theories and practice. A cursory view of results from a Google Scholar search for the phrase *theory-practice gap in management* yields a large collection of papers in which this phenomenon is explored. Brownlie et al. summarize this succinctly: "For many academic practitioners of business and management, closing this so-called gap has assumed the proportions of an heroic struggle between the high-mindedness of theory and the allure of pragmatic everyday trials and the tribulations of heroic practitioners struggling in 'the real world'" (Brownlie, Hewer, Wagner, and Svensson 2008).

In a scenario such as this, where there are many different "expert" theories that commonly compete with one another, not only for positioning in best-seller rankings but also in fundamental conceptual underpinnings, it is understandable that the less glamorous science-based management methodology as a field draws somewhat less attention, and that such gaps persist. As Rousseau (2006) points out, resistance on the part of some managers to engage in discussions and actions concerned with finding, delivering, and evaluating best practice methodologies has to do with the "belief that good management is an art—the 'romance of leadership'" and that by following this method, managers will lose the ability to "manage from experience."

Negative impact of this disorganized methodological approach as described by O'Toole provides a proxy argument for the need for a rigorous method: "What is lost in the cacophony of injunctions emanating from management consultants, advocates, gurus, and charlatans is the basic fact that virtually all management prescriptions are based on little if any actual, systematic evidence that they work—or if they work, under what conditions" (Meier and O'Toole 2008).

Given the melting pot of ideas that make up popular management theory, the only way to achieve consistent improvement is by learning how to separate the wheat from the chaff, in practices and beliefs, and in the rhetoric of the larger management research body of knowledge. Pfeffer (2005) outlines how this type of analytical thinking has benefited organizations and provided long-lasting strategic benefits. Indeed, Pfeffer maintains that creating organizational cultures where this kind of management thinking is encouraged and acted upon is one of the most important methods for building strategic competitive advantages that are unlikely to be easily duplicated.

Among the plethora of management methodologies and theories that promise competitive advantage, it seems that very few provide the user with the means to test whether or not the theory is the correct fit for the organization, or even whether the theory is working as it should. This is where EBMgt is different, as it encourages managers and employees to continuously view organizational behavior with a critical eye, aiming to find what is working or not and why.

Defining Management of Virtual E-Learning Teams

For our purposes, I define "management of virtual e-learning teams" as the management relationship and structures that exist to support leaders and managers working in online learning organizations. In other words, this chapter concerns investigation of methodologies for managers to maintain effective coordination, communication, and productivity of education workers—including teachers, tutors, lecturers, facilitators, and specialist support staff—geographically distributed, and who themselves are providing an online learning experience to distributed students. This is not the traditional approach to the management of teaching and learning, and represents a significant change in mode of delivery and management from what has been done up until now. This new mode of delivery presents significant opportunities for improving the level of specialization, and therefore expertise on the part of the educator, which will lead to improvements in engagement and learning outcomes for students.

Workers who rely on electronic communication channels to conduct their work instead of gathering at a central meeting place are often referred to as "telecommuters" or "virtual team members." Such a school, run via mostly electronic means, by decentralized managers working with decentralized educators, could be thought of as a "virtual school."

A large body of research exists on management of relationships between teachers and students working in "virtual classrooms," the so-called evidence-based education movement; however, management methodologies for virtual schools is thinner on the ground. A Google Scholar search for the keyword *e-learning management* yielded a far higher proportion of hits for research into pedagogical considerations of e-learning than for research into management methodologies for teachers in e-learning contexts. A similar result is found for searches of combinations of "management," "school," and "online."

This chapter addresses virtual *school* management methodologies, rather than virtual *classroom* management methodologies.

The Time Is Right for Virtual Schools, but Do We Know How to Run Them?

Wholly virtual schools are as of yet rare outside of distance education, although an increasing number of tertiary institutes operate online certificate and degree programs (Allen and Seaman 2007). The industry needs to adopt work-from-home options for educators in online programs. Shifting the management of such teams into at least a partial work-from-home, or telework, mode is a logical next step, as it has advantages to the organization (explored in subsequent sections). Therefore, it is reasonable for these kinds of organizations to exist in the near future. Growth in this mode of work has several core drivers.

The provision of telework options has recently gained legitimacy through an increasing recognition of financial benefits and through legislative pressure. Some of the financial benefits realized through telework are operational cost savings achieved by externalizing office space costs to workers. Offshore outsourcing is another trend in global business that has gathered momentum, with organizations employing telework as a means of accessing cheap labor forces in countries outside of the (highly developed) home country.

The *U.S. Federal Government Clean Air Act 1996* recognizes the potential environmental savings it can provide by reducing fossil fuel used by daily commuters to and from work, and these potential environmental impact reductions have also withstood rigorous modeling investigation.

Another driver of growth in telework labor is the human resource economic benefit. A 2008 survey of fourteen hundred chief financial officers conducted by Robert Half International suggests that telework is a significant drawing card in maintaining lower turnover rates and attracting better applicants for positions, with 13 percent of chief financial officers listing it as the best recruiting incentive, ahead of pay (Robert Half International 2008).

As suggested by Tamrat and Smith, it stands to reason that given all the benefits to organizations, individuals, and the environment that telework options can provide, it is only a matter of time before widespread telework becomes a reality in countries where there is sufficient telecommunications infrastructure (Tamrat and Smith 2002). For the Australian context, this is a particularly relevant point, given the Rudd government's proposed Fibre to the Home network that is intended to deliver broadband speeds of 100 megabits per second into 90 percent of households in Australia. Such a network would be a fundamental requirement for the rollout of widespread rich Internet-based curriculum.

Online and distance-based education also has significant benefits for organizations similar to those of any other telework situation; students save commuting time, reduce pollution, and can potentially use flexible contact hours. Providers save on classroom space and, by providing telework as an option for educators, also save on office space. For educational service providers, this represents a double incentive, and thus it stands to reason that given adequate market demand, and equivalent outcomes for students, this option will be pursued.

In regard to the effectiveness of online learning, a recent systematic review of research into the implications of teaching courses online found that in general, performance of online students was approximately equal to the performance of the students in the face-to-face mode, and that there is a general movement toward this mode of education (Tallent-Runnels et al. 2006). This study also found that through analysis of the situations in which student outcomes were reported as lower than in traditional modes of delivery, often there was a mismatch between the course design and the preferences and needs of the students. One preference on the part of the students was for increased rich media access to materials, rather than the overwhelmingly text-based delivery approach, which is typical of online education delivery modes.

The need for understanding of effective management methodologies in geographically distributed workplaces (teleworkplaces) is becoming increasingly important because of the increase in this kind of work mode and the use of online learning as an accepted and effective mode of education. Quality-focused organizations moving from a traditional delivery methodology to a mixed mode (telework, and online delivery) will require understanding of managerial styles that could potentially be somewhat different from those that are effective in managing traditional settings.

It is no longer important to consider whether or not widespread use of virtual education workplaces is a possibility. The benefits are clear, and the barriers are all but gone. The important question is not "If?" but "How?" The following section explores these implications on management practices and provides guidance for leaders in organizations with a view to pursue competitive advantage in this relatively undeveloped service area.

Literature Search Methodology

The aim of this review is to establish a basis for assessing current management practice in this area and provide some robustness to recommendations concerning management methodology for online education provision. To do this I conducted an iterative search using a keyword list generated through a casual reading on the topic. The search began with a very specific search on the core topic of this chapter and widened or narrowed depending on the success of the search.

The keywords used were *evidence-based, organization, management, methodology, online, telework, work from home, education, Web-based learning, virtual, leadership, eLeadership, eLearning,* and *virtual teams.*

Combinations of the keywords were used to find relevant peer-reviewed articles published after 2000, through Google Scholar search, ERIC, EBSCO, Science-Direct, ProQuest, INFORMS Pubs, and InformaWorld Online Databases. The pervasiveness of the search term *evidence-based management* in reference to the health-industry sector diluted all searches with this as a term, and the large body of knowledge generated in the evidence-based education sphere that relates to managerial links between teachers and students also obfuscates relevant results. Because of these factors, many articles that were retrieved in searches have been defined as irrelevant to the research topic and have been discounted from this review. Additionally, where possible in online searches, the terms *health, healthcare,* and *medicine* were used to exclude search results.

The search strategy was iterative and followed these steps;

1. Keywords entered into "Title and Abstract" search in online database; if possible, *peer-reviewed* constraint added and exclusion terms *health, healthcare* and *medicine* used
2. Relevant research collected; obviously irrelevant articles discarded
3. Collected articles divided into types: comparative analysis, experimental designs, literature reviews and case studies / descriptive
4. Upon review, search strategy updated to reflect the findings in this iteration (i.e., search broadened if not enough results were retrieved or narrowed if too many were retrieved)

Search Results

Research Question 1: "What is the efficacy of the evidence-based management methodology when applied to virtual teams in the online education sector?"

Search Keywords: evidence-based management, virtual OR *telework,* AND *education—health—healthcare—medical*

The results of searches in the databases listed earlier for different combinations of keywords were checked for relevance to this research question. For this search strategy iteration, zero search results were found to be directly relevant.

Indeed, there are no papers on the topic at hand (see Table 6.1). The single relevant hit that was found on Google Scholar was Pfeffer's paper *Hard Facts, Dangerous Half-Truths, and Total Nonsense,* a widely referenced text on the virtues of evidence-based management, which has already been referenced in this chapter.

With the goal of analysis of a wider body of literature, the search was then broadened to include all papers that involve evidence-based management of telework teams.

Research Question 2: "What is the efficacy of EBMgt in virtual team management contexts?

Table 6.1

Research that Informs Research Question 1 after Controlling for Relevance

	Hits
Google Scholar	1
ERIC	0
EBSCO	0
ProQuest	0
Science Direct	0
INFORMS Pubs	0
InformaWorld	0

Table 6.2

Research that Informs Research Question 2 after Controlling for Relevance

	Hits
Google Scholar	0
ERIC	0
EBSCO	0
ProQuest	0
Science Direct	0
INFORMS Pubs	0
InformaWorld	0

Table 6.3

Research that Informs Research Question 3 after Controlling for Relevance

	Hits
Google Scholar	40
ERIC	10
EBSCO	14
ProQuest	116
Science Direct	120
INFORMS Pubs	0
InformaWorld	38

Search Keywords: evidence-based management AND *virtual teams—health—healthcare—medical*

The results of searches for different combinations of keywords were checked for relevance to this research question. For this search strategy iteration, zero search results were found to be directly relevant (see Table 6.2).

No articles were found for this version of the search terms, so the search was widened to encompass other management topics in this area.

Research Question 3: "What management methodologies are effective for virtual teams?"

Search Keywords: management AND *virtual teams—health—healthcare—medicine*

This wider search iteration resulted in a much larger body of literature; however, many articles failed to mention the evidence upon which their conclusions were based, so they were discarded. Around thirty of the articles retrieved in the search (see Table 6.3) were comparative studies that were explicit about methodology; the rest were single case studies, and there were a small number that employed an experimental design. Paper topics admitted for review largely fitted into the following themes: manage by objective, team building, and managerial style.

Discussion of Search Results

Manage by Objective

Many articles point to the importance of a management-by-objective, or results-oriented, approach to developing team productivity (Kaczmarczyk 2008), and indeed, indicate that the success of telework programs requires it (Steinhardt 2007). A change in approach like this has several benefits for managers of telework teams. First, a management-by-objective approach allows for clearer and more explicit communication of work requirements and task demarcation to team members who work in time zones that make synchronous communications difficult or rare. It also simplifies the performance appraisal process, as both the manager and the worker can concentrate on the outcomes, which are shared and tangible, rather than on work processes, which in the telework scenario can be difficult to monitor. A recent quantitative study into the managerial factors that promote job satisfaction for teleworkers found eleven factors that correlated with high reported job satisfaction (Carr, Ilozor, and Ilozor 2001). Of the factors that related to management behavior (providing clear expectations, goals, objectives, and regular performance appraisal), all relate to the definition and communication of objective-based requirements.

Team Building

Team building, and particularly building perceptions of trust, also emerges as a topic of significant research interest in this area. A comparative study of the relationship between virtual-team effectiveness and factors such as perceptions of task interdependence and team-based reward structures conducted across thirty-one virtual teams found that where management structures were put in place such that members felt that their work was explicitly contributing to the group output and that individuals' tasks were interdependent with other members' work, team effectiveness was positively correlated (Hertel, Konradt, and Orlikowski 2004). A case study of Sabre Holdings, a multinational business to business e-commerce provider for travel-industry booking services, also found a similar result: management structures need to support and foster team members' feeling that they are included in group transactions, that their work is valued, and that they can trust their virtual workmates (Kirkman et al. 2002). The relationship between trust and team effectiveness has also been demonstrated in a quantitative study in which perceived levels of trust between team members were tracked longitudinally and correlated with objective measures of team performance (Powell, Piccoli, and Ives 2004).

Managerial Style

In terms of the interactions that managers have with their teams, there is very little in the way of quantitative research. As a detailed literature review suggests (Powell,

Piccoli, and Ives 2004): "The current literature provides no guidance in answering the following questions . . . Do traditional managerial control mechanisms remain applicable in the virtual environment? If so, what are the most appropriate managerial controls (formal versus informal)? . . . Can a set of behaviors that promote effectiveness of a wide range of virtual teams be identified? How can these behaviors be effectively enforced in virtual teams?"

A very recent study into the impact of inspirational leadership on geographically dispersed teams found that creating inspirational leaders (i.e., those who passionately share the vision for the project and respect the team members' contributions) plays a significant part in engendering positive motivation and attitudes in the team (Joshi, Lazarova, and Liao 2009).

In the area of managerial methodology, there is no comparative or quantitative experimental research to inform managers of virtual teams which managerial methodologies work in this context. Most articles focus on implementation issues and methodologies that could be part of a management approach as described earlier in this section. However, the literature seems to stop short of evaluating management methodologies as a whole. For that reason, and to inform choices about future directions for relevant research in this area, an investigation of the lack of research in this area was conducted.

The Place of EBMgt in Virtual-Team Management for Online Education

This section draws on research from the education management field to ascertain the readiness of the education sector to implement the concepts of EBMgt.

In the education field, the concept of using research-based evidence to underpin practice is not a new one. Heck and Hallinger conducted a longitudinal study of the impact and direction of research in educational leadership and suggest that "beginning in the 1950s, the 'theory movement in educational administration' focused attention on the need to improve scholarly activity through the application of scientific principles based on empiricism rather than ideological belief, personal experience, and prescription" (as quoted in Heck and Hallinger 2005). However, they go on to suggest that even given this long lead time, there is still a significant gap between what the research shows and what practices reflect.

Heck and Hallinger also describe another gap between what was suggested could have been achieved through research by the "theory movement" and the actual outcomes of the direction that the field of study has taken over the past decades. Indeed, they suggest that the field of study is still significantly underdeveloped, with many areas of managerial influence in the education sphere relatively nonexistent, and that the direction of much of the research in this field is moving away from scientific approaches and toward more humanistic and moral approaches (Heck and Hallinger 2005). They conclude that a lack of empirical rigor in the research of this field will negatively impact the future generations of researchers in this field. The implications of this for the application of EBMgt in this area should be obvious. If education managers and leaders can find only nonempirical evidence to base their decisions on, then progress toward a proper implementation of EBMgt will be difficult.

A lack of empirical evidence from the research community does not mean that there is nothing to be gained by implementing EBMgt. EBMgt should also be informed by internally generated evidence from measures of performance within organizations. This evidence can then be shared between like-minded managers in similar contexts. The importance of this bottom-up approach to the production of evidence to be used in the decision-making process is not to be underestimated and is explicitly suggested by Rousseau (2006) as a method for bridging the divide between those who produce the evidence and those who use it. As Levacic and Glatter (2001, 6) point out, "research may not be able to provide 'data for decisions' in a straight-forward problem solving sense. In addition, it may take a considerable time for studies to yield validated findings."

EBMgt, however, as defined by Pfeffer (2006), is not a specific set of rules to be implemented; it is more of a philosophical approach to finding and using relevant research where possible, as well as critically analyzing the performance of the organization and work groups using an empirical method. In this way, EBMgt encourages the kind of scientific approach that may furnish the body of knowledge with the kind of information that is desirable.

From this perspective, then, even given the problematic situation of there being not enough empirical work to base decisions on, an implementation of evidence-based practice could still be attempted. The benefits of this could be manifold, from the concrete—finding and using appropriate evidence if available will improve the long-term performance of the organization—to the ephemeral—engendering an empirical approach to decision making means that it is more likely that education managers may engage in practices that can produce the kind of data that the body of knowledge so needs. In other words, implementing the core considerations of EBMgt could help to cultivate the ground in which more scientific evidence could grow.

Conceptualizing an EBMgt Approach to Managing Virtual Teams

The lack of evidence from the education management field as to which management methodologies are most effective means that any movement toward evidence-based management in education will require a change in mind-set on the part of managers in this area. These managers can draw from research in areas such as e-leadership and virtual teams, but to do so will have to reconsider themselves as online service providers. Once this is done, a much broader scope of research can be applied, although the extent to which it is possible to generalize research from other fields into the online education space is not known and is an area of research exploration that is in need of attention.

Proposals for Further Research

This chapter has shown that at this time there is a dire need for research to guide managers and leaders in the implementation of EBMgt practice in education, and especially in the online education sector, where there is no literature on the topic available. In order to establish a baseline to guide researchers in this area, it would be worthwhile to conduct a large-scale survey of online education providers that utilize telework as an employment option to ascertain the level of engagement and implementation of relevant evidence in related areas (for example, the area of leadership of virtual teams is fairly well described in the literature and yields some useful perspectives on the dynamics of groups, which could be generalized to the industry sector in question). This research could also involve a comparative study of virtual-team management behavior in these organizations, with a view to establishing the existence of trends in managerial approaches. There is also a need for experimental research to be conducted. This could be done by pre- and post-testing the effect of changes to management methodology over a significant length of time, in a range of virtual teams. Follow-up research could correlate levels of team satisfaction with managerial styles in an attempt to find particular traits that produce positive results.

Conclusion

EBMgt shows promise to deliver better teamwork experiences in the emerging virtual team-based online education sector and encourages a critical approach in implementation. However, there is not currently enough empirical evidence to inform managers as to effective methodologies to apply in this area, and empirical methods in general are underutilized in this area of research. A wider search of this knowledge space has shown that related fields also have very little in the way of empirical evidence to support management methodology choices; however, a handful of generally accepted and empirically based practices for management in these serve as a rough guide for managers. A widely recognized knowledge gap in this area was discussed, and while researchers in these fields have been aware of the need for more empirical evidence for a very long time, little progress has been made in this direction. For EBMgt to be used in this area, researchers must address the need for more rigorous research.

References

Allen, Elaine, and Jeff Seaman. 2007. *Online Nation: Five Years of Growth in Online Learning.* Needham, MA: Babson Survey Research Group.
Brownlie, Douglas T., Paul Hewer, Beverly Wagner, and Goran Svensson. 2008. "Management Theory and Practice: Bridging the Gap through Multidisciplinary Lenses." *European Business Review* 20 (6): 461–470.
Carr, John, Doreen Ilozor, and Ben Ilozor. 2001. "Management Communication Strategies

Determine Job Satisfaction in Telecommuting." *Journal of Management Development* 20 (6): 495–507.

Heck, Ronald, and Philip Hallinger. 2005. "The Study of Educational Leadership and Management: Where Does the Field Stand Today?" *Educational Management Administration and Leadership* 33 (2): 229–244.

Hertel, Guido, Udo Konradt, and Borris Orlikowski. 2004. "Managing Distance by Interdependence: Goal Setting, Task Interdependence, and Team-Based Rewards in Virtual Teams." *European Journal of Work and Organizational Psychology* 13 (1): 1–28.

Joshi, Aparna, Mila Lazarova, and Hui Liao. 2009. "Getting Everyone on Board: The Role of Inspirational Leadership in Geographically Dispersed Teams." *Organization Science* 20 (1): 240–252.

Kaczmarczyk, Stanley. 2008. "Telework: Breaking New Ground." *Public Manager* 37 (1): 63–67.

Kirkman, Bradley, et al. 2002. "Five Challenges to Virtual Team Success: Lessons from Sabre Inc." *Academy of Management Executive* 16 (3): 67–79.

Levacic, Rosalind, and Ron Glatter. 2001. "Really Good Ideas? Developing Evidence-Informed Policy and Practise in Educational Leadership and Management." *Educational Management and Administration* 29 (14): 5–25.

Meier, Kenneth J., and Laurence J. O'Toole Jr. 2008. "The Proverbs of New Public Management: Lessons from an Evidence-Based Research Agenda." *American Review of Public Administration* 39 (1): 4–22.

Pfeffer, Jeffrey. 2005. "Hard Facts, Dangerous Half Truths, and Total Nonsense: Profiting from Evidence-Based Management." Advanced Institute of Management Research. www.aimresearch.org/uploads/File/Presentations/2005/Pfeffer2_LBS-General.pdf (accessed on November 1, 2009).

———. 2006. "Evidence of Profit." Human Resource Executive, HR Technology Conference Update. www.evidence-basedmanagement.com/research_practice/articles/pfeffer_evidence_of_profit.pdf (accessed on November 1, 2009).

Powell, Anne, Gabriele Piccoli, and Blake Ives. 2004. "Virtual Teams: A Review of Current Literature and Directions for Future Research." *Advances in Information Systems* 35 (1): 6–36.

Robert Half International. 2008. "More than Money: Survey Finds Salary Is Top Draw for Job Candidates but Benefits Nearly As Popular." Press release, February 6. http://rhfa.mediaroom.com/index.php?s=305&item=408 (accessed on November 1, 2009).

Rousseau, Denise. 2006. "Is There Such a Thing as Evidence-Based Management?" *Academy of Management Review* 31 (2): 256–269.

Rousseau, Denise, and Sharon McCarthy. 2007. "Educating Managers from an Evidence-Based Perspective." *Academy of Management Learning and Education* 6 (1): 84–101.

Steinhardt, Bernice. 2007. *Human Capital: Greater Focus on Results in Telework Programs Needed.* U.S. Senate Testimony, June 12. Washington, DC: U.S. Government Accountability Office.

Tallent-Runnels, Mary K., et al. 2006. "Teaching Courses Online: A Review of the Research." *Review of Educational Research* 76 (1): 93–135.

Tamrat, Elsabet, and Malcolm Smith. 2002. "Telecommuting and Perceived Productivity: An Australian Case Study." *Journal of Management and Organisation* 8 (1): 44–69.

7

Evidence-Based Public Management and ICT

A Broad Survey of the Literature

Aaron Osterby and Robert Hanson

The notion that *evidence-based public management* (EBMgt) is currently applied to endeavors in information and communication technologies (ICT) may seem unlikely to some. The brand equity of ICT, particularly in public policy arenas, is tarnished by widely reported project "failures" and a legacy of unmet expectations. Two famously difficult projects include the UK Department of Human Services (DHS) initiative to provide integrated health care informatics and the U.S. Federal Bureau of Investigation (FBI) efforts to rein hundreds of isolated systems into a unified resource for counterterrorism and criminal investigations.

Project execution of any kind will always have some level of risk. Civil engineers, for example, have had a five-thousand-year head start on ICT practitioners in the refinement of their discipline, but cost overruns in flood-control projects are not unheard of either. Given that the number, size, and complexity of large-scale ICT systems seem to be increasing (Goodyear and Nelson 2007) perhaps disproportionately to more-established disciplines, it seems appropriate to bring some attention to the state of evidence-based management in the field.

Approach

This chapter represents a broad manual scan for threads of EBM in the literature of organizational use of ICT. The scan used primarily Google Scholar and focused on systematic reviews; however, a good deal of citation referral led to valuable papers not included in the "systematic review" keyword searches. Greater attention was paid to those works that Google Scholar identified as often cited by other authors and to those works believed to be influential. The scan included noteworthy topics in ICT management and project success or failure including stakeholder management, agile software development, pay for performance, and portfolio management.

As such, the scan is not exhaustive and mostly serves to acquaint the reader with applications of evidence-based approaches and, where there was little indication of organized evidence-based threads, to discuss themes of the available evidence. As a result of this work, we propose areas for future systematic literature reviews.

Covering the Basics

The formal study of ICT in management and organizational contexts is a relatively young body of literature. As such, there are significant definitional issues to manage, not yet completely resolved. Fundamentally, there are many different kinds of ICT, and the diversification makes definition, much less generalization, challenging. There are also consistent concerns about a relatively shallow base of data for analysis, especially when compared to the volume of evidence relied on in evidence-based medicine (Dybå, Kitchenham, and Jørgensen 2005).

An important focus of the developing literature was on the question of how, if at all, information systems contributed value to the firms that used them (Turner and Lucas 1984; Kauffman and Weill 1989; Weill 1990, 1992; Hitt and Brynjolfsson 1996; Brynjolfsson and Hitt 2003), and how as general-purpose technologies' (Bresnahan and Trajtenberg 1995) investment return was dependent on organizational complements (Brynjolfsson and Hitt 2000; Baradwaj 2000; Melville, Kraemer, and Gurbaxani 2004; Weill and Ross 2004) like business process change, skill development, changing decision rights, and patterns of teamwork (McAfee 2006). Observation of suboptimal results in some cases continues to fuel searches for the "missing link" that establishes value focused on specific issues related to particular complements (Deveraj and Kohli 2003; Tippins and Sohi 2003).

Cautionary arguments include Nicholas Carr's provocative title "IT Doesn't Matter" (2003) and John Thorp's *Information Paradox* (1999), which questions the costs associated with technological expansion and highlights lack of measures to track translation of ICT investment to business value.

Causality between a lack of complementary organizational change and a failure of ICT to deliver value is based on a variety of evidence sources and accepted by best practice wisdom. Technology projects are more likely to fail when managed in isolation. The need to continuously reinforce this concept strongly implies a need to resist a countervailing force that either fails to recognize the evidence or fails to give it the weight it deserves in technology decision making.

This dynamic of organizational "climate" (Weill 1990) creates challenges for government (Goodyear and Nelson 2007) and for efforts at integrating information systems across organizational boundaries. If it is difficult to manage organizational change in one organization, it must be harder to manage between government agencies. These challenges are factors to consider when examining the fate of the process and technology integration projects by the FBI or DHS. For these reasons, evidence about ICT implementation "failure" in government may not easily generalize to the experience of small to medium-size enterprises, or even some relatively large multinational corporations.

A zealous drive toward technological implementation is referred to as the *technological imperative*. This drive is perhaps innate to humanity and is strongly supported by Western jurisprudence, which holds the role of inventors in high esteem. Apel (2003) finds references in Aristotle's philosophies and discusses protechnology principles in patent law and product liability law that establish the process of invention as a protected activity.

The power and malleability of scope that computers enable highlight an aspect of the technological imperative that requires active management and stewardship. This is particularly so given the realization that technology for technology's sake driven orthogonally to the strategy or culture of an organization can be counterproductive for firms.

Historical Perspective on the Technological Imperative

Evidence from history suggests that being motivated by the technological imperative along a route based on mythology may not bring value. In the mid-1800s, unseasonal rain led to the popular belief among white settlers both in Australia and in North America that cultivation influenced climate. At the time, the theory was accepted by scientists, land speculators, and emigrants in the western United States and among South Australian farmers. Climate change was attributed to the technology of the plow, which supposedly released moisture from the ground as new fields were cultivated. The belief that "rain follows the plow," as espoused by Charles Dana Wilbur, was the wisdom of the time, but however firmly held and ardently agreed, the belief was not based on the evidence. A few contemporaries of Wilbur's were careful to watch the evidence; they included South Australian George Goyder, who warned "that rain would not follow the plow" as early as 1865. Evidence that eventually dispelled the wisdom as mythology was unfortunately the quite tangible proof in disaster, when the high rainfall ceased in the 1930s, causing crops to fail and the tilled soils to blow away in the infamous Dust Bowl era that contributed to the depths of the Great Depression (Guyatt 2007).

We argue that Wilbur's proclamations were a manifestation of the technological imperative that was undefeated by the experience of Wilbur and the settler-farmers contemporary to his time. We are also struck by the comparison of the if-you-build-it-they-will-come ethic to a more conservative view of technology adoption frequently held by practitioners burned by previous experience.

Westward-Ho Meets First to Market

There is a certain element of frontier attitude, particularly among firms with a first-to-market mentality, that spurs a rush into new-technology adoption. A salient example can be found in the widely reported delays developing the Airbus A380. The project was a massive undertaking in both complexity and scale, spanning organizational silos, companies, and countries. Eventually, schedule slippages cost Airbus $6.1 billion over four years, which made it the most expensive project failure in commercial aviation (BBC 2006).

Industry observers see these failures coming from a management approach emphasizing speed to market but tripped up by a seemingly small change in a pivotal information technology (Newton 2006). Airbus SAS was created from consolidation of French, German, and Spanish partners with the UK-based BAE Systems. The French and UK elements upgraded their computer-aided design (CAD) software to the next available version, while German and Spanish elements remained on an earlier version (Rothman 2006). That meant French and UK design teams had a new feature that rendered three-dimensional models of the plane, but due to version incompatibility, some German and Spanish design changes were not incorporated into the master plans. The result was mayhem over some elements of the design.

Estimating Value to the Organization

From the point of view of the organization, however, generalizations about the impacts of technology on society are far less meaningful than the impacts of technology, or the impacts of a failure to effectively adopt technology on the existence of the firm and the welfare of its stakeholders. We are learning that the quality of the technology is important to success but is not the sole or necessarily primary driver of success when considering a nuanced view of how success is defined.

DeLone and McLean (1992) synthesized research to propose a model for information-systems success and ten years on (DeLone and McLean 2003) conducted follow-up research synthesis on adoption and empirical testing of their model. In the original success model, technical success is underpinned by systems quality. Semantic success is measured by information quality. Effectiveness success has dimensions for use, user satisfaction, individual impact, and organizational impact. Their main point is that success for an ICT system is multidimensional and interdependent. DeLone and McLean (2003) indicate that follow-up research suggests that the strongest causal link is between system use and individual impact; next, system quality and information quality both are causal links to individual impacts. In their 2003 revision of the model, DeLone and McLean add a service-quality element alongside systems and information quality and collapse individual and organizational benefits together into net effect.

Executive satisfaction is frequently used as a proxy for business value to the firm among practitioners. This is not very useful, considering that the returns from an investment in general-purpose technologies like ICT increase as organizations get used to them and incorporate them more fully into business practice, sometimes three to five years out from the implementation (McAfee 2006). Value conclusions based on point-in-time opinion of value therefore fail to use evidence that corresponds to one of the few well-proven causal links.

According to Grant Thornton (2009) surveys of U.S. federal government chief financial officers, information technologies are the third-greatest risk to accomplishing their missions, behind human capital and leadership issues (pp. 11–12). Grant Thornton analysts argue that the most effective way for chief financial officers to ensure the utility of business systems is to be part of the implementation team.

Software Reuse

Even if we cannot specifically quantify the value of an ICT component to the firm, it should be quite reasonable to forward the point that if there is some unknown but positive value to using it, reusing it for another purpose would increase its value. By this logic, *software reuse* is an accepted wisdom and one that underpins much of the discourse surrounding *service-oriented architecture*. This approach emphasizes the separation of software components into reusable packages that can be considered discrete services. In this way, information systems would be composed using some standard replaceable services and some new features peculiar to the business of the system at hand. The term is heavily used in marketing materials, however, so it features as one of the latest must-have technologies for subscribers to the technological imperative.

Mohagheghi and Conradi (2007) performed a systematic literature review on *systematic software reuse* as opposed to ad hoc reuse. They found support in the literature for the value of reusing software expressed in terms of reduced direct cost from person-hours, reduced rework, and lower fault density (p. 489). There is some evidence that reuse and successful standardization are correlated. The literature also reported that there was some reluctance on the part of management to invest in reuse. Not surprisingly, the literature was not able to convincingly detail actual economic benefits from software reuse, largely due to the issues discussed previously related to the challenges of establishing a return on investment figure for ICT systems.

Notably, Grant Thornton (2009) surveys of U.S. federal government chief information officers found that the IT workforce is a consistent top-level concern (p. 67), and since standardization is an enabling factor for integration, the concept of software reuse in the public sector would certainly bear some further consideration and more detailed analysis.

Stakeholder Management

Given that organizational acceptance and complementary change are so important in the dynamics of ICT systems in organizations, *stakeholder management* is an important concept. In the sales phase of a project, there is a need to engage interest, so expectations are raised. When the end result turns out to be a compromise of multiple stakeholder positions and resource constraints, there is disappointment. The nature of the process ensures that the end product is unlikely to fulfill every stakeholder's expectations (Gutierrez and Friedman 2005).

In this context, failure and success are especially slippery concepts, because what is failure to one stakeholder may be success to another. Failure, like expectation, is a subjective concept. We can say that not meeting expectations can translate into a perception of failure. Some research in the application of ICT to social services suggests that expectation management is crucial because some disappointment is inevitable.

Gutierrez and Friedman (2005) studied information-systems implementation among a variety of organizations in the continua of care for homeless people. The effort to adopt a Homelessness Management Information System was driven by the U.S. Department of Housing and Urban Development as a compliance measure related to the Annual Homeless Assessment Report. Gutierrez and Friedman lay out a number of the specific factors that Goodyear and Nelson (2007) describe in general terms as "additional constraints" (p. 309) faced by the managers of public sector ICT projects. Social services systems implementations pose technical requirements on communities of stakeholders that seldom match available expertise. The collection of stakeholders is diverse and can include interests that are in competition with each other, but for the system to deliver on its potential, the stakeholders need to cooperate. The system itself is intended to handle highly sensitive data that require elaborate rules to govern normal use, not to mention security from external threats to privacy of data regarding clients who may be victims of domestic violence, mentally ill, substance abusers, or have other illnesses or disabilities. To top it off, the system required by the Department of Housing and Urban Development is being implemented in a sector that has very high resource constraints (Gutierrez and Friedman 2005).

The Homelessness Management Information System highlights in very clear terms the importance of how an organizational "climate" (Weill 1990) can affect investment performance. We can predict from the detectable evidence that the system's implementation will encounter substantial difficulties and will fail to meet the expectations of some stakeholders. Gutierrez and Friedman noted that successful project managers of these projects recognize that—whether through intuition or evidence they do not say—and seek not to prevent the inevitable but instead to manage its effects. The conclusion of the study suggests that the most effective practices in "multiple distributed projects" (p. 514) embrace flexibility.

That implies that effective stakeholder management is not particularly aligned with a desire to have certainty about the estimated costs of a system implementation project.

Estimating Project Costs

The value to the firm of any new information system will involve some function of the cost of acquiring and deploying the system, but accurate estimates are difficult to come by. This element is perhaps not the most important cost in the life cycle of an information system, but it is likely the most watched, and in an environment where long-term investment performance is often not tracked, it can have disproportionate influence on the perceived value of a system. Executive satisfaction as a proxy for business value, therefore, must be seen as an important, but inconclusive, metric of success. Consider that projects with cost blowouts are likely to have a strong correlation with informal and subjective or, worse yet, randomized dartboard-based estimation methods.

Work by Jørgensen et al. (2000) points out that while much work has been done to develop formal estimation models, most evaluation studies show that the models are inaccurate. It seems that "intuitive" and "expert" processes have a significant influence on estimation processes, which would naturally depend on the skill and expertise applied from case to case. Jørgensen and colleagues describe an elaborate combination of models and human judgment, which in theory could improve the accuracy of estimates at the cost of additional effort. However, more recently Jørgensen and Shepperd (2007) conducted a systematic review of software development cost-estimation studies and concluded that available evidence does not suggest that the use of formal estimation models improves the accuracy of estimates (p. 40).

Simonsen and Hertzum (2005) propose a hypothesis that if workable could resolve the issue of uncertainty from the client's point of view by putting more risk onto the shoulders of vendors, using an evidence-based pay-for-performance approach, what they define as *evidence-based IT development.* They propose a new commercial contract model for measuring the agreed-in-advance, business-centric effects of using the system, and they provide examples like "[a health care worker's] time needed for documenting a treatment, X, is reduced by 90 percent." They point out the similarities of the idea with *performance-based procurement* in the construction industry, and the less widely used *objectives-based usability engineering* in software development. Simonsen and Hertzum note some of the pitfalls and propose further research in that vein. Certainly such a contract model, if viable, would present an attractive alternative where cost estimates are known in advance to be pro forma guesstimates. Not all clients would be able to engage in this kind of contract, however, and not all vendors would see the value in changing, considering that the status quo puts most of the risk onto the clients.

Another alternative approach to the difficulty in accurately estimating project costs is encapsulated in the idea of *agile software development. Agile,* as it is known, has trendy new street credibility since the popularization of the Internet and the dot-com ethic of the heroic programmer. But agile methods have been around for some time and include the earlier ideas of rapid prototyping, scrum, and adaptive software development, to name a few. The heart of agile methods is the iterative process of improving the product and then checking with the client for reactions and feedback. It is contended that, applied properly, this will result in a product that is more satisfactory to the client, which is a common success proxy. The process embeds a level of expectation management if the iterative review is fast enough. The promised benefits of this approach include improved quality and speed, but a truly agile approach will not be able to produce any accurate estimates of time and cost involved in getting to the proffered superior product.

Dybå and Dingsøyr's (2008) systematic literature review of studies examining the use of agile methods concluded that agile methods do exist but do not generalize to all type of projects and project teams. The found agile methods are well suited to small teams and small projects, especially where the organization climate encourages a high level of team autonomy.

Most project governance approaches work well for small projects and small teams. The various project methodologies work as expected along a continuum from large-scale and simple to small-scale and complex (Goodyear and Nelson 2007). In short, the evidence on agile approaches is not a convincing solution for projects on the scale of government systems and could be correctly characterized as *design-and-build projects,* which Goodyear and Nelson consider a very risky state of affairs for large-scale ICT projects.

Making Technical Decisions

Dybå, Kitchenham, and Jørgensen (2005) discuss the circumstances that software managers and developers encounter, with various client motivations that must be considered in the adoption of new technology in their projects. Because there is little evidence about important dimensions like suitability and risks, the resulting decisions tend to be suboptimal. They define *evidence-based software engineering* as a mechanism to assist practitioners in these decisions. They propose embedding the practice of literature reviews and empirical methods into engineering practice in order to apply evidence to technical decision making.

Brereton et al. (2007) followed up on the application of systematic literature reviews to software engineering with the aim of detecting benefits similar to those accruing to *evidence-based medicine.* They concluded that while systematic review appears relevant, some fine-tuning of the process could improve its value as a research tool and evidentiary base for practitioners. In addition to de rigueur discussions about definitional fragmentation, they point to a lack of conformity in search facilities across commonly used digital libraries as a missing element that, if provided, could add value.

Notably Dybå, Kitchenham, and Jørgensen (2005) say that practitioners using evidence-based software engineering will make individual judgments based on the situation, rather than uncritically conforming to standards or procedures (p. 62). This is a fairly radical notion and suggests that some research is required into the effectiveness of wisdom-based versus evidence-based approaches for practitioners. Given the identified shortcomings of the literature, one cannot assume that a process dependent on literature reviews provides better outcomes than the group wisdom expressed in organizational policy.

Caution is also required before mapping this thread of literature regarding technical decision to other decision domains within the spectrum of system delivery. The value for technical decision making may not generalize well to other parts of the process.

Project Management

How we frame the questions that are asked about our perceived challenges in finding our way with technology is revealing. While a base of evidence has been compiled supporting answers to questions related to the contribution of ICT to the value to the firm, in the popular discourse there is a strong focus on ICT project failure.

But what constitutes failure? The dominant view as proffered by the Standish Group's figures focuses on a *project deliverables–based view* (Standish Group 1994). A project is successful, generally, if it is completed for the predicted costs, at the predicted time, with all of the predicted features. That is a rather narrow view of success. On the one hand, there appears to be unexplored nuance about the validity of the predictions at the outset of the project, and on the other hand there is unexplored nuance as to the satisfaction of the stakeholders. It is reasonable to posit that, by this definition, there are successful projects with unhappy stakeholders and successful projects that spent more time and more money to deliver fewer features than is reasonable. In short, the Standish work does not account for a nuanced view of stakeholder expectation.

There is much made of the view that ICT implementation projects fail at a considerably higher rate than other projects, but does the evidence support that view? The oft-quoted Standish Group reports certainly suggest that it is true, and they have likely held great sway in practitioners' perception of the situation. They famously claim that typically challenged software projects encounter average cost overruns of 189 percent of the original budget (Standish Group 1994), but Jørgensen and Moløkken (2006) present some compelling criticisms of the validity of the Standish Group's approach that give cause to avoid uncritically citing the Standish Group figures as evidence of a crisis in software projects.

According to Grant Thornton (2009) surveys of U.S. federal government chief information officers conducted in 2004 through 2007, the value of project management improvements has fallen relative to other kinds of improvements. While project management improvements ranked as the number one initiative that would bring value in 2004 and 2005, in 2006 and 2007 system and process integration ranked higher, as did security improvements and reduction in operating costs (p. 75). That suggests that senior ICT leaders in the U.S. federal government may feel that project management for ICT is turning a corner.

Portfolio Management

Project management is not the only dimension of the issue. If flexibility is important and project management requires disciplined execution of a plan, something else is required in combination with projects to permit flexibility and options-based value.

It is possible for an efficient project to deliver a system that is ineffective for the organization. Our earlier example of the Airbus CAD software is one such example. No one criticizes Airbus for poor project approaches in upgrading the

CAD systems that were upgraded. The failure of Airbus management was in the selection of those French and UK projects to proceed when no similar projects were planned for Spain and Germany. That was a failure not of project management but of what is called portfolio management.

These projects are typical scenarios where well-meaning and locally valuable but suboptimal development of ICT capabilities resulted in a sprawling landscape of fragmented systems, lacking ability to account for how much human and financial capital was invested in ICT-related activities. This class of myopic vision amounts to what Raiffa defines as an error of the third type, or more simply "solving the wrong problem" (Raiffa 1968). Fundamentally, this can be expressed as a governance issue, and there is evidence that a portfolio-based view of collection of projects is a credible treatment for this kind of risk.

The shift from stand-alone project management to portfolio management creates the potential to harvest increased alignment among ICT-enabled business transformation initiatives. It also expands options. As we know, options have inherent value (Saha 2006). This is encapsulated in the notion of *organizational agility* and includes the value of deferring decisions to reduce uncertainty.

Bardhan, Bagchi, and Sougstad (2004) point to the need for managers to have a reliable process of prioritizing projects within portfolios and seek to extend the research evaluating the use of *real-options analysis* as a basis for informed prioritization. A real option represents the opportunity to make business decisions, such as choosing to invest in a particular project. As such, they are not traded as stock options are, but they can be valued in present terms principally the same way stock options are.

They propose a *real-options portfolio optimization algorithm*. The basis of their calculations still rely on a calculation of present value of expected benefits and present value of expected costs, so the usefulness of this approach will suffer if the estimations are inaccurate. As discussed earlier, project cost estimates are often unreliable, and the contribution of value to the firm is rarely well understood by managers. Nonetheless, Bardhan, Bagchi, and Sougstad's algorithm does include a treatment for benefits-realization volatility.

Considering that U.S. federal government chief information officers identified conflicting priorities among program units as their greatest barrier to improved effectiveness in each of the years 2005–7, advances that permit greater management of conflicting and complementary portfolio elements would seem to be quite relevant. It would be useful indeed to follow up on this approach to see whether there is empirical support for it working in practice.

Discussion

The largest base of literature, explicitly identifying itself as evidence-based management, appears to be *evidence-based software engineering*. This school of thought seems sustained by a small core of authors. Dybå, Kitchenham, and Jørgensen in their "Evidence-Based Software Engineering for Practitioners" (2005) seek to popularize an evidence-based approach among software engineers. The article lays out a step-by-step process of applying research practices to technology selection.

Interestingly to the topic of project failure, in early works Jørgensen tended to uncritically cite Standish Group project failure statistics (Jørgensen et al. 2000). In learning to apply evidence-based approaches, he subsequently published an article critical of the Standish Group methodology (Jørgensen and Moløkken 2006) that should cause any academic to pause to consider whether such a ubiquitously quoted study has really earned its place.

A radical notion put forward is that evidence-based decision making should supplant adherence to organizational standards and policy as the evidence warrants (Dybå, Kitchenham, and Jørgensen 2005). This is, of course, the logic of trusting evidence over assertion. In an analogy to evidence-based medicine, this calls to mind the history of Ambroise Paré (Drucker 2008), a pioneering French battlefield surgeon who led a movement of then blue-collar barber-surgeons to compile their own evidence, which turned out to contradict the Roman-era dogmatic beliefs of the white-collar physicians. While this is a romantic notion, it is likely that evidence-based software engineering has a long way to go before it is time to completely eschew the value of time-tested wisdom expressed in particularly industry-accepted standards. Consider, after all, the weight of acceptance of the value of standards. The United States' Clinger-Cohen Act of 1996 (40 U.S.C. 1401 et seq.) mandates that government organizations adopt certain principles of ICT management, including requirements to comply with standards and to work to determine what practices are considered best of breed. No doubt there is a hybrid solution in which the evidence supporting organizational standards is actively considered.

If we make an inference from the fragmented definitional issues with much of the literature on ICT, it should be that conclusions drawn about systems in one organization are unlikely to easily or completely apply to systems in another organization. This dynamic makes evidence-based management as a means to understand the relationship between people and information systems a compelling offer. This dynamic also would make for a great challenge for evidence-based management of ICT-related organizational changes in that, unlike in medicine, where the human body is relatively analogous from patient to patient, abstract ICT systems do not obey many scientific laws. Given that, it should be no surprise that two different but similar systems can be subjected to the same or similar techniques for changing their course and result in quite different outcomes.

Opportunities for Future Research

Given that chief information officers in the U.S. federal government rate human capital issues as their number one concern and that South Australia faces significant projected shortfalls in technology-related skill sets (Brett and Jackson 2007), it would make sense to focus research on areas that promise to leverage available skills.

Based on those criteria and the results of this literature scan, it would appear that software reuse should be high on the priority list for public sector interest. It promises to leverage human capital and would enable a level of integration and standardization but would face organizational uphill sledding considering the strong sense of cultural individuality commonly on display in government agencies.

Interesting dimensions to study would be why managers seem more reluctant to invest in used software (Mohagheghi and Conradi 2007). The implications for or against service-oriented architecture as a platform for reuse are interesting, considering that there is some literature directly from an evidence-based medicine perspective that includes evaluations of service-oriented implementations of the HL7 (Health Level 7) in the United Kingdom. HL7 standards form the lingua franca for information systems in the health care industry to exchange information in a mutually predictable way.

This work should proceed with some urgency, as a number of agencies are proceeding with service-oriented architecture solutions, while the technology is often criticized as hype laden.

Conclusion

There is indeed evidence of an emerging field of evidence-based management applied to ICT. As with any other new technique applied to the information systems of complex social organizations, caution is warranted. Analogies to evidence-based medicine are not complete. As noted above, the state of the literature in ICT management is much less comprehensive than the research in medicine. However, for the ICT management literature to improve, there is certainly a requirement for more data generation from the firms and government agencies that use ICT in their day-to-day business. For that reason alone, a greater adoption of evidence-based management would benefit academics. The challenge will be to influence stakeholders to establish that system of information processing in organizations that are more accustomed to technical fixes, do not really understand the value of their ICT systems, and have difficulty prioritizing technology investments.

Certain elements of popular wisdom seem to be upheld by the literature reviewed. In particular, it is very difficult to estimate development and implementation costs. The idea of performance-based pay for developers seems quite appropriate given the circumstances; however, there are hurdles to overcome for that procurement mode to be accepted. No doubt some hourly rate plus performance-based bonus incentives would have more traction. Agile programming seems to live up to its reputation as a lightweight approach. It is still possible that it is the optimal way to perform small projects, but the literature seems to discount it as ill suited for large projects.

Software project failure is a multidimensional topic. It seems clear that there will be a heavy reliance on the social science aspects of organizational management studies in order to substantially improve government system implementation performance. The state of evidence-based approaches being largely confined to technical disciplines suggests that there is a long process of maturity required for it to have a worthwhile impact on ICT project failure rates.

References

Apel, A. 2003. "The Virtue of Innovation and the Technological Imperative." Butterflies & Wheels.com, September 30. www.butterfliesandwheels.org/2003/the-virtue-of-innovation-and-the-technological-imperative/ (accessed April 26, 2009).

Baradwaj, March. 2000. "A Resource-Based Perspective on Information Technology Capability and Firm Performance: An Empirical Investigation." *MIS Quarterly* 24 (1): 169–196.

Bardhan, I., S. Bagchi, and R. Sougstad. 2004. "Prioritizing a Portfolio of Information Technology Investment Projects." *Journal of Management Information Systems* 21 (2): 33–60.

BBC News. 2006. "Q&A: A380 Delays." BBC News Business, October 30. http://news.bbc.co.uk/2/hi/business/5405524.stm (accessed April 24, 2009).

Brereton, P., B.A. Kitchenham, D. Budgen, M. Turner, and M. Khalil. 2007. "Lessons from Applying the Systematic Literature Review Process within the Software Engineering Domain." *Journal of Systems and Software* 80:571–583.

Bresnahan, T.F., and M. Trajtenberg. 1995. "General Purpose Technologies 'Engines of Growth'?" NBER Working Paper W4148, Cambridge, MA: National Bureau of Economic Research. October.

Brett, M., and J. Jackson. 2007. "A Review of South Australia's IT Workforce: Preparing for the Perfect Storm." Australia Information Industry Association, Adelaide, South Australia, December.

Brynjolfsson, E., and L.M. Hitt. 2000. "Beyond Computation: Information Technology, Organizational Transformation and Business Performance." *Journal of Economic Perspectives* 14 (4): 23–48.

———. 2003. "Computing Productivity. Firm-Level Evidence." MIT Sloan Working Paper 4210–01, Cambridge, MA: MIT University. June.

Carr, N.G. 2003. "IT Doesn't Matter." *Harvard Business Review* 81 (5), 41–49.

Clinger-Cohen Act of 1996. 40 U.S.C. 1401 et seq. cio-nii.defense.gov/docs/ciodesrefvolone.pdf (accessed November 1, 2009).

DeLone, W.H., and E.R. McLean. 1992. "Information Systems Success: The Quest for the Dependant Variable." *Information Systems Research* 3 (1): 60–95.

———. 2003. "The DeLone and McLean Model of Information Systems Success: A Ten-Year Update." *Journal of Management Information Systems* 19 (4): 9–30.

Deveraj, S., and R. Kohli. 2003. "Performance Impacts of Information Technology: Is Actual Usage the Missing Link?" *Management Science* 49 (3): 273–289.

Drucker, C.B. 2008. "Ambroise Paré and the Birth of the Gentle Art of Surgery." *Yale Journal of Biology and Medicine* 81 (4): 199–202.

Dybå, T., and T. Dingsøyr. 2008. "Empirical Studies of Agile Software Development: A Systematic Review." *Information and Software Technology* 50 (9–10): 833–859.

Dybå, T., B.A. Kitchenham, and M. Jørgensen. 2005. "Evidence-Based Software Engineering for Practitioners." *IEEE Software* 22 (1): 58–65.

Goodyear, M., and M.R. Nelson. 2007. "Leadership Strategies for Large-Scale IT Implementations in Government." In *Transforming Public Leadership for the 21st Century*, ed. R.S. Morse, T.F. Buss, and C.M. Kinghorn, 308–323. Armonk, NY: M.E. Sharpe.

Grant Thornton. 2009. *Hail to the Chiefs: A Compilation of Federal Government CXO Surveys 2006–2008.* Alexandria, VA: Grant Thornton.

Gutierrez, O., and D.H. Friedman. 2005. "Managing Project Expectations in Human Services Information Systems Implementations: The Case of Homeless Management Information Systems." *International Journal of Project Management* 23:513–523.

Guyatt, N. 2007. *Providence and the Invention of the United States, 1607–1876.* Cambridge: Cambridge University Press.

Hitt, L.M., and E. Brynjolfsson. 1996. "Productivity, Business Profitability, and Consumer Surplus: Three Different Measures of Information Technology Value." *MIS Quarterly* 20 (2): 121–142.

Jørgensen, M., G.M. Kirkebøen, D. Sjøberg, B. Anda, and L. Bratthall. 2000. "Human Judgement in Effort Estimation of Software Projects." In Beg, Borrow, or Steal Workshop, International Conference on Software Engineering, pp. 45–51, Limerick, Ireland, June 4–11, 2000.

Jørgensen, M., and K.M. Moløkken. 2006. "How Large Are Software Cost Overruns? A Review of the 1994 CHAOS Report." *Information and Software Technology* 48 (4): 297–301.

Jørgensen, M., and M. Shepperd. 2007. "A Systematic Review of Software Development Cost Estimation Studies." *IEEE Transactions on Software Engineering* 33 (1): 33–53.

Kauffman, R.J., and P. Weill. 1989. "An Evaluative Framework for Research on the Performance Effects of Information Technology Investment." Paper presented at the *Tenth International Conference on Information Systems.* Boston.

McAfee, A. 2006. "Mastering the Three Worlds of Information Technology." *Harvard Business Review* 84 (11): 141–149.

Melville, N., K. Kraemer, and V. Gurbaxani. 2004. "Review: Information Technology and Organizational Performance: An Integrative Model of IT Business Value." *MIS Quarterly* 28 (2): 283–322.

Mohagheghi, P., and R. Conradi. 2007. "Quality, Productivity and Economic Benefits of Software Reuse: A Review of Industrial Studies." *Empirical Software Engineering* 12 (5): 471–516.

Newton, R.S. 2006. "Lessons for All CAD Users from the Airbus CATIA Debacle." AECNews.com. http://aecnews.com/articles/2035.aspx (accessed April 24, 2009).

Raiffa, H. 1968. *Decision Analysis.* Reading, MA: Addison-Wesley.

Rothman, A. 2006. "Airbus Vows Computers Will Speak Same Language After A380 Delay." Bloomberg, September 28. www.bloomberg.com/apps/news?pid=newsarchive&sid=aS GkIYVa9IZk (accessed April 24, 2009).

Saha, P. 2006. "A Real Options Perspective to Enterprise Architecture as an Investment Activity." *Journal of Enterprise Architecture* 2 (3): 32–52.

Simonsen, J., and M. Hertzum. 2005. "Evidence-Based IT Development: Toward a New Contract Model for EPR Projects." In *Proceedings of the 3rd Scandinavian Conference on Health Informatics (SHI 2005),* ed. O. Hejlesen and C. Nøhr, 66–70. Aalborg, Denmark: Aalborg University, Virtual Centre for Health Informatics.

Standish Group. 1994. *Chaos Report.* West Yarmouth, MA: Standish Group.

Thorp, J. 1999. *The Information Paradox: Realizing the Business Benefits of Information Technology.* New York: McGraw-Hill.

Tippins, M.J., and R.S. Sohi. 2003. "IT Competency and Firm Performance: Is Organizational Learning a Missing Link?" *Strategic Management Journal* 24 (8): 745–761.

Turner, J.A., and C. Lucas Jr. 1984. "Developing Strategic Information Systems." NYU Working Paper IS-84–52. Information Systems Working Papers Series. New York: School of Computer Science, New York University. http://hdl.handle.net/2451/14566 (accessed March 12, 2009).

Weill, P. 1990. *Do Computers Payoff? A Study of Information Technology Investments and Manufacturing Performance.* Washington, DC: ICIT Press.

———. 1992. "The Relationship Between Investment in Information Technology and Firm Performance: A Study of the Valve Manufacturing Sector." Cambridge: Massachusetts Institute of Technology, Center for Information Systems Research, WP 239, May.

Weill, P., and J.W. Ross. 2004. *IT Governance: How Top Performers Manage IT Decision Rights for Superior Results.* Boston: Harvard Business School Press.

Part II

Evidence-Based Public Management

8

Evidence in Public Management

A Comparative Perspective

Terry F. Buss and Nathaniel J. Buss,
with Evan Hill

> *In 1884 at a Convention on Good Government, President*
> *Theodore Roosevelt announced that he intended to transform*
> *government, concentrating on better financial management, cost*
> *reduction, separation of politics and administration, engagement*
> *of professional managers, and adoption of scientific management*
> *principles as common to practice of business.*

Throughout the twentieth century and into the twenty-first, policy makers, particularly in Great Britain, Canada, New Zealand, Australia, and the United States, have struggled with management and civil service reform (see Figure 8.1), intending to improve their effectiveness, often calling for sound evidence to inform administration, policy, and practice (see also GAO 1995). Analyses from Canada and Britain are representative. In 1983, Canada's auditor general, for example, identified three constraints to effective government management (as cited in GAO 1997): political priorities had a major adverse impact on productive management; managers felt unduly constrained by administrative procedures and conflicting accountability requirements; and there were too few incentives for productive management but many disincentives. A report for Prime Minister Margaret Thatcher in 1988 found similar constraints (reported in State Services Commission 2005):

- Because of an emphasis on policy, focus on service delivery was insufficient.
- A shortage of management skills and experience among civil servants abounded.
- Short-term political priorities squeezed out long-term planning.
- There was too much emphasis on spending money and not enough on getting results.
- The civil service was too large and diverse to manage as a single organization.
- Central rules took away the flexibility managers needed to manage for results.

Figure 8.1

Management and Civil Service Reform Connected

The UK Cabinet Office provides the linkage between management and civil service reform. Civil service reform focuses on the following:

- Making savings (economies) in public expenditure
- Improving service quality
- Making government operations more efficient
- Improving the effectiveness of policy selection and implementation

The "what" of civil service reform is invariably managerial in nature:

- Finance: budget, accounts, audits
- Personnel: recruitment, posting, remuneration, security of employment, and so forth
- Organization: specialization, coordination, scale, (de)centralization
- Performance measurement systems: content, organization, use

These managerial components that characterize civil service reform function alongside other methods of improving government performance, including political reforms and significant changes in key policies.

Source: Cabinet Office 2009b.

Reforms fall naturally, but not entirely, into three approaches: performance management; good management practice; and performance, budgeting, and management integration.

Performance-Based Management

Performance management, also referred to as performance-based management, results-based or results-oriented management, or management for results or outcomes, is grounded in classic strategic management/planning models where an organization establishes a *mission*—its purpose; a *vision*—what it strives to become in the future; a set of *goals* and *objectives*—what it wants to achieve; *strategies*—how it will achieve its goals and objectives; and *performance measures* and *evaluation*—how it will hold itself accountable for achieving its goals and objectives (van Dooren, Bouckaert, and Halligan 2010). Under these models, if an organization attains its goals and objectives, as reflected in its performance on a set of measures, then policy makers take this as prima facie evidence of successful management. A serious flaw in the model, as discussed later in this chapter, is that really bad managers oversee programs that perform well, while really good managers preside over failing programs. Performance is not evidence of the quality of management.

Figure 8.2   **Strategic Management Model**

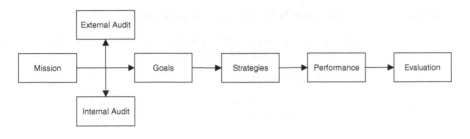

Good Management Practice

Policy makers have also attempted to improve agency and program management generally, independent of their performance in the strategic management context. Good management practice seeks to be effective, efficient, and economical—the three Es—and recently, equitable—now the four Es. In this model, evaluators assess good management against compliance with standards derived from best practices, lessons learned, benchmarks, guidance, and processes—in short, as we say in Australia, "ticking off the boxes." Policy makers view compliance with standards as evidence of good management or of a good manager. But standards reflecting good management practice are not, in themselves, based on evidence and so may not be the way to do things "right." They stipulate a priori what good management is. For example, a standard good management practice is to ensure that managers expend budgets in a timely fashion during a fiscal year. So many managers, seeking good performance evaluations, roll out cash regardless of whether the expenditures make sense, will be effective, or are wasteful. In addition, managers can manage against any standard in a myriad of ways, many of which can lead to poor results. For example, having clear goals and targets does not mean that they are actually good goals and targets. Compliance is not evidence of good management.

Performance, Management, and Budgeting Integration

In most governments, performance management, good management practice, and budgetary decision making are fragmented endeavors, often proceeding on independent tracks. Performance management is not often explicitly linked to good management, and neither of these typically translates into budgetary decisions about programs and agencies. Underperforming programs and bad management often do not lead to a comparable reduction in budget (Gilmour 2008). One reason for this is that in many governments, little spending is discretionary. Even on the discretionary side, programs that enjoy popular or political support may get a pass when tough budget decisions are pending (see, for example, Buss 2008). It is only natural

---

Figure 8.3

Strategic Management Criteria for Good Management

- Does the program have a limited number of specific long-term performance measures that focus on outcomes and meaningfully reflect the purpose of the program?
- Does the program have ambitious targets and time frames for its long-term measures?
- Does the program have a limited number of specific annual performance measures that demonstrate progress toward achieving the program's long-term measures?
- Does the program have baselines and ambitious targets and time frames for its annual measures?
- Do all partners (including grantees, subgrantees, contractors, cost-sharing partners, etc.) commit to and work toward the annual and/or long-term goals of the program?
- Are independent and quality evaluations of sufficient scope and quality conducted on a regular basis or as needed to support program improvements and evaluate effectiveness and relevance to the problem, interest, or need?
- Are budget requests explicitly tied to accomplishment of the annual and long-term performance goals, and are the resource needs presented in a complete and transparent manner in the program's budget?
- Has the program taken meaningful steps to correct its strategic planning deficiencies?

Source: U.S. Office of Management and Budget, www.expectmore.gov.

---

that policy makers attempt to merge these disparate activities into one integrated system, or at least give nod to the notion that this would be desirable. Although this approach is much better than either of the models mentioned earlier, it tends to retain the flaws of each when policy makers fold them into the same performance management system. So, just because policy makers integrate everything under one system, it does not follow that this is evidence of good management.

In this chapter, we review examples of the three approaches mentioned previously, looking at selected practices and initiatives in Great Britain, Canada, New Zealand, Australia, and the United States. This chapter provides a "high level" context in which to view evidence-based management (EBMgt) in government, while Chapters 9 and 10 show how the field works at the U.S. Department of Veterans Affairs and the U.S. Government Accountability Office, respectively. The range of examples is so vast that it proved impossible to discuss in depth all but a few of each country's accomplishments. Each country has a long history of management and civil service reform, and each has liberally borrowed from the others in an effort to improve its own management systems. Where possible, we report on problems with reforms as seen in credible evaluations and assessment, which unhappily are not plentiful or available. Each performance management system initiative over time, for some, has incrementally advanced public manage-

Figure 8.4

Evidence-Based Management Definitions

Results-oriented management of an organization or program entails articulating its mission and goals, developing plans and measures tied to the mission and goals, and reporting on program results. Strategic planning is the process organizations use to assess their current situation and future path, develop missions and goals, and devise strategies to achieve the missions and goals. Performance—or operational—planning is the process organizations use to determine how their strategic goals will be met through activities of their staffs. Performance measurement involves the development of measurable indicators that can be tracked over time to assess progress made in achieving predetermined goals. Performance reporting entails the comparison of actual performance achieved versus predetermined goals for a given period.

Source: GAO 1995, p. 12.

ment. Others see systems that are largely spinning their wheels over time. To make public management truly evidence based, policy makers must invest more heavily in program evaluation and not just in performance measurement on the one hand, and ground management itself more in evidence on the other.

Before proceeding, we note that this chapter is not about evidence-based policy. *Public policy* is a vision, goal, plan, or direction articulated by the executive, legislature, or courts that translates into *programs,* services, actions, or activities. We are concerned with program and agency management, not with policy development. Besides, public policy has its own evidence-based approach, as observed in Chapter 1.

Performance Management

Below we offer thumbnail sketches of country initiatives done in the past several decades to make two points: (1) performance management has been around a long while and (2) it continues to evolve as one government replaces another, each trying to improve on its predecessor (see also Halligan 2007; Pollit and Bouckaert 2004; Bouckaert and Halligan 2007). For many observers (e.g., Light 1997, 1995), though, it remains unclear exactly to what extent performance management has advanced, and even whether it has ever been fully implemented; in other words, are these questions of rhetoric or reality?

Australia

Australia, as is the case with other countries highlighted in this chapter, has a rich history of management reform initiatives from a performance management perspective.[1] Australia serves as an exemplar of decades of work. In 1976, a Royal Commission on Australian Government Administration—the Coombs

Commission—called for more accountability in the public service, greater efficiency and responsiveness in service delivery, devolution of management responsibility, and improved management capacity building. In 1983, the Reid Report, issued by the Public Service Commission, emphasized the importance of quality management. This was immediately followed by another report, *Reforming the Australian Public Service,* calling for efficiency, effectiveness, equity, and responsiveness in service delivery. Australia launched a "comprehensive management improvement effort that centered on changing public service culture; creating the structures, standards, and practices conducive to good management; and developing management skills in the public service." To do this, Australia implemented results-oriented management reforms, called Program Management and Budgeting, requiring departments to define program goals, plan how they would achieve those goals, measure program effectiveness and efficiency, report on program performance, and adjust program operations on the basis of performance data (GAO 1995, 14). Another report, *Financial Management Improvement Program (FMIP): A Diagnostic Study,* called for a shift from compliance-based to performance-based management and mandated evaluation of public programs (Hawke 2007). Later in 1990, this initiative was supplemented by another report, *Not Dollars Alone: Review of the Financial Management Improvement Program,* looking more comprehensively at performance management, and offering support for the initiative, but criticizing shortcomings of management for results. In 1984, a paper, *Finance Paper on Budget Reform,* called for a greater emphasis on program goals and objectives and improved performance and efficiency. In 1986, Prime Minister Hawke established the Efficiency Scrutiny Unit to promote cost savings across government. The Public Service Reform Act of 1984 increased flexibility, responsibility, and public scrutiny given to agency heads. In 1987, the Administrative Arrangements Act established a Public Service Management Advisory Board to advise the government on management issues and to act as a forum for good management practice. In 1992, a task force published a report, *The Australian Public Service Reformed: An Evaluation of a Decade of Management Reform,* declaring that reforms over the past decade were appropriate, well accepted by the civil service, and effective.

From 1987 to the present, Australia launched two "performance evaluation and management systems" (1987 to 1997 and 1997 to present) (Mackay 2004). The first set out formal program evaluation requirements that were intended to produce evaluations that could be used in the annual budget process. It produced a great deal of information for policy makers but was not much used by program managers (Task Force on Management Improvement 1992). The second reduced the formal requirements in place, opting instead for a set of principles that evaluations should be consistent with. A 2004 assessment of the system concluded that the second system failed to serve the needs of Parliament and was insufficient in promoting sound management (Mackay 2004).

In 1995, a Public Service Commission report, *A Review of the Public Service Act of 1922,* called for a new replacement act focusing much more on efficiency, results, and accountability. In 1996, a white paper for Parliament, *Towards a Best Practice Australian Public Service,* led to an act in 1999 (see later in this section) mandating managerial flexibility, streamlining, and cultural change to improve performance. In 1997, the government required all agencies to develop customer service charters. In 1998, the government issued a pamphlet, *Australian Public Service Reform: Building on Good Practice,* in which policy makers promoted customer-focused services and performance management. In 1999, policy makers launched the Senior Executive Leadership Capability Framework, which mandated, among other things, strategic thinking and results-oriented management. The Financial Management and Accountability Act of 1997, the Charter of Budget Honesty Act of 1998, and the Public Service Act of 1999 all mandated performance management. In 2002, policy makers empowered the Australian Public Service Commission to improve management practices by entering into partnerships with agencies. In 2007, a management advisory commission issued a report, *Reducing Red Tape in the Australian Public Service,* calling for cost-benefit reviews of regulation and administration. The recommendations were not fully implemented.

In 2006, the Australian Labour Party published its policy framework to guide the government after taking office: *Operation Sunlight* called for more transparency and accountability, all packaged in an outcomes framework. Portions of the framework are in play under the Labour Government today (see Blondal et al. 2008).

Under the Rudd government, a new performance management system took shape in Australia in November 2009 by redefining *federal financial relations.* The national government and states and territories meet under the auspices of the Council of Australian Governments. Collectively, the council decides how funding will be allocated to specific program areas, currently, health care, education, skills and workforce development, disabilities, affordable housing, and indigenous affairs. The programs receiving emphasis are those based on campaign promises made by the new government in 2007. Each program area includes a National Agreement, detailing how much funding is to be allocated, how it will be spent, and who is responsible. National Agreements also include goals and objectives, outcomes, outputs, and other indicators of performance.

At the same time, the Rudd government launched a new reform initiative, Reform of Australian Government Administration (2009). An advisory committee began gathering public comment through November 2009, believing that a high-performing civil service will include a values-driven culture; high-quality, forward-looking policy advice; high-quality service delivery; flexible and agile priorities; and effective and efficient operations. While the report states that improved public administration is its overall goal, it does not offer a management reform agenda.

Canada

Next, consider Canada.[2] The Glassco Royal Commission on Government Organisation, in 1962, concluded in its report, *Management of the Public Service,* that government was weakened by outmoded concepts of public administration and needed fundamental restructuring. The Lambert Commission of 1976–77 bemoaned inadequate managerial training and ability among the most senior public servants; while the D'Avignon Commission of 1979 recommended that management powers be delegated and performance judged by results. They argued that managers needed a "philosophy of management"—sorely lacking in their view, if managers were to improve administration, presaging the debate about what EBMgt really is, as noted in Chapter 1. Since the early 1980s, Canada has implemented numerous results-oriented management reforms. To increase accountability and clarify responsibility for program performance, Canada instituted performance agreements between upper and lower departmental management and reduced the number of management levels within departments. To support achievement of program performance goals, the government provided departments with greater authority over spending and the size of their staffs and simplified human resources regulations. These reforms, pursued under the Nielsen Task Force, failed, necessitating another subsequent reform initiative (Organization for Economic Cooperation and Development 1999b). In 1995, the Canadian government declared its Policy and Expenditure Management System, in place since 1980, a failure, in its review *The Government of Canada's Expenditure Management System* (Blondal 2001). Policy makers had hoped the system would improve planning, control expenditures, and devolve authority to ministers and managers (State Services Commission 2000).

Following this, Canada launched its Public Service 2000 initiative to get management and performance back on track:

> In *The Renewal of the Public Service of Canada* (1990), the White Paper's contents reflected the objectives established by the Prime Minister in 1989. The White Paper sounded many familiar themes, occasionally dressed up in contemporary language: reduction of red tape, empowerment of staff, devolution of authority, decentralization, and the elimination of unnecessary regulations that hinder effective management. It differed from earlier attempts in that it was the first administrative review to designate the quality of service to the public as a goal of public management. In order to achieve this goal, the government determined that a change in the culture of the Public Service was required. The old or existing culture had placed an emphasis on administrative systems, and conformity and control to produce "error-free" government [and] . . . has circumvented the initiative of public servants, sacrificed timeliness and placed insufficient emphasis on results and cost effectiveness. (Office of Prime Minister 1990, i)

This program led to the passage of the Public Service Reform Act of 1992. Eventually, in 1996, the government produced *Getting Government Right,* clarifying government's role in public management. In 1997, Canada began reforming its human capital management system under the La Releve Task Force. This evolved out of two separate whole-of-government program review initiatives, intended to reform financial management (Organization for Economic Cooperation and Development 1999b).

But evaluations of the Canadian efforts were not so enthusiastic. There was growth and development in the management machinery of federal government, as well as in the staffing levels at the central agencies. Yet A.W. Johnson reports that the "essentials of the management regime in place seem not to have changed" (as cited in Baehler 2003, 10). The reformed management practices and structures advocated had not materialized in any meaningful way.

Canadians continued to innovate with the Public Service Modernisation Act of 2003 and the Federal Accountability Act of 2006, both results oriented. The Federal Accountability Act of 2006 mandated a results-based expenditure-management system, requiring departments to manage against performance information. In 2005, the Management, Resources and Results Structure policy replaced the 1996 Planning, Reporting and Accountability Structure policy framework. The Management, Resources and Results policy "supports the development of a common, government-wide approach to planning and managing the relationship between resource expenditures and results, while serving as a consistent and enduring foundation for collecting, managing and reporting financial and non-financial information to Parliament."[3]

New Zealand

New Zealand also implemented management reforms designed to increase the accountability of government managers for achieving desired program results, as had Canada.[4] In 1962, the McCarthy Commission recommended that New Zealand set up the State Services Commission, whose director would take responsibility for much broader civil service reforms than had the predecessor Public Services Commission. The State Services Commission did not advance the field of performance management to any great extent. In 1984, New Zealand's management reforms initially focused on transferring government enterprises to the private sector, or running the government's enterprises in a more businesslike manner, largely as a solution to the economic crisis plaguing the country. In 1987, in a report by the Treasury, policy makers articulated five core principles of the New Zealand system (Cook 2004, 4; Boston 1996): clarity of objectives; freedom to manage; accountability; effective performance assessment; and adequate information flows. Taken together, they constituted a manifesto for a new model of government.

Later, New Zealand passed two key laws—the State Sector Act of 1988 and the Public Finance Act of 1989—designed to create a business orientation in as many other government functions as possible. The State Sector Act is especially important in that it transformed the State Services Commission from an employer of the civil service to an adviser and change agent in a new public management system (Organization for Economic Cooperation and Development 1999a). New Zealand sought to increase accountability for achieving desired program results by implementing performance agreements between departmental chief executives and their ministers and by requiring departments to report on performance against targets. In addition, the government provided departments with greater flexibility over spending and human resources management to achieve the specific results for which they were responsible. In the 1990s, New Zealand launched the Strategic Result Areas program, based on the acronym SMART (specific, measurable, achievable, realistic, and time bounded) with respect to its programs. In 1996, New Zealand's performance management system became famous and envied with the publication of an assessment by Allen Schick, *The Spirit of Reform* (1996). Even so, numerous criticisms of New Zealand's performance model abounded: lack of accountability, strategic management, and performance management (Baehler 2003).

From 1987 through 2004, policy makers completed five reviews of the New Zealand public management system (Cook 2004, 11), concluding for purposes here that "evaluative activity—assessing whether interventions have had the anticipated impact—is a key component in a results-oriented system. The New Zealand public management system does not have a strong history of evidence-based decision-making. As noted, recent work by the central agencies has suggested that before evaluative activity can be embedded in the public management system a culture of inquiry needs to be generated."

Cook further concludes, "Shifting the culture of the New Zealand public management system towards one focused on achievement of outcomes will be a slow process" (2004, 45), noting that the principles articulated for the system have not been fully realized.

United Kingdom

The British also have a long tradition of performance management initiative.[5] Rather than review this history, we begin in the 1980s, a period when many countries ramped up their efforts in the field. In 1979, government began privatizing nationalized industries under the Efficiency Scrutinies program, aimed at improving public management through efficiency studies. The Financial Management Initiative of 1982 intended to improve the performance management systems in agencies, seeking improvements in the allocation, management, and control of resources. In 1987–88, the Thatcher government, in *Improving Management in Government: Next Steps,* announced that much of the executive work would devolve to agencies, launching the Next Steps Initiative. Next Steps attempted to improve public service delivery by employing market-driven approaches, improved management of civil servants, and decentralized authority to manage service delivery. Next Steps yielded some impressive gains in performance in many service-delivery areas but experienced some difficulties, including (1) lack of clarity in relationships between agencies and programs, (2) uncertainty about accountability for performance, and (3) difficulties in developing and setting performance goals (GAO 1997, 6). If performance is considered evidence, then Next Steps failed to offer an effective EBMgt model.

The Clinton administration assessed Next Steps as a possible model for its Performance Based Organization initiative in 1997 and had a lot of positive things to say about. But Clinton never was able to fully implement his initiative as originally conceived.

In 1991, the government launched Competing for Quality and Citizen Charter initiatives. The Civil Service (Management Functions) Act of 1992 further delegated management authority downward to agencies and departments.

Tony Blair, upon taking the reins of government in 1997, launched a comprehensive evidence-based policy initiative, one that also had a subordinate management component. In 1998, under the Comprehensive Spending Review program, the government created Public Service Agreements covering performance standards and measures for different types of services developed in consultation across responsible agencies and frontline workers. These tied in to the Citizen Charter initiative begun under John Major's government. Public Service Agreements also describe "a small basket of national outcome-based performance indicators" used to measure progress on performance. The indicators include national targets. The administration also launched another Civil Service Reform Program in 1999, the key features of which were leadership, business planning, performance management, and diversity.

In 1999, in *Modernising Government* (Cabinet Office 1999a, 1999b), the government announced three key aims: strategic policy making; focusing on the public service users, rather than the providers; and high-quality and efficient public services, along with its new philosophy, "This Government expects more of policy makers. More new ideas, more willingness to question inherited ways of doing things, better use of evidence and research in policy making and better focus on policies that will deliver long term goals" (Cabinet Office 1999a, i). The Blair government (1997–2007) adopted the mantra "What matters is what works" as the basis for reforming public management. Rather than deriving policies from principles and political inclination, Blair stated that his government would adopt policy based on what was proven to work.

Modernising Government expressed the government's desire for the public service to become a "learning organization" (see also Redburn, Shea, and Buss 2008). The government implemented initiatives to support its vision, including best practice guides to policy development (Cabinet Office 1999b), an online tool, and the Policy Hub[6] to gather and disseminate information on EBMgt. Benchmarks for e-government and external advisory panels were set to identify and critique evidence to support decision making (Cabinet Office undated). This evidence was broad ranging, employing systematic and peer reviews. Most important, the Cabinet Office set up Delivery and Reform Teams (six in all) that specialized in strategic policy development, public service implementation, e-government transformation, management development, public service reform through best practice, and overall public service reform (House of Commons 2003).

Reports on the success of the Blair government were mixed. Flynn (1999) claims that government promoted experiment and evaluation, with successes quickly adopted. However, others argue that getting to know what works became the rationale for vastly expanded research staffs and budgets in government, rather than public sector improvement (Solesbury 2001; see also Light 1995, 1997).

Interim evaluations and case studies of the *Modernizing Government* agenda reveal little evidence of the success or failure of the Blair government's initiative. In 2000, the Cabinet Office reported that further work was required to achieve the Blair government's vision, in particular, training for ministers and senior civil servants on the importance of evidence-based policy, improving the use of pilots to test the impacts of policies, improving the use of existing government data, and the introduction of employee incentives to reward good practice and achievements (Cabinet Office 2000). In a 2001 report, *Customer-Focused Government: From Policy to Delivery,* policy makers tried to develop momentum to make public series more citizen-centric. In 2002–3, the Public Administration Select Committee of the House of Commons (2002–3) issued a report, *On Target? Government by Measurement,* concluding that the government's five aspirations for its performance system—(1) a clear statement of what government was trying to achieve, (2) a clear sense of direction and ambition, (3) a focus on delivering results, (4) a basis for what is and is not working (in short, evidence), and (5) better accountability—were not being fulfilled and that front-line civil servants recognized this. In 2003, the Comptroller and Auditor General (2003) reported that some sectors of the public service, particularly the Office of Science and Technology, did "modernize" their research to include evidence-based approaches. However, this report also found that further effort was needed to improve the way research was commissioned, specifically to clarify research aims and communication of research findings.

United States

The history of U.S. performance management is exemplified by at least one new significant proposal advanced under nearly every administration.[7] New approaches tend to acknowledge the shortcomings of previous models and address any critical public or political concerns. Federal interest in performance budgeting began in the early 1920s, as a result of recommendations from the earlier Taft Commission of 1912. Rising government spending and debt associated with World War I led Congress to pursue a budget system that would also act as a tool for controlling federal spending. The Budget and Accounting Act of 1921 had a twofold approach: It delegated more definitive authority and responsibilities over the budget to the executive and established many basic measurements to facilitate greater congressional oversight. It also authorized use of the line-item veto by the president. Prior to 1921, the federal government operated without a comprehensive presidential budget process. The earlier budgeting process, dominated by Congress, treated each bureau individually, limiting analysis of overall federal budget priorities. The act of 1921 assigned responsibility for budget programming to the executive, directing the president to provide Congress with expenditure estimates and appropriations necessary to operate the government. The act also created two new institutions—the Bureau of Budget, now the Office of Management and Budget (OMB), and the General Accounting Office, now the Government Accountability Office (GAO)—to provide a more intense oversight function. Congress intended for OMB and the GAO to have discretion over bureaus and for OMB to act as an extension of the president in developing a budget. Nevertheless, the reach of these policies was limited: they ignored the numerous dimensions of budgeting, including political priorities, constituencies, and external pressures, as well as other approaches that enhance effectiveness of budget formulation. In 1937, President Franklin Roosevelt created the Committee on Administrative Management, which in a series of reports, *Administrative Management in the Government of the United States,* looked at among other topics fiscal controls and accountability, especially in the context of GAO.

While the policies of the 1920s improved spending controls, they failed to establish a comprehensive understanding of performance budgets. That task was taken up by the Commission on Organization of the Executive Branch of the Government (Hoover Commission), in 1949, which called for employing performance budgeting throughout the federal government. For the first time, the commission's recommendations acknowledged that the value of performance budgeting consisted not in gathering data as an end in itself, but rather in using that information to inform decisions. The federal budget should be based on the "general character and relative importance of the work to be done or upon service to be rendered, rather than upon the things to be acquired, such as personal services, supplies, equipment, and so on" (as quoted in Grifel 1993, 404). In short, this approach focused budgeting on workloads, unit costs, and functions as tools that help inform management practices.

The commission recommended wholesale reorganization of the executive branch, enacted through the Budget and Accounting Procedures Act of 1950. The act directed the president to present a budget to Congress showing "obligations by activities," a format that further institutionalized the system of measuring budget outputs. It also expanded the managerial powers of the executive further under the notion that the president needed to have substantial budget authority in order to implement policies effectively. Nevertheless, while the act contributed a new understanding of budgeting as a management tool, it still failed to include program assessment.

In 1965, President Lyndon Johnson launched the Planning-Programming-Budgeting-System (PPBS) to address the shortcomings of previous efforts. PPBS advocated developing multiple budget alternatives, establishing program objectives, and pursuing multiyear planning to improve the quality of budgeting decisions, under three functions: strategic planning in setting objectives and evaluating alternative scenarios; management control of goals, objectives, projects, and activities; and operational control of budget execution and auditing. While earlier budgeting frameworks focused on control and management, PPBS merged these into one framework.

PPBS, mandated throughout the federal government, assumed that different levels of program performance could be quantified through policy analysis, and that would help policy makers make the best decisions, an assumption that tended to minimize the political nature of budgeting. Agency objectives were linked to measured outputs, which provided a picture of the benefits and costs of various ways of achieving those outputs, which in turn assumed a causal link between those outputs and desired results. Additionally, multiyear planning was based on agency need, "program structure," activities planned, and national resources. PPBS spawned a colossal amount of analysis, which slowed down agencies and provided limited meaningful information for budget deliberations.

In 1973–74, President Richard Nixon advanced the Management by Objectives model, which sought to better link agency objectives to budget proposals. Management by Objectives made managers responsible for achieving outputs and outcomes rated through agreed-upon processes. In theory, managers were accountable for achieving objectives determined by supervisors, while agency heads responded to presidential objectives of national priority. More importantly, Management by Objectives was the first significant effort to articulate a model for measuring and achieving outcomes rather than outputs.

Similarly, in 1976, President Jimmy Carter promoted the Zero Based Budgeting (ZBB) system, which advocated a reevaluation of all expenditures annually. ZBB had its origins in state government. Its champion, President Carter, believed ZBB had been a successful technique for improving performance in the state of Georgia, when he served as governor. Essentially, ZBB requires that every year, policy makers assume nothing about the budget and start from an evaluation of all programs. To make budget decisions, ZBB was based on discrete packages, each of which included detailed proposals describing what could be achieved with discrete increments of funding. Accordingly, agencies would advance discrete packages prioritized for different levels of spending for a specific program. While this approach appeared useful in theory, the process proved to be too time-consuming and expensive to execute and eventually lost political support. Although Carter later modified this policy to start the evaluation process at a specified percentage of department funding, it was still difficult to compare the same increments across different agencies. ZBB sought to create a clear link among budgetary resources, decisions, and results but failed to recognize the practical limits of agencies' ability to manage excessive performance information and the ultimately political nature of budgetary processes.

President Ronald Reagan rescinded ZBB in 1981. David Stockman, OMB director, required agencies to conduct economic analyses as part of the budget process. Critics suggested that this was ineffective because analyses lacked objectivity. In 1988, President George H.W. Bush expanded on Reagan's work in Executive Order 122637—Productivity Improvement Program for the Federal Government, calling for improvements in quality and productivity. Also during this period, Total Quality Management (TQM) began to infuse itself in government (Durant and Wilson 1993).

The 1990s augured in the age of performance-based management activity. The Chief Financial Officers Act of 1990 made chief financial officers responsible for developing and implementing performance management systems. Immediately upon taking office in 1993, President Bill Clinton began implementing National Performance Review (NPR), later the National Partnership for Reinventing Government (1998).[8] President Clinton described his platform as a call for "reinventing government," a proposal mirrored on similar reforms he had championed as governor of Arkansas and similar to the Texas Performance Review. Initially, NPR, under the direction of Vice President Al Gore, focused on administrative initiatives such as reducing red tape by streamlining processes and eliminating unnecessary regulatory overkill, improving customer service by creating more marketlike dynamics, decentralizing decision-making processes to empower employees, and other measures. NPR's organizing principle was attainment of high-quality customer service.

Earlier in 1994, the Republican Party, running under the banner *A Contract with America*, won control of Congress, ousting the Democratic Party after being in power in the House for forty years. The Contract called for smaller, more responsible, and more efficient government and reform of "welfare state" programs. In 1995, Republicans went so far as to temporarily shut down the federal government by withholding approval of appropriations in an effort to slow government spending. In 1996, Clinton, in a *State of the Union* address, apparently joining the Republicans, declared that the "era of big government was over."

Critics of NPR suggest that the multiple purposes of NPR led to major inconsistencies in goals, methods, focus, and strategies (Kettl 1995). Others suggest that the reinventing movement misrepresented the problem and misjudged the consequences (Moe 1994). Most important, there is some evidence that policy makers failed to "adjust their strategy to account for basic differences between NPR and past reforms" (Thompson 2000, 508). But NPR was only the executive branch approach to performance.

It was Congress, in passing the Government Performance and Results Act (GPRA) in 1993,[9] along with the Chief Financial Officers Act of 1990, the Government Management Reform Act of 1994, and the Information Technology Management Reform Act of 1996, that took a much more aggressive role in promoting EBMgt in government. GPRA's intent is "to shift the focus of federal management and accountability from what federal agencies are doing to what they are accomplishing." The act notes in section 2 that:

1. waste and inefficiency in Federal programs undermine the confidence of the American people in the Government and reduce the federal government's ability to address adequately vital public needs;
2. Federal managers are seriously disadvantaged in their efforts to improve program efficiency and effectiveness, because of insufficient articulation of program goals and inadequate information on program performance; and
3. congressional policy making, spending decisions, and program oversight are seriously handicapped by insufficient attention to program performance and results.

Congress clearly states in the act's purpose that this is a performance-management approach intended to improve:

1. the confidence of the American people in the capability of the federal government, by systematically holding federal agencies accountable for achieving program results;
2. program performance reform with a series of pilot projects in setting program goals, measuring program performance against those goals, and reporting publicly on their progress;
3. federal program effectiveness and public accountability by promoting a new focus on results, service quality, and customer satisfaction;
4. service delivery, by requiring that federal managers plan for meeting program objectives and by providing them with information about program results and service quality;
5. congressional decision making by providing more objective information on achieving statutory objectives, and on the relative effectiveness and efficiency of federal programs and spending; and
6. internal management of the federal government.

But what is important for purposes here is that Congress infused the act with EBMgt language by requiring strategic plans to include a description of program evaluations used in establishing or revising general goals and objectives, with a schedule for future program evaluations,[10] and means to be used to verify and validate measured values.

GPRA employs a classic strategic planning model. Agencies develop mission, vision, and value statements; conduct internal organizational audits and external assessments; devise goals and objectives; craft strategies for goal attainment; create performance measures—including outputs, outcomes, and targets—for accountability; and undertake program evaluations to determine what works. GPRA requires three- to five-year plans with annual performance updates.

From an EBMgt perspective, GPRA succeeded in focusing agencies on performance. So, the system is now heavily evidence based. The promise of improving management and conducting formal program evaluations has not been fully realized within this model. Also, GPRA does not concentrate on programs, but rather on agencies at a much higher level of aggregation. As we note in a subsequent section, GPRA failed to produce program-specific performance data of much use to policy makers and managers. Periodic surveys of federal managers on their use of performance information under GPRA, for example, show that "while significantly more federal managers reported having performance measures for their programs than they did 10 years ago, their reported use of performance information to make management decisions has not changed significantly" (GAO 2009).

Many credit David Osborne for not only inspiring NPR and GRPA, but also for auguring a new movement, the new public management, which forms the intellectual undergirding for performance management. In 1988, Osborne published *Laboratories of Democracy,* highlighting the innovative efforts of many governors across the country at improving public services in innovative ways. And, in 1992, Osborne and Ted Gaebler described innovative state and local efforts to become more efficient and effective in *Reinventing Government.* A House of Lords report, *The Public Service,* summed up the movement well: "The doctrines of NPM involve a focus on management, performance appraisal and efficiency; the use of agencies which deal with each other on a user-pay basis; the use of quasi-markets and contracting out to foster competition; cost-cutting; and a style of management which emphasizes, among other things, output targets, limited term contracts, monetary incentives and freedom to manage" (1997–98, 2). While NPR and GPRA have been roundly criticized, the new public management probably represents the most widely used performance management in government, bar none.

Good Management Practices

In the new millennium, government began to add more of a management component to its focus on performance management. Previous efforts mentioned management, but if one looks closely, they really were about goal attainment, efficiency, and financial management. Most new initiatives tended to focus on ensuring that managers had the capacity to manage, and, where there were gaps, to fill them. So, policy makers began to illuminate the management black box, all but absent in strategic and performance management models. Self-assessment to identify good and bad practices became widespread, extensive use of technical assistance and advising began, and development training on how to manage abounded.[11] Evidence, as noted above, became compliance with guidance and process.

United Kingdom

In 1967, a parliamentary committee in a report, *The Fulton Committee Report on the Civil Service,* came to the following conclusion (as cited in House of Lords 1997–98):

> The Civil Service was essentially based on the cult of the amateur or generalist. . . . The Committee considered that the Civil Service lacked skilled managers. One reason for this was that most of the work of most Senior Civil Servants was not managerial, but rather related to matters such as the preparation of explanatory briefs and answers to parliamentary questions. To improve management skills, the Committee recommended that administrators should become more specialized, and more training in management should be given to scientists and specialists. The Committee also recommended that the principles of "accountable management" be introduced. (According to those principles, the performance of individuals [or units] is measured as objectively as possible, and those individuals [or units] are then held responsible for tasks they have performed. Accountable management requires cost centers to be identified, and costs to be precisely allocated to the official in charge of each one.) To improve management even

further, the Committee recommended several more innovations: the establishment of a new Civil Service Department; the creation of a management services unit in each department to promote new management techniques; a planning and research unit to undertake major long term planning; and the creation of departmental planning units to acquire facts and to consider and administer policy.

As is the case with the other countries discussed in this chapter, the United Kingdom pressed on for decades trying to improve public management. In 2005, the Cabinet Office rolled out its Capability Review Program, a government-wide initiative to assess the organizational capabilities of its ministries with an eye toward correcting deficiencies and promoting effective management practices, among other things (Cabinet Office 2009a). [Shortly thereafter, the government began implementing a new budget philosophy, "value for money" (see National Audit Organization 2007).] Assessments were independently completed and published. The assessment model looked at three areas—delivery, leadership, and strategy. The model also included a performance management component, in line with other approaches discussed in the previous section. Of interest here is the strategy component. Evaluators assessed all senior management to determine whether they made major decisions based on evidence. In short, evaluators looked to see whether policy makers had institutionalized evidence-based management practices. Evaluators assessed how well senior management systematically improved performance.

Also as part of the program, policy makers undertook an assessment of public administration in the United Kingdom against other comparable governments (United States, Canada, Australia, New Zealand, Germany, France, Sweden, Finland) (Accenture 2008). Such benchmarking, of course, is a central tenet in good management practice approaches. Assessors developed a framework representing good practices derived from standards and guidelines of the Organization for Economic Cooperation and Development, European Union, UN Public Administration Network, World Economic Forum, and World Bank. Using an EBMgt approach—examining existing studies—assessors found that the United Kingdom met or exceeded the best management practices of other governments. Policy makers and consultants give the Capability Review Program mixed reviews as to its utility and effectiveness from policy makers and evaluators. First-round assessments of ministries showed that performance management rated 2.1 on a 5-point scale on average across the government, while EBMgt averaged 2.6 (Cabinet Office 2009a, 48–49). Subsequent reviews showed performance and EBMgt indicators improving, indicating that senior management were taking the exercise seriously. In a review of the program by the National Audit Office, analysts concluded the following (Cabinet Office 2009a):

- In the "delivery" category, Capability Reviews are not linked to departments' reported performance. The Cabinet Office defines capability in terms of a department's ability to deal with future challenges. This implies that in future it will be possible to explain current delivery in terms of earlier capability, as time series of data build up. For the moment, our analysis of departments' performance data for 2005–06 to 2007–08 shows a divergence between reported performance and review team assessments of each department's delivery capability during the same period (Cabinet Office 2009a, 7).

- Departments cannot yet show any clear impact on outcomes as a result of their responses to Capability Reviews.
- Capability Reviews are beginning to provide evidence of improvement in capability, if not in actual delivery.
- Departments have struggled to develop reliable metrics that would indicate their progress from improved capability to improved outcomes.
- It is unusual to examine an organization's leadership, strategy and processes in isolation from its operational results. The lack of a link between Capability Review scores and reported performance will appear increasingly anomalous and could undermine the credibility of both.
- Capability Reviews are missing opportunities to improve further by not benchmarking performance with organizations outside the civil service.

It seems, then, that the Capability Review, although a sophisticated framework for improving management's using evidence, has a long way to go before it succeeds in doing so.

The government continues to try to fold Capability Review into other areas. In the 2009 paper *Working Together: Public Services on Your Side,* government set out priorities for public service reform to which Capability Reviews contribute. *Working Together,* overall, concerned partnering with citizens to have greater input into service delivery. These include: introducing simpler, more transparent department performance assessments; better assessing departments' capabilities; and improving the quality of leadership and management.

New Zealand Model

In 2001, the Cabinet introduced new expectations, setting the stage for the Managing for Outcomes (MfO) initiative (see also Kibblewhite and Ussher 2002).[12] MfO required all agencies to adopt a more strategic and outcomes-focused approach to management and reporting. New Zealand, like many other countries, emphasizes management systems that demonstrate how activities of government agencies contribute to results, or outcomes. MfO mandated marshaling of better evidence to strengthen decision making by "better gathering and use of evidence to determine whether the design and delivery of major interventions could be improved; and better management of capability, including further management system development to support gathering of high priority performance information." In addition, MfO identified, developed, and managed capabilities (people, systems, resources, structures, culture, leadership, and relationships) to plan for, deliver, and assess results, and to develop an ongoing program to embed MfO into management practices and culture.

The Pathfinder Project (from its Web site) "led the development of management for enhanced outcomes. The Project developed a suite of basic techniques, together with practical guidance on developing outcome-based management systems. Systems go beyond only measuring performance or outcome. Instead, they put outcomes at the heart of business decisions on strategy, the best output mix, capability development, and resource allocation decisions." The project, completed in 2003, received excellent evaluations from consultants (Baehler 2003).

In 2008, New Zealand launched the Gateway Process, another EBMgt compliance approach to good management practice.[13] From the Gateway Web site: "Programmes and projects provide an important vehicle for the efficient and timely delivery of government aims. Procurement expenditure through programmes and projects is therefore a significant, and increasing, proportion of total government expenditure. Good and effective management and control of programmes and projects is therefore essential to the successful delivery of government objectives. The Gateway Process is designed to provide independent guidance to Senior Responsible Owners (SROs), programme and project teams and to the departments who commission their work, on how best to ensure that their programmes and projects are successful."

- There is deployment of best available skills and experience on the program or project.
- There is understanding by the stakeholders covered by the program/project of the program/project status and the issues involved.
- There is assurance that the program/project can progress to the next stage of development or implementation and that any procurement is well managed in order to provide value for money on a whole-life basis.
- There are more realistic time and cost targets for programs and projects.
- There is improvement in knowledge and skills among staff through participation in reviews.
- There is advice and guidance to program and project teams by fellow practitioners.

Canada

In 1997, the Canadians launched a good management initiative, in a report, Results for Canadians.[14] The prime minister designated the Treasury Board and its Secretariat (TBS) as the management board, with a mandate to work with and support agencies in improving management practices, especially in service delivery and human resources management. TBS interacts with headquarters operations as well as with interdepartmental councils in federal regions. It works with departments to set realistic standards and management frameworks in informatics and comptrollership. And it provides support to improve management practices through sharing of best practices to guidance in the conduct of gap analysis, to the funding of special initiatives aimed at improved management.

In 2001, the TBS crystallized its policy to *actively monitor* public management practices. "The management board must monitor the overall situation in departments and agencies. This monitoring requires TBS staff to actively and constructively engage internal audit, evaluation and other departmental and agency managers in order to maintain an ongoing awareness of the effectiveness of control systems. This awareness will allow early action where unacceptable risks or vulnerabilities have been identified." The policy defines a regime to actively monitor management practices and controls throughout government with these results:

- better information sharing and improved understanding of the effectiveness of management practices and controls, both within departments and across government;
- timely assessments and preventative or remedial actions in areas where control deficiencies or failures have been identified; and
- improved assessments of the effectiveness of TBS policies, and earlier identification of the need for adjustments to existing TBS policies or for new policies.

In 2003, TBS introduced the The Management Accountability Framework (MAF)[15] as a framework for discussions between deputy heads and TBS on management issues. MAF sets management standards for senior management, organized around ten key elements that define management and establish expectations for good management practices.

As the Canadians envision it (McCormack 2007, 16):

> The MAF can be viewed through three lenses: as a vision for good management, establishing a framework for accountability; as a process (assessment, engagement, dialogue and reporting); and as an analytical tool to identify strengths and weaknesses within departments and across government. Through the MAF, departments are evaluated against a set of indicators and measures that assess, among other things, the quality of management, resources and results structures; the capacity to undertake and use programme evaluations; and the overall quality of reports to Parliament. Discussions between senior officials identify management priorities, a process that draws attention to issues in a structured way that can lead to improvement.

In 2004, thirty-five agencies participated in an assessment process to identify strengths and weaknesses in management practices, allowing deputy ministers to identify management priorities, which then became part of individual performance management agreements. In 2005, MAF was aligned with the government's planning and reporting cycle. Policy makers gather information on results (internal, service, and program) and make departmental decisions. MAF links information on program resources and performance to strategic outcomes. To the best of our knowledge, MAF has not yet been rigorously evaluated (McCormack 2007).

European Union

In 2000, the European Union launched the Common Assessment Framework (CAF).[16] From its Web site: "CAF is an easy-to-use, free tool to assist public-sector organizations across Europe in using quality management techniques to improve performance. CAF provides a self-assessment framework which is conceptually similar to the major Total Quality models, in particular the Excellence Model of the European Foundation for Quality Management (EFQM), especially designed for public-sector organizations, taking into account their characteristics."

The CAF has four purposes, consistent with EBMgt, employing a compliance approach to:

* introduce public administrations to the principles of TQM and gradually guide them, through the use and understanding of self-assessment, from the current "Plan-Do" sequence of activities to a full-fledged "Plan-Do-Check-Act (PCDA)" cycle;
* facilitate the self-assessment of a public organization in order to arrive at a diagnosis and improvement actions;
* act as a bridge across the various models used in quality management; and
* facilitate bench-learning between public-sector organizations.

CAF apparently has not been adopted widely in Europe, but it is important as an example of an attempt to develop universal standards to assess public management practice.

Linking Performance, Management, and Budgeting—United States

The United States has made the most "conceptual" progress in linking performance, management, and budgeting in a whole-of-government approach under the George W. Bush administration. For many critics, however, the initiative fell considerably short of expectations.

President's Management Agenda

The Bush administration's President's Management Agenda (PMA) is the only whole-of-government EBMgt approach that explicitly links program performance, evaluation, management, and budgeting in the same system. Policy makers developed PMA through an understanding and analysis of what was effective and ineffective in previous management reforms efforts, especially GPRA and NPR. Policy makers grounded PMA in the following principles:[17]

* *Shift the burden of proof.* Today, those who propose to shift priorities or adjust funding levels are expected to demonstrate that a program or activity should

be changed. It is time, instead, that program proponents bear the burden of proof to demonstrate that the programs they advocate actually accomplish their goals, and do so better than alternative ways of spending the same money.

- *Focus on the "base" not the "increment."* Policy and budget debates focus on the marginal increase (or cut) in a program—failing to look at whether the program as a whole (the base) is working or achieving anything worthwhile. We need to reverse the presumption that this year's funding level is the starting point for considering next year's funding level.
- *Focus on results.* A mere desire to address a problem is not a sufficient justification for spending the public's money. Performance-based budgeting would mean that money would be allocated not just on the basis of perceived needs, but also on the basis of what is actually being accomplished.
- *Impose consequences.* Underperforming agencies are sometimes given incentives to improve, but rarely face consequences for persistent failure. This all-carrot-no-stick approach is unlikely to elicit improvement from troubled organizations. Instead, we should identify mismanaged, wasteful or duplicative government programs, with an eye to cutting their funding, redesigning them, or eliminating them altogether.
- *Demand evidence.* Many agencies and programs lack rigorous data or evaluations to show that they work. Such evidence should be a prerequisite to continued funding (pp. 6–7).

With our focus on EBMgt, two major PMA components: the Budget and Program Integration initiative with the Program Assessment Rating Tool (PART), a system for linking program performance with budget decision making as its centerpiece (see also, Redburn, Shea, and Buss 2008); and the Human Capital Assessment and Accountability Framework,[18] a system that builds capacity in the civil service to undertake "results-oriented management" to further the performance agenda, were initiated. In addition, the Bush administration launched the Freedom to Manage Initiative to clear statutory impediments to efficient management.

PART

In 2002, the Bush administration rolled out its PART program in Rating the Performance of Federal Programs[19] (p. 50):

The PART evaluation proceeds through four critical areas of assessment—purpose and design, strategic planning, management, and results and accountability. [The PART is essentially a questionnaire completed by program managers and submitted to OMB for assessment.] The first set of questions gauges whether the programs' design and purpose are clear and defensible. The second section involves strategic planning, and weighs whether the agency sets valid annual and long-term goals for programs. The third rates agency management of programs, including financial oversight and program improvement efforts. The fourth focuses on results that programs can report with accuracy and consistency.

Answers to questions in each of the four sections result in a numeric score for each section from 0 to 100 (100 being the best). These scores are then combined to achieve an overall qualitative rating that ranges from Effective, to Moderately Effective, to Adequate, to Ineffective. Programs that do not have acceptable performance measures or have not yet collected performance data generally receive a rating of Results Not Demonstrated. While single, weighted scores can be calculated, the value of reporting, say, an overall 46 out of 100 can be misleading. Reporting a single numerical rating could suggest false precision, or draw attention away from the very areas most in need of improvement. In fact, the PART is best seen as a complement to traditional management techniques, and can be used to stimulate a constructive dialogue between program managers, budget analysts, and policy officials. The PART serves its purpose if it produces an honest starting point for spending decisions that take results seriously.

In addition to the components above, the PART also requires that agencies establish and report performance measure data on outcomes, outputs, and efficiency, along with targets the program intends to meet on an annual basis (see Figure 8.5). Programs must also report what management plans they have in place to correct deficiencies in program management, and what actions they have completed to improve performance. Finally, programs publish annual budget data in the report.

Policy makers included rigorous evidentiary requirements throughout the PART. For example, the PART asks program managers to provide evidence to show that where there were management deficiencies, program managers had taken meaningful steps to address them. Under the "Results and Accountability" section, the PART asks program managers to justify performance by providing independent program evaluations. Policy makers intended that programs conduct evaluations based on experimental design (see Chapter 2 for a discussion), considered the Cadillac of performance assessment (OMB 2004; GAO 2004a,b). They must also furnish a comparison between their program and other government or private programs as further evidence of program performance.

Once they are completed, OMB posts the individual program assessments produced on its Web site in an easily assessable format. The PART assessments are only ten to fifteen pages in length. In addition to the PART posting, Web visitors may access agency strategic plans, annual performance reports, congressional budget justifications, and detailed budget data. So, for the first time in the United States, most critical information on program performance is easily available in one central place (www.expectmore.gov).

With the Bush administration out of office, the PART has attracted much criticism. Barack Obama's head of management at OMB, Jeffrey Zients (2009), summed up the problems on the PART in testimony before Congress on October 29, 2009 (see also Metzenbaum 2009): "The test of a performance management system is whether it is used. Despite the extent and breadth of these historic efforts, the current approach fails this test. Congress doesn't use it. Agencies don't use it. And it doesn't produce meaningful information for the public. Most metrics are process-oriented and not outcomes-based. We do not track progress on goals that

Figure 8.5 **PART Process**

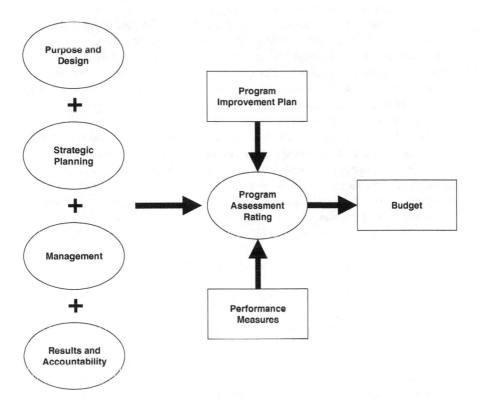

cut across agencies. Overall, too much emphasis has been placed on producing performance information to comply with a checklist of requirements instead of using it to drive change."

In spite of the PART's sophistication, the initiative had problems from an EBMgt perspective: it did not advance the practice to a new level, but ended up combining a lot of practices from the past. Evidence reported in the PART remains performance data about achieving goals and targets, and management evidence is about compliance (for a variety of views on the PART, see Redburn, Shea, and Buss 2008; Norcross and Adamson 2007; Stalebrink 2009; Gueorguieva et al. 2009; Gilmour 2008).

The PART called for independent program evaluations, using experimental or quasi-experimental design that would count as evidence to give the PART real teeth. Yet few programs were able to conduct evaluations of any kind, let alone rigorous scientific ones. For many programs, an experimental design approach simply was not applicable, and for others, resource constraints prohibited funding of studies (see also Chapter 2). The administration softened this evidentiary requirement to such an extent that it became rather meaningless for most programs, in the view of its critics (Heinrich 2007; see also GAO 1998).

The administration had originally hoped that the PART would provide convincing evidence to build a case to increase or decrease budget based on performance. The large number of mandatory spending programs and the political protections for many discretionary programs greatly dampened this expectation. Eventually, the administration began to talk about the PART as just one input into the budgetary process, the others being politics and expediency. Linking budgets to performance and management had all but been abandoned.

The PART never clearly spelled out the explicit relationship linking GPRA's strategic plan, annual Performance and Accountability Report, and Annual Performance Plan requirements. Even the PART's relationship to the President's Management Agenda scorecard assessments on whole-of-government initiatives was never articulated. As will be seen later in this chapter, management components of the Human Capital Assessment and Accountability Framework were never tied into the management components of the PART.

Human Capital Assessment and Accountability Framework

The Human Capital Assessment and Accountability Framework (HCAAF) supports PMA by requiring agencies to have in place human capital systems that foster performance-based management evidenced in five areas:

- *Strategic Alignment*—aligns human capital management strategies with an agency's mission, goals, and objectives through analysis, planning, investment, measurement, and management of human capital programs.
- *Leadership and Knowledge Management*—ensures continuity of leadership developing and maintaining organizational knowledge and learning.
- *Results-Oriented Performance Culture*—promotes high-performing workforce through effective performance management systems.
- *Talent Management*—establishes a system to attract, acquire, develop, promote, and retain quality talent in workforce.
- *Accountability*—monitors and evaluates the results of human capital management policies, programs, and activities against merit system principles.

HCAAF is a framework used by the Office of Personnel Management (OPM) and agency policy makers to ensure that agencies have appropriate systems in place to manage performance. HCAAF asks policy makers to evaluate their agency against a set of standards deemed to be state-of-the-art in human capital management (see Table 8.1). Each standard includes a set of metrics, critical success factors, and expected results. Performance indicators provide evidence that the agency meets acceptable standards. HCAAF combines performance management and good management practice in one instrument.

Table 8.1

The HCAAF System

Component	Explanation
Standard	A standard describes the critical human capital management outcomes for agencies to strive toward in each of the five human capital systems.
Metrics	These are measurements that provide a basis for comparison. Strategic human capital management requires a reliable and valid set of metrics that provides an accurate baseline against which individual agency progress can be assessed. Required outcome metrics are provided for the three systems that implement strategic human capital plans and programs: Leadership and Knowledge Management, Results-Oriented Performance Culture, and Talent Management.
Critical Success Factors	Each system is based on critical success factors that make up the overall system. Critical success factors are the areas on which agencies and human capital practitioners should focus to achieve a system's standard and operate efficiently, effectively, and in compliance with merit system principles. For example, Change Management and Diversity Management are two critical success factors associated with the Leadership and Knowledge Management system.
Results	The results describe the desired effects when key elements of a critical success factor are effectively implemented. Results are presented in two categories: effectiveness results and compliance results. Compliance results refer to specific statutory or regulatory requirements.
Key Elements	Each critical success factor contains several key elements that are similar to the Elements of Yes that were initially developed as part of the HCAAF. Key elements describe what you would expect to see in an effective critical success factor.
Suggested Performance Indicators	The suggested indicators (both effectiveness indicators and compliance indicators) describe examples of visible evidence of the existence of key elements and compliance with merit system principles. Cumulatively, the indicators identify how well the agency is doing relative to key elements. The suggested performance indicators are linked to the key elements and are not meant to be an all-inclusive list. Human capital practitioners may need to search for other indicators if agency approaches differ from the list of suggested performance indicators provided. Agencies may decide which suggested performance indicators provide the best evidence that they have implemented practices that lead toward achieving the standard.

Source: Office of Personnel Management, "Human Capital Assessment and Accountability Framework (HCAAF) Resource Center." www.opm.gov/hcaaf_resource_center/2-4.asp.

Unlike the PART, HCAAF has drawn little attention for its contribution, or lack thereof, to the performance management movement (see NAPA Fellows 2009). It appears not to have drawn any criticism, as has not been the case with the PART.

The Obama Administration

The new Obama administration appeared intent on undoing the PART performance management system, announcing, in *A New Era of Responsibility: Renewing America's Promise,* that "the Administration will fundamentally reconfigure the PART. We will open up the insular performance measurement process to the public, the Congress and outside experts. The Administration will eliminate ideological performance goals and replace them with goals Americans care about and that are based on congressional intent and feedback from the people served by Government programs. Programs will not be measured in isolation, but assessed in the context of other programs that are serving the same population or meeting the same goals" (White House 2009, 2).

Nonetheless, unlike other U.S. administrations, the Obama administration is the first in almost a century not to come to office with a management or civil service reform strategy. With the other problems facing the administration—financial crisis, health care crisis, wars in Iraq and Afghanistan—some believe that the era of performance management and good management reform in the United States may be over. This indictment may be premature: In June 2009, OMB announced guidance for preparing the fiscal year 2011 budget. The administration announced that it wanted each agency to focus on priority performance goals for its programs (Orszag 2009). In general, the Obama performance management system will have the following characteristics (see also Metzenbaum 2009):

- Senior leader ownership of performance management process
- Cascading goals and measurements
- Outcome-oriented, cross-agency goals and measurements
- Relentless review and accountability
- Transparent process
- Management dashboards
- Customer-facing performance information
- Rigorous evaluations
- Performance leadership

Dilemmas in Evidence-Based Management

Because PMA is the most advanced performance management system, we draw on Zients's assessment above and explore some of the PART's limitations as a way to motivate a discussion of what a better system might look like (see also Chapter 16). To a certain extent, initiatives from other countries mirror these limitations.

Good Performance Is Not Good Management

Good performance as measured against goal attainment is not evidence of good management. We analyzed the PART data for 1,009 federal programs to see what the relationships among program design, program management, strategic management, and performance results were. Recall that in the PART, policy makers required evidence for all four factors. We discovered in a multiple regression analysis that strategic management explained nearly 50 percent of the variance in performance results, while program management explained less than 10 percent. Program design was not significant. We also found that about one-fifth of the programs had good management but bad performance results, and one-fifth of the programs had bad management scores but good results. The same results were generally true for strategic management as well. There appears to be only a weak (if any) causal link between management and results.

There are a variety of explanations for these findings; several stand out. First, it is unlikely that a standard set of management indicators can possibly apply to all managers in all programs. The PART does not allow for variation due to program context or circumstance:[20] one size may not fit all. Second, it is not clear why the "evidence" required under the PART is really supportable in the absence of evidence-based research. Just because a management practice sounds good does not mean that it is. Third, of course, from a methodological point of view, it could be that the PART is not really measuring management or performance with its measures, but something else—in short, it may have validity issues. Fourth, perhaps the PART management scores were too political or subjective, masking good and bad management.

It may be that the more recent focus on management is misplaced. For some, the conclusion may be that what we should care about is performance, regardless of how we get there (e.g., Davenport and Harris 2007).

Performance and Budgeting Are Not Linked

As noted, there is only a weak association between performance and budget decision making. So, we know how programs are performing, but we are unwilling for the most part to increase, decrease, or terminate programs accordingly. Also as noted, program spending is mostly mandatory, and discretionary spending is politically protected. At the same time, we are quite willing to launch new programs without much evidence that they will work as intended.

In this context, management may appear to some to be irrelevant as an issue in most public programs.

Rigorous Program Evaluation Is Absent

Some believe that rigorous evaluation will save the day, in either the performance management or the good management context (see Chapter 2 for a discussion of this issue). In another analysis of the PART, we found that only 60 percent of programs had reported evaluations, and of these less than half produced results suggesting high quality. As observed, the Bush administration backed off the evaluation standard that would have given the PART a true evidentiary base. So, without evaluation, we cannot say whether programs worked; we can only say from the other components of the PART that they met their goals. But we note that many programs report only outputs—number of things produced—and a few outcomes—which are easy to measure but do not add much to our knowledge of whether the programs worked. So again, not only is management somewhat irrelevant, it also appears to be the case that on the performance management side, a lot of programs are poorly assessed against goals and objectives. For example, Medicare, one of the largest federal programs, has only a few outcome measures, like what percentage of elderly people got flu shots.

Management Practice Guidance Is Neither Evidence Based Nor Good Management

There is virtually no evidentiary basis for the good management guidelines promulgated in most government Web sites. In the field of management, for example, public managers are told to manage collaboratively with their staff, stakeholders, and just about everyone else (see Morse and Buss 2008). Yet, we do not really know whether it makes sense to manage all programs using collaborative models or more traditional authority ones. This is because the context in which managers find themselves does not lend itself to cookie-cutter approaches, and managers have difference skills, experiences, and personalities that work with some models but not others. As a result, imposing checklists of good management practices to determine whether managers are good managers does not make sense. If this were not enough, there is a great deal of disagreement among researchers on what constitutes good management practice: if one takes the most recent crop of management books and compares their advice to managers, one finds them to be totally contradictory. Some commentators posit that much of the wisdom on management comes from faddism—management trends frequently come into style, and then are replaced by newer ones (e.g., Brindle and Stearns 2001; Watson 2009)—and the confusion over best practices and lessons learned, which are not evidence.

Conclusion

We conclude that to foster EBMgt in government, the following would need to happen:

- Require rigorous program evaluation to promote accountability.
- Improve program performance measures to include outcomes and impacts.

- Link budget decisions to program performance, and link individual performance assessment to program performance in a meaningful way.
- Ground management practice in evidence-based research.
- Make management assessments context sensitive.

How likely is this to happen? Not very. Performance management and good management practice, from their early history to the present, suggest that evidence-based management may have peaked, and continues to decline as an approach, in spite of government initiatives to promote it. Thirty years of effort by major world governments shows a lack of interest or an unwillingness to conduct rigorous evaluation, link performance to budgets, develop evidence-based management practice, infuse evidence-based practice in decision making, and account for context. There seems to be no major thrust in play to get governments to change.

However, governments have become much more adept at strategic management, setting goals and measuring performance. Some might even say that this activity now approaches a science. Performance management as goal attainment seems institutionalized in government.

So, the question becomes, if goal attainment is really not a function of good or bad management, and evidence for management is unhelpful or irrelevant in goal attainment, why bother with EBMgt? We vote for increased rigor on the performance management side.

Notes

1. Materials accessed from the Australian Public Services Commission at http://www.apsc.gov.au/.
2. See Treasury Board Secretariat at http://www.tbs-sct.gc.ca/.
3. See http://www.tbs-sct.gc.ca/rma/mrrs-sgrr_e.asp.
4. See State Services Commission at http://www.ssc.govt.nz/display/home.asp.
5. See Cabinet Office at http://www.cabinetoffice.gov.uk/.
6. See www.nationalschool.gov.uk.
7. This section draws heavily from our work in Redburn, Shea, and Buss (2008).
8. http://govinfo.library.unt.edu/npr/library/papers/bkgrd/brief.html.
9. http://www.whitehouse.gov/omb/mgmt-gpra_gplaw2m/.
10. Program evaluation' means an assessment, through objective measurement and systematic analysis, of the manner and extent to which federal programs achieve intended objectives.
11. Much of this training in practice centers on leadership development (see Morse and Buss 2008). Some question whether this furthers good management practice.
12. http://www.ssc.govt.nz/display/document.asp?docid=3530&pageno=1#P9_0.
13. http://www.ssc.govt.nz/display/document.asp?docid=6580&pageno=1#P9_0.
14. Material in this section drawn from the Treasury Board Secretariat at http://www.tbs-sct.gc.ca/.
15. http://www.tbs-sct.gc.ca/maf-crg/images/maf-rcg-01-eng.gif.
16. http://www.eipa.eu/en/pages/show/&tid=67.
17. http://www.whitehouse.gov/omb/assets/omb/budget/fy2002/mgmt.pdf.
18. http://www.opm.gov/hcaaf_resource_center/.

19. http://www.gpoaccess.gov/usbudget/fy04/pdf/budget/performance.pdf.
20. PART does separate out different types of programs—block grants from loan programs, for example.

References

Accenture. 2008. *An International Comparison of the United Kingdom's Public Administration.* London: National Audit Office, Her Majesty's Stationary Office.
Advisory Group on Reform. 2009. *Reform of Australian Administration.* Canberra, Australia: Department of Prime Minister and Cabinet. www.pmc.gov.au/consultation/aga_reform/index.cfm (accessed November 1, 2009).
Baehler, Karen. 2003. *Toward Mutual Adjustment: Pathfinder Project Evaluation.* Wellington: State Services Commission, New Zealand Government.
Blondal, Jon. 2001. "Budgeting in Canada." *OECD Journal on Budgeting* 1 (1): 1–15.
Blondal, Jon, Daniel Bergvall, Ian Hawkesworth, and Rex Deighton-Smith. 2008. "Budgeting in Australia." *OECD Journal on Budgeting* 8 (2): 1–15. www.oecd.org/dataoecd/59/24/42007191.pdf (accessed November 1, 2009).
Bouckaert, Geert, and John Halligan. 2007. *Managing Performance: International Comparisons.* New York: Routledge.
Boston, Johnathon. 1996. *Public Management: The New Zealand Model.* Auckland: Oxford University Press.
Brindle, Margaret C., and Peter N. Stearns. 2001. *Facing Up to Management Faddism.* Westport, CT: Quorum Books.
Buss, Terry F. 2008. "Reforming CDBG: An Illusive Quest." In *Reengineering Community Development,* ed. Donna Fabiani and Terry Buss, 223–235. Armonk, NY: M.E. Sharpe.
Cabinet Office. 1999a. *Modernising Government.* London: British Government. www.archive.official-documents.co.uk/document/cm43/4310/4310.htm (accessed November 1, 2009).
———. 1999b. *Professional Policymaking for the Twenty-first Century. Report by Strategic Policy Making Team, Cabinet Office.* London: British Government.
———. 2000. *Adding It Up: Improving Analysis and Modeling in Central Government.* London: British Government.
———. 2009a. *Assessment of the Capability Review Program.* London: British Government.
———. 2009b. *Civil Service Reform.* London: British Government. www.cabinetoffice.gov.uk/media/124376/civilservice_reform_paper.pdf; www.nationalschool.gov.uk (accessed November 1, 2009).
———. Undated. *Evidence-Based Government Initiatives.* London: British Government. www.nationalschool.gov.uk (accessed November 1, 2009).
Comptroller and Auditor General. 2003. *Getting the Evidence: Using Research in Policy Making,* London: Stationery Office, British Government.
Cook, Anna-Luis. 2004. *Managing for Outcomes in the New Zealand Public Management System.* Wellington: Treasury Ministry, New Zealand Government.
Davenport, Thomas H., and Jeanne G. Harris. 2007. *Competing on Analytics.* Cambridge, MA: Harvard Business School Press.
Durant, Robert, and Laura A. Wilson. 1993. "Performance Management, Total Quality Management, and Quality Improvement." *American Review of Public Administration* 23 (3): 215–245.
Flynn, N. 1999. "Modernizing British Government." *Parliamentary Affairs, Oxford* 52 (4): 582–597.
GAO. *See* Government Accountability Office.

Gilmour, John B. 2008. "Implementing OMB's PART." In *Performance Management and Budgeting,* ed. F. Stevens Redburn, Robert Shea, and Terry Buss, 21–48. Armonk, NY: M.E. Sharpe.

Government Accountability Office. 1995. *Managing for Results.* GAO/GGD-95–120. Washington, DC: Government Accountability Office, May 2.

———. 1997. *Performance-Based Organizations: Lessons from the British Next Steps Initiative.* GAO/T-GGD-97–151. Washington, DC: Government Accountability Office, July 8.

———. 1998. *Program Evaluation: Agencies Challenged.* GAO/GGD-98–53. Washington, DC: Government Accountability Office, April 24.

———. 2004a. *Performance Budgeting: Observations on the Use of OMB's PART for FY2004.* GAO-04–174. Washington, DC: Government Accountability Office, January.

———. 2004b. *Performance Budgeting: OMB's Performance Rating Tool Presents Opportunities and Challenges for Evaluating Program Performance.* Washington, DC: Government Accountability Office, March 11.

———. 2005. *Managing for Results: Enhancing Agency Use of Performance Information for Management Decision Making.* GAO-05–927. Washington, DC: Government Accountability Office, September 9.

———. 2009. *Results-Oriented Management: Strengthening Key Practices at FEMA and Interior Could Promote Greater Use of Performance Information.* GAO-09–676. Washington, DC: Government Accountability Office, August 17.

Grifel, Stuart. 1993. "Performance Measurement and Budgetary Decision Making." *Public Productivity and Management Review* 16 (4): 403–407.

Gueorguieva, Vassia, et al. 2009. "The PART and GPRA." *American Review of Public Administration* 39 (3): 225–245.

Halligan, John. 2007. "Reintegrating Government in Third Generation Reforms of Australia and New Zealand." *Public Policy and Administration* 22 (2): 217–238.

Hawke, Lewis. 2007. "Performance Budgeting in Australia." *OECD Journal on Budgeting* 7 (3): 1–15

Heinrich, Carolyn J. 2007. "Evidence Based Policy and Performance Management: Challenges and Prospects in Two Parallel Movements." *American Review of Public Administration* 37 (3): 255–277.

House of Commons. 2003. *Whither the Civil Service?* London: House of Commons. www.parliament.uk/commons/lib/research/rp2003/rp03–049.pdf (accessed November 1, 2009).

House of Lords. 1997–98. *The Public Service.* London: House of Lords. www.publications.parliament.uk/pa/ld199798/ldselect/ldpubsrv/055/psrep01.htm (accessed November 1, 2009).

Kettl, Donald F. 1995. "Building Lasting Reform." In *Inside the Reinvention Machine,* ed. Donald Kettle and John DiIulio, 9–83. Washington, DC: Brookings Institution.

Kibblewhite, Andrew, and Chris Ussher. 2002. "Outcome Focused Management in New Zealand." OECD paper. Organization for Economic Cooperation and Development, Paris. www.oecd.org/dataoecd/62/60/43513908.pdf (accessed November 1, 2009).

Light, Paul C. 1995. *Thickening Government.* Washington, DC: Brookings Institution.

———. 1997. *The Tides of Reform.* New Haven, CT: Yale University Press.

Mackay, Keith. 2004. *The Development of Australia's Evaluation System.* ECD 4. Washington, DC: Operations Evaluation Department, World Bank.

Management Advisory Committee. 2007. *Reducing Red Tape in the Australian Public Service.* Canberra: Australian Public Service Commission. www.apsc.gov.au/mac/redtape.htm (accessed November 1, 2009).

McCormack, Lee. 2007. "Performance Budgeting in Canada." *OECD Journal on Budgeting* 7 (4): 1–18. www.oecd.org/dataoecd/42/16/43411424.pdf (accessed November 1, 2009).

Metzenbaum, Shelley. 2009. *Performance Management Recommendations for the New Administration.* Washington, DC: IBM Center for the Business of Government. www.businessofgovernment.org/publications/grant_reports/details/index.asp?gid=330 (accessed November 1, 2009).

Moe, Ronald. 1994. "The 'Reinventing Government' Exercise." *Public Administration Review* 54 (2): 111–122.

Morse, Ricardo, and Terry F. Buss, eds. 2008. *Innovations in Public Leadership Development.* Armonk, NY: M.E. Sharpe.

NAPA Fellows. 2009. "A Certified Assessment of Human Resources Systems." In *Innovations in Human Resource Management,* ed. Hannah Sistare, Myra Shiplett, and Terry F. Buss, 245–262. Armonk, NY: M.E. Sharpe.

National Audit Organization. 2007. *Value for Money in Public Sector Corporate Services.* London: National Audit Organization, Her Majesty's Stationary Office.

Norcross, Eileen, and Joseph Adamson. 2007. *An Analysis of the OMB PART for FY2008.* Washington, DC: Mercatus Center, George Mason University.

Office of Management and Budget. 2004. *What Constitutes Evidence of Program Effectiveness.* Washington, DC: Office of Management and Budget. www.whitehouse.gov/omb/assets/omb/performance/2004_program_eval.pdf (accessed November 1, 2009).

Office of the Prime Minister. 1990. *The Renewal of the Public Service of Canada.* Ottawa: Government of Canada.

Organization for Economic Cooperation and Development. 1999a. *Government Reform: of Roles and Functions of Government and Public Administration New Zealand. Country Paper.* Paris: Organization for Economic Cooperation and Development. www.oecd.org/dataoecd/48/39/1910905.pdf (accessed November 1, 2009).

———. 1999b. *Project on Strategic Review and Reform: Canada Country Paper.* Paris: Organization for Economic Cooperation and Development. www.oecd.org/dataoecd/9/28/2731224.pdf (accessed November 1, 2009).

Orszag, Peter R. 2009. "FY 2011 Budget and Performance Plan." Memo 09–20. Washington, DC: Office of Management and Budget, June 11.

Pollit, Christopher, and Geert Bouckaert. 2004. *Public Management Reforms.* London: Oxford University Press.

Public Administration Select Committee of the House of Commons. 2002–3. *On Target? Government by Measurement:* London: House of Commons.

Redburn, F. Stevens, Robert Shea, and Terry Buss, eds. 2008. *Performance Management and Budgeting: How Governments Can Learn from Experience.* Armonk, NY: M.E. Sharpe.

Schick, Allen. 1996. *The Spirit of Reform.* Wellington: State Services Commission, New Zealand Government.

Solesbury, William. 2001. "Evidence Based Policy: Whence It Came and Where It's Going." ESRC UK Centre for Evidence Based Policy and Practice Working Paper 1. ESRC UK Centre for Evidence Based Policy and Practice, London.

Stalebrink, O.J. 2009. "National Performance Mandates and Intergovernmental Collaboration." *American Review of Public Administration* 39 (6): 619–639.

State Services Commission. 2000. *Canadian PEMS and NZ SRAs: A Comparative Study.* Working paper 3. Wellington: State Services Commission, New Zealand Government.

———. 2005. *Getting Better at Managing for Outcomes.* Wellington: State Services Commission, New Zealand Government.

———. 2008. *The Capability Toolkit: A Tool to Promote and Inform Capability Management.* Wellington: State Services Commission, New Zealand Government.

Sunnydale Institute Study Team. 2007. *Take-Off or Tail-Off? An Evaluation of the Capability Review Program.* London: Sunnydale Institute, National School of Government.

Task Force on Management Improvement. 1992. *The Australian Public Service Reformed: An Evaluation of a Decade of Management Reform.* Canberra: Task Force on Management Improvement.

Thompson, James R. 2000. "Reinvention as Reform: Assessing the National Performance Review." *Public Administration Review* 60 (6): 508–521.

Van Dooren, Wouter, Geert Bouckaert, and John Halligan. 2010. *Performance Management in the Public Sector.* New York: Routledge.

Watson, Don. 2009. *Bendable Learnings: The Wisdom of Modern Management.* Sydney: Random House Australia.

White House. 2009. *A New Era of Responsibility: Renewing America's Promise.* Washington, DC: The White House. www.whitehouse.gov/omb/assets/fy2010_new_era/A_New_Era_of_Responsibility2.pdf (accessed November 1, 2010).

Zients, Jeffrey. 2009. Testimony before the Senate Budget Committee. October 29. http://www.whitehouse.gov/sites/default/files/omb/assets/testimony/Zients_102909.pdf (accessed November 1, 2010).

9

Organizing for Continuous Improvement

Evidence-Based Management at the VA

NAPA Fellows and Staff

Congress and an array of federal departments and agencies, including the Department of Veterans Affairs (VA), face a very large and complex organizational and management challenge in improving care and benefits for veterans, including those now returning from Iraq and Afghanistan. To accomplish its mission and goals in an era of change, the VA and its partners must pursue a broader systematic organizational strategy of continuous improvement. This strategy will involve a series of successive and coordinated *evidence-driven alterations* to the administration of service and benefits for veterans. For the change to be sustained and successful, it must be supported at the top and managed centrally, with clear accountability by all for specific results under their control and a continuous focus on how their work contributes to better outcomes for veterans.

The change strategy must be guided by a clear vision, translated into specific performance goals and targets for achievement, and grounded in sound evidence. At the highest level, the goal is to transform the VA into a veteran-centered organization that produces better service and outcomes.

This chapter describes the actions required for a successful organizational change. It is grounded in evidence-based models that have been used successfully within the VA and elsewhere. These models contain practical steps for building and sustaining such a strategy in the VA.

Long-term success in providing better support for recovery and reintegration requires:

- Sustaining and strengthening collaboration between the VA and the Department of Defense (DOD) to support transitions and support recovery and reintegration of separated service members;
- Integrating the management and operations of the Veterans Benefits Administration (VBA) and the Veterans Health Administration (VHA) as needed to ensure "no wrong door" for the veteran seeking help or information;

- Balancing centralized review of information system investments with open-ness to innovation at lower levels;
- Establishing a cost-effective tracking, communications, and outreach strategy for veterans, with appropriate interventions and access to continuing support; and
- Finding cost-effective ways to provide long-term support for full recovery and reintegration of returning injured veterans, including in some cases long-term institutional care of the most severely injured.

Addressing these challenges will require a major reorganization of roles and responsibilities within the VA or between the VA and DOD.[1] However, it will require creative leaders and managers, with sufficient authority and control over resources to manage the change process over an indefinite period. The VA, working with its partners, also must retain flexibility to adjust systems and management priorities and reallocate resources in response to changes in the numbers and geography of needs arising from military conflicts and the tension between rising medical care costs and competing demands for resources. It also will require broadening the use of the existing evidence-based learning capacity now in the VA—represented by the QUERI process in the VHA, for example.[2] This will promote continual learning from experience and adjustment of strategies for improving service when, for example, piloting and evaluation identify new, cost-effective means of targeted outreach, or new scientific understanding emerges of how to diagnose and treat specific illnesses and injuries.

Fortunately, the VA has in its own recent experience a documented model of successful change that includes the elements needed for sustained organizational improvement.[3] The VHA reorganization during the last decade demonstrates that the VA can manage large-scale change successfully. The success of that effort has been attributed to a combination of strong individual leadership with a well-defined vision of what the change was intended to accomplish and how to bring it about; a new management approach that combined delegation to strong regional administrators held accountable for specific results in line with the vision of improved health care; and a system of evidence-based evaluation research and testing of new clinical practices that has allowed the organization to learn and improve at a rapid pace.

According to Kenneth Kizer, the undersecretary for health who led the change, systemic change at the VHA is still a work in progress.[4] More managerial accountability is needed, as well as greater flexibility to make difficult decisions that are inherent in organizational change. Kizer has noted that, given the numerous attempts at reforms in the years prior to his tenure and their ultimate failure, an attitude toward change efforts permeated the workforce and could be summed up as, "Well, this too will pass. It won't be long before we get back to the old way of doing things."[5] It is not easy for large organizations to sustain a process of continuous learning and improvement. That is why the best, most successful organizations consciously design and build institutional support for strategic performance-driven management grounded in sound evidence.

Public organizations face special challenges in systematically changing to more effective modes of operation, given—among other factors—the complexity of their missions, the constant and often conflicting demands of various constituencies, and frequent changes in their top leadership. The net result of these pressures can be an organizational tendency to react to the latest crisis rather than to plan against long-term performance objectives. The prevailing environment can contribute to a defensive and overly cautious resistance to change. A conscious strategy for learning and improvement can help buffer and offset these inevitable, performance-eroding pressures.

A Strategy for Continuous Improvement

At the broadest level, those responsible for improving the system of care and benefits for veterans face the challenge of organizational transformation. Success depends on the following elements:

- Leadership that is prepared to communicate a clear, consistent, and compelling vision that is aligned with the organization's statutory mission and is reinforced by a steady focus on results, measurement, and reporting systems to track progress toward desired outcomes.
- Developing and using a balanced array of performance metrics to guide change and provide accountability for results internally and externally.
- Ensuring that personnel with the appropriate skills are employed and given sufficient authority, autonomy, and incentive to achieve the goals. Internal and external relationships must ensure coordination among actors and units and must give each person a "line of sight" to the larger purposes.
- Establishing regular processes for planning and managing strategically, enabling continual improvement by learning and then adapting to the new information.

For challenges such as those presented by returning veterans from Afghanistan (Operation Enduring Freedom) and Iraq (Operation Iraqi Freedom), a successful response also will depend on how effectively the VA collaborates with its partners in the federal and state governments and among the many nongovernmental organizations interested in helping veterans and their families. Of particular importance to providing a continuum of care to wounded veterans and a seamless transition from active service for others is the fostering of a deeper, more effective partnership with DOD and the military services.

Managing Organizational Change

Managing the complex set of changes required to make the VA fully veteran centered is a major challenge. As noted, transformation efforts can fall short for many reasons: fear of change, lack of thorough planning, waning commitment, insufficient accountability, and poor timing.

The core set of contributors to successful change identified by nearly all stud
ies includes:

- *Commitment* of leadership in both words and actions over a sustained period
  of time;
- *Information and communication* to all involved, explaining what the change
  is about, the desired outcomes, their role in the effort, and why it matters to
  them;
- An *enabling environment* that promotes the change by training new skills or
  imparting knowledge; creating new or modifying existing work processes;
  opening communication and data-sharing channels to support those work
  processes; and removal of barriers, negativity, and resistance to change;
- *Enforcement* of new business rules, requiring *accountability* through use of
  performance metrics, and offering *incentives* for achievement of milestones
  and goals; and
- Most recently, marshaling *evidence* to support management and policy.

The VA has had plans and champions at various times for integrating its administration and systems under the banner of "OneVA." Earlier versions of the
VA's strategic plan placed the OneVA concept high in priority for development
and implementation, and numerous concept papers and planning documents were
developed for the OneVA vision. However, the department has never had sustained
success in turning those plans into progress. VA managers note that, historically,
the department has not lacked for good plans to address a variety of issues that
would move it toward becoming more veteran centered. Execution of those plans
has fallen short because many of the components of successful change have been
lacking.

Goal Setting and Performance Improvement

Intense activity and rapid change increase the risk that personnel at all levels of an
organization will lose sight of the larger goals to which their efforts are contributing. The goal setting and performance improvement (SOC) process may be an
example of this. It has been guided by the recommendations of previous commis-
sions and groups, and, to move more quickly, each of the process lines of action
has concentrated on how to implement the specific categories of recommendations
within its assigned area.

While this approach has speeded the launch or piloting of new initiatives, there
does not appear to be a clear statement as yet of what would constitute overall
success of the joint effort. Nor is there in place a framework of targeted outcomes
or indicators of progress that will allow DOD and the VA to judge which of their
efforts have contributed to improvements in care and benefits for veterans.[6]

The techniques of strategic planning and performance measurement are well understood and have been applied effectively in both DOD and the VA, as evidenced by the major successful restructuring of the VHA in the 1990s. A strategic discussion at the outset of the SOC process would have required some time. The main obstacle to using these techniques in the SOC effort has been the pressure to achieve and demonstrate results quickly.

It is possible that an early effort to develop such a plan and an explicit strategy would have revealed fundamental differences in perspective and mission among DOD, the military services, and the VA that would have hindered their initial progress. Deliberation regarding the basic objectives of the effort, such as whether to focus on short-term recovery or long-term reintegration into civilian society, and whether to concentrate on veterans of the current conflicts or to pursue changes that would benefit all veterans, would have raised difficult issues. In the absence of such exchanges, these underlying differences in philosophy and culture are yet to be addressed, with unclear implications for the future course of the effort.

Basic questions ultimately will be asked about whether the changes resulting from the SOC's efforts have been successful in the most fundamental terms, that is, numbers of service members reintegrated successfully into civilian life; numbers of seriously injured veterans restored to fullest possible functioning and health; and effectiveness of specific strategies for early diagnosis and treatment of trauma-related mental illness. Clear goals and strong performance measurement would enable the VA and DOD to answer these questions more precisely and to use the answers to improve their efforts to facilitate transitions, as well as to demonstrate accountability to external stakeholders including Congress and the administration. An appropriate array of performance metrics, developed from well-established evidence-based practices in the field, also would support internal management decisions regarding the best use of resources, technology investment, and program design.

Within the VA, both the VHA and VBA administrations have used performance measurement extensively to guide their program management. The VHA has more experience than most of the VBA in using performance metrics to set and monitor goals for senior managers and in applying these metrics to systematic improvement of programs.

To be fully successful, the performance framework for improving transitions must encompass both benefits (the VBA) and health care (the VHA). To drive successful change, the VA and its partners need to establish a performance framework change that will:

- set goals for improved outcomes for each category of veteran, including access to appropriate care and assistance, health and recovery, employment and earnings, and quality of life;
- provide the VA and its partners with a common strategy for achieving improved outcomes by identifying actions that build on existing assets and deploy them more effectively;
- design and apply performance measures, supported by data collection, analy-

sis, and reporting infrastructure, based on baseline performance levels and including interim and long-term improvement targets;
- establish joint administrative responsibilities for performance measurement, including data quality and reliability, related to transitions;
- develop program measures for health and quality-of-life outcomes for recovering veterans in order to assess program effectiveness and guide improvement;
- establish baselines against which to judge progress and provide regular feedback on results to those working to improve outcomes;
- support random controlled trials of critical treatment and services changes as they are introduced and use these to guide decisions about program design; and
- link information on results to transition program management, personnel ratings and rewards, program redesign, and policy and budget development.

Authority and Incentives

Productive and lasting change may emerge from the joint DOD/VA SOC process, as well as from independent work by the two departments to aid the adjustment, recovery, and reintegration of veterans. Congress has not waited, however, to institutionalize interdepartmental policy development and collaboration through joint centers and other joint management structures to deal with seriously injured veterans. The National Defense Authorization Act of 2008:

- Directs the VA and DOD secretaries to jointly develop and implement a mechanism to provide for the electronic transfer from DOD to the VA of DOD documents necessary to establish or support eligibility of a member for benefits under laws administered by the VA at the time of the member's retirement, separation, or release from service;
- Establishes the DOD-VA Interagency Program Office for a Joint Electronic Health Record and requires that the office develop and prepare a joint record that complies with applicable federal interoperability standards, deployed on September 30, 2010; and
- Mandates joint DOD-VA standards for transition of recovering members and veterans from care and treatment by DOD to care and treatment by the VA before, during, and after separation from service, VA access to military health records, and surveys and other mechanisms to measure patient and family satisfaction with DOD and VA care and services.

Such mandates impose a new layer of organizational and management challenges regarding divided authority and accountability; conflicting missions and incentive structures; and oversight by multiple congressional committees. Control of these joint structures will, in the absence of other determinants, likely lead to dominance by whichever department receives congressional spending authority for the operation of these structures.

Divided or disconnected management functions—as between the VHA and the VBA, or between DOD and the military services, or between DOD and the VA at different stages of the transition—create coordination problems that may impair effective service to individual veterans. To the extent that activities are managed by a cluster of personnel with overlapping roles and responsibilities to different organizations, as appears to be the case with care for the seriously wounded, there is more potential for confusion and conflict. Sorting out proper roles and relationships will require both coordination across congressional committees and close collaboration between DOD and the VA and between the VHA and the VBA.

An Evidence-Based Strategy for Continuous Improvement

To make the Department of Veterans Affairs fully veteran centered, and therefore more effective in serving the veteran, is a long-term, complex process of organizational change. Sustained high-level leadership of the required organization-wide changes will depend on establishing a new capacity directly responsible to the secretary for the change. The secretary should establish a process of performance-driven management and evidence-based improvement, modeled in part on the successful performance-based reinvention of the VHA in the previous decade.

Effective transformation of the VA to a veteran-centered department will require revision of the performance plans of the VA offices to focus on efforts that promote this objective and measure veteran satisfaction with their encounters with the VA as important "process goals." A performance-driven management structure and philosophy can be supported by specific techniques that the VA and its partners can use to promote continuous improvement in outcomes for veterans. For example, experience in both private and public sectors suggests that techniques such as developing program "logic models," organization "strategy mapping," "balanced scorecards," and "value stream mapping" can drive constructive change. Many large private companies and some public organizations that recognize the need for continuous improvement in their competitive environment have used such processes successfully. Their success depends on visionary leadership to achieve positive, focused change. Illustrative versions of a strategy map and a balanced scorecard to support improved service to returning veterans, including exemplary measures, are presented later in this chapter in the context of other recommendations.

Previous organizational change research shows that successful change in large organizations occurs as follows:

1. Create a sense of urgency regarding the idea that the VA must become a veteran-centered service organization to be fully effective—personnel will start verbalizing a recognized need to change;
2. Build the guiding team—designate a group who have sufficient power

and authority to guide the change and who are in a position to direct collaborative efforts crossing intradepartmental boundaries;

3. Elaborate a clear, simple vision of what a new veteran-centered VA would look like and set a strategy—the guiding team develops the vision and strategy for the change effort (see Figure 9.1);

4. Communicate the vision and strategy to transform the VA over time into a veteran-centered and more effective organization—personnel begin to accept the change because they are informed about what it is and how it will affect them;

5. Empower VA managers to advance the strategy by removing obstacles—more personnel are able to act and begin to do so; they have fewer obstacles or perceive less risk;

6. Produce short-term successes, including early implementation of recommendations included in this chapter, to demonstrate progress and create more support—personnel will be energized by successes and momentum will increase, while detractors begin to diminish;

7. Do not let up, but stay committed to achieving more successes and institutionalizing the changes—so that over time more people make changes and see successes; and

8. Make the change stick by encouraging a new culture within the VA that places services to the veteran at the heart of everything the department does—the new behaviors continue, despite the influence of tradition or leadership turnover, the earlier and continued successes keep the momentum up for sustaining the change, and it becomes the new cultural norm.

Recommendations

1. The VA should create a new performance-driven culture and management style to transform the VA into a veteran-centered organization.

The illustrative strategy map in Figure 9.1 shows at a high level how the principal recommendations in this chapter and related organizational and resource allocation decisions (first line) can support proposed strategies to improve service to returning veterans, and how these service improvements in turn can contribute over a period of years to improved outcomes for veterans.[7] In this case, the focus is on returning veterans, but similar maps could be developed as guides to change for all or other categories of veterans.

Such maps are one tool used by managers and leaders of transformative change in large private and public organizations.[8] Strategy maps describe how an organization adds value. For a private sector organization, the desired outcomes typically include profitability and revenue growth. For a public sector organiza-

Figure 9.1   **Illustrative Strategy Map: Improving Service to Returning War Veterans**

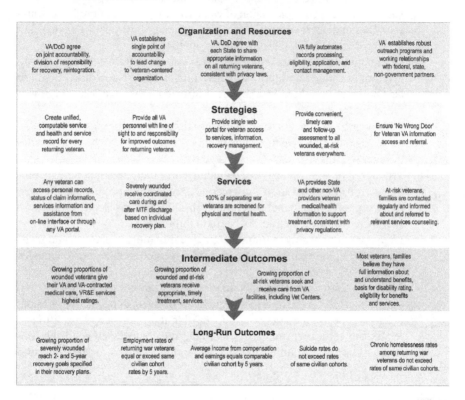

tion like the VA, desired outcomes relate to its mission and strategic objectives, in this case improving the lives of veterans. This version of the map, like the report as a whole, addresses only actions and strategies consistent with current policy and legislation.

It is up to VA leadership, under the direction of the president and Congress, to decide which metrics and targets it will use to assess progress toward its goals, and to assess which changes in organization and use of resources and which strategies and service changes are most likely to lead to improved outcomes.

As the change progresses, more detailed strategy maps can be used to capture the logic of the change, that is, how each action or strategy contributes to specific improvements expected to support fuller recovery and reintegration of returning veterans. At this level of detail, it should be possible to monitor the effects of particular elements of each strategy on intermediate outcomes and, in turn, on improvements in veteran welfare. For the most important relationships, it will be useful to conduct rigorous evaluations employing randomization and other statistical controls for other influences on the result.

2. The VA, Congress, and the president need to provide leadership for institutionalizing the change and achieving a veteran-centered department.

- The secretary of the VA should be held accountable for sustaining a commitment to achieving a veteran-centered department. Examples of actions to demonstrate commitment by the secretary include:

  - creation of joint project teams across the administrations;
  - identification of business leaders to direct the teams;
  - commitment of resources;
  - setting timelines with milestones and goals;
  - clear performance metrics and targets at all levels of the organization; and
  - accountability for goal achievement, including penalties for nonperformance and rewards for progress.

- OMB should require that the VA's budget submission and performance reports document its progress toward achieving its objectives, and
- congressional oversight hearings should be held to examine the department's progress in achieving its objectives designed to accomplish a veteran-centered VA.

3. The secretary should establish a new Office for Veteran-Centered Change Leadership.

The secretary should establish a new senior executive officer, who is a direct report, responsible for coordinating change leadership, supported by a small analytical and monitoring staff. The Office for Veteran-Centered Change would be responsible for advising the secretary on how to implement and sustain an overall strategy and specific changes to transform the VA into a veteran-centered service organization and to ensure timely, appropriate, effective treatment and benefits for those veterans in need. The office would monitor progress and report to the secretary, Congress, and the public on measures of the changes' effectiveness, including improved outcomes. It would advise the VA undersecretaries for health and benefits and the chief information officer on how they should prioritize and coordinate their efforts to ensure these improvements. The head of the office would continuously advise the secretary on how to improve service to veterans based on rigorous evaluation of elements of the change strategy, demonstrating what works and is cost effective.

4. Congress should establish a new permanent, expert, external
advisory board on veteran-centered change and require periodic
reports on the progress in achieving veteran-centered service.

This board would advise the secretary and report to the public and Congress on administrative changes that would support veteran-centered service and improved care and benefits for veterans. The committee should include members with expertise in (1) service delivery, especially those services using the Internet creatively, (2) marketing (how to reach and spark the interest of new veterans, (3) health care delivery (especially those in integrated systems and mental health care systems), and (4) needs of veterans and/or veteran's services organizations (VSOs). This advisory board should have access to VA staff with expertise in veterans benefits and programs.

5. The VA should develop and use new performance metrics to
monitor progress and drive change.

These measures should reflect a balance of perspectives consistent with an overall strategy to improve outcomes for veterans. They also should include direct measures of the extent of recovery and reintegration by returning veterans, consistent with the goals of the joint VA-DOD effort to improve these outcomes.

Specific proposed metrics are included in the illustrative balanced scorecard in Figure 9.2. A scorecard similar to this can be used by senior managers of the change to assess in the short term whether it is on track and whether it is likely to produce long-term outcomes consistent with the aims of the transformation, such as those listed in the strategy map (Figure 9.1).

Such instruments are "balanced" in the sense that they look at the process of change from differing perspectives, including that of an internal manager; of the customer, that is, veteran; of those responsible for promoting organizational learning and employee growth; and of the financial manager. As with the strategy map, it will be the responsibility of VA leadership to determine how best to measure progress and what targets to set for change in a given year, consistent with resource levels and other environmental factors.

6. The VA should link new performance metrics to employee rewards.

Incentives and recognition should be provided to employees at all levels based on excellence in both individual and team performance in achievement of organizational results. These results would include progress on the metrics identified in the balanced scorecard and other measures of improved service appropriate to each program and level of responsibility. Experts on the federal government's merit system principles increasingly recognize that some system processes do not effectively support excellence, flexibility, urgency, and clarity of mission.[9] The VA is conducting a limited pay-for-performance pilot, and its experience may help to inform a broader application of modern merit principles to its system for rating and rewards.

7. The VA should use Web 2.0 technology for internal and external collaboration.

Following the lead of other public sector service-oriented agencies, the VA should pursue a range of initiatives that would support veteran-centered service and would help implement and accelerate the necessary reorientation of the department. Implementation of this recommendation would include the following:

Employee "Idea Factory"

An internal collaborative site, similar to one used by the Transportation Security Administration, should be established where any employee can (following ground rules and with attribution) propose any new practice or policy change (not requiring legislation) that would improve service to returning or all veterans, have these screened and presented for a vote of the collaborating employees, and then reviewed for possible adoption.

Partners Wiki

A platform should be provided for any subgroup or existing network of non-VA service providers and other public or private agencies working on behalf of veterans to use to organize a collaboration regarding a particular problem related to improved service for veterans in a particular region or state or with a particular need. Products would be proposals that could be formally endorsed or informally advanced for consideration by the VA in a fully transparent, open-ended process. Expected results would include a growing number of collaborative networks that could help disparate providers find each other, form constructive partnerships, and solve problems related to veteran service.

Veteran Feedback Site

An interactive site should be built where a veteran could pose a query or post a complaint and receive both an initial automated response and, as needed, personalized follow-up and response or referral. A sampling of veterans would receive follow-up survey questions to assess their satisfaction with the response received and whether any problem identified had been corrected. Analysis of the resulting data would identify weaknesses in the existing services system and support remedial action.

Figure 9.2

Illustrative VA Seamless Transition Balanced Scorecard: Improved Service to Returning War Veterans

Objectives	Initiatives	Measures	FY 2010 Targets
Internal			
Build integrated information technology systems to facilitate service delivery for and information sharing with the veteran.	Accelerate the migration to electronic records.	Percentage of claims with electronic records	XX% of claims with electronic records
	Update the Web-based Veterans on Line Application Process (VONAPP).	Percentage completion against timeline	YY% completed in Y time
	Align future IT application development with OneVA goals.	Percentage of IT business planning documents that explicitly link to OneVA goals	ZZ% of IT business plans linking to OneVA goals
Improve the VA's outreach to veterans.	Develop and employ e-mail communication channels with veterans.	Percentage of inquiries handled through e-mail	XX% of inquiries handled through e-mail
	Add communication channels used in the VA's general information outreach.	Number of new communication channels, including e-mail, Web 2.0, partnering with other agencies (e.g., job fairs)	ZZ new communication channels
	Develop targeted outreach efforts to identified subgroups.	Number of contact lists by characteristics of interest (e.g., female, amputees, rural)	XX contact lists developed for targeted outreach
Form linkages with non-VA partners.	Identify existing public contact opportunities with veterans other agencies engage, and encourage those agencies to share basic information about VA benefits.	Number of outreach MOAs with other agencies (e.g., DoL, SBA) and organizations Number of joint outreach efforts engaged in (e.g., job fairs)	YY MOAs developed with non-VA agencies and organizations ZZ joint outreach efforts the VA participated in

| Identify at-risk veterans and facilitate their entry into the VA's continuum of care. | Assess who, of those identified as at-risk for mental health illness, has not received care, and follow up with that veteran as appropriate. | Number of PDHRA referrals to VA care facilities, including Vet Centers
Percentage of referred patients seeking mental health care from VA facilities or Vet Centers (rate of follow-up) | XX referrals made to VA care facilities
ZZ% of referred patients seeking mental health care from VA facilities |
| | Request that DOD provide an option to the service member to enroll in VA health care as part of the PDHRA program for those service members, including National Guard and Reserve, who anticipate separating from the military. | Percentage of those who opt to auto-enroll in VHA at the time of the PDHRA | XX% of veterans auto-enrolled n VHA at time of PDHRA |

Veteran Outcomes

| Improve access to health and mental health care | Develop a strategy for providing training to state and community providers to increase their capability to effectively treat veterans for combat-related mental illness, including PTSD, depression, and mild TBI | Number of state and community health providers trained on best practices in care for veteran-specific issues | YY non-VA mental health care providers trained by the VA in care for veteran-specific issues |
| | Build upon existing collaborative partnerships currently being used in the Veterans Integrated Service Network (VISN) networks that include aspects of referral and communication and data sharing between the VHA and community and state providers, with priority for those areas underserved by mental health providers. | Number of referrals to VA health care from state and community services
Percentage of injured veterans in need of community-based rehabilitation and support services receiving such services | ZZ increase in referrals to VHA from state and community providers
XX% of veterans in need of support services and care receiving such services |

(continued)

Figure 9.2 *(continued)*

Improve quality of life for veterans by using veteran-centered care management tools to facilitate recovery and reintegration of returning war veterans.	Use a scaled-down version of the Federal Individual Recovery Plan to a broader group of less severely injured veterans, including those with mental health illness, who are receiving case management services. Make full use of applications of the online portal system MyHealtheVet to house the online recovery plan, provide screening tools and educational materials to veterans and family members, and allow tracking and management of a veteran's clinical and nonclinical goals over time by care coordinators.	Proportion of injured or at risk veterans receiving case management services Proportion of wounded OEF/OIF veterans with a recovery and reintegration plan Proportion of veterans and their families using the online web portal for tracking and managing health care Proportion of severely injured veterans who met FIRP short and long-term goals	ZZ% of injured or at-risk veterans receiving case management services XX% of wounded OEF/OIF veterans with a recovery and reintegration plan YY% of veterans and their families using online portal ZZ% of severely injured veterans meeting short and long-term goals Unemployment at or below comparable civilian cohort rate

Learning and Growth

Increase rate of innovative change supporting a veteran-centered approach.	Leverage/expand use of Web 2.0 IT applications.	Use new collaborative sites to identify and vet proposed policies and practices Use Veteran Feedback Interactive Site to monitor and respond to service failures	Collaborative sites established by XX At least YY innovative practice and policy changes adopted ZZ% of veterans using new interactive site report satisfaction with VA follow-up
Continue progress toward developing new PTSD and TBI treatments.	Pursue collaborative studies among research bodies, both governmental and nongovernmental, on PTSD and TBI.	Number of collaborative studies resulting in evidence-based findings for treatment of PTSD and TBI	Reach YY% of milestones set for treatment development

Financial

Manage administrative costs of transitions.	Improve VA and DOD budget allocations to reduce administrative overlap	Average outreach spending for each returning veteran visiting VA facilities	Reduce spending per returning veteran to no more than ZZ% of total cost

Ensure prompt payment of fee-basis providers.	Ensure timeliness standards are met for payment of contract providers.	Average days from invoice to full payment	Reduce average from XX to YY days

PTSD, post-traumatic stress disorder; TBI, traumatic brain injury; OEF, Operation Enduring Freedom (Afghanistan); OIF, Operation Iraqi Freedom (Iraq)

8. The VA should promote continuous learning that is research driven and evidence based.

As previously noted, a model for this exists in the VHA's Quality Enhancement Research Initiative (QUERI) process[10] and performance metrics, and in its Performance Measurement Development and Life Cycle process.[11] Using a similar research and testing approach, the department's strategy for improving services to returning veterans should be modified as new evidence becomes available on more cost-effective ways to achieve better outcomes for veterans. As the organization learns from systematic evaluation of what works and is cost effective, the more detailed versions of a strategy map like that shown in Figure 9.1, used to model and guide the change, should be revised to reflect this learning.

At all times, attention must remain on what is of practical benefit to veterans by aiding their full recovery and reintegration.

Notes

This chapter was drawn from National Academy of Public Administration (NAPA), *After Yellow Ribbons: Providing Veteran-Centered Services* (Washington, DC: NAPA, October 2008). The academy panel conducting this study was chaired by William G. Hamm, managing director of LECG. Other panel members included Virginia T. Betts, commissioner, Tennessee Department of Mental Health and Developmental Disabilities; Dennis M. Duffy, former acting assistant secretary for policy, planning, and preparedness, Department of Veterans Affairs; Frank A. Fairbanks, city manager, Phoenix, Arizona; Thomas L. Garthwaite, executive vice president and chief medical officer, Catholic Health East, Newtown Square, Pennsylvania; Donald F. Kettl, professor of political science, Stanley Sheen Endowed Term Chair in Social Sciences, director, Fels Center of Government, University of Pennsylvania; Bernard D. Rostker, senior fellow, the RAND Corporation; and Daniel L. Skoler, consultant and contract adjudicator. NAPA staff assisting with this report were Rick Cinqueqrana, F. Stevens Redburn, Sherrie Russ, Leslie Overmyer-Day, Betsy Kidder, Guy McMichael, Caroline Epley, Ednilson Quintanilla, and Martha S. Ditmeyer.

1. Collaboration with the Department of Defense is addressed in the report NAPA, *After Yellow Ribbons* (Washington, DC: NAPA, 2008).

2. Compare, for example, L. McQueen, B.S. Mittman, and J.G. Demakis, "Overview of the Veterans Health Administration (VHA) Quality Enhancement Research Initiative (QUERI)," *Journal of the American Medical Association* 11, no. 5 (September–October 2004): 339–343.

3. Phillip Longman, *Best Care Anywhere: Why VA Health Care Is Better Than Yours* (Sausalito, CA: PoliPoint Press, 2007).

4. K. Kizer, Presentation to the Institute of Medicine Roundtable on Evidence-Based Medicine (Washington, DC: National Academies of Science, April 29, 2008).

5. G. Young. *Transforming Government: The Revitalization of the Veterans Health Administration,* the 2000 Presidential Transition Series (Washington, DC: PricewaterhouseCoopers Endowment for the Business of Government, 2000), p. 25.

6. The SOC was considering, as of July 2008, whether to adopt a "balanced scorecard" approach to guide its future efforts. As noted in the recommendations at the end of this chapter, a joint DOD-VA scorecard on transition management would be useful if it captured the vision and performance metrics needed to guide the DOD-VA partnership.

7. This section is adapted from J.P. Kotter, *The Heart of Change* (Cambridge, MA: Harvard Business School Press, 2002).

8. Robert S. Kaplan and David P. Norton, *Strategy Maps: Converting Intangible Assets into Tangible Outcomes* (Cambridge, MA: Harvard Business School Press, 2004).

9. The panel is grateful to Dr. Nancy Kingsbury, managing director for applied research and methods at the Government Accountability Office, for sharing a working document on modern merit principles developed by a team at the Government Accountability Office that she led.

10. McQueen, Mittman, and Demakis, "Overview."

11. Compare the *FY 2008 VHA Executive Career Field Performance Plan—Final,* updated November 16, 2007. Washington, DC: Veteran's Health Administration.

10

Evidence-Informed Public Management and Evidence Development at the Government Accountability Office

Nancy J. Kingsbury, Nancy Donovan, Judy A. Droitcour, and Stephanie L. Shipman

Evidence-based management (EBMgt) and evidence-based policy (EBP) have been portrayed as basing policy decisions and the selection of organizational strategies on science and rigorous evidence rather than on anecdote and unsubstantiated belief.[1] But managers and policy makers alike may lack evidence that is good enough or relevant to decisions affecting organizational or government goals. The extent or quality of existing evidence concerns the size and significance of problems, data on program outcomes, and evaluations of program effectiveness and impact. It is not always possible, for example, for managers to use a strict evidence-informed approach to

- identify new obstacles to a goal or new ways to prioritize long-standing problems,
- choose new goal-oriented programs or strategies that actually work, or
- determine whether a program's effectiveness is grounds for its continuation.

New concerns about data may surface as problems change and new opportunities arise. To support managerial decisions in the public sector, evidence development must be dynamic and ongoing.

The GAO has over time engaged in many evaluation, performance measurement, and auditing efforts relevant to an evidence-informed approach.[2] Here we focus primarily on the importance of evidence development and illustrate key approaches to it, such as

- fostering the clarification of research questions and needs,
- developing innovative data-collection techniques and new evaluation strategies, and
- encouraging capacity building and disseminating information on best practices for evaluation and evidence development.

Approaches to evidence development such as these may become especially relevant as the pace of change accelerates in the twenty-first century, presenting new problems, new opportunities, and a changing environment. Because evidence development may struggle to keep pace with change, an evidence-informed approach might be best conceptualized as management's multipronged effort to

- recognize uncertainty and develop appropriate decision rules or criteria (considering, for example, risk-management principles as well as what evidence exists);
- encourage or foster evidence development as an ongoing and changing effort within the organization; and
- network and communicate with others to encourage a greater appreciation of changing problems, potential solutions, and evidence issues and to exchange information in a broader, evidence-informed approach.[3]

The Limitations of Available Evidence

Available evidence may be limited, whether it be data on program outcomes, information on the size or significance of a problem or opportunity, or program evaluations—especially evaluations attempting to estimate an intervention's impact.

Acquiring valid and reliable measures of program outcomes is still a struggle for many federal agencies almost a decade after the Government Performance and Results Act first required annual reporting on federal program performance (see also Chapter 8).[4] Tracking program outcomes can be difficult in the intergovernmental arena, because whether and how federal, state, and local governments collect data can vary. In a classic, flexible, state grant program, for example, state and local grant recipients control the use of federal financial assistance, and federal agencies are not always able to require them to collect and report outcome or performance data. Even when a federal agency is permitted to require reports on services provided, service providers may gather data in different ways in different states or localities.[5] Creating a picture of national progress across jurisdictions can be formidable.[6]

As for information on the size or significance of a problem or opportunity, available evidence on new or fast-developing problems and opportunities is key. Information may be limited to early signals of a problem's potential significance. Data that do exist may not adequately describe the emerging reality. Such limitations may become increasingly important with the fast pace of twenty-first-century technological change, as agencies struggle to keep pace. (One example is the fast-changing highway safety problem emerging from driver cell phone use, driver texting, and driver use of other features of portable devices.[7]) The foresight literature highlights the need to address problems as they emerge, before they become entrenched and difficult to reverse (as illustrated in Figure 10.1).

Literature on organizational "clockspeed" suggests that because government agencies may have slower clockspeeds than other industries, data collection to

Figure 10.1 **What Falling Behind a Worsening Problem Could Mean If Not Effectively Countered by Early Action**

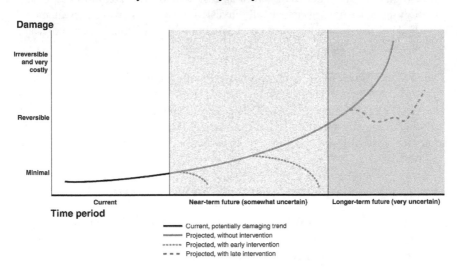

Source: GAO, *Highway Safety: Foresight Issues Challenge DOT's Efforts to Assess and Respond to New Technology-Based Trends*, GAO-09-56 (October 2008); adapted from David W. Rejeski, "S&T Challenges in the 21st Century: Strategy and Tempo," in *AAAS Science and Technology Policy Yearbook 2002*, ed. Albert H. Teich et al. (2008).

support management or policy may lag behind fast-developing private sector developments.[8] But even long-term, long-recognized problems are not always well studied, and evidence on them may be lacking, especially if they are inherently difficult to study. For example, obtaining reliable information on the size of a problem such as illegal immigration is difficult for at least two reasons: (1) some illegal immigrants may intentionally avoid census takers and researchers, and (2) direct questions about immigration status may be too sensitive to ask (or if asked, may not be answered correctly).

Finally, rigorous program evaluations are often lacking, especially rigorous evaluations of program effectiveness and impact. The reasons for this deficit include the following:

- Impact evaluations may be difficult when a program is designed to influence systems separate from the government—for example, credit and labor markets, health care services, and food production. The federal government neither controls these systems nor has strong oversight of them. It is especially difficult, therefore, to isolate the effects of federal programs on outcomes as distinct from these other influences. Moreover, because of the changing societal contexts, older studies of program effectiveness still in use may no longer apply, even if the programs themselves have not changed.[9]

- In addition, as became clear through the Office of Management and Budget Program Assessment Rating Tool assessments of available evaluation data, few agencies have systematically invested in rigorous program evaluation.[10] Federal program evaluation has sometimes been disjointed, episodic, and underresourced.[11]

The GAO's Efforts to Advance Evidence Development

The GAO's efforts to advance evidence development at the federal level have included clarifying question definition, developing innovative techniques and strategies, fostering the development of evaluation capacity, and disseminating best practices.

Framing the Question: Logic Models and Conceptual Frameworks

The GAO has pointed to the importance of articulating questions that need to be answered, when they need to be answered, and with what precision.[12] Other tools organize information to answer questions program managers and policy makers pose. Logic models and conceptual frameworks can help (see also Chapter 9). Listing management and policy questions that flow from a program's logic model can specify how the program's strategy might achieve the desired results and depict features of the environment that can support or hinder achieving them.

Conceptual frameworks can make existing levels of evidence in relation to governance options transparent and may highlight needs for further evidence. Figure 10.2 illustrates a GAO framework developed to communicate evidence and governance issues relevant to new technologies affecting highway safety. This framework guided the GAO in communicating governance options taken and evidence available on technological developments in crash avoidance, driver cell phone use, and other potentially distracting technologies for drivers.

Developing Innovative Techniques and Strategies

The new techniques and strategies facilitating evidence development range from a grouped-answers approach for collecting sensitive data to synthesizing existing evidence, whether retrospectively or prospectively.

The Grouped-Answers Approach to Sensitive Data Collection

Estimating a problem's scope can yield important evidence for a manager, whether in deciding to prioritize a problem (given competing problems and limited resources) or in planning how to address it. However, this can be challenging, as when the problem is sensitive or involves a hidden population, such as the illegal immigrant population. In such instances, quantitative information can be limited. Surveys

Figure 10.2 **Framework for Identifying Evidence and Governance Options Relevant to New Technologies for Highway Safety**

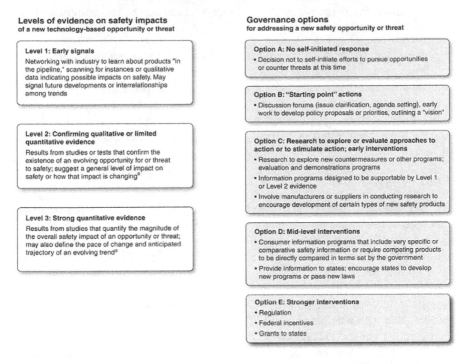

Levels of evidence on safety impacts
of a new technology-based opportunity or threat

Level 1: Early signals
Networking with industry to learn about products "in the pipeline," scanning for instances or qualitative data indicating possible impacts on safety. May signal future developments or interrelationships among trends

Level 2: Confirming qualitative or limited quantitative evidence
Results from studies or tests that confirm the existence of an evolving opportunity for or threat to safety; suggest a general level of impact on safety or how that impact is changing[a]

Level 3: Strong quantitative evidence
Results from studies that quantify the magnitude of the overall safety impact of an opportunity or threat; may also define the pace of change and anticipated trajectory of an evolving trend[a]

Governance options
for addressing a new safety opportunity or threat

Option A: No self-initiated response
• Decision not to self-initiate efforts to pursue opportunities or counter threats at this time

Option B: "Starting point" actions
• Discussion forums (issue clarification, agenda setting), early work to develop policy proposals or priorities, outlining a "vision"

Option C: Research to explore or evaluate approaches to action or to stimulate action; early interventions
• Research to explore new countermeasures or other programs; evaluation and demonstrations programs
• Information programs designed to be supportable by Level 1 or Level 2 evidence
• Involve manufacturers or suppliers in conducting research to encourage development of certain types of new safety products

Option D: Mid-level interventions
• Consumer information programs that include very specific or comparative safety information or require competing products to be directly compared in terms set by the government
• Provide information to states; encourage states to develop new programs or pass new laws

Option E: Stronger interventions
• Regulation
• Federal incentives
• Grants to states

Source: GAO, *Highway Safety: Foresight Issues Challenge DOT's Efforts to Assess and Respond to New Technology-Based Trends*, GAO-09-56 (October 2008).

may include interviews with many foreign-born persons, for example, but questions typically do not ask about immigration status because of sensitivity issues. To overcome such obstacles, the GAO's methodologists created grouped-answers approaches. The two-card method, for example, groups answers to an immigration question in boxes shown on a flash card in a personal interview (Figure 10.3). Specifically, this method shows each foreign-born respondent a flash card with answers grouped in three boxes (A, B, and C) and then

- asks the respondent to just pick the box that contains his or her current legal status (along with other statuses) while
- avoiding questions about whether any respondent is unauthorized, thus protecting privacy.

Estimating illegal immigrant status for the population, or major categories within it—male/female or employed/unemployed—is possible because the grouped-answers approach (two-card version)

- divides respondents into two subsamples,
- shows subsamples 1 and 2 slightly different cards (as in Figure 10.3), and
- compares the percentages of people who picked key boxes, as indicated by the arrow in Figure 10.3.

An estimate of the percentage with illegal status in the population represented by those surveyed is obtained by calculating the difference between the percentage of subsample 1 respondents picking Box B, and the percentage of subsample 2 respondents picking Box A.

The degree to which foreign-born respondents accept the grouped-answers approach has been tested in federally funded private sector personal interview surveys.[13]

Cross-Design Synthesis

Existing data on an intervention's effectiveness may be limited, even when rigorous randomized trials have been conducted. One reason is that existing trials may be limited to special populations or to interventions performed by premier providers who may not represent the full community of practitioners.[14] GAO methodologists developed the cross-design synthesis to help public managers in health care deal with this problem. This evaluates what works outside a research setting—that is, when an intervention is applied to a broader range of patients, students, or clients or applied by a broader range of providers and practitioners than have participated in controlled studies. This method draws together studies such as (1) randomized controlled trials, which provide tightly controlled comparisons, and (2) analyses of representative databases, whose results are more generalizable. This assessment of varied study strengths and weaknesseses in existing studies is then combined with the design of a framework for synthesizing results across designs.[15]

Prospective Evaluation Synthesis and Foresight Frameworks

Emerging problems and new opportunities for addressing them can represent a special evidence-development challenge. The GAO's methodologists developed the prospective evaluation synthesis to systematically marshal the best possible information on likely outcomes of proposed programs or legislation and adequacy of proposed regulations.[16] The combination of techniques this approach uses includes analysis of alternative proposals and projections to answer prospective questions.

Additionally, the GAO recently devised a foresight-evidence framework for assessing and guiding the choice of research methods for evaluating emerging, fast-changing problems, opportunities, or interventions. Assessment criteria include: (1) technical adequacy, (2) timeliness, and (3) ability to measure change over time—potentially in frequently repeated applications (requiring reasonable cost).[17] Research depicting how drivers are using portable electronic devices, such as cell phones, in 2010 may present useful results, but—if such devices continue

Figure 10.3   **Grouped-Answers Approach: Legal Status Cards 1 and 2, Compared**

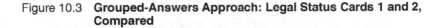

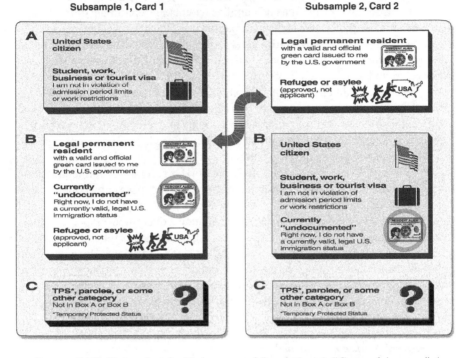

Source: GAO, *Estimating the Undocumented Population: A "Grouped Answers" Approach to Surveying Foreign-Born Respondents,* GAO-06-775 (September 2006).

Note: The actual size of each card is eight and a half inches by eleven inches.

to evolve rapidly and drivers use them in new ways that can potentially worsen highway safety—a snapshot for one point in time (2010) would not remain timely or relevant for very long. In such situations, repeated studies are needed. This can be challenging, given limited resources—especially in cases in which, as in highway safety, large or lengthy studies are needed to provide real-world data about rates of serious or fatal crashes (because such crashes are infrequent). Still, new technology may facilitate the ability to field meaningful, repeated, or ongoing studies of highway safety.[18]

Efforts at Capacity Building and Disseminating Best Practices

Developing Evaluation Capacity in a Federal Agency

In 2003, the GAO identified four elements of evaluation capacity in five federal agencies. They had demonstrated evaluation capacity early in the implementation of performance reporting under the Government Performance and Results Act (GPRA) by establishing a culture committed to self-examination, data quality, analytic expertise, and collaborative partnerships.[19] Importantly, the five agencies (the Administration for Children and Families within the Department of Health and Human Services, the Coast Guard, the Department of Housing and Human Development, the National Highway Traffic Safety Administration within the Department of Transportation, and the National Science Foundation) used diverse strategies to develop and improve their ability to evaluate their programs' results. Some developed a commitment to learning from evaluation in response to demands for accountability, others in order to support policy debates. Some agencies improved their administrative systems to improve data quality and reliability; others turned to specialized data collection to obtain the data they needed. All five contracted with experts for specialized analyses to complement the relevant subject matter.

What is key is that, in an increasingly networked federal government, all five agencies leveraged their own evaluation resources and expertise by collaborating with or actively educating and soliciting the support of their program partners and stakeholders. The networked aspect of the federal government is perhaps most obvious in state grant programs, where achieving federal goals relies on the policy choices and management expertise of state and local officials. However, even relatively autonomous agencies must form collaborative partnerships to achieve their goals; for example, the Coast Guard shares information and decision making through port security committees made up of federal, state, and local agencies and private shipping companies.

The Federal Evaluators Network

Along these lines, the GAO has supported the development of the Federal Evaluators network, an informal association of three hundred evaluation officials in the legislative and executive branches, organized in 1999 to share information and concerns about evaluation methodology, policy, and practice.[20] The group meets a few times annually. Its closed Listserv, FEDEVAL, promotes discussion of program and policy evaluation and related issues. In addition to sharing evaluation methods and policy resources, the group advises OMB examiners on federal evaluation policies.

Toward a Broader View of Evidence-Informed Management

Because public sector decisions are based on more than evidence, and because existing evidence may be weak or limited, management's using evidence effectively may require broadening what might be called a strict evidence-based perspective. That is, an effective, evidence-informed approach might broaden the range of evidence beyond what has been considered highest-quality evidence. It might include, for example, early signals of emerging problems and a trend's likely trajectory; it might expand decision-making criteria beyond the evidentiary, potentially including risk-management criteria or a foresight approach.[21] Additionally, a manager pursuing an effective and realistic evidence-informed approach could find it helpful, as needed, to

- encourage the identification or development of additional or improved evidence on program outcomes, the size or significance of key problems and opportunities, and the effectiveness of programs and strategies, and
- communicate within the organization and, as appropriate, outside it about problems and opportunities, ongoing decisions and options, existing evidence (and its quality), and what is being done to obtain further evidence.

The three broad activities summarized in Figure 10.4—making decisions, developing evidence, and networking and communicating—may be crucial if an evidence-informed approach is to be effective and realistic. The three activities are likely to be interrelated and to support one other.

The GAO has devoted various efforts to improving federal practice and data through one or more of the activities listed in Figure 10.4. For example, all three activities were highlighted in a recent GAO report on new opportunities and challenges in highway safety that discussed issues such as (1) the possible use of risk-management approaches in making decisions when evidence is limited and (2) the need for federal agencies to communicate with others about emerging problems even before definitive evidence or specific strategies are developed for addressing an emerging problem.[22] The report highlighted the need to increase agency communications to congressional policy makers with respect to emerging, fast-developing trends—even when evidence on such trends is somewhat limited. This is partly because agency-congressional communications can sometimes result in new options that might not otherwise be considered. Expanding communications or networks to include new industries and other agencies may be an important source of data when new trends cross the boundaries of an agency's traditional mission or focus. (For example, in the case of highway safety, distracted driving was known to be associated with increasing driver use of portable electronic devices, but as of 2008, the National Highway Traffic Safety Administration had not expanded its networking to emphasize the cellular communication industry.)

Conclusions

GPRA has been instrumental in prompting agencies to develop their ability to report on program outcomes and effectiveness. However, the reality of fast-paced change in the twenty-first century, the complexity of factors influencing program outcomes, the difficulty of studying sensitive issues, and the issue of underresourced evaluation programs all suggest that managers may continue to face a lack of good-quality, currently relevant evidence on both (1) problem size (including emerging and long-term problems) and (2) program effectiveness (including those that are

Figure 10.4   **Three Broad Interrelated Activities: An Evidence-Informed Approach**

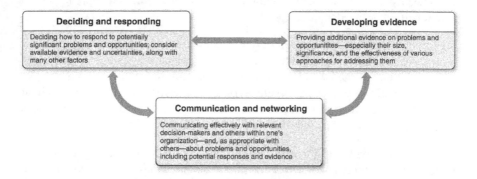

Source: Adapted from GAO, *Highway Safety: Foresight Issues Challenge DOT's Efforts to Assess and Respond to New Technology-Based Trends*, GAO-09-56 (October 2008).

newly proposed as well as, in some cases, long-established programs). To accelerate the development of evidence-informed management, further discussion within the public administration community may be needed to

- highlight the need for evidence development, the distinctive ways it can serve management and policy, and the potential for approaches (1) using logic models and conceptual frameworks to articulate questions about a problem; (2) developing, testing, or using new tools for difficult-to-study issues; and (3) working to enhance evaluation capacity within organizations; and
- further define or conceptualize evidence-informed management to include guides to functioning in this mode even when desired evidence is lacking— including, for example, managers' placing a greater emphasis on risk management, networked governance, and communicating within and outside their organizations about problems and programs for which evidence is limited.

Notes

1. The views expressed here do not necessarily reflect the position of the Government Accountability Office.

2. These efforts include publications such as the GAO's *Performance Measurement and Evaluation: Definitions and Relationships,* GAO-05–739SP (May 2005); *Managing for Results: Agencies' Annual Performance Plans Can Help Address Strategic Planning Challenges,* GGD-98–44 (January 30, 1998); and *GAO Cost Estimating and Assessment Guide: Best Practices for Developing and Managing Capital Program Costs,* GAO-09–3SP (March 2, 2009).

3. Donald F. Kettl, *The Next Government of the United States: Challenges for Performance in the 21st Century,* Transitions of Organizations Series (Washington, DC: IBM Center for the Business of Government, December 2005).

4. GAO, *Results-Oriented Culture: Implementation Steps to Assist Mergers and Organizational Transformation,* GAO-03–689 (2003), Washington, DC: GAO.

5. GAO, *Grant Programs: Design Features Shape Flexibility, Accountability, and Performance Information,* GAO/GGD-98–137 (1998), Washington, DC: GAO.

6. GAO, *Grant Programs: Design Features,* GAO/GGD-98–137 (1998). Washington, DC: GAO See also GAO, *Improving the Flow of Program Information to the Congress,* GAO/PEMD-95–1 (1995), Washington, DC: GAO.

7. GAO, *Highway Safety: Foresight Issues Challenge DOT's Efforts to Assess and Respond to New Technology-Based Trends,* GAO-09–56 (2008), Washington, DC: GAO.

8. David Rejeski, "S&T Challenges in the 21st Century: Strategy and Tempo," in *AAAS Science and Technology Policy Yearbook 2003,* ed. Albert H. Teich et al., pp. 47–57 (Washington, DC: American Association for the Advancement of Science, 2003). The concept of organizational clockspeed was put forward in Charles H. Fine, *Clockspeed: Winning Industry Control in the Age of Temporary Advantage* (Cambridge, MA: Perseus Books, 1998). In addition to these challenges, other issues in producing rigorous analysis for decision making are discussed in Carolyn J. Heinrich, "Evidence-Based Policy and Performance Management," *American Review of Public Administration* 37, no. 3 (2007): 255–277.

9. For example, the relevance of study findings for the Perry Preschool Project conducted in the 1960s to current preschool programs has been questioned because preschool programs are more available today. Thus, we would not expect to see effects as large today as when the study compared project participants to children who were not attending preschool at all.

10. See "Increased Emphasis on Program Evaluation," OMB Memo M-10–01, Washington, DC, October 7, 2009; and American Evaluation Association, Evaluation Policy Task Force, *EPTF Evaluation Roadmap for a More Effective Government* (Fairhaven, MA: American Evaluation Association February 2009), www.eval.org/.

11. Ibid.

12. GAO, *Improving the Flow of Program Information,* GAO/PEMD-95–1 (1995), Washington, DC: GAO.

13. GAO, *Estimating the Undocumented Population: A "Grouped Answers" Approach to Surveying Foreign-Born Respondents,* GAO-06–775 (2006), Washington, DC: GAO.

14. GAO, *Cross-Design Synthesis: A New Strategy for Medical Effectiveness Research,* GAO/PEMD-92–18 (1992), Washington, DC: GAO.

15. GAO, *Cross-Design Synthesis,* GAO/PEMD-92–18 (1992), Washington, DC: GAO and GAO, *Breast Conservation versus Mastectomy: Patient Survival in Day-to-Day Medical Practice and in Randomized Studies,* GAO/PEMD-95–9, Washington, DC: GAO.

16. GAO, *Prospective Evaluation Methods: The Prospective Evaluation Synthesis,* GAO-PEMD 10.1.10 (1990), Washington, DC: GAO.

17. GAO, *Highway Safety: Foresight Issues,* GAO-09–56 (2008), Washington, DC: GAO.

18. Ibid.

19. GAO, *Program Evaluation: An Evaluation Culture and Collaborative Partnerships Help Build Agency Capacity,* GAO-03–454 (2003), Washington, DC: GAO.

20. For more information, see www.fedeval.net/about.htm.

21. One version of such an approach is illustrated by the "precautionary principle" in Europe, which concerns acting "to reduce potential hazards before there is strong proof of harm, taking into account the likely costs and benefits of action and inaction. The principle is applied in situations of potentially serious or irreversible threats to health or the environment." Poul Harremoes et al., *Late Lessons from Early Warnings: The Precautionary Principle 1896–2000* (Luxembourg: Office for Official Publications of the European Communities, 2001), p. 13.

22. GAO, *Highway Safety: Foresight Issues,* GAO-09–56 (2008), Washington, DC: GAO.

Part III

Applications and Research

11

Managerial Capacity and Performance

An Evidence-Based Analysis

Kenneth J. Meier and Laurence J. O'Toole, Jr.

In the 1960s Dwight Waldo urged public administration to become a profession similar to medicine rather than an academic discipline like biology or chemistry (Waldo 1968, p. 10). Professions are pragmatic—they take knowledge developed elsewhere and apply it to real-world problems; in this sense, public administration has become a profession. In all realms of professional practice, however, problems change, rules of thumb become outdated, and practitioners can become estranged from academics. The evidence-based movement in medicine seeks to refocus the practice of medicine on its scientific basis and systematically determine if existing standards of practice are effective. Over the past ten years, we have used the evidence-based movement in medicine as our guide to do systematic research on what works in public management and what does not.

Our version of EBMgt relies on the use of a grounded theory of management that generates precise predictions about what managerial techniques should affect organizational performance. It then takes advantage of large N social science methods to systematically evaluate some of the prevailing nostrums of public management. Some of these are likely to have validity, while others clearly do not. Our work has investigated a variety of concepts central to public management that should bear on public program performance, including managing in the organization's networked environment (Meier and O'Toole 2001), human resources management (O'Toole and Meier 2009a), the quality of public management (Meier and O'Toole 2002), the role of personnel and managerial stability (O'Toole and Meier 2003), organizational contracting (O'Toole and Meier 2004), and organizational buffering (Meier and O'Toole 2008a, 2008b).

This essay brings together our work on one such concept—*managerial capacity* (see also Chapter 10). We emphasize this theme for two reasons. First, management capacity is the sine qua non of EBMgt. Any organization willing to systematically examine its processes with the objective of improving its performance (and validating the efficacy of managerial actions) must have the analytical capacity to do so. Managers whose days are fully booked with operations or crises cannot be expected to take the time to engage in the systematic analysis required by EBMgt.

Second, creating management capacity requires that greater investments be made in the organization's management cadre, including the size of that cadre. This basic principle of investing in rather than pruning management runs counter to what we see as the predominant orientation resulting from the new public management and other "reforms" (Meier and O'Toole 2009b). Lean organizations that minimize administrative overhead are in vogue; *bureaucracy* retains its negative connotations. Such prescriptions are essentially advocated on faith or catalyzed by anecdotal reports without systematic evidence that such managerially slimmed-down organizations actually improve the performance of government.[1] These arguments, we think, are ripe for the application of EBMgt.

Managerial capacity is an element in our broader theory relating public management to public program performance. Essentially, we see different managerial functions as having different, and typically positive, contributions to performance. External management, or management's interacting with the interdependent environment, can play important roles in buffering the organization from negative environmental influences, tapping resources and opportunities for the organization from the environment, or both. Internal management can provide additional help in generating outcomes. The extent of managerial effort matters, we have hypothesized, as does the quality of management itself.[2] We treat managerial capacity, as the next section explains more carefully, as the managerial talent and effort that *could be* mobilized in an organization when needed.

Defining Managerial Capacity

Management capacity has attracted interest from public management researchers and practitioners, and efforts have been made to develop data on the relative capacity of different governmental agencies and different units of government (Ingraham, Joyce, and Donahue 2003). But these data have not thus far been tied clearly to information about program outcomes, and that tie must necessarily be developed if we are to implement fully EBMgt. This lacuna points to the basic dilemma of linking capacity to performance—where the best capacity measures have been developed (U.S. states and U.S. federal executive departments), there are few if any performance indicators that are comparable across organizations. Some might point to the national government's Program Assessment Rating Tool scores for federal agencies as a possible source of such data (see also Chapter 8). Unfortunately, there is no publicly available information on just how the scores are determined by the Office of Management and Budget's examiners; nor is there any assurance that different examiners are applying the same standards and criteria to different programs. At best only certain aspects of the Program Assessment Rating Tool could be plausibly associated with outputs or outcomes, and there is some evidence that the scores reflect partisan concerns (Gilmour and Lewis 2006).

Stepping back from these well-developed indicators, we believe there is reason to think that more generic measures of management capacity might be effective.

Protecting public organizations and programs from disruption is clearly a core managerial function (for a classic depiction, see Thompson 1967), despite the emphasis in recent literature on the proactive and entrepreneurial aspects of public management. Protection and defense are important, even if currently underemphasized, aspects of management, and evidence has been offered on behalf of the role of these elements in contributing to performance. Studies of strategic management explore a "defender" approach to dealing with the organizational environment (Miles and Snow 1978), and defenders can outperform other strategic stances in some settings (Meier et al. 2009). Personnel stability, including managerial stability, also contributes to outcomes (O'Toole and Meier 2003). Most significantly for present purposes, subtle managerial efforts internally can have impacts in protecting the core organizational tasks from performance disruptions (Meier and O'Toole 2009a). The idea here is akin to the notion of "disturbance handler," as characterized by Mintzberg (1972). Even if environmental shocks enter the organization and threaten to wreak havoc, managers are far from impotent; they can reallocate staff and resources toward the highest-priority tasks, with the organization thereby continuing to deliver results with minimal disruption, at least for a while and at least within some limits.

Management capacity can mean different things (for a recent review of the literature on capacity, including the complex ways that the concept has been used, see Gazley and Christensen 2007). Ingraham, Joyce, and Donahue (2003) observe that the notion of "capacity" has been defined in varied ways (see also Malysa 1996) but is typically considered a concept with multiple dimensions (p. 15). As they indicate, "by *capacity*, we mean government's *intrinsic ability* to marshal, develop, direct, and control its financial, human, physical, and information resources" (p. 15; emphasis added in the latter instance). Ingraham, Joyce, and Donahue then go on to stipulate four "key levers" that, they argue, drive or feed into capacity. We build from their general definition but treat the "levers" aspect more abstractly.

In particular, these researchers reference governments' "intrinsic ability" to get things done, and this framing of the concept draws one's attention not to actual operations but to "potential" or "reserve" available for handling the varied tasks of management. Management capacity, therefore, is not management effort or practice but rather what *could be* mobilized if needed. An analogy drawn from the field of physics comes from the distinction between kinetic and potential energy, the former constituting energy in operation or execution, the latter the possible energy available in a system.

How might one assess the management capacity of an administrative system? The answer is not obvious, since capacity cannot be directly and operationally observed—it constitutes a potential for action rather than action in practice. Capacity, further, probably has multiple dimensions, and there is no real evidence regarding which aspects might be most important and under which circumstances. Accordingly, we work from a general notion that reaches to potential that could be mobilized in varied ways. The relative size of the administrative corps of a system should tell us something of the capacity of that system, but some of the administrative personnel have regular line responsibilities and are not easily mobilized or deployed to deal in nonroutine ways with challenges to the organization. Much of our empirical research focuses on school districts, and so in it we consider the relative size of a district's central office staff as a rough measure of management capacity in the organization. Central staff have regular responsibilities, but in the typical educational system the central office is the locus for financial planning, human resources analysis, data gathering, and system leadership. Central administrators would be more likely to have organization-wide views and also be less likely to be solidly booked with running day-to-day operations. These perspectives and related functions are those that, we could expect, are crucial for maximizing the operational capacity of the system in times of stress (see Yukl 2006, pp. 364ff.).[3] Accordingly, we consider whether this measure of managerial capacity of school districts can contribute to performance under a variety of situations.[4] We should note that the organizations studied are relatively lean in terms of managerial capacity. The average district from 1995 to 2002 had only 1.89 percent of total employees allocated to central office administration (standard deviation of 1.42 percent). Ninety percent of all school districts had between 0.71 percent and 3.54 percent central administrators.

Central office staff are obviously not deadweight in such administrative systems. Under normal circumstances, they are occupied with a variety of tasks, including manifold analytical functions as well as efforts to diagnose and address chronic problems facing the organizational system, whether legal, political, or production related. One example of this last-mentioned type of chronic challenge, for the case of school districts, would be efforts to devise programs to improve student attendance. Doing so would likely boost performance on other indicia over the longer term. In a sense, however, our conceptualization of management capacity considers central staff as representing a kind of (partial) slack in the managerial resources available for near-term production, and thus as a potential for action that may not be fully realized except under relatively unusual circumstances—when tasks can be reassigned and central staff can directly address immediate performance-related needs. Indeed, the central office (headquarters) is also the location where one might expect some slack in human resources, such as it is, to be stockpiled—if there is any conscious effort to build such slack into the system. The logic of storing slack in administrative capacity is based on the notion of flexibility, innovation, and relative payoffs. Adding a single person to a line production position is likely to increase production by a marginal amount, but that person is unlikely to be usable for other functions should the need arise. Similarly, adding a person as a line administrator could well improve day-to-day responsiveness, but these skills would not necessarily be transferable in times of emergency. Storing slack within the central office, however, provides the greatest flexibility because one can move a central manager from seeking grants one week to assessing the profitability of food services the next week to an emergency fill-in for a line manager the next. Theoretically, organizational slack of this sort is best stored at the managerial levels where it translates into increased management capacity.

Earlier research and theorizing on slack can help to clarify this notion. Thompson (1967) and Galbraith (1973; see also Pfeffer and Salancik 1978) have argued that slack can serve as a buffer to help organizations absorb and survive the effects of shocks. This notion of slack is conceptualized as resources that can, if needed, be mobilized as inputs for the technical core during turbulent times. It is likely infeasible to assign most central office personnel to line production in the technical core, at least on short notice. But a complementary function can be performed by human resources available centrally. Cyert and March (1963) point out that slack can also be seen as resources available on behalf of innovation (see also Doig and Hargrove 1990, p. 3). Organizations with slack are likely to be more innovative— particularly so when the slack is managerial. Innovative organizations are more likely to sustain their level of performance when shocks occur. Organizational slack, therefore, including managerial slack, should be positively associated with performance in organizations experiencing shocks.

The Empirical Studies

We have explored the impact of managerial capacity in four studies related to the performance of Texas school districts, along with one study from a very different empirical context that serves as corroboration for those focused on Texas. Organizations delivering public education have been underresearched by public administration scholars (Raffel 2007) but constitute an important set of empirical settings. Indeed, they are the most common public organizations in the United States. Nevertheless, they have some distinct characteristics. School districts are highly professionalized, with elaborate certification processes for various occupations. The organizations themselves are decentralized, with substantial discretion vested at the street (classroom) level. Despite this common structure, districts themselves are highly diverse. They range from urban to rural, rich to poor, and homogeneous to heterogeneous, as one would expect, given that Texas contains 8 percent of all school districts in the United States.

We approach our examination of managerial capacity with different sorts of investigations. Of the four school-district studies referenced in this chapter, the first examined budget cuts. In a preliminary study of budget reductions that exceed 10 percent or more of the total budget, we found that performance impacts were relatively small in the first and second years. Perhaps, we thought, the ability to do this was related to management capacity. The second study pursued the notion of crisis management by examining how school districts coped with the problems created by two hurricanes striking the region in 2005. The third study tied capacity to our series of studies on managerial networking—top managers' interactions with a variety of external parties—to determine if capacity was a precursor for effective networking efforts. The fourth school-district study moved to a more abstract level to examine the process of organizational buffering and its effect on various dimensions of performance. We explain each analysis and then offer some general conclusions. A final investigation conducted with local governments in England shows that the sorts of performance effects that managerial capacity displayed in the other studies also appear elsewhere.

Capacity and Budget Crises

The first study, in which we explored the performance-related effects of managerial capacity, dealt with a moderately predictable crisis, a budget cut (O'Toole and Meier 2009b). Using the criterion that a budget reduction of 10 percent or more is significant enough to create an organizational crisis, we examined how Texas school districts over an eight-year period responded to the cuts. We estimated the size of the budget cut based on the historical trend of the organization (that is, a budget equal to last year's in an organization growing at the rate of 10 percent per year was considered a budget cut). The first performance indicator examined was the Texas Assessment of Academic Skills (TAAS), the standardized test that all students in Texas take. It is a high-stakes exam, and students must pass it to graduate from high school. The budget cut itself had only a modest impact on this core performance criterion, a decline of one-half point in the first year and an additional point in the second year.

The budget reduction had a more substantial impact on two other performance indicators—the percentage of students who take either of the two standard national college-entrance examinations (the SAT and the ACT) and the percentage of students who score above 1110 on the SAT or its ACT equivalent. For the former, the estimation shows that a budget shock cut the test-taking rate by approximately 1.39 percentage points in the first year, a sizable drop. The reduction in this performance criterion may be due in part to systems' efforts to maintain and protect other key kinds of educational activities. There is no statistically significant impact of the budget shock, however, in the following year. The results also showed that the rate at which test-taking students score at a reasonably high level—a level designated by the state of Texas as "college ready"—also drops, in this instance by approximately 1.28 percentage points in the first year of the budget hit and then another 0.8 percentage points in the next. The total impact on the college-ready student cohort is a matter of real concern. On average only 19 percent of students meet this criterion; a reduction of 2.08 percentage points over two years, therefore, translates in to an 11 percent drop in students meeting this criterion.

In an effort to determine if managerial capacity could dampen the negative impact of these budget shocks, we (O'Toole and Meier 2009b) examined whether central office staff interacted with a budget cut to mitigate its negative impact. We found that organizations with larger central office staffs were able to overcome both the first- and second-year negative impacts of a budget cut on each of the performance indicators. Management capacity, thus, was linked to buffering the impact of these budget shocks.

How did superintendents protect TAAS and College Board scores from these budget cuts? We traced the budget decisions of the superintendents and followed up with some interviews. Essentially superintendents made a series of logical decisions that resulted in a set of minor adjustments in funding and the allocation of personnel in the system. Instructional expenditures were generally protected (they suffered smaller cuts than other areas) while maintenance and nonoperating expenses were reduced significantly. Among instructional resources the reallocations were made in predictable ways. Superintendents held down teachers' salaries and let class sizes grow. When teachers left, more expensive teachers (those with bilingual or special education specialties) were replaced by less expensive teachers (regular education teachers). The sum of these minor decisions protected most of the instructional function from the budget cuts and allowed the district to maintain its relative performance. These impacts were particularly effective in terms of the TAAS exam (Meier and O'Toole 2009a).

We should qualify the budget-cut findings. The study examined only short-term effects—that is, impacts over a one- or two-year span. Quite clearly, organizations can delay the maintenance tasks of the organization only so long before they become a limit on productivity. We also did not investigate what happened with multiple budget shocks; again, even an organization with the very best managerial capacity has limits to what it can do without resources.

The Hurricanes Study

Although budget cuts are somewhat predictable and likely to be expected on occasion, natural disasters are not. In 2005 the Gulf Coast of the United States was pummeled by two major hurricanes within a few weeks. Hurricane Katrina displaced some forty-five thousand students from Louisiana to Texas school districts (of these, thirty-six thousand remained the full year). The general perception was that Louisiana students were not as well prepared as Texas students. Hurricane Rita then led to a massive evacuation of the Texas Gulf Coast; the evacuation and the hurricane damage resulted in districts losing twelve hundred total class days. Both hurricanes had a negative impact on district performance. Performance was assessed on the statewide standardized test (now called the Texas Assessment of Knowledge and Skills, TAKS).[5] TAKS scores dropped in response to both the influx of students and the missed class days. Not all districts suffered equally, however; many were able to weather these two shocks (so to speak) and score as well as or better than predicted based on previous TAKS scores and a variety of other factors.

Analysis of more than seven hundred districts with five hundred or more students showed two key factors in mitigating the negative impact of the hurricanes. First, greater *managerial capacity* interacted with the impact of the disasters. At low levels of managerial capacity, the impacts of both hurricanes were negative and statistically significant. At higher levels of managerial capacity, the performance-related impact of the hurricanes essentially dropped to zero. Again follow-up interviews showed that managerial capacity allowed the districts to make key decisions by either quickly sorting and assigning incoming students or realigning curriculum to make up for missing classes. To illustrate, one district used its existing migrant-worker assess-ment process to sort and assign the Katrina students; another district, which had been rapidly growing, decided to rush the completion of a new school to be able to absorb the influx of students. In many cases, individuals from the central office were temporarily assigned various tasks to deal with the influx of students and buffer the schools as much as possible. In addition to managerial capacity, teacher stability had a similar impact on the negative relationship. In districts with higher turnover among teachers, both the influx of Katrina students and days missed due to Rita reduced TAKS scores by a statistically significant amount. As teacher turnover declined, and thus as human capital in the organization increased, these negative impacts became smaller until they were essentially zero (Meier, O'Toole, and Hicklin 2009).

Networking

Although our initial studies focused on management capacity in crisis situations, it is unlikely that organizations will staff additional managers in anticipation of an unspecified crisis when they might be needed. Crisis managers also have a day job—or, in this case, some other set of functions that they perform on a day-to-day basis. To probe the impact of capacity in these settings, we examined the interaction of capacity with managerial networking (Meier and O'Toole 2008a). We know from earlier studies that such networking by top managers is related to better organiza-tional performance. The theoretical logic for this study linking such networking to managerial capacity was that a top manager's interaction with other environmental actors (what we term *managerial networking*) is essentially an effort to gain coop-eration or resources from important actors in the organization's environment. At the same time, such interactions can be considered a two-way street (O'Toole and Meier 2004). Each of the environmental actors is likely to also want something in turn from the school superintendent—the top manager. Viewed in game-theoretic terms (Scharpf 1997), top managers have far more possible interactions than they have the time and resources to undertake. Management capacity can be seen as playing two possible roles in managerial networking. First, such capacity provides the analytical ability to scan the environment, determine the possible network in-teractions, and assess which of those interactions might be the most useful to the organization. Second, management capacity also means that the superintendent has the ability to implement any agreement with a network actor, and network actors are more likely to undertake joint efforts if they can see that the agreement will actually be implemented. In short, managerial capacity both evaluates potential network actions for their payoffs to the organization and provides an incentive to other actors to participate in the process.

Prior studies showed that managerial networking was positively related to organizational performance, particularly for overall performance and high-end tasks. When central office bureaucracy is interacted with managerial networking, we found that central office bureaucracy appears to have no impact on student TAAS scores in normal times, a strong positive impact on attendance, and a negative impact on high College Board scores. As the level of managerial capacity increased, however, it also interacted with networking so that the impact of networking on both TAAS scores and attendance rates increased dramatically. Similarly, as managerial networking increased, managerial capacity positively affected the standardized test scores, increased its impact on attendance by about 30 percent, and reduced its negative impact on College Board scores by about 56 percent.

The overall findings for managerial capacity—a variable showing strong positive impact on addressing problems such as attendance and dropouts, positive on indicators for disadvantaged students, but negative for high-end performance (that is, College Board scores)—suggest that managerial capacity may reflect a key organizational trade-off. Schools can either invest their slack resources in managerial capacity (which will address one set of problems) or commit these resources to dealing with high-end performance (advanced placement instructors, etc.). Neither option is an incorrect decision but rather reflects a choice by managers to address one set of challenges rather than another. The choice, however, has consequences for how the organization can respond to opportunities in the environment and also to environmental shocks.

General Buffering

Our final Texas management capacity study to be discussed was more academic in objective. Management capacity, as we see it, performs a buffering role for the organization. It is used to protect the organization from negative shocks and may contribute to proactive action. As such, capacity plays a stabilizing role for the organization. In Meier and O'Toole (2008b) we created a generic measure of organizational buffering (or the capacity to manage environmental turbulence). Essentially we looked at the history of the organization from 1988 to 1994 and generated a prediction about how loosely coupled the organization's production was. A loosely coupled organization, in theory, can take a shock from the environment and dissipate it faster than can a tightly coupled organization. Designing such loose coupling into the system—essentially creating some slack capacity—is a management function and, we think, is also closely related to managerial capacity.

The analysis attempted to ascertain two things about organizational buffering—did it matter in terms of performance, and what was the appropriate functional form? The functional form question is more academic and related to our theory of public management. That theory hypothesizes that buffering's relationship with performance should take the form of a reciprocal function, and it should interact with both management and the environment.[6] In a sense, we were interested in using an evidence-based approach for academic reasons.

Did the loose coupling of the organization affect its performance in future years (after 1995)? We found that loose coupling was positively associated with organizational performance for seven of ten performance measures (only SAT scores, ACT scores, and percentage of high College Board scores were not affected). An interesting pattern is that the impact is higher for more disadvantaged students (poor students and black students) and lower for more advantaged clientele (much the opposite of the relationships for managerial networking). Loose coupling not only affects performance, but also affects performance for the more disadvantaged clientele. This finding is very consistent with the managerial capacity studies that show a strong impact on factors such as attendance and dropouts, indicators that are more likely to affect disadvantaged students.

To determine if the relationship between buffering and performance is linear and additive or is the more complex reciprocal form that interacts with other variables, we applied the principle of Occam's razor—unless the more complex specifications were demonstrably superior, we would accept the simpler linear, additive form as correct. Estimating a reciprocal function, a reciprocal function that interacted with management, and a reciprocal form interacting with the environment did not produce results that were consistently better than the linear additive form. While we concluded that the evidence most supported a linear additive model for buffering, we qualified that conclusion because we specified only a single form of buffering and applied it to only one set of cases. More empirical tests are needed before definitively rejecting the rich qualitative literature that suggests that buffering affects performance in a highly nonlinear, interactive format.

A Corroborative Study on Management Capacity

Local governments in the United Kingdom provide an opportunity to determine if the ability of managerial capacity to mitigate shocks was a more general phenomena. English local governments are multipurpose organizations that provide most government services other than health care (but including education). Local governments operate under a national performance appraisal system whereby the national government rates the performance of local governments by combining a variety of objective measures with some judgments by the appraisers. These measures of performance for individual services can then be combined to obtain an overall assessment of government services in the local authority.

We (Andrews et al. 2009) examined these local governments that have been experiencing yet another sort of shock: an unexpectedly high influx of immigration. The United Kingdom's response to the first wave of European Union accession in 2004 was to extend the basic freedom of movement for citizens of countries within the European Economic Area seeking employment in the United Kingdom to potential economic migrants from the accession countries (the Czech Republic, Estonia, Hungary, Latvia, Lithuania, Poland, Slovakia, and Slovenia), with few conditions or restrictions. Differences in the performance of countries' economies then resulted in a substantial, unanticipated influx of immigrants from these coun-tries to the United Kingdom as workers sought better opportunities. The number of immigrants was seventeen times the forecasted level and exceeded 1 million over a three-year period. This flood of immigration has been a shock to local governments because under UK law the immigrants are entitled to the basic government services afforded all residents, and suddenly there were many more people to serve—people with different needs, different language skills, and different expectations.

Our studies of the years 2006–7 showed that the influx of immigration (the number of new arrivals from these countries relative to the population size) had a statistically significant and negative impact on the performance of local govern-ments. Because the measure of performance was a standardized scale, it does not have an easy substantive interpretation like test scores for schools. Again we analyzed the data to determine if managerial capacity, in this case measured as the percentage of funds spent on the central office (personnel data were not available), made a difference. The findings were strikingly consistent with the findings from Texas school districts. English local governments with greater managerial capac-ity could handle a substantial influx of new immigrants and effectively have no reduction in services provided.

Conclusion

The findings summarized in this chapter provide a rather strong body of evidence that management capacity can make important contributions to public organiza-tional performance. Additional capacity may seem to be a drag on organizations' production—and in fact may be so during quiet or routine times—but can be cru-cial in supporting and protecting core tasks during nonroutine events, especially unexpected jolts or shocks that inevitably pound public organizations from time to time, and can provide other advantages as well.

In a world of organizations as open systems, many sorts of disruptive forces could buffet such agencies. These include budget cuts, the sudden arrival of displaced persons as organizational clients, and large waves of international migration that could overwhelm systems for the delivery of public services—the three sorts of shocks we have analyzed. The evidence-based conclusion is rather clear: managerial capacity has the potential to protect public organizations from performance drops, at least in the short term, for reasons that were outlined earlier in this chapter. To the extent that public organizations and public managers operate in environments that expose their agencies to such potential disruption, it would seem to be wise to develop sufficient managerial capacity to protect the system from interruption or shoddy performance. Some redundancies are built into many sorts of systems when the consequences of failure are unacceptable—the examples of nuclear power plants and jet aircraft are illustrative. Why not perform similar risk-based assessments of administrative systems as well?

The evidence we have summarized here also points to additional assistance that managerial capacity may provide. Three of our studies showed that once shocks enter the organizational system, more managerial capacity can vitiate the disruptive effects. But one other of our investigations points toward a supplementary benefit: sometimes enhanced capacity buffers or protects the organization so the shocks from the external world are turned away even before entering the organization. Loose coupling, a form of managerial capacity, not only protected organizations in most of their production; it also did so especially well for outcomes of particular relevance for more disadvantaged clients of the organizations. This finding is not so surprising, since marginalized groups typically have weaker support systems and fewer resources to provide help, and thus benefit especially from stability in and from public services. Still, it is important to have the finding validated through an evidence-based approach. Many other apparent maxims of good management turn out to be unverified, and are sometimes unverifiable in principle.

Finally, one of our empirical studies suggests yet an additional contribution that managerial capacity can make. Our investigation of the interactive effect of capacity with managerial networking—beyond the additive impacts of each—validates the idea that enhancing capacity can also leverage more from other kinds of managerial effort. While further empirical work should be conducted on this issue, for instance, to see if other functions like internal management are also improved as capacity is increased, it makes theoretical sense for those leading public organizations to consider these sorts of subtle performance-related impacts that follow from a marginal improvement in capacity.

Lean management is not always smart management. This lesson comes through clearly from a sustained, evidence-based research program like this one. Estimating the appropriate level of managerial capacity for a particular public organization facing its own unique array of challenges and constraints is no easy chore, but it should be done with careful attention to the manifold ways that capacity can help.

Notes

This chapter is part of an ongoing research agenda on the role of public management in complex policy settings. That agenda has benefited from the helpful comments of George Boyne, Stuart Bretschneider, Gene Brewer, Amy Kneedler Donahue, Sergio Fernandez, H. George Frederickson, Carolyn Heinrich, Patricia Ingraham, J. Edward Kellough, Laurence E. Lynn Jr., H. Brinton Milward, David Peterson, Hal G. Rainey, and Bob Stein on the research program. Needless to say, this article is the responsibility of the authors only.

1. For an explanation as to why organizations that contract out functions must nonetheless possess substantial good management internally to do so successfully, see Rainey (2010).

2. We have built much of our joint research agenda on management and performance from an inductively generated formal model:

$$O_t = \beta_1(S+M_1)O_{t-1} + \beta_2(X_t/S)(M_3/M_4) + \varepsilon_t$$

where O is some measure of outcome; S is a measure of stability; M denotes management, which can be divided into three parts: M_1, management's contribution to organizational stability through additions to hierarchy/structure as well as regular operations, M_3, management's efforts to exploit the environment of the organization, and M_4, management's effort to buffer the unit from environmental shocks (with M_2 denoting the M_3/M_4 ratio); X is a vector of environmental forces; ε is an error term; the other subscripts denote time periods; and β_1 and β_2 are estimable parameters (O'Toole and Meier 1999). Each M is conceived as having a quantity or effort component as well as a quality component; in our empirical work we have measured the quantity dimension for each managerial function and separately developed an overall measure of managerial quality. We have estimated the effects on performance of a number of such management-related functions. Managerial capacity is not included in the model, since it refers to potential management rather than actual ongoing managerial effort. But when it is mobilized, as, for instance, during times of crisis or nonroutine disturbance, we conceive of it as adding to one or more of the M terms in the model.

3. Doig and Hargrove (1990, p. 3), quoting March (1981, pp. 28–29), consider the notion that "administrators are vital as a class but not as individuals. . . . What makes an organization function well is the density of administrative competence." Doig and Hargrove's own position is partially different from this one, but one of their dimensions of leadership behavior has relevance for the kind of function we are examining: "systematically scan[ning] organizational routines, and points of internal and external pressure, in order to *identify areas of vulnerability* . . . followed by remedial action" (emphasis in original).

4. Other measures of managerial capacity might consider education levels, skills sets of managers, or even years of experience.

5. The Texas Assessment of Knowledge and Skills (TAKS) replaced the Texas Assessment of Academic Skills (TAAS) in 2003.

6. One can make this point more specifically by referencing the second term of our general model, as depicted in note 2. The second, or environmental, term is $\beta_2(X_t/S)(M_3/M_4)$. Rearranging the elements of this term produces $\beta_2(X_tM_3)/(SM_4)$. The denominator of this term, or the SM_4 combination, is our formal depiction of buffering. As the rearranged term shows, we hypothesized this buffering term interacting with both management and the forces in the environment.

References

Andrews, Rhys, George A. Boyne, Kenneth J. Meier, Laurence J. O'Toole, and Richard M. Walker. 2009. "The Micro-politics of European Immigration: Local Government Capacity and Public Service Performance in England." Unpublished paper, Cardiff University (Wales).

Cyert, Richard M., and James G. March. 1963. *A Behavioral Theory of the Firm.* Englewood Cliffs, NJ: Prentice Hall.

Doig, Jameson W., and Erwin C. Hargrove, eds. 1990. *Leadership and Innovation.* Baltimore: Johns Hopkins University Press.

Galbraith, Jay R. 1973. *Designing Complex Organizations.* Reading, MA: Addison-Wesley.

Gazley, Beth, and Robert K. Christensen. 2007. "Salvaging Capacity's Usefulness: Analysis of Meaning and Measurement." Paper presented at the Public Management Research Conference, Tucson, AZ, October 25–27.

Gilmour, John D., and David E. Lewis. 2006. "Assessing Performance Budgeting at OMB." *Journal of Public Administration Research and Theory* 16 (2): 169–186.

Ingraham, Patricia W., Philip G. Joyce, and Amy Kneedler Donahue. 2003. *Government Performance: Why Management Matters.* Baltimore: Johns Hopkins University Press.

Malysa, Lani Lee. 1996. "A Comparative Assessment of State Planning and Management Capacity: Tidal Wetlands Protection in Virginia and Maryland." *State and Local Government Review* 28:205–218.

March, James G. 1981. "How We Talk and How We Act: Administrative Theory and Administrative Life." In *Leadership and Organizational Culture,* ed. T.J. Serfiovanni and J.E. Corbally. Urbana: University of Illinois Press.

Meier, Kenneth J., and Laurence J. O'Toole, Jr. 2001. "Managerial Strategies and Behavior in Networks: A Model with Evidence from U.S. Public Education." *Journal of Public Administration Research and Theory* 11 (July): 271–295.

———. 2002. "Public Management and Organizational Performance: The Impact of Managerial Quality." *Journal of Policy Analysis and Management* 21 (Fall): 629–643.

———. 2008a. "Beware of Managers Not Bearing Gifts: How Management Capacity Augments the Impact of Managerial Networking." Paper presented at the annual meeting of the American Political Science Association, Boston, MA, August 28–31.

———. 2008b. "Management Theory and Occam's Razor: How Public Organizations Buffer the Environment." *Administration and Society* 39 (8): 931–958.

———. 2009a. "The Dog That Didn't Bark: How Public Managers Handle Environmental Shocks." *Public Administration* 87 (3): 485–502.

———. 2009b. "The Proverbs of New Public Management: Lessons from an Evidence-Based Research Agenda." *American Review of Public Administration* 39 (January): 4–22.

Meier, Kenneth J., Laurence J. O'Toole, Jr., and Alisa Hicklin. 2009. "I've Seen Fire and I've Seen Rain: Public Management and Performance after a Natural Disaster." *Administration and Society* 41 (8): 979–1003.

Miles, Raymond E., and Charles C. Snow. 1978. *Organizational Strategy, Structure, and Process.* New York: McGraw-Hill.

Mintzberg, Henry. 1972. *The Nature of Managerial Work.* New York: HarperCollins.

O'Toole, Laurence J., Jr., and Kenneth J. Meier. 1999. "Modeling the Impact of Public Management: Implications of Structural Context." *Journal of Public Administration Research and Theory* 9 (4): 505–526.

———. 2003. *"Plus ça Change:* Public Management, Personnel Stability, and Organizational Performance." *Journal of Public Administration Research and Theory* 13 (1): 43–64.

———. 2004. "Parkinson's Law and the New Public Management? Contracting Determinants and Service Quality Consequences in Public Education." *Public Administration Review* 64:342–352.

———. 2009a. "The Human Side of Public Organizations: Contributions to Organizational Performance." *American Review of Public Administration* 39 (5): 499–518.

———. 2009b. "In Defense of Bureaucracy: Public Managerial Capacity, Slack, and the Dampening of Environmental Shocks." Unpublished paper.

Pfeffer, Jeffrey, and Gerald R. Salancik. 1978. *The External Control of Organizations: A Resource Dependence Perspective.* New York: Harper and Row.

Raffel, Jeffrey A. 2007. "Why Has Public Administration Ignored Public Education, and Does It Matter?" *Public Administration Review* 67 (1): 135–151.

Rainey, Hal G. 2010. *Understanding and Managing Public Organizations.* 4th ed. San Francisco: Jossey-Bass.

Scharpf, Fritz W. 1997. *Games Real Actors Play: Actor-Centered Institutionalism in Policy Research.* Boulder, CO: Westview Press.

Thompson, James D. 1967. *Organizations in Action.* New York: McGraw-Hill.

Waldo, Dwight. 1968. "Scope of the Theory of Public Administration." In *Theory and Practice of Public Administration: Scope, Objectives, and Methods,* ed. James C. Charlesworth, 1–26. Philadelphia: American Academy of Political and Social Science.

Yukl, Gary. 2006. *Leadership in Organizations.* 6th ed. Upper Saddle River, NJ: Prentice Hall.

12

State Agency Attention to Scientific Sources of Information to Guide Program Operations

Edward T. Jennings, Jr. and Jeremy L. Hall

The quest for evidence-based public management (EBMgt) faces a variety of challenges, including issues regarding the validity, reliability, interpretation, and application of studies providing evidence of the consequences of management practices. Despite those challenges, we can expect that EBMgt will continue to grow in importance in the years to come, as policy makers and managers pursue cost-effective strategies to achieve desired outcomes in public programs. Indeed, the appeal of evidence-based practice can be found as much in the terminology as in any demonstrated results. Who, for example, would want to say that their practices are not based on evidence?

The introduction to this volume offers a definition of EBMgt, but it is useful to discuss it here. The two important concepts in the term — *evidence based* and *management*—provide a good place to start. The concept seems to originate in the field of medicine, where there is considerable scientific evidence regarding the efficacy of different treatments, as discussed in a symposium in 2005 (Steinberg and Luce 2005). That symposium not only revealed the extensive attention to evidence-based medicine, but also discussed a variety of caveats regarding its use (see also Chapter 2 on methodological issues in EBMgt). There does not seem to be much debate about what *evidence-based* means in medicine, where the experimental model of scientific research is widely used and nonexperimental designs are rarely accepted. At the federal level, Medicare uses evidence from systematic reviews to establish policies and procedures that govern health care practice. In addition, the current health care reform discussion in Washington has drawn attention to the role of evidence, including comparative effectiveness in making medical decisions under potential federally directed programs.

In the field of public administration, the meaning of *evidence* is much more contested territory. In the medical arena, few would suggest that a case study would provide sufficient evidence on which to base practice. The editors of this volume, however, in the call for papers, suggested that EBMgt, as an approach, derives principles of good management from scientific research, meta-analysis, literature reviews, case studies, and practitioner experience, then translates them into effective practice. This is quite similar to a definition of best practices approaches, rather than EBMgt. Hall and Jennings (2008) conceptualize these differences in a tiered approach. It seems to miss the point of EBMgt, which is to move beyond case studies and personal experience to provide evidence that is valid and reliable, grounded in systematic research based on principles of scientific study. If it is evidence based, the research should be able to stand up to internal and external validity threats. Or, as Hall and Jennings (2008) point out, when experiments are not possible or appropriate, the next best alternative may be acceptable. That is asking a lot in public administration, where the academic discipline is still riven by disputes over what constitutes knowledge. Many practitioners are not trained in scientific method, and many lack graduate training in the field.

We write from the perspective that EBMgt is management based on scientific research into the causes and consequences of programmatic alternatives and administrative arrangements. While there is considerable scientifically based research that is relevant to programmatic operations across a wide range of public programs, the scientific analysis of management practices is much thinner, but growing (Davies, Nutley, and Smith 2000; Meier 2008). When we talk about evidence relevant to programmatic operations, it is useful to think about examples. One is in the area of pharmacy management for state Medicaid programs. States have an interest in ensuring that Medicaid recipients are receiving the most cost-effective drugs for their medical conditions. The Drug Effectiveness Review Project helps them do this by providing analyses of the effectiveness of all of the drugs in particular drug classes (Gibson and Santa 2006; Hoadley et al. 2006). Those reviews consider the full range of scientific evidence that is available for each drug under review. The reviews distinguish among studies on the basis of a variety of characteristics, in particular, the validity and reliability of the findings. The reviews are shared with state policy makers and program managers who make locally based decisions about how to use that information to guide the management of Medicaid and other state programs.

This raises an interesting question about what we mean by management. Management encompasses all of the traditional functions of human resources, organization, finances, planning, capital, and communications. When we look at the widely discussed Government Performance Project, for example, we find that its initial iterations focused on the management of finances, capital, human resources, and information. Integrating these different management-capacity dimensions was seen as taking place through managing for results (Ingraham and Donahue 2000). The terminology changed a bit in later iterations of the project, but the conceptual underpinnings were still the same. Management involved money, people, infrastructure, and information (Pew Center on the States 2008).

Management, however, also involves directing agency-specific program operations. The multiple forms of management capacity are brought together to produce programmatic operations that lead to programmatic outputs and outcomes. In the discussion that follows, our focus is management of programmatic operations, rather than the more general management functions that transcend agency boundaries.

For EBMgt to work, several things have to happen. There has to be systematic evidence on which to base management practices. The evidence has to be valid and reliable. It has to be relevant and usable. The evidence has to be organized and presented in a form that is easily understandable by managers. The evidence must be communicated to managers. Managers must be receptive to the communication and able to understand the message. Managers have to act on the evidence. This leaves a long train of opportunities for things to go wrong.

Whether there is a strong research base for EBMgt is an open question. One thing is clear—there has not been much writing about EBMgt. A Google search on August 5, 2009, using the search term *EBMgt* yielded 2,690,000 entries. Unfortunately, a scan of the first five pages of listings yielded none that was about EBMgt generally. Instead, there were many about evidence-based medicine, about evidence-based public health, and with respect to particular policy practices, as in education and criminal justice. There was one about EBMgt in the private sector. In other words, none addressed general public management functions of human resources management, budgeting, planning, and information that were identified above.

Despite that lack of attention to general management functions, there is a large set of studies relevant to programmatic operations. That research comes from the normal scientific inquiry in such areas as natural resources and the environment, medicine, mental health, agriculture, and other arenas of policy activity. It is also a product of the explicit attempt over the last thirty years to generate evidence for policy and conforms generally to the broader effort to rationalize government (Stone 2002). In addition to major national social science experiments involving income maintenance, early childhood education, and other policy questions, there have been countless social experiments and other studies carried out at the state and local level. These studies are often context bound and driven by specific questions of interest at the local level, without much consideration for the cumulative body of evidence in the field. The Coalition for Evidence-Based Policy catalogs and makes available the evidence from a variety of these studies (Coalition for Evidence-Based Policy 2006). It references randomized control studies bearing on programs in the areas of early childhood development, education, youth development, crime and violence prevention, substance abuse treatment and prevention, mental health, employment and welfare, and international development.

Is the evidence bearing on programmatic operations valid and reliable? The case can be made that much of it is. As the Coalition for Evidence-Based Policy makes clear, there are various randomized control studies on which managers can draw. The broader scientific evidence bearing on a range of public problems is also sound. Beyond that, there are numerous nonrandomized control trial studies that offer systematic empirical evidence relevant to program practices. These show up in public policy and administration journals and specialized journals focusing on particular programmatic areas.

The fact that there is a lot of evidence does not mean it is accessible or usable. The field of medicine, where evidence-based practice is widespread, does not simply rely on physicians and other medical practitioners to be aware of individual studies and take them into account in practice decisions. Instead, there are extensive, organized efforts to develop practice guidelines based on systematic reviews of evidence. The developers of evidence-based guidelines always face the questions of when the evidence is sufficient and how it should be interpreted. It is also important to properly frame evidence around instrumental questions and establish boundaries for guidelines so that they are properly interpreted for practice. The typical process by which they are developed involves evaluating a body of evidence, rating the strength of the evidence derived from individual studies, assessing the consistency of results, determining the magnitude of effects, establishing the population for which the evidence is relevant, and deciding how strong the evidence should be when making a particular type of decision (Steinberg and Luce 2005).

Research Methods

There is little information on how widely evidence-based practices are pursued. Indeed, in keeping with our observation about what has to happen for EBMgt to occur, we do not know very much about how attentive managers are to scientific evidence (or other types of information) in their decision making. Efforts to develop EBMgt can benefit from careful explorations of the experience with evidence-based program and policy practices. In the remainder of this chapter, we examine state agency administrators' experience with evidence-based policy and program operations to identity implications and lessons for EBMgt.

In 2008, we executed a survey of six hundred state government agencies to determine where they obtain information to guide decisions to improve programmatic operations. We conducted the survey by mail and online. For each state, we surveyed the following agencies: alcohol and substance abuse, children and youth services, developmental disabilities, economic development, environmental protection, fish and wildlife, hazardous waste management, natural resources, state police, tourism, transportation and highways, and vocational rehabilitation. Our purpose was to determine the degree to which agencies consult a variety of sources for ideas or information to improve operations, how much weight they place on those sources, the degree to which they believe that scientific evidence is available with respect to their programs, and factors that influence their programmatic decisions. The responses to the survey shed light on (1) whether, and how often, agencies seek information or evidence to support program or policy decisions, (2) where agencies turn for information and evidence to support program or policy decisions, (3) how much weight various information sources and types of information and evidence receive in the decision process, and (4) how information use varies by agencies' substantive policy focus. If agencies are not attuned to scientific evidence bearing on programmatic operations, they are unlikely to be responsive to evidence bearing on other dimensions of management.

Results from our survey are enlightening. We received a total of 234 paper and

Table 12.1

Percent of Agencies Responding by Type

Agency	# of Agency Responses	# States Surveyed	% of Agencies Responding	Rank
Alcohol and Substance Abuse	21	50	42	5
Children and Youth Services	21	50	42	5
Developmental Disabilities	14	50	28	8
Economic Development	15	50	30	7
Environmental Protection	18	50	36	6
Fish and Wildlife	27	50	54	1
Hazardous Waste Management	13	50	26	9
Natural Resources	7	50	14	11
State Police	26	50	52	2
Tourism	8	50	16	10
Transportation and Highways	24	50	48	3
Vocational Rehabilitation	23	50	46	4
	217	600	36.2	—

electronic responses for an initial response rate of 39 percent. We dropped seventeen responses to ensure reliability and validity, leaving a remaining total of 217 responses for analysis and a final response rate of 36.2 percent. Naturally, response rates varied by state and agency type. The number of selected agencies responding from each state ranged from 2 (16.7 percent) to 9 (75 percent). In addition, the rate of response for each agency type also varied. Fish and wildlife agencies were most responsive, with 54 percent responding, followed by state police (52 percent), and transportation and highways (48 percent); natural resources (14 percent) and tourism agencies (16 percent) were the least responsive (Table 12.1).

Findings

We asked the agencies to tell us the degree to which they consult each of nineteen different sources for information to improve their operations. We also asked them how much weight they place on each of these sources. The nineteen potential sources of information we included are:

- Accrediting bodies
- Professional associations
- Professional literature
- Research and formal evaluations
- Scientific studies
- Consultants
- Think tanks

- Innovation award programs
- Internal agency staff
- Other agencies in your state
- Comparable agencies in other states
- Federal government agencies
- Associations of government officials (such as NGA, CSG, NASBO)
- Governor
- Legislators
- Legislative staff
- Local government officials
- Interest groups
- News media

Sources on this list are both internal and external to state government, formal and informal, political and apolitical. We asked about this broad array of information sources to provide a context for comparing agency evidence use relative to other types of information and the varied attention it would receive in decision making. The frequency of use and weight are indicators of the relative influence each information source holds in agency decision making. We used a scale ranging from *never* (0) to *very often* (4) to ask respondents to indicate the degree to which their agency consults each source to inform policy and programming decisions. We used the same scale to assess how much weight they place on different sources. The responses provide insight into the relative importance of scientific and professional sources of information among a wide array of information alternatives. It also provides an opportunity to examine variance among agencies operating in different fields of public service.

As can be seen in Table 12.2, there is considerable variation in the extent to which state agencies consult different information sources and the importance they attach to those sources. The most frequently used information sources are internal agency staff, comparable agencies in other states, research and formal evaluations, and professional literature. The least frequently used are the news media, think tanks, innovation award programs, and local government officials. These match up very closely with the importance attached to different sources of information. As Table 12.2 also indicates, agency respondents place the greatest importance on information from their own staff, research and formal evaluations, comparable agencies in other states, and the governor. Thus, while the governor is not among the most frequently consulted sources of information, when he or she is consulted, he or she receives great attention.

We also find considerable variation in the degree to which different types of agencies depend on different sources of information. Table 12.3 reports by agency type the results of our question asking how much weight respondents placed on different sources of information. The data tell a number of interesting stories. First, several agencies stand out because of the higher level of attention that they give to

Table 12.2

Average Score and Agency Differences for Each Information Source: Consultation Frequency (A) and Weight (B)

Information Source	A: Frequency of Consultation ANOVA: Between Groups Results			B: Weight Assigned to Information ANOVA: Between Groups Results		
	Mean Score	F	Sig.	Mean Score	F	Sig.
Accrediting Bodies	2.13	2.006	0.030	2.50	1.756	0.064
Professional Associations	2.87	1.292	0.231	2.78	2.132	0.020
Professional Literature	2.97	1.296	0.229	2.95	1.322	0.214
Research and Formal Evaluations	3.00	2.866	0.002	3.20	2.608	0.004
Scientific Studies	2.68	5.106	0.000	2.97	3.840	0.000
Consultants	2.25	5.824	0.000	2.43	2.219	0.015
Think Tanks	1.45	3.206	0.000	1.64	2.120	0.021
Innovation Award Programs	1.57	1.055	0.400	1.79	1.493	0.136
Internal Agency Staff	3.55	1.656	0.086	3.40	2.192	0.016
Other Agencies in Your State	2.63	1.932	0.037	2.66	0.875	0.566
Comparable Agencies in Other States	3.13	2.383	0.009	3.01	2.861	0.002
Federal Government Agencies	2.79	2.400	0.008	2.82	1.721	0.071
Associations of Government Officials	2.22	2.560	0.005	2.24	1.681	0.080
Governor	2.64	3.575	0.000	3.12	2.148	0.019
Legislators	2.33	1.985	0.032	2.74	0.495	0.905
Legislative Staff	2.08	1.176	0.306	2.30	0.871	0.570
Local Government Officials	2.05	2.094	0.022	2.24	1.261	0.249
Interest Groups	2.52	3.004	0.000	2.44	1.666	0.000
News Media	1.12	1.620	0.096	1.23	2.007	0.030

scientific studies. These include fish and wildlife, natural resources, environmental protection, and alcohol and substance abuse. Noticeable for their low levels of attention to scientific studies are economic development, vocational rehabilitation, state police, and hazardous waste management. Some of the agencies that are highly attentive to scientific research are also highly attentive to research and formal evaluations more generally. These would include fish and wildlife, natural resources, and alcohol and substance abuse. Interesting is the fact that agencies that score relatively low on attention to scientific studies are not necessarily also the low scorers on attention to research and formal evaluations. Agencies attaching relatively low weight to research and formal evaluations are hazardous waste management and environmental protection.

Agencies do not place the same weight on information from the governor. The organizations placing the most weight on information from the governor relative to information from other agencies are economic development, environmental protection, transportation and highways, and tourism. Governors are notable for the attention that they give to economic development and growth. Three of these

Table 12.3

Average Weights for Information Source by Agency Type

Agency Type	Accrediting Bodies	Professional Associations	Professional Literature	Research and Formal Evaluations	Scientific Studies	Consultants	Think Tanks	Innovation Award Programs	Internal Agency Staff
Alcohol and Substance Abuse	2.50	2.78	3.17	3.39	3.22	2.56	1.78	1.89	2.89
Children and Youth Services	2.47	2.89	3.05	3.37	2.95	2.47	2.11	2.05	3.32
Developmental Disabilities	2.54	2.38	2.77	3.00	2.77	3.08	1.31	1.31	3.31
Economic Development	2.23	2.54	2.69	3.08	2.08	2.62	1.77	1.69	3.31
Environmental Protection	1.87	2.33	2.53	2.80	3.40	2.20	1.33	1.67	3.53
Fish and Wildlife	2.55	2.95	3.41	3.55	3.64	2.14	1.32	1.55	3.68
Hazardous Waste Management	1.83	2.33	2.50	2.42	2.67	2.25	1.50	1.42	3.17
Natural Resources	2.43	2.57	3.29	3.43	3.43	2.29	2.43	2.14	3.43
State Police	3.04	3.08	2.96	3.29	2.63	2.00	1.54	1.83	3.63
Tourism	2.60	3.60	2.80	3.80	3.00	2.80	1.80	2.40	3.60
Transportation and Highways	2.63	2.84	2.68	3.05	3.11	2.53	1.89	1.68	3.26
Vocational Rehabilitation	2.47	2.79	2.89	3.11	2.63	2.63	1.74	2.32	3.42

agencies—economic development, tourism, and transportation and highways—contribute to state economic growth strategies and are also potential sources of political rewards. The literature highlights the central role that flashy projects, usually infrastructure based, play in local politics, with leaders seeking to provide evidence of their effectiveness in office through tangible outcomes (Wolman 1996;

Table 12.3 *(continued)*

Other Agencies in Your State	Comparable Agencies in Other States	Federal Government Agencies	Associations of Government Officials	Governor	Legislators	Legislative Staff	Local Government Officials	Interest Groups	News Media
2.44	2.78	2.78	2.22	2.94	2.61	2.22	2.22	2.39	1.11
2.68	3.16	2.79	2.47	2.95	2.74	2.47	2.16	2.58	1.05
2.62	2.77	2.77	2.08	2.46	2.23	2.00	1.54	2.92	0.92
2.77	2.54	2.15	2.38	3.62	2.62	2.46	2.69	1.54	0.92
2.67	3.00	2.87	2.47	3.53	2.87	2.13	2.47	2.40	0.73
2.55	2.82	2.64	2.06	2.82	2.73	1.91	2.18	2.80	1.20
2.83	3.00	2.83	2.33	3.17	2.83	2.08	2.67	2.58	1.17
2.71	2.86	3.14	2.57	3.00	2.71	2.57	2.14	2.86	1.43
2.75	3.33	2.71	2.00	3.25	3.00	2.58	2.33	2.08	1.79
2.60	2.60	2.40	2.60	3.40	2.60	2.20	2.60	2.20	2.00
2.47	2.79	3.16	2.68	3.47	2.89	2.53	2.42	1.84	1.37
2.84	3.47	3.11	1.68	2.84	2.58	2.11	1.74	2.74	1.11

Buss 1999; Dewar 1998). The fourth, environmental protection, often deals with issues that have important economic consequences. It is perhaps for these political reasons that these agencies are especially attentive to the governor.

There is another way we can look at this. Are there distinctive patterns in attention to information from different sources? Does attention to sources cluster in particular ways? Are agencies differentially attentive to the clusters? To examine this, we performed factor analysis on the responses to the questions about frequency with which information is sought from the source and the weight attached to information from the sources.

That analysis yielded four factors, which we label political, scientific/professional, agency/client, and innovation (see Table 12.4). The *political* factor information sources include associations of government officials, the governor, legislators, legislative staff, local government officials, and news media. The *scientific/professional* factor includes accrediting bodies, professional associations, professional literature, research and formal evaluations, and scientific studies. The *agency/client* factor includes internal agency staff, other state agencies, peer agencies in other states, federal agencies, and interest groups. Finally, the *innovation* factor includes consultants, think tanks, and innovation award programs. The factors clearly differentiate the patterns of agency attention to the different sources of information.

This is as we would expect. The scientific/professional sources are the most likely place to look for systematic evidence on what works and professional consensus or disagreement about that evidence. The political sources are those that are most likely to provide guidance on directions and priorities for agency programs. The agency/client sources are the ones where experiential information is most likely to be found. These sources often provide compelling stories. Finally, the innovation factor consists of sources where agencies can learn about new ideas, exciting developments, and creative approaches. These are also the sources that our findings suggest are likely to be the least central to agency decision making, perhaps as a result of inertia or incremental pressure to preserve the status quo.

Agencies differ in the degree to which they tune in to these different factors. We generated factor scores to identify the extent to which agencies emphasize information from each of the four areas. ANOVA indicates statistically significant differences among agency types for each of the four common factors. Table 12.4 ranks the factor scores by agency type to better convey differences among agency types. These data reveal interesting differences in agencies' information focus.

According to the factor scores, the agencies that give the most attention to professional/scientific information are fish and wildlife, natural resources, alcohol and substance abuse, and tourism. Except for tourism, this is not a surprise. Each of the agencies is in a field of considerable scientific research. It is natural, and sometimes mandatory, that the agencies would be attuned to that research. Tourism ends up among the agencies that score high on the professional/scientific scale because these agencies rely on a great deal of research into consumer behavior. Surveys and market studies are stock in trade for tourism managers. On the other hand, at the bottom of the professional/scientific scale are hazardous waste management, economic development, developmental disabilities, and vocational rehabilitation. These agencies rely much more heavily on their own staff, counterparts in other states, federal agencies, and clients for guidance, as can be seen by the fact that

Table 12.4

Agencies Rank-Ordered by Factor Scores

	Political F1 (Mean)		Professional/Scientific F2 (Mean)
Vocational Rehabilitation	-0.619	Hazardous Waste Management	-0.823
Developmental Disabilities	-0.554	Economic Development	-0.637
Alcohol & Substance Abuse	-0.214	Developmental Disabilities	-0.408
Fish & Wildlife	-0.212	Vocational Rehabilitation	-0.291
Hazardous Waste Management	-0.075	Environmental Protection	-0.255
Children & Youth Services	-0.037	Transportation & Highways	0.066
Environmental Protection	0.083	Children & Youth Services	0.113
Tourism	0.284	State Police	0.135
Transportation & Highways	0.301	Tourism	0.205
State Police	0.457	Alcohol & Substance Abuse	0.278
Natural Resources	0.482	Natural Resources	0.507
Economic Development	0.531	Fish & Wildlife	0.786

	Agency/Client F3 (Mean)		Innovation F4 (Mean)
Economic Development	-0.685	Fish & Wildlife	-0.809
Tourism	-0.474	Environmental Protection	-0.694
Transportation & Highways	-0.445	State Police	-0.443
Alcohol & Substance Abuse	-0.283	Hazardous Waste Management	-0.018
State Police	-0.267	Economic Development	0.151
Children & Youth Services	-0.029	Tourism	0.157
Natural Resources	0.022	Vocational Rehabilitation	0.253
Fish & Wildlife	0.257	Developmental Disabilities	0.330
Environmental Protection	0.262	Transportation & Highways	0.331
Developmental Disabilities	0.298	Alcohol & Substance Abuse	0.443
Hazardous Waste Management	0.522	Children & Youth Services	0.488
Vocational Rehabilitation	0.619	Natural Resources	0.551

three of them score highest on the agency/client scale. The other, economic development, scores highest on the political scale.

Vocational rehabilitation, developmental disabilities, alcohol and substance abuse, and fish and wildlife score quite low on attention to political sources of information. This is not surprising. These are agencies that are seldom the target of significant political attention outside the client groups that they serve. Governors and legislators do not get too excited about hunting seasons, sport-fishing quotas, the treatment of addicted individuals, or other responsibilities of these agencies. On the other hand, governors pay a lot of attention to a number of the agencies that score high on the political factor—economic development, natural resources, state police, transportation and highways, and tourism—and that focus on the allocation of resources through highly visible projects. All of these agencies except state police play a role in the economic development and growth initiatives of governors and are often the target of legislative interest because of their capacity to deliver the goods to constituents back home.

Discussion and Conclusions

The survey findings do not tell us how much evidence-based practice takes place in public agencies. But they do offer good insight into the relative importance of scientific studies and systematic research in the decision-making process to guide programmatic operations. If evidence is to guide operations, managers have to be aware of it, pay attention to it, and give it priority. Our survey findings are quite mixed in this regard. First, agencies do pay attention to research-based information, but it has to compete with other sources that are considered to be important. Nothing is more important in efforts to improve program operations than the guidance provided by internal agency staff, suggesting that experience is critical in decision making. Nonetheless, professional literature, research and formal evaluations, and scientific studies rank high as sources of information to guide operations in some agencies. Thus, at least with respect to program or operations management, agency managers do give attention to and use systematic evidence.

We temper this with the recognition that attention to scientific/professional sources of information varies considerably across the agencies. While some score high on this dimension, others score quite low. This, however, does not mean that their program management lacks a scientific basis. For some of them, that scientific basis may come from other sources. Hazardous waste and environmental protection agencies both score relatively low on the scientific/professional scale. Conversely, they score high on the agency/client scale. To a significant degree, this reflects their dependence on federal rules and regulations, which themselves are typically grounded in scientific evidence. Indirectly, then, these agencies use an evidence base to guide their operations. One important question this raises is whether agencies can be expected to attend to EBMgt when they have no established tradition of evidence-based practice within their substantive field of policy or practice.

Our evidence bears on program operations, not on general management functions. We expect direct use of systematic research to guide general management activities to be much more limited. Agencies that use formal research to guide program operations are staffed to a significant degree by scientists trained in scientific research. They come from basic disciplines whose knowledge is relevant to programmatic activities. This will be much less the case for general management functions. Few, indeed, are the managers who have scientific training in policy and management research. They are not inclined toward management research and are likely to give it quite limited attention.

This suggests to us that translators and certifiers will be critical in the attempt to put public administration on a stronger research footing. As we noted earlier, the field of medicine, where evidence-based practice is widespread, does not simply rely on physicians and other medical practitioners to be aware of individual studies and take them into account in practice decisions. Instead, there are extensive, organized efforts to develop practice guidelines based on systematic reviews of evidence. A comparable effort will be required to move public management in an evidence-based direction. Even with that, EBMgt will be much more limited than evidence-based medicine because the evidence base is so much thinner.

These differences suggest several important questions about how managers and agency officials should approach the field of EBMgt. Will it be necessary to issue legislative mandates that agencies base their practices on evidence, as Oregon has done? Will it become necessary to create new certifying bodies within or across states to review evidence and report out practice guidelines? If these are the preferred alternatives, what will become of local discretion? Just as the argument in health care goes—that the doctor best knows his or her patient—state and local governments are best equipped to understand the problems confronting their jurisdictions. It will be important that, however they proceed, states preserve the incentive to innovate and thus ensure that Justice Brandeis's laboratory continues to turn out innovative approaches that may be added to the evidence base and diffused. Overreliance on evidence of existing practices runs the risk of de-emphasizing potentially better innovative alternatives on which evidence is not yet available.

References

Buss, Terry. 1999. "To Target or Not to Target, That's the Question: A Response to Wiewel and Finkle." *Economic Development Quarterly* 13 (4): 365–370.

Coalition for Evidence-Based Policy. 2006. "What Works and What Doesn't Work in Social Policy? Findings from Well-Designed Randomized Controlled Trials." http://www.evidencebasedprograms.org/ (accessed August 25, 2009).

Davies, Huw T.O., Sandra M. Nutley, and Peter C. Smith. 2000. *What Works: Evidence-Based Policy and Practice in Public Services.* Bristol, England: Policy Press.

Dewar, Margaret E. 1998. "Why State and Local Economic Development Programs Cause So Little Economic Development." *Economic Development Quarterly* 12 (1): 68–87.

Gibson, Mark, and John Santa. 2006. "The Drug Effectiveness Review Project: An Important Step Forward." *Health Affairs* 25 (2): 272–275.

Hall, Jeremy L., and Edward T. Jennings, Jr. 2008. "Taking Chances: Evaluating Risk as a Guide to Better Use of Best Practices." *Public Administration Review* 68 (4): 695–708.

Hoadley, Jack, Jeffrey Crowley, David Bergman, and Neva Kaye. 2006. "Understanding Key Features of the Drug Effectiveness Review Project (DERP) and Lessons for State Policy Makers." National Academy for State Health Policy Issue Brief, March.

Ingraham, Patricia W., and Amy Kneedler Donahue. 2000. "Dissecting the Black Box Revisited: Characterizing Management Capacity." In *Governance and Performance: New Perspectives,* ed. Carolyn J. Heinrich and Laurence E. Lynn, Jr., 292–318, Washington, DC: Georgetown University Press.

Meier, Kenneth J. 2008. "The Scientific Study of Public Administration: A Short Essay on the State of the Field." *International Review of Public Administration* 13 (1): 1–10.

Pew Center on the States. 2008. *Grading the States.* http://www.pewcenteronthestates.org/gpp_report_card.aspx (accessed August 19, 2009).

Steinberg, Earl P., and Bryan R. Luce. 2005. "Evidence Based? Caveat Emptor!" *Health Affairs* 24 (1): 80–92.

Stone, Deborah. 2002. *Policy Paradox: The Art of Political Decision-Making.* Rev. ed. New York: W.W. Norton.

Wolman, H., with D. Spitzley. 1996. "The Politics of Local Economic Development." *Economic Development Quarterly* 10 (2): 115–151.

13

Leadership Development in the UK National Health Service

An Evidence-Based Critique

Paul Kearns

This chapter applies the concept of evidence-based public management (EBMgt) to public health care. This is an issue of global relevance as the inexorable rise in demand for health care continues to outstrip available resources. Spending on health care in France and Germany is 11 percent of GDP, while the United States spends 17.6 percent.[1] In a speech to the American Medical Association in June 2009, President Obama compared the U.S. health care system with the country's ailing car industry, stating, "If we do not fix our healthcare system, America may go the way of General Motors—paying more, getting less, and going broke."[2] The United Kingdom's Office for National Statistics reported that between 1997 and 2007 a 117 percent increase in spending on the National Health Service (NHS) had produced only a 52.5 percent increase in health care output. The case for efficient and effective public management, using an evidence-based approach, has never been more pressing.

So who and what is an evidence-based public manager? The most obvious answer has to be—"someone who has evidence that their management methods are effective." So, what qualifies as meaningful and credible evidence of effectiveness? The public sector cannot normally resort to the profit motive and, even if it did, the recent collapses of General Motors and large banks are stark reminders that profits can hardly be described as evidence of effective and sustainable management practices. In the worst cases, the achievement of shortsighted profit targets can even mask underlying management problems, such as managers afraid to admit that they do not understand the financial derivatives they are buying. Flawed management practice, though, should always be seen as a symptom of flawed leadership. The definition of leadership adopted here is one that says effective leaders are those who can show that their decisions are based on evidence intended to create the most sustainable value for society: with *evidence* and *value* being synonymous.

Value is also a very practical proposition from a management perspective: it is all about outcomes—producing the best possible product or service at the best possible cost. This chapter adopts these fundamental EBMgt principles and applies them in a critique of one of the largest public management bodies in the world, the UK's NHS. In particular, I review its attempts over the last decade to improve its leadership and along the way offer some general lessons for those who aspire to become leading exponents of the theory, the practice, and indeed the art of EBMgt.

Evidence as "Value Created"

What is the job of a manager? At its most basic level, it is to manage people and other resources to achieve a set of organizational objectives. Yet if the leaders of the organization do not set ambitious objectives, then the manager's potential is already restricted, whereas leaders whose goal is simply to create as much value as possible will stretch management capabilities to their limit. Value maximization means that managers have to constantly check that their management practices are contributing to never-ending improvements in outcomes.

When an organization is very small and simple, it is relatively easy for a manager to see a direct connection between his or her decisions and outcomes. A window cleaner who employs one assistant can easily check his productivity and work standards and manage them accordingly; cause and effect are crystal clear, and the window cleaner knows only too well that a valuable employee attracts more valuable business. As soon as operational processes become more complex, though, the individual manager starts to lose sight of the direct connection between his or her own managerial decisions and the end result. For example, in health care, the radiologist will not necessarily see whether the patient ultimately received the best treatment available or even if the patient survived.

Matters can also become much more complicated in public management because the desired outcomes can often be ambiguous and even conflicting. A doctor might want to keep a patient in the hospital for an extra few days just to make sure the patient has fully recovered. This can easily conflict with the hospital manager's need to maximize patient throughput or minimize costs. The value question is always one of balancing genuine, professional concerns with the strictures of hard finance. Such tensions and potential conflicts will usually be viewed as an inevitable and unavoidable fact of managerial life; conventional managers become inured to this daily battle for resources. Often the root causes of these apparent dilemmas lie within differing value sets and perspectives—the doctor values excellent medical care, while the ward manager values a well-balanced set of accounts and the achievement of his or her targets. Of course, these goals do not have to be mutually exclusive, and if EBMgt is ever to attain real meaning, then it has to offer a better way of reconciling such opposing forces. The only way to do this is to aim for a common definition of value rather than one that is dependent on each individual's particular perspective.

So what might a common definition of value be? Let us return to the doctor and ward manager and ask them what they believe their objectives are. The doctor says she will aim to treat as many patients as possible, to the quality of care she believes is appropriate. The ward manager agrees that the hospital should treat as many patients as possible, to an acceptable quality of care, but this has to be within the limits of the budget. These two viewpoints do not appear to be too far apart; the only sticking point appears to be what constitutes "appropriate quality of care." The doctor believes she is paid to be the arbiter of "quality," but the manager knows that this is always liable to put him under cost pressure to avoid overspending. So how can this be better resolved using EBMgt?

Let us assume that the doctor treated 1,000 patients last year at an average cost of £5,000 per patient. The ward manager, who aspires to practice EBMgt, asks the doctor to indicate which of these patients received the right quality of care, and let us assume the doctor is happy to be openly questioned and challenged, as required by an EBMgt culture. This doctor is prepared to admit that no one is perfect and so acknowledges that 5 patients had to be readmitted because of inadequate care during their first stay. They also recognize that these 5 are "double counted" as "new" patients in the total patient count for that year. This means that in reality the hospital treated only 995 patients. Moreover, the annual budget of £5,000,000 was meant to treat 1,000. So the real average cost per actual patient is not £5,000 but £5,025 (£5,000,000 ÷ 995). The extra, opportunity cost incurred of £25,000 (5 readmitted patients at £5000 per head) could have treated 5 new patients, thereby achieving more value for society from existing resources. So far, so simple, and by the doctor's own admission, the hospital is providing society with only 99.5 percent of expected value for money. Now the question is, How can this hospital create more value through EBMgt?

There is a very simple EBMgt equation that will point us in the right direction every time this question is asked. Figure 13.1 presents a simple, generic definition of value that can satisfy all of the stakeholders simultaneously—the doctor, the manager, the patient, the taxpayer, and the government. There may still be disagreements among stakeholders about how much they want to spend on health care, but the purpose and criteria of success are all captured here.

Figure 13.1 shows two snapshots, A and B. A is the *baseline* picture, the current level of performance of the whole of the NHS expressed as its total cost of £100 billion per year. B is the level of value the NHS wants to achieve by the year 2014, based on a five-year business plan to reduce spending by approximately £6 billion per year. While such figures are usually viewed as inputs (costs), the evidence-based manager will view them as an indicator of output (value)—the number of patients treated effectively for the money expended. Dividing total expenditure by the number of patients treated annually produces the average patient cost. In our earlier example we took a figure of £5,025 as A and the £5,000 target as B. Immediately this compares like with like; the before and after measures are identical. All that has to be decided now is how to get from A to B.

Of course, we might refer to "average" figures here, but it must be emphasized that evidence-based management is all about individual managers working from their own "personal" data—data they already regard as credible. A non-evidence-

Figure 13.1 **Value Added**

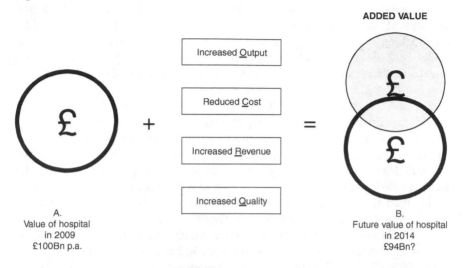

A.
Value of hospital
in 2009
£100Bn p.a.

B.
Future value of hospital
in 2014
£94Bn?

based manager who already has an average patient cost of £4,995 might focus his or her attention elsewhere because he or she is already ahead of target. The evidence-based-practice manager, however, will see the £4,995 as just their own, next, personal baseline as a basis for further improvement.

The generic, added-value equation in Figure 13.1 reveals that there are only four ways a manager can do this—only four ways a manager can improve or add value—

O   The quantity of patients treated could be increased, in this case by 0.5 percent (i.e., 1,000 unique patients are treated for £5,000,000), to achieve the target of £5,000 per patient.

C   Costs could be managed more tightly. Here the manager could save 0.5 percent, or £25,000, thereby achieving the same target of £5,000 per patient.

R   If the hospital was privately run, patients could be charged 0.5 percent (£25) more. As this is an NHS hospital, this option is not available on this occasion.

Q   The manager could improve the quality of care. Here the manager could ensure that the quality of care was such that no patient had to be readmitted and so no extra costs would be incurred.

Choosing any one of these options would achieve the immediate value objective, but this model is intended to be both dynamic and sustainable in the long term. So EBMgt is not about target setting; it expects managers to see all operational performance data as evidence of what else needs to be improved. They should already be thinking about how to move on to an even greater level of value. The more conventional managers would be tempted to hit their targets by trading off one variable for another, such as accepting lower quality to achieve a cost saving. For example, they might purchase cheaper but inferior drugs, consumables, or equipment, but this could actually reduce value by increasing the incidence of readmissions. So value is a holistic concept that does not allow trade-offs. It also incorporates the most "moral" personal values; evidence-based managers have integrity and so do their best to add value rather than cut corners. In other words, EBMgt is intrinsically more ethical than conventional, profit-driven management.

It is also a solid basis on which to establish more constructive working relationships. Let us return to the relationship between the doctor and the manager. The doctor will obviously want the best for her patient, including the best drugs and equipment, but the goal of value demands that the doctor do her best as well to make sure she operates within the budget available and is not tempted to just prescribe more drugs to save time.

The whole point of the value equation is that

- there is a common understanding of what "success" looks like among all stakeholders;
- the focus has to be on just these four value variables, which avoids wasted or unfocused management effort;
- no trade-off between objectives is allowed, which demands the best use of management capabilities;
- everyone involved has to see the connection between his or her own practices and ultimate value, whether or not they can see all the connections to the end of the process.

This might all seem like a statement of the blindingly obvious and of little consequence in the field of EBMgt, until we start to look at some real figures from the UK NHS (see Figure 13.2) that show

- an increase in annual spending of £52 billion from £44 billion to £96 billion between 1997 (baseline A) and 2007 (B);
- a 117 percent increase in the NHS's annual budget (approximately 85 percent, adjusted for inflation, at an average annual inflation rate of 2.5 percent);
- a rise in NHS spending from approximately 6.5 percent to 8.4 percent of GDP; and
- an "increase in health care output" over the same period of just 52.5 percent (although what constitutes "output" is still problematic.

On the face of it, there appears to be evidence here of a huge loss of value of the order of 30 percent. If that were applied to total expenditure in this period, of

Figure 13.2   **NHS Spending and Health Output**

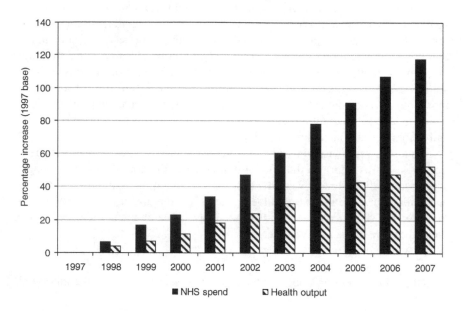

£745 billion, it would amount to a loss of £223.5 billion in value. So how might this evidence be used to create more value, ensuring that every pound spent on health care has at least a corresponding increase in health outputs? One of the immediate hurdles with which any EBMgt advocate will have to contend is skepticism about the veracity and accuracy of the evidence itself, even when it appears so clear that something has to be done to change the situation.

Evidence, Statistics, and Damn Lies

Evidence itself, regardless of its quality or veracity, will never be enough. There are several reasons why this is so:

- there is no single, absolute definition of what constitutes valid evidence;
- one man's "evidence" is another man's "statistics and damn lies"; and
- in an organizational context, particularly a public management organization, political expediency can easily trump and traduce evidence-based philosophy, policy, and practice.

So a guiding principle for any evidence-based manager is "your evidence is only as good as its credibility with your stakeholders." In the case of the NHS, the only thing that should matter is patient outcomes. There is no point saying to a patient that infection control is improving after they have just acquired an infection while in the hospital; generalized statistics have little meaning to individuals, and general "improvements" offer scant consolation to victims. General evidence also offers little specific guidance to the hospital manager, whose own ward is meticulously cleaned and sterilized, when the infections are acquired in admissions or the radiology department. Evidence works best when it means something to all of those who have to act on it, that is, everyone involved in the total patient process.

Statistics can always be disputed, and there is a natural human tendency, when put under pressure, to try to defend one's actions by selecting only those statistics that support one's case. A professional approach to EBMgt therefore requires an ability to distinguish between what we might term high-grade and low-grade evidence. It is unlikely that there will ever be an absolute standard that satisfies everyone. For example, some people will continue to choose homeopathic remedies for their ailments despite the lack of any solid evidence of their efficacy. So evidence-based managers should not set out on a search for the holy grail of incontrovertible proof or "truth." Such an endeavor might have a certain appeal, but the real world is one where there are always differing and conflicting perspectives, opinions, and political imperatives. The best managers can hope for is that the evidence they use gives them the greatest confidence that their actions will be effective and the highest probability that they will actually add as much value as they can. The evidence should also convince as many stakeholders as possible that this is the case. So what does that mean in practice?

Let us change tack for a moment and consider a different sector of public management, where evidence is everything: the police. When a crime is committed, police investigators look for evidence to identify, apprehend, and prosecute the perpetrator; police evidence is largely unearthed after an observable and verifiable fact (e.g., the body of the possible murder victim is in front of their very eyes). On rare occasions, they gather evidence of criminal intent before the fact (e.g., the threatening letter to the victim). This neatly highlights a dilemma in EBMgt—when is the best time to gather and use evidence—after the problem has arisen, or before, to prevent it from happening in the first place?

In a health care context, evidence is sought to indicate that the treatment has worked (e.g., the rates of cancer deaths drop over time). However, doctors are also trained to adopt an evidence-based approach right from the beginning, as part of the diagnostic that has to precede any prescription or treatment. They will take a patient history, as well as a family history, and look for symptoms of illness or disease to make an accurate diagnosis. This has to be exactly the same mind-set and approach adopted by evidence-based managers. They have to work through a simple sequence:

1. collect evidence that a problem, or potential problem, exists;
2. diagnose the root causes of the problem;
3. prescribe the best possible solution;

    4. implement the solution; and

    5. check for evidence that the solution worked, and, if it did not, start again at step 1 by revisiting all available evidence.

This sequence has been a standard tool in management problem solving for many years, at least since the 1920s, when Walter Shewart referred to it as the "New Way" in management, and is usually referred to as the plan-do-check-act cycle. The whole cycle is predicated on the need to measure the evidence before *planning* to do anything about it. It is logical and could be regarded as common sense except that we have already highlighted some practical problems with deciding what constitutes high-grade evidence and the temptation to use generalized data for diagnosing and treating specific, individual problems.

One example of this tendency would be a doctor's prescribing antidepressants for all patients with symptoms of depression, without taking a proper history or bothering to understand individual circumstances. Worse still, imagine walking into a doctor's office and, before you even have a chance to sit down, your general practitioner hands you a prescription for antibiotics, on the assumption that regardless of your ailment, these are bound to have some benefit. Far-fetched? Apparently not. Guidance from the National Institute for Health and Clinical Excellence[3] advises "doctors to tell patients suffering from respiratory infections that they do not need antibiotics. . . . Patients should be reassured that antibiotics will 'make little difference to symptoms and may have side-effects.'"

Some doctors persist in offering patients antibiotics for virus-related illnesses when they know this is inappropriate. One estimate[4] suggests that up to 80 percent of common viral infections are still treated with antibiotics that are inappropriate.

We can spot exactly the same human tendency among senior managers who are prepared to make the wild assumption that the serious loss of value draining from the NHS's annual budget is deemed to be due to a lack of "leadership," whatever that means. This generalized and simplistic "diagnosis" is precisely what has led to a prescription for leadership development programs across the whole of the NHS. This common failing in conventional management thinking is compounded by the belief that the impact of such programs or projects can be decided only after the fact, the equivalent of a police postmortem, without having established any sort of baseline first. This is the antithesis of EBMgt and can be regarded as a serious contraindicator, just as drugs can have serious side effects or prove to be totally misprescribed.

So EBMgt demands a discipline whereby the manager does not rush to act unless and until the baseline evidence is measured and used for a clearheaded diagnosis. Moreover, all stakeholders should know what the baseline is, even if they are not totally convinced that it is the right measure. The plan-do-check-act philosophy underpinning EBMgt is based on continuous, never-ending improvement. It teaches us that even if the initial measure chosen was "wrong," success will always be achieved, eventually, if there are enough iterations of trial and error.

This follows the same logic that an infinite number of monkeys with an infinite number of typewriters will produce the works of Shakespeare. In practice we do not have infinite resources, but there are rarely as many iterations required as we might imagine, because plan-do-check-act reveals when mistakes are being made, and this in itself tends to reduce the number of mistakes that human beings make. However, nothing is to be swept under the carpet.

This could also be called "evaluative" management, where managers start a cycle of improvement by evaluating their priorities and then *check*ing the evidence to ascertain whether improvement is actually occurring. This is where EBMgt hits another hurdle, though, due to conventional management's poor understanding of the purpose and role of evaluation.

Evaluation Should Always Be at the Beginning, Not the End

When managers are asked to evaluate any project, they tend to have a preconceived notion that evaluation happens after the project is completed, rather than before it started. So the usual questions would be, Was the project on time and budget? and Did it produce what was originally planned? They might even send out questionnaires or conduct a survey of different stakeholders to gather as wide a range of views as possible, but all of this would be after the fact. How much more useful it would have been to ask these questions at the beginning. The views of the different stakeholders could have significantly influenced the design of the project. Proper evaluation always asks really tough questions about the potential value of the project right at the beginning and should play a critical part in its design.

If we apply this thinking to anyone planning a leadership program, they should articulate what the value of "better leadership" might look like in terms of the four value variables in Figure 13.1. Will better leadership mean more patients, lower costs, increased revenue, or better quality of patient care? This might sound like just another hypothetical question, but under EBMgt, it is a serious question demanding specific measures attributed to and owned by the individuals concerned, in this case probably chief executives of individual hospitals and primary care trusts. In fact, it is even more important to undertake a very rigorous, pre-intervention diagnosis for leadership development, because whatever "science" underpins this field of study, it is much younger and less exact than the field of medicine, which has been predicated on evidence-based practice for many, many years.

In 2004 the NHS's Leadership Centre,[5] which was part of its Modernisation Agency, justified the running of its own leadership programs by declaring that "improved leadership will improve patient's care, treatment and experience; improve the health of the population." This was a bold assertion considering no evidence has been offered in support. Yet the same body commissioned a "Guide to evaluating leadership development,"[6] which defined evaluation as "the assessment of how well something is working against the criteria that have been established for it at the outset." It seems here that the purpose of evaluation, its role in management, and its emphasis are still more concerned with showing that something worked after the event, rather than as acting as part of a diagnostic design process to ensure that a program has the highest probability of success from the outset. Evaluation should ensure that the "criteria" established "at the outset" are the right criteria, the same four value variables shown in Figure 13.1. If these criteria had been established at the beginning of the NHS leadership program, even in general terms (e.g., the NHS needs to improve health output per pound spent by at least 30 percent), then leadership would actually start to mean something to the NHS managers who were undertaking the leadership training. The acid test for checking whether development programs are following these fundamental principles is to ask two distinct questions that are a distillation of the very essence of evaluative EBMgt:

- Do we have performance measures for the people we are planning to develop?
- What would an x percent improvement in value (using output, cost, revenue, and quality variable measures) be worth in pounds?

So, for example, every chief executive of an NHS hospital could be asked what their average cost per patient is (or any value metric deemed to be a priority) and evidence produced to show their performance relative to their peers. This could be in the form of the simple, bell-shaped (normal distribution) performance curve shown in Figure 13.3.

Of course, the primary purpose in actually drawing this curve is to create a comparative picture where every participant can see where they are in relation to their colleagues and peers. It does not matter what shape the curve is, whether it is "normal" (Gaussian) or even if it is skewed or shifted to one side. It is just a starting point, and the only thing that matters, from a management perspective, is whether the managers or leaders accept and agree where they are starting from (i.e., they know why they have a score of 3 and what it represents—such as long waiting lists, for example) and are prepared to be held accountable for improving their score. Needless to say, falsifying the waiting lists is not an option, even though this is precisely what some NHS managers have done in the past.

To construct one example of this curve, all we need is the average patient costs for all the organizations run by all the chief executives in the NHS. The resulting scores can then be converted to a frequency range from 1 to 10 (where 1 is the highest average cost and 10 is the lowest). Only then can we ask a sensible question about leadership capability and at the same time maintain a clear distinction between "management" and "leadership." There would be many distinguishing characteristics of the real leaders. Leaders would not offer excuses for their "low" scores or rush to blame anyone else. They would own the problem and look for the root causes rather than just aim to keep their political masters satisfied.

What this curve does is create the evidence base for articulating what the problem is. Here there are two key questions being asked:

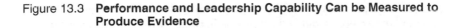

Figure 13.3 **Performance and Leadership Capability Can be Measured to Produce Evidence**

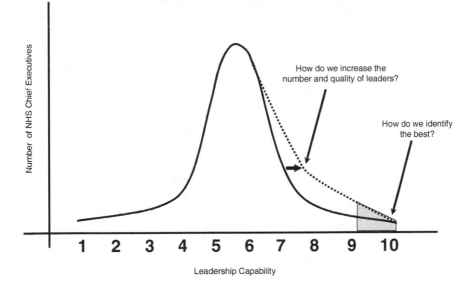

- How are we identifying effective leaders?
- Could we increase the number of chief executives with the requisite qualities of leadership we want?

For example, any manager can try to trim costs, and the best will make significant improvements. However, they will start to hit a wall when they try to involve, say, consultant surgeons whose actions influence their costs. When this happens, a higher order of influence is called for; the leaders of the organization have to create an environment in which the managers can mount a valid challenge to the consultants' costs. Managers cannot assert themselves if the de facto power base is not in their favor.

Leadership discussions held in a vacuum, without evidence of current performance, would be of academic interest only. However, before a connection can be made between one piece of evidence and leadership capability, the NHS has to be prepared to collect potentially sensitive and even incriminating data. The curve in Figure 13.3 is designed to raise levels of accountability, not hide them. It is also designed to instigate an open and honest discussion about what needs to happen. In essence, EBMgt will never happen unless the right culture and climate have been created. Where politics or a seeking-to-blame culture militate against such simple evidence gathering, such a well-tried and tested technique will be regarded with suspicion and encourage excuses rather than solutions.

In fact, this is probably one of the primary reasons that evidence-based management is still the exception rather than the rule in twenty-first-century management. However, experienced evidence-based managers will already have anticipated this reaction and so will advise that everyone on the curve has to be prepared to improve from where they are. Acceptance of this is the only thing that matters. Evidence-based managers do not prejudge the situation. Even though such strong evidence might tempt them to jump to the conclusion that the chief executives achieving the highest scores must, by dint of that fact, be the best, de facto "leaders," they will resist this temptation. The only guidance that the curve in Figure 13.3 offers is the basis for a mature and intelligent discussion. The chief executives with the lowest scores will be asked why they think that is the case, not to blame them, but to ascertain the root causes of their problems so that appropriate measures can be taken to resolve them.

At the same time, the chief executives with the highest scores will also be asked how they can improve. They may have inherited a particularly good hospital, or there may be other fortuitous circumstances that have produced their good scores. This curve is nonjudgmental, and its sole purpose is to elicit further efforts to create more value from the chief executives themselves. Yet it is the organizational culture that will determine whether it is effective or not, not the evidence presented, per se. Only when the discussion has reached this stage can the next question be asked, which is, What would an x percent improvement look like in terms of hard pounds in value (e.g., the opportunity cost of ensuring that patients are not readmitted).

The NHS's approach is the very antithesis of evidence-based leadership development (or any other development activity, for that matter) in that it has produced a pre-prepared prescription looking for an assumed ailment. If there is a root cause of poor leadership in the NHS, then no evidence has been produced to support such a contention. The very fact that it still persists with leadership development suggests that if there is poor leadership in the NHS, it is not necessarily within the target audience for these particular leadership programs.

Evidence-Based Management Is Common Sense Writ Large

The NHS is not the only organization guilty of this failure to follow common sense; it is a universal management problem. The reason EBMgt is so high on the agenda today is because so little high-grade evidence has ever been produced to demonstrate that leadership training actually creates any value at all. But this is another general problem in management, and it applies particularly to matters of "people" management. While information technology systems can generate as much data as we are ever likely to need for management purposes, there is a distinct lack of people-management data that reveal anything about the connections between effective people management and value creation. If the NHS suddenly decided to adopt an EBMgt approach to its leadership, it would have an immediate problem in trying to produce a comprehensive series of performance curves like the one shown in Figure 13.3.

The real irony is that the evidence in Figure 13.2 demonstrates that previous leadership efforts seem to have failed, and yet need for improvement is resulting in even more pressure on the NHS to look at its leadership capability. Here we see a classic illustration of the real difference between non-evidence-based approaches and EBMgt. Where evidence is not used during the diagnostic phase, a vicious cycle is generated. There can be no escape from this cycle and no observable progress made without a establishing an evidence-based baseline. Where evidence is gathered and used intelligently as a diagnostic, then true EBMgt will be witnessed immediately in the automatic instigation of a virtuous cycle.

Gathering baseline data (A) before a leadership development intervention commences offers a reference point by which to gauge B at some time in the future. Of course, the anticipated results at B might not materialize, but then that only sets up a further set of questions, another iteration, in a relentless search for added value. Evaluation is not a static concept in EBMgt; it is part of a continuous cycle of learning. It does not try to prove anything, either, especially as EBMgt accepts that there will never be absolute proof that a particular intervention transformed A into B. What it does offer, though, is a much higher probability that the original criteria were the right criteria and that the learning hypothesis holds water (e.g., sending managers on a leadership course will improve their leadership capability at least in terms of patient costs).

As the Office for Public Management / NHS guide to evaluation did not follow this sequence, it should be no surprise that the leadership development efforts of the NHS at the time were terminated shortly after the guide was published in 2005. In fact, much of the work of the Modernisation Agency itself was disbanded and resurfaced in a new incarnation, the NHS Institute for Innovation and Improvement, which is still in existence and provides leadership programs for NHS managers without any baseline value measures in place.

But this is not the only NHS body trying to promote and develop leadership. The latest manifestation of leadership development guidance and activity for the NHS is revealed in a document entitled "Inspiring Leaders: Leadership for Quality. Guidance for NHS Talent and Leadership Plans,"[7] issued as "best practice guidance" by the Department for Health, Workforce Directorate on January 22, 2009. There is no evidence to support the claim that this should qualify as "best practice," and, as the purpose of this initiative is obviously to improve leadership, it is surprising to read on and find that they already believe they have "fantastic and talented leaders in the NHS," despite the evidence in Figure 13.2 suggesting otherwise. The illogicality and contradictory nature of these statements indicates an organization in a chronic state of denial, failing to face up to the evidence and lessons from its experience. It could be described as a nonlearning organization. Not only is this a vicious circle but a dishonest and self-reinforcing one at that, where "fantastic and talented leaders" producing poor results apparently need more of the same "leadership treatment."

Perhaps the cornerstone of EBMgt has to be an honest appraisal of the situation the organization is in. Certainly dishonest EBMgt is a perfect oxymoron. No progress can be made in the management of the NHS until it uses whatever evidence it already produces more effectively. Just how much of a quandary it is in can be seen in the following statement,[8] on its own Web site as recently as March 2009, where it states that the NHS is already "the world's largest publicly funded health service. It is also one of the most efficient, most egalitarian and most comprehensive."

But it readily admits, under the heading "Performance," that "Measuring the efficiency of healthcare systems is notoriously difficult. The NHS—in common with other healthcare systems—has never consistently and systematically measured changes in its patients' health. As a result, it's impossible to say exactly how much extra 'health' is created for each pound spent."

So how can any progress be made in an organization that finds it so difficult to cope with the evidence that is staring it in the face?

Applying the Principles of EBMgt to the NHS

EBMgt cannot be transplanted into an organization against its will. EBMgt is as much a societal and organizational philosophy as it is a set of management methods and practices. EBMgt has to be an essential ingredient in the organization's vision. So what is the vision of the NHS? No one really knows, as even its core principles offer no definition of its real purpose or its value to society. Its aim was always to provide health care for free (for "free" read "taxpayer funded") at the point of need, but nowhere does it mention at what cost or at what quality level. In other words, this is a very narrow view of its remit and does not include a full value proposition of the best health care at the best cost.

As with all mission statements, declaring a clear purpose is a double-edged sword. It provides the clarity that everyone craves yet comes with personal accountability that is perhaps not so warmly welcomed. That is why mission statements are so often fudged or omitted altogether, but there are always consequences. How can doctors be criticized for offering "expensive" treatments (e.g., new cancer drugs) when the mission statement does not mention cost? That is why a mission statement has to be a clearheaded value proposition, fully and simultaneously encompassing all of the variables of output, cost, revenue, and quality. Only then will there be a solid foundation on which to build the necessary culture, structures, systems, and processes that underpin organizational management.

The NHS, on paper at least, is run by a management structure that leads all the way up to the prime minister's office, as shown in Figure 13.4.

This appears to be a typical hierarchical management structure, albeit for one of the biggest organizations in the world, with clinicians delivering services being managed by managers. Yet the reality is different. No big decisions are taken without consulting and negotiating with the doctors, who are represented by one of the most well-organized unions in the United Kingdom, the British Medical Association. It would probably be more accurate to say that the clinicians run the NHS with the

Figure 13.4   **The Organization Structure of the UK NHS** (Simplified)

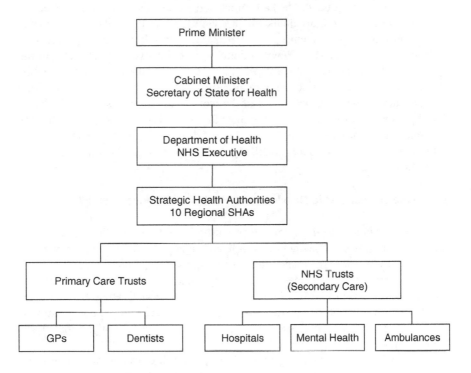

acquiescence of the managers. In this context, the maximization of value is always going to be a huge challenge, but if the NHS is ever to be pulled back on the right financial track, there are two items on the leadership agenda:

- The NHS needs leadership that is prepared to rebalance the power structure between management and clinical staff.
- The value proposition of the NHS has to be restated, with crystal clarity, that cost is now a key part of the value equation and that it can only be adequately addressed by clinicians and managers working from a common understanding of the right balance between quality and cost of care.

Both of these will require gauging the performance of all NHS employees against value criteria rather than simplistic targets such as the number of surgical procedures. This will be a significant step forward. In April 2006, the then health secretary, Patricia Hewitt, declared, "Despite the headlines, actually the NHS has just had its best year ever."[9]

She was disingenuously referring to simplistic data, and her comments were immediately ridiculed for flying in the face of the experiences of thousands of

UK citizens who were on waiting lists for treatment or who could not get to see a doctor when they needed to. She had committed the cardinal sin of using selective data to try to convince individuals who knew otherwise. Politicians, who refer to such figures as "improvements in the NHS," are certainly not looking at it from a value perspective. Patricia Hewitt's definition of "best year" might refer to patients treated, but we have already seen that the value equation, of more patients per pound spent, has deteriorated dramatically. Judged on the basis of value, 2005 could accurately be described as one of the worst years in the history of the NHS. Pouring money into an organization, especially one in crisis, is no way to increase its value. An acknowledgment that the law of diminishing returns applies in the public sector is long overdue, and EBMgt will help to highlight what economists have always known.

The Value of Leadership Development Programs Is Questionable

Providers of leadership development programs might suggest that the need for such interventions is self-evident. A simplistic logic might support the view that a relentless search for performance improvement, particularly in the public sector, is bound to require better leadership. Such arguments, however, run counter to the prevailing wisdom in EBMgt. An evidence-based approach would be characterized by two simple criteria—an accumulation of evidence that the organization is failing to exploit opportunities for creating value and a causal analysis that points to inadequate leadership.

This is where EBMgt can be relatively impartial. It does not take a particular view or stance on any specific management method, technique, or tool; it simply asks, Where is the evidence that value has been created? If an organization chooses to send managers to have an experience of fire walking or hanging upside down from trees on an outdoor management development camp, there should be no criticism of the means chosen, only the process of how this "solution" stemmed from an organizational diagnostic of current performance. If no connection between the two is discernible, the evidence-based manager will not condemn their methods as ineffective, but will only insist that they are patently non-evidence based. However, the evidence-based manager would go further and ask whether any organization can afford to be deemed to be engaging in such activities. If the organization wants to defend its management development methods, it will of course present whatever data it regards as important, but if it is not related to value, then it can rightly be put into the low-grade category.

If there is any resistance among seasoned managers to what they might view suspiciously as the "new concept" of EBMgt, it might be because they regard their decision-making processes as based on reliable management data and information. They might never have referred to this as "evidence" in the past, or even regarded it as anything other than common sense, but they will have responded to what operational data tell them.

If EBMgt were nothing more than just another badge for this type of management, then it is unlikely to be welcomed as an innovation in management thinking. Yet it is so easy to see the damage that can be done through the limited lens of conventional management.

The absence of EBMgt is not peculiar to or just a problem for the NHS, or the public sector per se; it is a very serious issue of global proportions. A lack of interest in evaluative EBMgt means that we do not know which management practices create value and which do not. It is a failure to recognize this that creates the downward spiral of repeated management mistakes and deteriorating effectiveness. In turn, this breeds organizational stasis through a climate of nonaccountability that inevitably ensues. The tools and techniques of EBMgt will not bring about the necessary transformation, though; only strong leadership that understands exactly how to get the best value out of EBMgt will be able to do that.

Conclusion

As with many "innovations" in management thinking (management by objectives, total quality management, balanced scorecards, and strategy maps) more often than not, behind the hype and the headlines are just simple, commonsense methods and approaches (see also Chapters 3, 8, and 9). Even though they are touted as "new ways" of thinking and working, they tend to be a conglomeration of very old tools and techniques (the Gaussian distribution in Figure 13.3 is more than 150 years old). Hopefully, they will have generated value, but if that was enough, then why has EBMgt surfaced as a critical question in the twenty-first century?

Maybe one of the answers is that when a management concept is perceived to be "new," it immediately becomes disconnected from its forebears. Also, inadequate management education can result in partial knowledge and senior executives getting "the wrong end of the stick," with each new idea meaning many different things to different people. So for some organizations total quality management has morphed into "Six Sigma," or even just "Lean" (as it has in the NHS), without any clear understanding among the most senior management group of either the inherent connections among each of these elements or the requirement for a change in management philosophy and culture and not just operational practices.

EBMgt is in danger of suffering the same fate unless it is able to express itself as a single, coherent combination of management philosophy, business strategy, and management practice. What currently stands in the way of any further progress is a commonly accepted definition of what constitutes "evidence." If there are different types of data competing for the title of "best evidence," then the term *EBMgt* will eventually be meaningless. If those designing and running leadership programs, for example, regard "happy" participants as meaningful evidence of either leadership capability or effectiveness, then the challenge for serious EBMgt advocates is to demonstrate that this is no more useful or relevant, in management terms, than a placebo is in medicine.

The leadership and management development industry is unlikely to roll over in the face of such challenges, though, not just because of vested interests but because there will be plenty of participants in leadership programs at prestigious management schools who are bound to have received some benefit from their education. Evidence-based managers should not decry such anecdotal testimonials but rather challenge the diagnostics that led the executive to the management school in the first place. Whatever benefits the participants might feel they have gained from participating in a program if it was not predicated on EBMgt, it will represent a missed opportunity. There will of course always be serendipitous benefits in most management education interventions, but serendipity should be no competition for a clearheaded, focused EBMgt approach that aims to maximize value.

Until all of these issues are resolved, organizations will have no option but to resort to practices that can only be described as either non-evidence based or at least low-grade-evidence based. No self-respecting chief executive would admit to supporting non-EBMgt, even though there are plenty of examples where this is precisely what is currently happening. An admission of ignorance is obviously too much to expect, so there will have to be tactics developed in the EBMgt community to break this impasse.

While determined political leadership should be the answer in the public sector, the political sensitivities involved with trying to turn around large public organizations like the NHS are probably just too big a task unless and until they become a "burning platform." One minuscule silver lining in the current dark clouds of global recession might just be that these platforms are starting to ignite as we speak.

Perhaps the last and most worrying conclusion is that maybe the management textbook has yet to be written for organizations as large as the NHS. There has probably also been an implicit assumption, during the inexorable growth of our largest corporations in the boom years before the banking collapse of 2007–8, that an organization is infinitely scalable. The NHS appears to be one organization that has tested that assumption to the absolute limit.

There is a view now that some of the banks became too big to fail and that in the future, that will mean they should not be allowed to become that big again. The same argument could be applied to the NHS and maybe to other large public sector organizations. If these large organizations start to adopt EBMgt, they might survive long enough to be able to say, with some confidence, whether that is the case or not.

Notes

1. Anatole Kaletsky, "Healthcare, Not Bailouts, Could Break America," *Times* (UK), June 18, 2009, www.timesonline.co.uk/tol/comment/columnists/anatole_kaletsky/article6523512.ece (accessed November 1, 2009).

2. BBC News, "Obama Warns Doctors over Reforms," June 15, 2009, http://news.bbc.co.uk/1/hi/world/americas/8100605.stm (accessed November 1, 2009).

3. David Batty and agencies, "Watchdog Tells Doctors to Prescribe Fewer Antibiotics," Guardian.co.uk, July 23, 2008, www.guardian.co.uk/society/2008/jul/23/nhs.health (accessed November 1, 2009).

4. Oxford University, "Antibiotic Resistance: Doctors' Antibiotic Prescribing Practices Still Contributing to Problem," *ScienceDaily,* July 27, 2007, http://www.sciencedaily.com/releases/2007/07/070726091218.htm (accessed November 1, 2009).

5. Happi, "In a Nutshell: Modernisation Agency," January 16, 2004, www.happi.org.uk/content.php?id=61 (accessed November 1, 2009).

6. Office for Public Management & NHS Leadership Centre, 2005. London: National Health Service.

7. UK Department of Health, "Inspiring Leaders: Leadership for Quality," January 20, 2009, www.dh.gov.uk/en/Publicationsandstatistics/Publications/PublicationsPolicy-AndGuidance/DH_093395 (accessed November 1, 2009).

8. UK National Health Service, "About the NHS," April 12, 2009, www.nhs.uk/NHS-England/aboutnhs/Pages/About.aspx (accessed November 1, 2009).

9. BBC News, "NHS 'Enjoying Best Year'—Hewitt," April 22, 2006, http://news.bbc.co.uk/1/hi/health/4935358.stm (accessed November 1, 2009).

14

Evidence-Based Management of Social Services

Providing the "Right" Services for Complex Needs

Denise de Vries

The integrated and efficient delivery of social and health services to the most marginalized sections of our society remains a difficult problem for government. At the behest of and in partnership with the South Australian Aboriginal community, this research brought together the Australian Research Council, Australian Housing and Urban Research Institute, Neporendi Aboriginal Forum Inc., Achieve SA, the Department of Human Services, Flinders University, and the University of South Australia to design, develop, and test a participatory process to match services to perceived need. A software tool has been developed to guide a "conversation" between service providers and users that assists the service provider in addressing the more complex needs of the user. The software system includes a knowledge base that has a three-layer architecture with an interface positioned between the data and the metadata for the management of the complex structure of the concepts, issues, and resources involved. This intermediary level is the *mesodata* layer. The mesodata layer provides complex structures in which to store domain values and their interrelationships. The domain structures enable different orderings that form the bases of filters for enhanced querying and information retrieval. This enables the interrelationships between the factors to be analyzed and provides not only statistical evidence but also clusters or sequences of factors and their (perceived) importance to the service users. From this richer analysis, information is provided that

- allows for enhanced participation and enables service providers to "case manage" complex needs,
- highlights what works, why, and how, and
- facilitates the distribution and scheduling of resources.

Evidence: What Works, Why, and How?

Performance-based measurements have been used to improve management since the early twentieth century using systematic management techniques researched by people such as Taylor (1911), Mayo (1946), Weber (1968), and others. Evidence-based practice (including evidence-based guidelines, evidence-based decision making, evidence-based policy making, and so forth) has developed from health systems and patient care as a way of doing practice. It was developed as a method for teaching critical assessment skills to medical residents, providing a way of assessing, intervening, and evaluating based on a set of assumptions and values, so as to strengthen the scientific base used by physicians in decision making (Mullen et al. 2008).

In this project, the coming together of researchers from multiple disciplines also brought together different views of how to gather evidence and knowledge: the systemic thinking methodology, using a soft-systems mapping approach inspired by Checkland and Scholes (1990), including narratives and rich pictures; the systems-engineering iteration model for requirements acquisition, as in agile (Martin 2003) and XP (eXtreme Programming) software development (Beck and Andres 2004); Christopher Alexander's pattern language (Alexander et al. 1977) to articulate and maintain stability in patterns; mesodata techniques (de Vries 2006) to build taxonomies and develop context-sensitive knowledge. These differing approaches crystalize to a participatory design approach that includes all stakeholders to discover what works, why it works, and how it works.

Background to Research Project

Our multidisciplinary team contributed to redressing social inclusion issues by designing, developing, and testing a software management tool together with Neporendi Aboriginal Forum Inc.[1] Aboriginal researchers and the South Australian Department of Human Services (McIntyre-Mills 2008).

The challenge was to address comorbidities (the coexistence of substance abuse and mental health problems) and a number of other issues through the development of a meaningful process that was tested by those who experience the areas of concern and who are affected by the decisions taken.

Current Department of Human Services management is confronted with the expectation of provision of a high quality of service to an increasingly diverse clientele. Service providers can no longer be compartmentalized and specialized. In the area of social services, a service user rarely has a single issue to resolve, yet the service agencies typically still concentrate on single-issue solutions without regard to related matters. For example, a public housing provider may allocate housing without considering whether it is near a person's place of employment or training or if it is near public transport routes, thus inadvertently creating more problems for the service user.

Neporendi's clientele is representative of the issues faced by indigenous communities in other areas of Australia, such as high levels of health-related issues, unemployment, homelessness, limited education opportunities, and domestic violence. The effects of domestic violence are extensive: for example, the criminalization of the offenders has financial, physical, and psychological consequences for the women, children, and men involved. It also has intergenerational consequences. Social inclusion, homelessness, unemployment, gambling, family violence, and drug misuse are facets of complex, interrelated problems requiring a coordinated governance response across the public, private, and nongovernment sectors.

Research Methods

As a starting point, the experience and knowledge of one hundred stakeholders—both service providers and service users—were acquired. Their wisdom and implicit knowledge were gathered through conversations, narratives, and rich pictures[2] rather than interviews. A systemic, iterative conversational approach is different from an interview where the researcher asks the questions according to a linear set of questions. The conversational approach allows people to choose how they wish to answer questions and control the direction of the topic. They can start a conversation from their perceptions, rather than from the viewpoint of the researcher.

This iterative approach acquires a broad view of the universe of discourse in the preliminary phases and elicits many facets that are often not taken into account when designing software systems, for instance, intangible aspects such as emotions, self-esteem, and so forth that typically are excluded from computer systems but are necessary for the success of a system in this particular universe of discourse.

These data were then used to design a generic computer system model that can be used as a tool by both clients and providers of community agencies to find possible solutions to issues facing the client. These solutions are anticipated to be plans of action and are conceptually "pathways to well-being."

The requirement that the tool be *generic* means that even though the concepts and issues being considered in this project are specific to its context, the process by which decisions are made are universal. It is the *process* of decision making, planning, and resourcing that is modeled within the computer system. Combined with decision making, the computer system comprises a knowledge base to provide storage and retrieval of problems, issues, resources, and solutions, which are then analyzed to inform management policy.

Building the Knowledge Base

The overarching architecture for devising pathways within the system is to formulate solutions by investigating existing problem-solving methods. These methods generate "action plans" that invoke concepts and issues that are already described by previous knowledge and experience.

As can be seen in Figure 14.1, the foundation of the system is the knowledge base. Thus, the data modeling also begins with modeling these components of data. The preliminary interviews of fifty clients and fifty providers resulted in classifications of "states" of well-being as well as indicators for each of the states and the rela-

Figure 14.1   **Architecture of Knowledge Base**

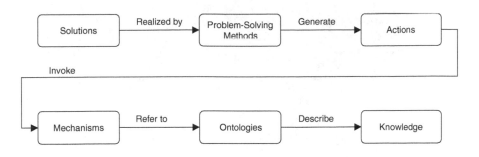

tionships, or influences, each had on another. Further to these classifications, more specific information about each of the identified classes and issues was gathered by structured interviews aimed particularly at getting data regarding both tangible and intangible concepts and the relationships between them.

The resultant data were qualitatively analyzed and summarized to a list of concepts. To store these concepts in an ontology, a further questionnaire was developed to gather more detailed data about how the key issues and related terms are regarded by people in their lives and to ascertain the scale of importance they have in an action plan. This iteration of data acquisition included prompting questions inspired by Christakis's (Christakis and Bausch 2006) structured design process. As this process has been developed for groups of participants, the heuristics for voting could not be applied in this case; however, the key points for the definition stage of inquiry were.

A graphical overview was created (Figure 14.2), which shows the key concepts and interrelationships identified in the first round of interviews. Participants were given this graphic with the discussion and consideration points pro forma (Figure 14.4).

These discussion points not only provide the frequency of issues facing the target population but also provide us with data enriched with the participants' perceptions of the different interrelations among them, including importance (impact), chronological sequence or co-occurrence, as well as factors that can facilitate or hinder an individual's life. None of the concepts was a priori classified as "good" or "bad," and results showed that some may be either a help or a hindrance depending on the individual's situation. From these responses, in particular the mapped pathways, plus more issues (Figure 14.3), both an ontology of the universe of discourse and a repository of "patterns of solutions" were modeled.

Ontology structures reflect the complexity of and relationships within a concept domain. Currently ontologies are viewed as resources that are positioned *outside* a user's information system and are used as an aid for the design of metadata, for translation of concepts, or for transformation of related concepts.

Figure 14.2 **Issues Identified at First Iteration**

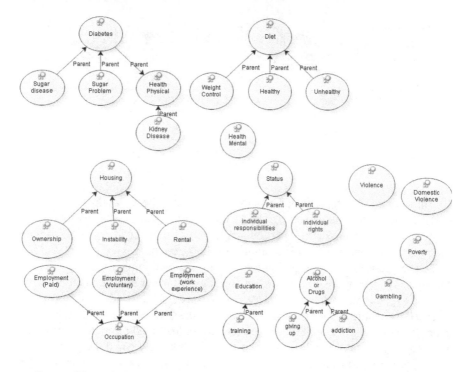

Source: The author.

In this research, a three-layered architecture is used with an interface positioned between the data and the metadata for the management of the complex structure of the ontology.

This intermediary level is the *mesodata* layer (de Vries 2006; de Vries et al. 2004; de Vries and Roddick 2004; La-Ongsri et al. 2008; Rice et al. 2006; Roddick and de Vries 2006). This mesodata layer, separate from the metadata and data, provides complex structures, such as graphs, queues, and circular lists, in which to store domain values, the interrelationships of the attribute values, and the strength of those relationships, as well as supplying the "intelligence" required to operate and manipulate them. The domain structures enable different orderings that form the bases of filters for enhanced querying and information retrieval.

The mesodata layer facilitates data capture, as it allows a greater variety of terms to be captured within the database as it builds an ontology or taxonomy (dependent on system requirements). Such a model means that synonyms and related terms can all be recorded rather than selecting from a constrained pre-defined list, as is normally the case. This in turn empowers people to say in their own words what they really mean to say rather than having to choose another's

Figure 14.3   **Issues Identified at Second Iteration**

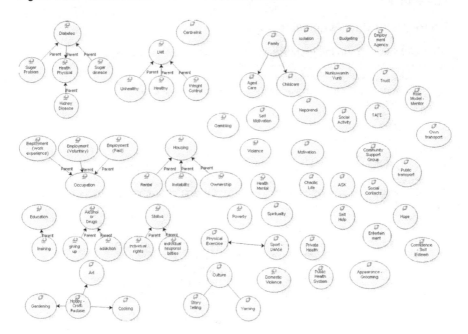

Source: The author.

words. Analysis can then be generalized or specialized on these terms, dependent upon the situation.

In addition to the ontology of the domain, the knowledge base also contains the patterns of solutions. Christopher Alexander (Alexander 1979; Alexander et al. 1977), using architectural patterns, developed a "pattern language" to provide a lingua franca for describing these patterns, or rules of thumb, to enable laypersons to communicate with architects and town planners. Alexander's definition of a pattern is "Each pattern is a three-part rule, which expresses a relation between a certain context, a problem, and a solution."

Patterns are also identified, or tagged, to show the strength of their success. Some are more true, more profound, more certain than others (Alexander et al. 1977).

The conceptual design of the system has the following components:

- Knowledge base containing the ontology of issues and concepts
- Repository of patterns of solutions
- Resource requirements for implementing the patterns
- Pathfinder based upon the discussion and selections of the users
- Statistical and data-mining routines to analyze pathways created and resources used

Figure 14.4

Pro forma for Data Acquisition

1. Select a bubble in the graphic and consider the issue or concept named.
2. How does the bubble help other aspects of life?
3. How does the bubble hinder other aspects of life?
4. How important is the bubble? (Use a scale like the one below.)
   ____ Not at all
   ____ A bit
   ____ Doesn't matter
   ____ Quite important
   ____ Very important
5. If I solve this problem or have this asset first, does it make solving other problems easier?
6. Do these things always happen together? Or one after another?
7. How do I achieve it?
8. How do I avoid it?
9. Where can I get help for it?
10. Who can I help and how, if they need this or have this problem?
11. Is it sometimes good and sometimes bad—in what situations?
12. Are there other names/terms for the same thing?
13. What can stop me from (or make it really hard) getting/achieving it?
14. Are there conditions I have to meet to achieve/get it? (such as age, sex, children, income, employment, etc.)
15. Is this a smaller or larger part of another issue? (like Physical Health is a parent of Diabetes)
16. If one thing happens, does another thing usually follow? (both good and bad)

Task

- Please look at the drawing of the factors that influence well-being.
- Please write under the headings and draw your own pathways.
- Add issues/needs/solutions as you discuss and think about things.
- You can work as a group or alone—people can choose.
- Add as many more questions/descriptions as they/you want.
- Add balloons/bubbles as well, if you want to.

Pathways to Well-being Software

The software prototype developed for this project guides a conversation between a service provider case worker and a service user to assist in decisions of what actions to take and which resources are necessary to improve the well-being of the service user. Its aim is to provide a pathway for integrated services. The steps are as follows:

1. Listen to a variety of stored narratives of scenarios in the knowledge base and identify with one of them. This is not an automatic process, as it is an individual's perception of his or her own life. The only information

required to present suitable archetypes is a person's age and gender. This step establishes a baseline from which to begin building. The pathway (pattern of behavior) connected to the stored narrative enables the service user to identify with an "other" who has resolved his or her own situation. The stored pathway is used to begin the conversation to compare and then personalize the pathway.

2. The service user identifies issues and factors that are present in his or her life. These may be tangibles or nontangibles, such as children, homelessness, or lack of confidence. In addition, the user is asked how closely related he or she feels each factor is to the others and in which chronological order they came. The user is also asked to rank each of these in order of importance or impact.

3. Similarly, the immediate needs of the user are identified and the user asked to rank them in order of time requirement, importance, and interrelatedness.

4. The next step is for the service user to commit to an action. These actions are divided into two classifications: actions to include in the service user's life and those to exclude. The exploratory discussion for this step typically involves what-if scenarios to evaluate changes in the service user's behavior. Each action requires one or more resources, which may be provided by the organization itself or by referrals to other agencies. A resource may also be a book, a URL to an informational Web site, or a brochure.

From these steps both the service provider and the service user have an overview of multiple aspects of the service user's life as well as a printed guide to which actions he or she will take and which resources to use to resolve the issues.

In sessions following the preliminary one, a pathway may be reviewed and refined or a new pathway defined. These subsequent refinements also capture which actions and resources have been followed and which have been successful.

Evolving Knowledge

As the primary goal of the software is to find what works, how, and why, there is little personal information kept about the individual (Wahlstrom et al. 2008). Only the relevant demographic information, including sex, year of birth, SLA (statistical local area),[3] and number of dependents (aged or children), is stored with a unique identifier.

The data collected pertain to issues faced, the interrelationships among those issues, the services user's perceptions of the impact and required order of resolution, and the successes and failures of resources used.

These data continuously update the typical "patterns of behavior"[4] and refine them to better reflect the actual service users in the target areas of the service providers and the suitability of the services being provided in the area (Figure 14.5).

Figure 14.5 **Sequence of Evolving Knowledge**

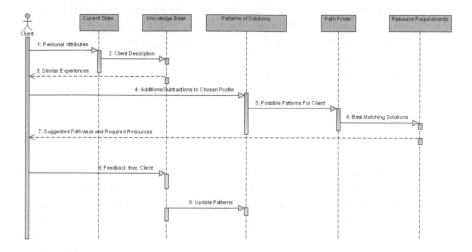

Source: The author.

Knowledge Management

In addition to the data-collection functions, the software also has tools to apply known data-mining and statistical methods on the collected data, which provide evidence of what the issues are and which resources are required to solve the issues (see also Chapter 17 on knowledge management issues). The analysis goes beyond standard statistical reporting, as associations, clusters, and strengths of interrelatedness are also quantified, enabling management to analyze contributing factors and consequences to issues that are faced and thus fine-tune and evolve their policies, services, and resources to what is required.

Quantitative analysis provides information such as the frequency of referrals to a particular service provider and trends over time of selected values. Qualitative analysis can highlight previously unknown factors, affecting good service delivery. For example, in this research, the need for a *friendly* reception and being *treated with respect* at a service provider was rated as an important *need* and had a great influence on whether the service was used at all.

Association-mining applications (Ceglar and Roddick 2006) elicit correlations between values, providing a picture of the probability of co-occurring problems and needs, showing which services should be evaluated for integration. Clustering applications such as K-means, DBSCAN, and self-organizing maps (SOM) (Berkhin 2006) show the spatial attributes of the data such as the prevalence of a particular service requirement in various SLAs.

Figure 14.6 **Evidence-Based Policy Development**

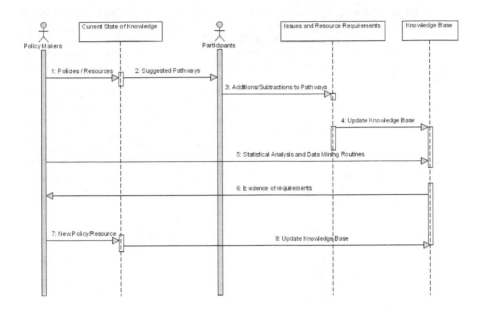

Source: The author.

These reports are together the bases for further research and consideration when forming policy and implementing changes to the management of resources. These updates, in turn, are recorded in the knowledge base (Figure 14.6), completing the cycle of knowledge management.

The benefits of knowledge management to an organization, including staff and clients, are:

- improved responses based on matching services with the users in terms of their demographic characteristics as well as their immediate assessed needs,
- streamlined and timely identification of and contact with appropriate service providers,
- minimum backtracking, as an individual service pathway is created to enable continuous progression,
- minimum staging, as the client is not moved in sequential stages from one service provider to another, obviating a needs assessment at every stage, and
- organizational data to analyze determined network gaps or inefficiencies, patterns of use, and social and operational costs.

Notes

1. Neporendi Aboriginal Forum Inc. is a nonprofit corporation providing a referral service for Aboriginal and non-Aboriginal people of all ages seeking assistance with food, accommodation, employment, training, health, well-being, and legal issues.

2. Rich pictures are advocated as one suitable means of expression. They are cartoonlike representations that allow people to express their experiences and accentuate points that stand out in their mind.

3. The SLA is a general-purpose spatial unit. In census years, the SLA consists of one or more whole collection districts. In noncensus years, the SLA is the smallest unit defined in the Australian Standard Geographical Classification. The SLA is the base spatial unit used to collect and disseminate statistics other than those collected from the population census.

4. The weighted concepts and issues are stored in mesodata structures within the database. These structures are weighted, fully connected graphs that enable enhanced queries to select sets of data in which values are *semantically* close to one another.

References

Alexander, Christopher. 1979. *The Timeless Way of Building.* Cambridge, MA: Harvard University Press.

Alexander, Christopher, et al. 1977. *A Pattern Language: Towns, Buildings, Construction.* New York: Oxford University Press.

Beck, Kent, and Cynthia Andres. 2004. *Extreme Programming Explained: Embrace Change.* 2d ed. Boston, MA: Addison-Wesley.

Berkhin, P. 2006. "A Survey of Clustering Data Mining Techniques." In *Grouping Multidimensional Data: Recent Advances in Clustering,* ed. J. Kogan, C. Nicholas, and M. Teboulle, 50–65. Berlin: Springer.

Ceglar, Aaron, and John F. Roddick. 2006. "Association Mining." *ACM Computing Surveys* 38 (2): 25–30.

Checkland, Peter B., and J. Scholes. 1990. *Soft Systems Methodology in Action.* Chichester: Wiley.

Christakis, Alexander, and Kenneth C. Bausch. 2006. *How People Harness Their Collective Wisdom and Power.* Greenwich, CT: Information Age Publishing.

de Vries, Denise. 2006. "Mesodata: Engineering Domains for Attribute Evolution and Data Integration." Ph.D. diss., School of Informatics and Engineering, Flinders University.

de Vries, Denise, et al. 2004. "In Support of Mesodata in Database Management Systems." In *15th International Conference on Database and Expert Systems Applications (DEXA 2004).* Zaragoza, Spain: Springer-Verlag.

de Vries, Denise, and J. Roddick. 2004. "Facilitating Database Attribute Domain Evolution Using Mesodata." In *3rd International Workshop on Evolution and Change in Data Management (ECDM2004).* Shanghai: Springer-Verlag.

La-Ongsri, Somluck, et al. 2008. "Accommodating mesodata into conceptual modelling methodologies." *Information and Software Technology* 50 (5): 424–435.

Martin, Robert Cecil. 2003. *Agile Software Development: Principles, Patterns, and Practices.* Upper Saddle River, NJ: Prentice Hall.

Mayo, Elton. 1946. *The Human Problems of an Industrial Civilization.* 2d ed. Boston: Division of Research Graduate School of Business Administration Harvard University.

McIntyre-Mills, Janet. 2008. *User-Centric Policy Design to Address Complex Needs.* New York: Nova Science Publishers.

Mullen, Edward J., et al. 2008. "Implementing Evidence-Based Social Work Practice." *Research on Social Work Practice* 18 (4): 325–338.

Rice, Sally P., et al. 2006. "Defining and Implementing Domains with Multiple Types Using Mesodata Modelling Techniques." In *3rd Asia-Pacific Conference on Conceptual Modelling (APCCM '06),* ed. Markus Stumptner et al. Hobart, Tasmania: ACS.

Roddick, John F., and Denise de Vries. 2006. "Reduce, Reuse, Recycle: Practical Approaches to Schema Integration, Evolution and Versioning." In *4th International Workshop on Evolution and Change in Data Management,* ed. Fabio Grandi. Tucson, AZ: Springer.

Taylor, F.W. 1911. *The Principles of Scientific Management.* New York: Harper and Brothers.

Wahlstrom, K., et al. 2008. "Legal and Technical Issues of Privacy Preservation in Data Mining." In *Encyclopedia of Data Warehousing and Mining,* 2d ed., ed. John Wang. Hershey, PA: IGI Publishing.

Weber, Max. 1968. *Economy and Society: An Outline of Interpretive Sociology.* New York: Bedminster Press.

Part IV

Future Directions

15

Governing with Foresight

Institutional Changes to Enhance Fact-Based Presidential Decision Making

John M. Kamensky

The federal government is facing increasing challenges without the capacity to manage them effectively. Donald Kettl, a public administration expert at the University of Pennsylvania, explains that "the problem often has to do with organizational structures and processes that no longer match reality" (Kettl 2000, p. 488). America's state and local governments are in similar positions.

Over the past two decades, the federal government's response has been to increasingly emphasize "managing for results," agency by agency and program by program (see Chapter 8 for a review). However, many of the federal government's challenges reach beyond the abilities of individual agencies and programs, and the White House does not have institutional mechanisms to foster the needed transformation to cross-program and cross-agency realities.

Consensus is growing that the federal government's machinery for governing is no longer adequate to address the extended range of national—not just federal—strategic challenges it faces. Several perceptive observers have called for a new national debate about better approaches. Former comptroller general David Walker, for example, advocated creating a set of national indicators to measure progress and extend existing requirements for agency strategic planning to a government-wide strategic plan (GAO 2005, p. 65). The Government Accountability Office (GAO), which Walker formerly headed, has assessed a possible alternative, the use of "national strategies"—topical, cross-agency strategic plans that have been developed largely in the national security arena—for potential application in other policy areas. There is also a growing use of the "performance-stat" model, which has been successfully used at the state and local levels as a mechanism to foster cross-agency actions around common outcomes (Behn 2007). This model has been proposed for use in the Executive Office of the President by John Podesta, chief of staff.

This chapter explores how such approaches could be used to upgrade the Obama administration's management agenda and bolster the president's capacity to lead the nation. Several recommendations for applying these approaches are offered.

Context

Under pressures of increasing complexity and interconnectedness—between agencies, between levels of government, and among the public, private, and nonprofit sectors—the issues facing governments are changing too rapidly for existing governmental institutions to keep up. Some careful observers have found little if any institutional capacity to focus on crosscutting outcomes and have determined that there is an increasing lack of national consensus on priorities and future directions. In contrast, other observers note that over the past two decades a foundation for addressing these complexities has begun to evolve. At the federal level, agencies have developed strategic plans, performance measures, and assessments of the performance of major programs that they administer, all major thrusts of the evidence-based management (EBMgt) movement. Some evidence also shows increasing citizen interest in engaging with governments on policy development as well as on implementation of programs and services. For example, in Boston, citizens are involved in measuring the health and performance of the city and its neighborhoods, and recommend ways to improve public safety as well as cultural life and the arts (Ho 2007, p. 23). At the same time, there is an increasing technical capability to connect people via the Internet to share data and insights gathered from experience.

Kettl has observed the increasing ineffectiveness of traditional vertical relationships in government and a trend toward replacing them with networks. However, he notes that "for public administration, the challenge is reconciling the management and accountability challenges of these networks with the bedrock that hierarchical authority has long provided. How can government ensure accountability in extended service networks where administrative responsibility is widely shared and where no one is truly in charge? How can government, structured and staffed for an era where vertical relationships dominated, build the capacity to manage horizontal partnerships effectively?" (Kettl 2000, p. 494).

The GAO's 2005 report *21st Century Challenges* mirrors Kettl's observations and offers an answer to his question: "The government is still trying to do business in ways that are based on conditions, priorities, and approaches that existed decades ago and are not well suited to 21st century challenges. . . . Government . . . must fundamentally reexamine not only its business processes, but also its outmoded organizational structures, management approaches, and in some cases, outdated missions. . . . Government must have the institutional capacity to plan more strategically, identify and react more expediently, and focus on achieving results" (GAO 2005, p. 64).

Developing Key National Indicators to Monitor Progress

Then comptroller general Walker hosted a forum in 2003 to begin a conversation about how to create some institutional capacity to plan more strategically by creating a set of key national indicators to assess the nation's position and progress. In launching this conversation, he noted, "More and better public information may be needed to effectively resolve current and future national challenges" (GAO 2003b, p. 1). He continued, saying: "There has been a long history—checkered by success and failure—of attempts to create sources of information that would inform our public dialogues and serve as a context for governance and civic choices." Walker cautioned, "A fully operational set of credible measures of our progress and prospects will take years to develop, require broad involvement of American society, and involve substantial resource commitments" (GAO 2003b, p. 2). Nevertheless, in a subsequent study of similar efforts in other countries and among U.S. state and local governments, he concluded that the effort would be worthwhile: "To be a leading democracy in the information age may very well mean producing unique public sources of objective, independent, scientifically grounded, and widely shared quality information so that we know where the United States stands now and how we are trending, on both an absolute and relative basis—including comparisons with other nations. By ensuring that the best facts are made more accessible and usable by the many different members of our society, we increase the probability of well-framed problems, good decisions, and effective solutions." (GAO 2004b, p. 2).

The comptroller general's initial forum sparked an informal effort at the National Academies of Science to begin laying a foundation for a national effort. While the federal government invests about $4 billion a year in gathering statistical information, that information is not readily accessible to most citizens and is targeted toward experts. The National Academies hosted a small group for several years as it reached out to experts to develop baseline questions that may be of interest to broader groups—citizens, media, and civic leaders. It also sought nonprofit foundation support for a more permanent organization. The group created connections to both international as well as U.S.-based grassroots efforts.

The group developed about 1,000 specific questions that were subsequently grouped into about 20 categories, such as economic, social, and environmental (see Appendix A). These questions were used to identify about 500 baseline indicators that would then be shared more widely in public forums to determine their relevance and usability. It also engaged similar ongoing state and local efforts, such as those embraced by the Community Indicators Consortium, a nonprofit that includes more than 170 subnational indicator initiatives.

The group was incorporated in early 2007 as the State of the USA, Inc. (SUSA), as a nonpartisan, nonprofit, public-private partnership that "seeks to illuminate our nation's progress with key quantitative metrics on the economy, the environment and society. Its initial goal is to create a state-of-the-art website that incorporates high-quality information and data from a broad range of public and private sources." It has initial foundation grant funding of about $3 million.

SUSA's purpose is "to provide nonpartisan, non-ideological and accurate information for a range of audiences—from nonprofits, government policymakers and commercial organizations to city planners, educators, engaged citizens and the media—to help Americans to assess our nation's position and progress in addressing important problems. By aggregating information, rather than collecting it, and by disseminating information, instead of interpreting it, SUSA will focus on filling the void for trusted, accessible and valuable facts in a transparent and highly actionable fashion" (SUSA 2007b, p. 2).

How SUSA approaches its goal of being a trusted source of quality information is important. As a result, the State of the USA's guiding principles include:

- Process characterized by openness, inclusiveness, and transparency
- Content shaped by extensive dialogue and diverse perspectives
- Combine audience value, political legitimacy, and scientific credibility
- Independent reporting of quality, reliable data
- Nonpartisan, nonideological, fair and balanced
- Assembly, not collection; dissemination, not interpretation
- Grounded in a broad-based public/private partnership

Of these principles, particular emphasis is being placed on providing an open and transparent process when identifying and reporting information. SUSA says it will try to pose answers to key questions such as:

- What key facts measure national progress?
- What is the difference between quality facts and spin?
- What is going well and what is not?
- Who is being affected and how?
- Compared to what?
- How can government be held accountable?
- How could independent quality information be used?

SUSA president Christopher Hoenig notes that existing technologies offer unique opportunities to make key indicators available to tens of millions of Americans in an engaging and useful form. Hoenig also notes the challenge of consolidating data in understandable format. He cited efforts going back to President Herbert Hoover that attempted to address this problem (National Academy for Public Administration 2007).

Hoenig observes that "the democratic system in the U.S. is predicated on civic involvement—on American citizens setting national priorities directly by the selection of their elected representatives and indirectly through their market choices. SUSA will facilitate more meaningful participation in these processes by providing citizens with reliable, objective and accessible information about their neighborhoods, their states and their nation" (SUSA 2007b, p. 4). When SUSA's Web site went live in early 2009 Hoenig said be hoped that "the data provided by SUSA will also help to ensure that decision-makers at all levels are responsive, accountable and effective. A common factual frame of reference, based on unbiased and high-quality key indicators as envisioned by SUSA, will allow for stronger civic dialogue."

Having an institutional capacity to create a broader public understanding of the position and progress of the nation will be an important element in creating a concerted focus on current and future national challenges. However, the Executive Office of the President has no existing institutional capacity to act on such information. Selected institutional elements focus on selected areas that cross agency boundaries in isolated sectors: the Office of Science and Technology focuses on science and technology, the Council on Environmental Quality focuses on the environment, and the Council of Economic Advisors focuses on the economy. However, there is no overarching mechanism to set a strategic direction for the federal government.

Creating a Government-wide Strategic Plan

There have been proposals to improve the strategic direction of the federal government by creating a government-wide strategic plan that sets and prioritizes goals among the government's programs. The GAO observes, "The federal government lacks a government-wide strategic plan to provide a framework for addressing crosscutting goals" (GAO 2005, p. 66).

In 2011, the Government Performance and Results Act (GPRA) will have been in place for eighteen years (see also Chapter 8). That law requires agencies to develop strategic plans and annual performance plans and to report annual progress against those plans. It also requires the Office of Management and Budget (OMB) to prepare an annual progress report for the entire government. OMB has been a reluctant contributor. In the early stages of the law's implementation, OMB developed a "derivative" government performance report by extracting information from individual agency reports. It then discontinued the reports because it believed there was no audience for the report and that preparing it was a waste of effort. OMB asserts that the president's annual budget contains the required information (GAO 2004c).

In 2004, GAO conducted a ten-year retrospective assessment of the implementation of GPRA and concluded, "A strategic plan for the federal government, supported by key national indicators to assess the government's performance, position, and progress, could provide an additional tool for government-wide reexamination of existing programs, as well as proposals for new programs . . . a strategic plan can provide a more comprehensive framework for considering organizational changes and making resource decisions" (GAO 2004c, pp. 104–105). The GAO suggested, "To provide a framework to identify long-term goals and strategies to address issues that cut across federal agencies, Congress should consider amending GPRA to require the President to develop a government-wide strategic plan" (GAO 2004c, p. 110).

In reaction to the GAO's suggestion, OMB deputy director Clay Johnson III under the Bush administration wrote, "With respect to your recommendation to produce a government-wide strategic and performance plan, we believe that the President's annual Budget represents the Executive Branch's government-wide strategic and performance plan. The President's Budget provides a strategic cross-cut of the President's priorities, and the Budget is providing increasing emphasis on performance" (GAO 2004c, p. 238). The GAO responded, "A government-wide strategic plan should provide a cohesive perspective on the long-term goals of the federal government and provide a basis for fully integrating, rather than primarily coordinating, a wide array of federal activities" (GAO 2004c, p. 111).

No consensus has emerged on how to bridge these GAO and OMB perspectives. However, there seems to be a practical alternative.

Using "National Strategies" to Foster Cross-Agency Strategic Direction

While the Bush administration's OMB resisted a comprehensive government-wide strategic plan, it had supported ad hoc cross-agency planning efforts around specific issues such as coordinating agencies that fight forest fires, and so forth, as well as several ongoing crosscutting issues (see Appendix B). In addition, the Bush White House adopted the use of "national strategies" as ways of marshaling government-wide—and sometimes national—efforts around specific challenges facing the nation, including the national strategies on homeland security, cybersecurity, and pandemic influenza. Use of national strategies has increased in the past decade, most commonly around homeland security issues (Kamensky 2006).

After the 9/11 terrorist attacks, President Bush recognized the criticality of developing a national—not just a federal—approach to fighting terrorism. He expanded the use of a relatively new policy vehicle—which the White House calls a "national strategy" document—as a way to create an overarching strategic plan around a specific need or outcome. One of the first, the ninety-page *National Strategy for Homeland Security,* was issued in July 2002 and updated in October 2007. It addresses the threat of terrorism in the United States and focuses on the domestic efforts of the federal, state, local, and private sectors. It identified three major goals—prevent terrorist attacks, reduce vulnerability, and minimize damage and recover from attacks. These are underpinned by six critical mission areas, each of which has five to twelve accompanying initiatives. For example, one critical mission area is "emergency preparedness and response," and related initiatives include the creation of a national incident management system and ensuring seamless communication among emergency responders. These are implemented via presidential directives (such as Homeland Security Presidential Directive 5), which in turn drive specific activities such as the development of the National Response Plan.

National strategy documents have been issued in the past. Their use seemed to have started under President Bill Clinton in the mid-1990s, for example, the *International Crime Control Strategy* in 1998. In fact, some were required by law, such as the 1997 *National Military Strategy of the United States of America*, but these were not signed by the president and largely dealt within the bounds of a specific agency. For example, the national military strategy was signed by the chairman of the Joint Chiefs of Staff and focuses on the armed forces—force structure, acquisition, doctrine, and so forth. Other agencies had developed crosscutting national strategies. For example, the Office of National Drug Control Policy's national strategy and the attorney general's interagency counterterrorism and technology crime plan preexisted the Bush administration.

About a dozen national strategy documents that address terrorism or related issues already exist (see Appendix C). But what is a "national strategy" document? Congress asked this question of the GAO, which concluded, "National strategies are not required by executive or legislative mandate to address a single, consistent set of characteristics . . . we found there was no commonly accepted set of characteristics used for an effective national strategy." As a helpful next step, the GAO developed a set of six "desirable" characteristics as part of its review (GAO 2004b):

- Purpose, scope, and methodology
- Problem definition and risk assessment
- Goals, subordinate objectives, activities, and performance measures
- Resources, investments, and risk management
- Organizational roles, responsibilities, and coordination
- Integration and implementation

The GAO developed these characteristics based on existing strategies, as well as the best practices that agencies had developed in drafting their strategic plans under GPRA. It found that national strategies differ from other federal government planning documents in that they were national—not just federal—in scope. They often had international components, and the federal government did not control many of the sectors, entities, or resources involved in implementing them. It also found a rough hierarchy among the various terror-related strategies and cross-references among them. For example, the *National Security* strategy provided an overarching strategy for national security as a whole, while the *Homeland Security* strategy provided more specific approaches to combating terrorism domestically.

However, more important than defining national strategies is an answer to the question, "So what?" National strategies, says GAO, "will not ensure a strategy-driven, integrated, and effective set of interagency, inter-organizational programs to implement these strategies" (GAO 2003a, p. 2). There is no single central entity that can control implementation, accountability, oversight, or coordination. That is the nature of a federal system of government. Moreover, if there are not common incentives that inspire joint federal-state-local-nongovernmental goals (such as those present in the pandemic flu initiative), the national strategies may revert to being of interest only to the federal government and become primarily a federal responsibility. So while this lack of a single point of accountability may concern the GAO, it may not concern others. Like most planning efforts, just the process of developing a plan may be the most valuable part of the process. It creates a dialogue among stakeholders around developing a common direction, developing relationships, and improving cooperation. GAO concerns about accountability and implementation may be important, but accountability may not be the only measure of success.

Creating a White House "Performance-Stat"

One response to the GAO's concerns about cross-agency accountability may be to adapt a successful management model being used at the local and state levels. Generically called "performance-stat," this model directly addresses the account- ability and implementation concerns noted by the GAO.

At the local and state levels, this model has been called "Comp-Stat" by the New York City Police Department, where it originated in the 1990s, "Citi-Stat" in the city of Baltimore, and "State-stat" in Maryland. As described by Professor Robert Behn, this management approach is a leadership strategy that a chief executive can use to mobilize action across a range of agencies to produce specific results. Its components include (1) an ongoing series of *regular, frequent, periodic, integrated meetings* during which (2) the chief executive and/or the principal members of the chief executive's leadership team plus (3) the individual leaders of different agencies (4) *use data* to analyze the agencies' past *performance* and contributions in relation to the strategic goal being examined, to (5) *follow up* on previous decisions and commitments to improve *performance,* (6) to establish the next set of *performance* objectives, and (7) to examine the effectiveness of overall *performance* strategies.

The meetings are organized by a small analytic staff reporting directly to the chief executive. That staff organizes the meetings, helps set the agenda, ensures that the right data and people are available during the meetings, and ensures follow- through on commitments made at the meetings. Creating an institutional "home" for fact-based decision making focused on strategic issues, such as those reflected in national strategies, would create accountability and focus. These approaches are increasingly being used both in industry and in selected areas in government (Davenport and Jarvenpaa 2008).

However, in the end, Behn (2007) notes, "The key aspect of this way of thinking about public management is a clear, express, detailed focus on performance." He says it has to be explicitly embraced by the top leader before it can be an effective leadership strategy.

The Y2K council, created to address the technological threat posed by date conversion to the year 2000, is an example of such a successful leadership strategy. John Podesta, a former White House chief of staff, suggested in 2007 that this ap- proach should be seriously considered by the new Obama administration (Center for American Progress 2007). In fact, several of the former presidential candidates had promised to use some variation of performance-stat if they were elected, but without necessarily defining any institutional characteristics.

Conclusions

Academics, practitioners, and other observers increasingly agree that the federal government is unable to define a long-term agenda, set key national priorities, focus on cross-boundary outcomes, and ensure accountability for achieving those outcomes. They agree on a need to rethink the governance structures that inform and guide the nation's strategic direction.

The Obama White House needs to be better organized institutionally to develop foresight based on facts and drive effective strategic action. Several efforts under way may be useful building blocks for President Obama in the future. The effort that may make the most immediate contribution is the development of key national indicators. The State of the USA's efforts to create a go-to Web site with relevant statistical data could contribute greatly to informing a national dialogue around strategic directions that the nation might pursue. Similar efforts, such as Virginia Performs (Council on Virginia's Future 2009) and the Boston Indicators Project, are already under way in states and localities, so there are potential models to adapt.

However, having good data will not be enough. The White House would need to be reconfigured to act on such information with greater strategic foresight. Specific "action" mechanisms—such as strategic plans or national strategies, and a performance-stat—would be useful institutional innovations to give President Obama the capacity needed to govern with greater foresight.

Recommendations

Recommendations to define a long-term agenda, set key national priorities, focus on cross-boundary outcomes, and ensure accountability for achieving those outcomes to be considered by the Obama administration include the following.

Support the creation and sustain the continuation of a set of nonpartisan key national indicators that have wide public support and understanding. A set of publicly accepted key national indicators of national performance and progress achieved would undergird a national consensus about strategic actions needed to meet key challenges facing the nation. Creating and fostering both the indicators and a national dialogue that engages citizens in defining the indicators and setting priority focus areas would be an important step. Once those indicators are created, ensuring that they are maintained and refined will be equally important. Whether this is done by law or via other approaches would be a separate decision.

Develop a government-wide, longer-term, outcome-oriented perspective by creating either a strategic plan or a small handful of targeted, key national strategies. The White House needs an institutional mechanism to focus on longer-term national challenges and create a set of widely shared priorities. The budget process is the current mechanism for doing this. However, its approach is too limited to be effective. Also, the budget development process does not allow adequate stakeholder engagement; it is too hierarchical, too bound by the existing agency and program structures, and too secretive. Either a strategic plan or a coordinated set of national strategies that focus on critical issues of national significance would provide a framework for strategic trade-offs. Developing such strategies should be done openly and should involve both stakeholders and citizens.

Establish a National Performance Council, supported by a small analytic staff that would adapt the performance-stat model to ensure focus and commitment to action on key national strategies. Once consensus is reached on national priorities and strategies, another institutional mechanism is needed that reaches across agency boundaries to create a collaborative engagement around strategies to achieve agreed-upon outcomes. A focal point is also needed to ensure accountability and action, as well as to mediate differences in approach. Establishing such a council would create a neutral broker for collaborative efforts among agencies and stakeholders. It would also monitor progress of strategies compared to the commitments made. To have the clout necessary to be effective, the council would need to work collaboratively with OMB to ensure appropriate budget and performance integration. A council with these characteristics would create the institutional capacity for the president to be more strategic and action oriented around longer-term challenges.

Appendix A. List of Major Issue Areas as Proposed in Version 1.0 of the State of the USA Indicators

- Animals, Plants, and Ecosystems
- Business
- Children and Families
- Civic Involvement
- Crime and Safety
- Ecosystem Goods and Services
- Education
- Employment and Labor Markets
- Financial Markets
- Government Finance
- Health
- Housing
- Income and Poverty
- Landscape
- National Security
- Population
- Prices and Inflation
- Production and Output
- Research and Development
- Soil, Water, and Air
- Values and Culture
- The World Economy

Source: State of the USA 2007a.

Appendix B. OMB Crosscutting Programs, FY 2008 Budget

- Homeland Security
- Statistical Programs
- Research and Development
- Federal Investment
- Credit and Insurance
- Aid to State and Local Governments
- Integrating Services with Information Technology
- Federal Drug Control
- California—Federal Bay—Delta Program

Source: U.S. Office of Management and Budget 2007.

Appendix C. List of National Strategies

Table 15.1

List of National Strategies

Strategy	Issued by	Date
National Military Strategy	Chairman of the Joint Chiefs of Staff	September 1997
National Drug Control Strategy	President	February 2002
National Strategy for Homeland Security	President	November 2003; updated October 2007
National Money Laundering Strategy	Secretary of the Treasury and Attorney General	July 2002
National Security Strategy	President	May 1997; updated September 2002
National Military Strategic Plan for the War on Terrorism	Chairman of the Joint Chiefs of Staff	October 2002; updated January 2005
National Strategy to Combat Weapons of Mass Destruction	President	December 2002
National Strategy for Combating Terrorism	President	February 2003; updated September 2006
National Strategy for the Physical Protection of Critical Infrastructure and Key Assets	President	February 2003
National Strategy to Secure Cyberspace	President	February 2003
National Strategy for Pandemic Influenza Preparedness and Response	President	November 2005
National Strategy for Maritime Security	President	October 2005
National Strategy for Victory in Iraq	President	December 2005
National Strategy to Internationalize Efforts Against Kleptocracy	President	August 2006
National Border Patrol Strategy	Commissioner, Customs and Border Protection (CBP)	September 2004

Sources: GAO 2003; George W. Bush White House Web site.

References

Behn, Robert. 2007. "Designing PerformanceStat: Or What Are the Key Strategic Choices that a Jurisdiction or Agency Must Make When Adapting the Compstat/CitiStat Class of Performance Strategies?" Paper presented at the Association for Public Policy Analysis and Management, Washington, DC, November 8–10.

Center for American Progress. 2007. "The Citi-Stat Model: How Data-Driven Government Can Increase Efficiency and Effectiveness." www.americanprogress.org/issues/2007/04/citistat.html (accessed April 4, 2008).

Community Indicators Consortium. 2007. "Creating Stronger Relationships between Community Indicator Projects and Government Performance Measurement Efforts." April. www.communityindicators.net/documents/Linkages%20Final%20Report.pdf (accessed November 1, 2009).

Council on Virginia's Future. 2009. "Measuring Virginia." www.vaperforms.virginia.gov/.

Davenport, Thomas, and Sirkaa Jarvenpaa. 2008. Strategic Use of Analytics in Government. Washington, DC: IBM Center for the Business of Government.

GAO. See U.S. Government Accountability Office.

Harris, Blake. 2000. "The Lessons of Y2K." Government Technology, December 1. www.govtech.com/gt/94602 (accessed April 9, 2008).

Ho, Alfred. 2007. Engaging Citizens in Measuring and Reporting Community Conditions: A Manager's Guide. Washington, DC: IBM Center for the Business of Government.

Kamensky, John. 2006. "Making Big Plans: Bush Expands Use of 'National Strategies.'" PA Times, October.

Kettl, Donald F. 2000. "The Transformation of Governance: Globalization, Devolution, and the Role of Government." Public Administration Review 60 (6): 488–496.

———. 2007. Panel on Executive Organization and Management. Minutes, May 18.

State of the USA. 2007a. "Informing Society in the 21st Century." OECD World Forum, June 29.

———. 2007b. The State of the USA: Educating Americans About the Position and Progress of the United States. Brochure.

U.S. Government Accountability Office. 2003a. Combating Terrorism: Observations on National Strategies Related to Terrorism. GAO-03–519T, March, Washington, DC: GAO.

———. 2003b. Forum on Key National Indicators: Assessing the Nation's Position and Progress. GAO-03–672SP, May, Washington, DC: GAO.

———. 2004a. Combating Terrorism: Evaluation of Selected Characteristics in National Strategies Related to Terrorism. GAO-04–408T, February, Washington, DC: GAO.

———. 2004b. Informing Our Nation: Improving How to Understand and Assess the USA's Position and Progress. GAO-05–1, November, Washington, DC: GAO.

———. 2004c. Results-Oriented Government: GPRA Has Established a Solid Foundation for Achieving Greater Results. GAO-04–38, March, Washington, DC: GAO.

———. 2005. 21st Century Challenges: Reexamining the Base of the Federal Government. GAO-05–325SP, February, Washington, DC: GAO.

U.S. Office of Management and Budget. 2007. "Fiscal Year 2008." Analytical Perspectives, "Crosscutting Programs." Washington, DC: OMB. www.whitehouse.gov/omb/budget/fy2008/pdf/apers/crosscutting.pdf (accessed November 1, 2009).

16

Driving Improvement in Federal Policy Outcomes

Lessons for a New President

Kathryn Newcomer and F. Stevens Redburn

The Obama administration, eager to improve government's performance, has the challenge of identifying what is worth retaining and what is not of the procedures established by the Bush administration—ideally throwing out the bathwater but keeping the baby. The Obama administration also has an opportunity to redeploy the assets it inherited and draw lessons from recent experience about what will be most effective in achieving presidential policy priorities.

Who should be responsible for guiding the federal government's performance in the Obama administration? How can the new president achieve real improvements in federal policy outcomes? We propose answers to these questions and offer concrete recommendations to the president on how to improve executive branch performance to achieve desired policy outcomes. Our guidance is based on our review of the experience of the last decade, with efforts to bring performance information to bear in improving how programs are managed and in improving decisions on policy design and use of resources (see Newcomer 2007, 2008; Government Accountability Office 2006; Frederickson and Frederickson 2006; Moynihan 2008).

As elaborated later in this chapter, we believe that:

- the president must set the tone and indicate to his cabinet and senior officials that performance improvement is a high priority;
- agency heads, not the Office of Management and Budget (OMB), must lead in improving performance, and agency executives must be held accountable for improving outcomes;
- at the highest level, priorities for program assessment should be set so that assessments focus mainly on programs important to the president's major policy priorities;
- gains in transparency and standards for assessing how well programs perform should be preserved and built on; and

- the assessment process's analytic and reporting burdens on both OMB and agencies should be reduced and better targeted.

Since enactment of the Government Performance and Results Act (GPRA) in 1993 (see also Chapter 8), the efforts of successive administrations have built a legacy of assets useful to the next administration: an armature of strategic plans and performance measures supported by an infrastructure of staff and processes in the agencies, built incrementally and now quite sophisticated. These have provided the executive branch with enhanced capacity to drive improved results at a time when there will be a growing premium on making better use of budget resources.

Despite these advances, our review of the experiences of those involved in managing program assessment and performance improvement at various levels across government suggests that these efforts have led, to date, to only limited improvement in government programs. This has raised questions about their cost-effectiveness, that is, about whether the time and energy devoted to assessing performance is justified by the returns in improving performance.

The advice provided here reflects lessons captured during the authors' interviews with more than forty staff and officers, both in OMB and in the agencies, held between March and September 2008. Synthesizing these views and our own, we offer a set of goals and recommended strategies to improve government performance in the new Obama administration.

Lessons from Recent Experience

The most important lessons from recent experience—expressed by a variety of participants in the process, including career staff of agencies, OMB examiners, and others, and drawn from our own observations—are summarized next.

Conflicting Purposes

Tracking performance measures and assessing program effectiveness have the potential to be used to improve programs and to inform budgetary allocations within the agencies, OMB, and Congress, but it is very difficult to select a set of measures or to design assessment tools that can achieve both objectives. Both processes require a large number of choices about what and how to measure, and how to draw appropriate comparisons, thus introducing the potential for differences of opinion about criteria for judgment.

The Bush administration developed and used the Program Assessment and Rating Tool (PART) as its principal means of driving performance improvement (see especially Redburn, Shea, and Buss, 2008; and Chapter 8). The two biggest concerns about the PART process expressed by OMB examiners were a lack of time to conduct and review the assessments, and conflicting priorities conveyed to them about their responsibilities tied to the budget and their role in PART reviews.

According to some examiners, there are fundamental differences between what the PART measures and the most important performance measures in agencies' strategic plans. Both OMB examiners and agency representatives reported frustration arising from disconnects between the focus of the PART instrument and agencies' strategic plans produced under GPRA. As one budget examiner summarized, "The outcomes defined by PART are not necessarily related to how agencies measure progress toward their strategic goals or how they define effectiveness—this has led to skepticism of the process by those [in the agencies] who view their plan measures as more meaningful" (confidential interview conducted by authors).

PART assessments have been used by OMB in two distinct ways that involve different information and actors: (1) to support accountability and (2) to support program improvement. Another way of viewing this is to distinguish between performance information that is useful for a broader audience, including the public and Congress, and performance information that is useful for agency program managers and partners in gauging and improving the effectiveness of their activities. For both purposes and audiences, better information is still needed to determine program effectiveness and cost-effectiveness.

Both agency and OMB participants in performance assessment recognize that trade-offs are made regarding the use of performance data for *strategic* decision making versus *operational* decision making. Data useful for informing agency planning and resource allocation and for legislative reauthorization deliberations are not likely to be the same data that line managers need to improve program implementation. Yet data collection is costly, and trade-offs are likely to be made in favor of compliance with needs for data required for strategic purposes, including decisions about policy and budget. When line managers view the data as intended for strategic purposes, their involvement and support for assessment may diminish.

Burden

Another aspect of the performance challenge is linked to the lack of agency staff capacity to measure results at the activity level; this is an area of particular concern among agencies with a large number of grant programs with distinct measures. The quality and consistency of information on program effectiveness is still inadequate in most policy domains. More, and more rigorous, program evaluations are needed to test the effectiveness of policies and programs, but these assessments require more resources for most agencies.

The prevailing view among agency staff and OMB examiners is that evidence of the relationship between the collection of performance data and improvements in government performance is not there—yet. Some agency officials are skeptical, or even cynical, about the benefits reaped by program managers and executives from program assessment and evaluation, especially when compared to the heavy costs entailed in both and when the resulting data are not used to inform decisions. There are very few examples of telling use of the information for program improvement.

There are also legitimate complaints that some one-size-fits-all sophisticated and costly evaluation requirements have been communicated to agencies, although it should be noted that a good deal of flawed communications have traveled downward within agencies.

There is evidence of "compliance creep," with the issuance of more and more reporting requirements. Any performance reporting requirements should be simple and manageable and, particularly, should not overprescribe. Unnecessary requirements cause executive agencies to spend additional resources to tailor or redesign their systems to meet the new requirements. This takes human resources and scarce funds for program management away from other needed tasks.

Use of Performance Assessments

Performance information, including program assessments, has the potential to be used by two distinct audiences or sets of users: one external to executive agencies and the other internal.

The external path of influence is through the decision-making process, beginning with budgeting and including interest groups, others in the public, and Congress. OMB officials sought the views of Congress during development of the program assessment process (PART), but Congress showed little interest and has paid little attention to PART results. OMB has made some use of PART results in developing and justifying elements of the president's budget. However, the Congress's apparent lack of interest has been a disincentive for agency leaders to fully invest in the process operated within OMB. More broadly, the expectation that making program assessments widely available would change legislative and budget decisions has not been fulfilled. The experience of both OMB examiners and agency staff is that while a great deal of time and money has been spent on getting the results on the Web—which has increased transparency—the public is not making use of this information yet.

The internal path for performance data to be used is through agency administration of programs, including use in improving program management. By focusing agencies on results and highlighting aspects of program management that are weak and need improvement to yield better results or improve efficiency, the program assessments required by OMB have had some positive influence on program performance. The observed average improvement in PART scores over the last five years may or may not be convincing evidence of this, but examiners and agency staff can provide numerous examples of how the assessment process contributed to better program administration and improved results (for example, see Gilmour and Lewis 2006).

Anecdotes aside, most observers agree that the OMB-led processes have failed to result in use by agency managers to improve either policy outcomes or program performance to a degree sufficient to justify the amount of effort that has gone into performance assessment and reporting. The yield on the assets is still disappointingly low.

Figure 16.1   **Federal Performance Management**

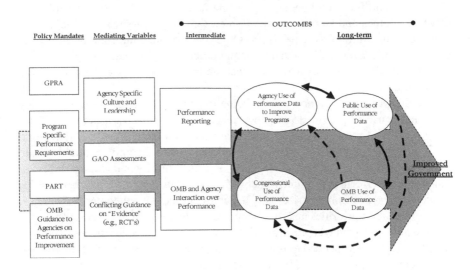

Figure 16.1 provides a snapshot of the complex paths through which use of performance data within the agencies may be increased. The arrows depict the potential for the use of performance data by both the OMB and Congress to increase the use of performance data within the agencies. In addition, there have been a variety of other factors in the environment that affect use of performance data—including legislative requirements, such as GPRA and other laws, and guidance and assessments provided by the Government Accountability Office, for example. The big question that has not been empirically tested is whether or not the use of performance data by the agencies, OMB, Congress, or the public results in improved government—and improved services rendered to the American people.

What's Next?

The president and his team in the executive agencies must be at the leading edge of the next frontier for achieving real, measurable, and significant improvement in federal program and policy performance. Political executives and senior managers must take ownership to ensure achievement of the key policy outcomes prioritized by the president.

The president has the means to hold agencies properly accountable for improved productivity in achieving mission-driven outcomes. For agencies to take more responsibility, OMB and the president's staff must step back and give agency leaders the flexibility to manage and to determine how they measure progress toward mission-related outcomes. Reporting of performance information upward—to the

White House and OMB for budget and policy making, to Congress, and to the public—should focus on how agency programs contribute to achieving mission-driven outcomes and should be used to monitor and judge success in advancing major administration policy priorities. Other performance information important to program managers and relevant to many other policy objectives should be the responsibility of the agency to develop, use, and report as they and their stakeholders require.

Incentives to use performance information to improve program and policy outcomes must be provided to agency leadership. A top-down, command-and-control system for driving performance management is simply not going to work; a more organic, empowering system is needed. Positive incentives should reward use of performance data, and a delegation of both authority and responsibility for making real performance improvements to agency leadership is needed. Asking agency leaders to commit periodically to achieving specific outcomes that connect to administration priorities and to show more productive use of the resources they receive through the budget process—without dictating to them the means of achieving those results—is needed to provide a higher rate of return on assets devoted to performance assessment than has been achieved in the past.

Suggested Initial Actions

Following are some actions that we believe should be taken by the Obama administration so the president can gain leverage quickly in improving executive branch performance to achieve desired policy outcomes:

- The president should identify a limited number of policy priorities and clarify that obtaining improved performance in these high-visibility policy and programmatic areas will be a critical priority for his administration.
- The president should assign accountability to agency executives to demonstrate progress in achieving his policy priorities and should require agency executives and senior leaders to expeditiously design and implement their strategies and processes for achieving improved outcomes in the new administration.
- The president should announce his commitment to transparency of performance reporting and a systematic, standardized approach to program assessment to support accountability.
- The president should use OMB strategically to support efforts to achieve high-priority policy and programmatic outcomes and should refocus OMB program assessments on a small set of high-priority targets for improved outcomes.

First Indications of the Obama Administration's Approach

During the first ten months of the Obama administration, there were signs that there would be a focus on the use of performance data to improve the performance of the federal government. President Obama appointed a chief performance officer for the federal government within OMB, Jeffrey Zients, and called for the retention of the performance improvement officers within the agencies—offices established by an executive order under the previous administration. In line with recommendations offered here, in the spring budget guidance to agencies, former OMB director Peter Orszag asked all major federal agencies to identify a limited number of high-priority performance goals reflecting the near-term implementation priorities of each agency's senior managers. In congressional testimony on September 24, 2009, Zients stated that "these goals communicate the priority targets that each agency's leadership wants to achieve over the next 12 to 24 months. Once this list is final, we will regularly review with agencies the progress they are making and the problems they are encountering. We will expect each agency to reach beyond their own organizational boundaries to get feedback about priorities and strategies and to enlist expertise and assistance to reach their targets." Zients also announced in September 2009 that OMB would develop a federal performance management framework that would be designed to serve the needs of agency managers, the public, and Congress—a tall order! It is clear that the Obama administration plans to replace the PART tool used in the Bush administration and to push for a strategic use of performance data and analysis moving forward.

Conclusion: Toward a More Strategic Approach

A strategic approach is needed to both performance planning and reporting. Authority and responsibility for ensuring that relevant and reliable data are collected and used to inform decision making in the agencies must be delegated to the agencies. The following represent general conclusions of the foregoing analysis of the previous administration's experience and the Obama administration's initial plans.

Goal 1: Strategic Presidential Leadership

The president must identify a limited number of policy objectives and ask his team to focus attention on improved performance in these high-visibility policy and programmatic areas. These priorities are likely to span the responsibilities of multiple agencies, which must collaborate effectively to achieve progress. Thus, for these major policy objectives, strategic performance planning, progress monitoring, and reporting need to be crosscutting. Relevant leaders and executives from all pertinent agencies must be brought together to collaborate and build integrated leadership and management processes to deliver the desired results.

The president should use OMB strategically, as elaborated below, and require only selective programmatic assessments that focus on sets of policies and programs that support the prioritized policy objectives—rather than asking OMB to manage the assessment of all programs.

Goal 2: Executive Accountability

The president should assign accountability to agency executives to demonstrate progress in achieving his policy priorities. Agency leaders should be charged with

- reporting regularly on performance to track achievement of major administration policy priorities, and coordinating with but not delegating this responsibility to staff offices;
- revisiting agency strategic plans, which should include consultation with relevant congressional stakeholders, and streamlining performance measurement and reporting processes to be in sync with refreshed agency strategic objectives;
- collaborating productively with state and nongovernmental service providers to prioritize and select appropriate measures to track achievement of outcomes related to their missions and achievement of their collaborative efforts;
- identifying a prioritized set of valid and reliable performance indicators that are deemed credible and useful internally, and supporting use of these measures throughout their agency to improve internal learning and management;
- streamlining performance reporting systems within their agency to reduce burdens where possible, and eliminating measurement where measures are not credible or useful;
- identifying a staff and consolidated system to administer and service performance reporting for purposes of program assessment, budgeting, and publishing of agency plans and performance accountability reports, consistent with OMB and GPRA requirements;
- clarifying to agency staff at all levels how agency strategic performance goals should be used to direct workforce staffing, and ensuring that all employees are involved and educated about how their work contributes to achievement of agency goals;
- leading processes within their agencies modeled after a "Citistat" or "State-stat" approach, in other words, regular discussions among senior managers about agency performance as measured by a limited set of valid, reliable, and frequently reported outcome measures, to focus regular attention to progress on the administration's highest-priority objectives;
- empowering and rewarding program managers for using performance information to improve programs;
- embracing transparency and a systematic, standardized approach to program assessment, key strengths of the PART process, by publishing results of program assessments and supporting explanation and evidence on the Web;
- supporting and funding strategic use of program evaluation methods by executives and program managers to address questions about both program implementation and results; and

- rewarding, publicly and frequently, achievement of mission-driven program outcomes, and providing rewards for performance (not simply for reporting) at all levels of the agency.

Goal 3: Strategic and Effective Use of OMB

The Executive Office and OMB should provide authority along with responsibility for achievement of mission-driven outcomes to agency leaders but should support political and career executives so that they can tailor strategies to their agency cultures rather than strive to meet one-size-fits-all management or performance reporting requirements.

The Office of Management and Budget should be used to support the agencies as they track outcomes and assess programs that correspond to presidential priorities, but OMB should not be the sole driver or primary arbiter of program performance ratings. OMB has strong leverage on the agencies through both its policy and budget formulation and its management oversight roles, but it does not have the needed capacity to adequately or fairly assess all federal programs on a regular basis and should not continue in this role.

OMB should continue and even strengthen its role in:

- crafting a government-wide performance and accountability plan;
- convening and supporting task forces of relevant multiagency stakeholders on crosscutting policy priorities;
- educating agency executives on performance measurement and reporting; for example, OMB staff, rather than contractors, should provide mandatory training for all political appointees on legislative and regulatory requirements regarding performance measurement and reporting;
- identifying efficiencies in meeting legislative performance reporting for all agencies to reduce reporting burdens; and
- facilitating collaboration and sharing of effective practices among agencies on generation and use of performance data, and effective use of information technology to facilitate performance reporting.

Note

An earlier version of this chapter was produced as a collaboration between George Washington University and the National Academy of Public Administration. We are grateful to the academy fellows who provided advice during this effort: Jonathan Breul, Harry Hatry, Phillip Joyce, Donald Kettl, Nancy Kingsbury, Paul Posner, Robert Shea, and Hannah Sistare. The recommendations were developed in consultation with the members of the advisory group but do not necessarily reflect the views of all members or of the academy as an institution.

References

Fredrickson, David G., and H. George Frederickson. 2006. *Measuring the Performance of the Hollow State.* Washington, DC: Georgetown University Press.

Gilmour, John B., and David E. Lewis. 2006. "Does Performance Budgeting Work? An Examination of the Office of Management and Budget's PART Scores." *Public Administration Review* 66 (5): 742–752.

Government Accountability Office. 2006. *Managing Results: Enhancing Agency Use of Performance Information for Management Decision Making.* GAO-06–927. Washington, DC: U.S. Government Accountability Office.

Moynihan, Donald P. 2008. *The Dynamics of Performance Management: Constructing Information and Reform.* Washington, DC: Georgetown University Press.

Newcomer, Kathryn. 2007. "How Does Program Performance Assessment Affect Program Management in the Federal Government?" *Public Performance and Management Review* 30 (3): 332–350.

———. 2008. "Measuring Government Performance." *International Journal of Public Administration* 30 (3): 307–329.

Redburn, F. Stevens, Robert Shea, and Terry F. Buss, eds. 2008. *Performance Management and Budgeting.* Armonk, NY: M.E. Sharpe.

17

Knowledge Management and Evidence

Anna Shillabeer

Knowledge management (KM) is concerned with understanding, organizing, and providing information. It is the study of how ideas, knowledge, and information are created, represented, communicated, and applied in a range of contexts. *Evidence* is defined as "information or signs indicating whether a belief or proposition is true or valid" (Hawker and Elliott 2005) and "data on which to base proof or to establish truth or falsehood, information etc., that gives reason for believing something" (Free Dictionary 2009). Evidence and KM are intertwined; neither exists in isolation. KM is the natural precursor for the provision of evidence, and evidence is similarly a natural product of KM. Issues with KM and the provision of evidence are becoming more frequently documented. Within government, policies are often developed at a frenetic pace to keep in line with global issues, and decisions are expected by an increasingly information-rich society to be justified and fully evidenced. More and more knowledge is required for this, and completeness is imperative to ensure against criticism and rebuttal from any person with Internet access to the vast numbers of documents available around the world. Too often we see careers destroyed by a single piece of information produced as evidence contrary to previous statements or recollections of events. Knowledge is rarely lost, but managing the ever-increasing volumes of knowledge that can be used as evidence is nontrivial.

Even with the realization that evidence and knowledge are inextricably linked and that a process of KM is what provides this evidence, there is still debate within government circles regarding implementation of formal knowledge processes leading to a state of flux within the practice of public management. Some believe that formalized, objective KM processes for the production of evidence are critical, while others believe that empirical subjective analysis of information will suffice; hence, there is debate between empirical and evidence-based decision-making camps. Experienced managers have "seen it all" and rely on what's gone before to advise; the less experienced "know it all" and rely on academic research learned at college, but are these two that dichotomous, and does either really have the optimal solution? Few would question that evidence to justify decisions should be broad, detailed, relevant to the issue, and timely and these needs can be satisfied by knowledge collaboration from all managerial types. Experience offers a context and history, and new ideas allow for creative applications of that experience to solve new problems; however, that experience and academic teaching are not often brought together to create a complete picture or broad evidence base upon which to develop decisions. This often results in an ongoing trial-and-error approach to public management strategic decision making.

An added constraint is that experience or training on which decisions are made stays with the individual. It is at the discretion of the individual to discern when to present that knowledge; however, it may not be within their jurisdiction or ability to do so effectively, and the motives for revealing or concealing knowledge that may be considered evidence may not be honorable. A more formal method of managing government-level knowledge can facilitate knowledge sharing, facilitate creative applications of that knowledge, provide accountability for decision making, and overcome the silo mentality pervading government. KM benefits government, as its products are informative in nature, whether policies, public fact sheets, application forms, sitting member contact details, guidelines, statutes, or any other, and the raw products for these items are data, information, and knowledge from a variety of sources.

While competitive advantage between agencies is a valuable resource, increasingly competitive employment markets promote a similar mentality in civil servants, who hoard rather than share ideas and knowledge in an effort to impress management and gain professional advantage at a time of their own choosing. At the agency level, this does not necessarily harm the operations of the agency, as most employees cannot wait to share their "genius"; however, problems surface when an employee moves to another agency or corporate entity, taking with him or her the valuable ideas, confidential knowledge, operational intelligence, and evidence for decisions developed and gathered while in a prior engagement. Adding to the mix is the effect of illegal activity, including data tampering, which changes or deletes data, removing the ability to find or rely upon that data for decision making; and espionage, where knowledge leaves the agency and is used for financial, political, or other gain, potentially without this being realized. While knowledge is not necessarily lost, a strategic advantage may be.

So, how can KM facilitate the provision of evidence to augment management and policy making? And what is the state of play for KM implementation within public management? These questions will be answered in a discussion of knowledge as evidence and an overview of the advantages and issues in implementing KM in public management.

Knowledge Assets

Knowledge is one of the most valuable assets for a manager to protect. Many millions of dollars are spent each year on computer security to maintain the confidentiality, availability, and integrity of corporate data and to prevent the devastating effects of computer crime, including hacking, malware, and espionage. There are also laws in force, for example, Sarbanes Oxley legislation in the United States, to ensure that corporate and public agency data are protected and managed in an appropriate manner (Sarbanes-Oxley Act 2002). Many businesses, for example, list brokers, focus on the provision of data for marketing or research purposes and enjoy multimillion-dollar turnovers. Knowledge is big business and recognized as a key factor in the success or otherwise of any agency or business entity (BEI Consulting 2003; Yelden and Albers 2004; Al-Hawamdeh 2002). However, it is too often not considered an asset that must be managed strategically, and audits do not assess the value of knowledge as they do machinery, products, or patents. Another often-overlooked resource is time. Governments move fast, and decisions need to be made faster to stay ahead of events, resulting in a need for rapid sourcing and assimilation of knowledge on which to base decisions. There is a constant battle to increase productivity and reduce time to publish information, but as with any process, this is only as fast as the slowest link, and unfortunately knowledge retrieval is usually the slowest step. There are many reasons for this.

Knowledge is maintained mentally and is not documented or shared. This is particularly the case with persons who perform tasks in isolation, who have been with the agency for long periods, or who have specialist skills or technical knowledge. This presents difficulties when knowledge is being collected; a large number of people must be individually consulted, and a high reliance is placed on recall, with little consideration of natural information filtering. If knowledge holders are on leave, then the decision must either be delayed or made without that input. People naturally omit reporting of tasks that are considered common sense or that are repetitive, monotonous, or reflexive, but this information may not be known to decision makers who are removed from the functional core of daily operations. This leads to decisions based on incomplete evidence, which potentially are not made with consideration of all critical factors, thus compounding the potential for failure of objectives or misrepresentation of presumed facts.

The application of agile software development and project management methodologies do not focus upon the production of specifications or documentation. Although these artifacts are considered a core deliverable for software projects, in environments that dictate tight development and delivery timelines and cost cutting wherever possible, this requirement can be overlooked. The result of this is loss of knowledge pertaining to system development and maintenance, leading to increased costs for support and the potential for bugs and information leaks to be introduced during maintenance that will cause lost productivity and potential homeland security threats into the long term. This impact is especially relevant to mission-critical software and systems holding classified information, which are common in strategic government sections.

Staff turnover, which is natural and expected, contributes to the first point, where mental knowledge ceases to be available once the holder of the knowledge leaves the agency. Often this knowledge is carried to new employment and utilized there, not always intentionally for means detrimental to the original agency but almost always to the benefit of the new employer. Decisions based upon this knowledge into the future will be flawed due to the incomplete foundation upon which the decision is built, and the lost knowledge may prove to be irreplaceable.

Many civil servants use local computer drives to store agency information, falsely considering them to be more secure than a public drive or because they provide faster access and avoid delays in such scenarios as a network connection being unavailable due to maintenance or criminal activity. The result is isolated data fragments that may not adhere to government guidelines, cannot be amalgamated into a central analysis, and may not be available for audit. An associated issue is the architecture of data storage, which can lead to information unavailability. Such issues as file or folder naming and directory structures can lead potentially to a situation where the knowledge is known to exist but cannot be found easily, if at all.

The need to ensure completeness of information without knowing what knowledge is held or how it is stored is a problem. If there is no system for logging information, then it may not even be realized that knowledge is held, and no search for or consideration of knowledge associated with a historic issue, solution, or prior decision will be incorporated into successive decisions. The solution requires extensive information auditing and documentation and often business process reengineering by specialist information consultants, requiring budgeting for what may be considered a noncore need.

While technology is designed to solve problems, often the same technology is the cause of issues. From the earliest computers in the 1950s there have been several hundred operating systems and information management programs. Windows alone boasts thirty-four versions (Wikipedia 2009). Since 2000 alone there have been 133 new operating systems or versions, and this represents only the digital data storage devices. A significant number of these new systems and versions are catering to the growing mobile technology markets. This is another hidden repository for knowledge, as these devices are used personally and are often not consciously considered to be within the agency knowledge domain. There are also microfiche, floppy disks, images, hard copies, and a plethora of other formats. This wide range gives us freedom of choice and allows us to make decisions on what is best for a particular application, but unfortunately this leads to an equally diverse range of information formats that are all too frequently not compatible and reduces the potential for amalgamation and analysis of all available knowledge in a timely manner. When versions of software are superseded, the speed with which the information created and managed by that tool becomes unreadable can be alarming. Imagine if today you were given a floppy disk, made less than ten years ago, that contains vital information. How long would it take to access that data and incorporate it into decision making?

Agency managers spend a significant amount of time and energy searching for knowledge due to the reasons mentioned previously. This means that one of their most valuable resources, time, is not used as productively as it should be, and time that is wasted in agency knowledge hide-and-seek could be much better channeled into core business functions. Some estimate that agencies can improve productivity by up to 30 percent through applying better KM practices (PowerKnow 2009). Knowledge that is lost due to personnel attrition is also costly in terms of both time and cost to replace the individual or retrain others to perform unallocated tasks and rebuild the lost knowledge base previously held by that one person. In financial terms, one estimate suggests this can equal two years' salary (PowerKnow 2009), but as knowledge development and retention vary among individuals, the same quality or amount of knowledge may never be replenished and hence a historical context can never be realized.

Apart from savings in time and financial cost, there is a long list of tangible and intangible benefits to protecting the knowledge assets of an agency (BEI Consulting 2003), including:

- Improved customer relations and level of service
- Reduced costs and faster times for maintenance tasks
- Reduced civil servant stress and improved morale
- Improved accuracy in estimates
- Improved quality, quantity, and standardization of outputs
- Faster policy development and higher acceptance
- More effective use of agency knowledge
- More effective and efficient decision making
- Improved facility to adhere to legal requirements
- Improved development and application of evaluation metrics
- Greater staff retention
- Overall reduced costs and improved productivity

Many of these are areas upon which government agencies focus and strive for improvement through traditional personnel-based initiatives and significant ongoing investment that often outweighs the small gains realized. Out of a need to increase financial viability or simply survive times of crisis, many agencies have employed crushing cutbacks, leaving little more to be squeezed from diminishing budgets and overloaded staff. The business case for implementing KM is substantial, but what methods and tools are available to facilitate the integration of KM into standard practice and agency philosophy?

Knowledge Management Practice

When KM practices began in the mid 1990s, KM was touted as an effective method for managing the ever-growing amount of data collected, but not yet used by government and business entities. It was primarily developed to partner analysis techniques, such as data mining, to provide an analytical capacity to facilitate a practical method of organizing data and turning it into meaningful information that could be applied to decision making and evidence-based investigations. Sydney University scholars define KM as "the design, implementation and review of social and technological activities and processes to improve the creating, sharing, and applying or using of knowledge within an organisational framework" (University of Technology Sydney 2009)—a small statement that encapsulates the field but also obscures the work and expertise required to implement such a simple-sounding ideal. There are a number of frameworks available to guide KM implementation (see, for example, Yelden and Albers 2004; Clarke 2004); many were developed for specific applications, such as semantic Web management, but all can be distilled into four steps:

- Knowledge acquisition
- Knowledge organization
- Knowledge sharing
- Knowledge application

Knowledge Acquisition

This is a natural consequence of agency processes; every e-mail, invoice, meeting minutes, training manual, and report contains information that when combined with experience and considered thought becomes knowledge that can be referenced and used in the future. However, this step is not merely concerned with collecting information and data on a daily basis that can become knowledge but on the process of transforming that data and information into actionable knowledge. Knowledge is not information and information is not data without transformation and elaboration.

Clarke's cognitive continuum is often cited in knowledge acquisition discussions, as it clearly demonstrates the need for both experiential and new influences to achieve the highest levels of cognitive processing (Clarke 2004). It suggests that the process of acquiring knowledge is at least three-dimensional and requires development of considered understanding of an artifact within specified contexts over time, leading to a collective wisdom that is ingrained within the fabric of government. Most government entities struggling with KM are trapped by an inability to move from first base and spend their KM time researching to form an understanding of what knowledge is available to them and gathering knowledge artifacts for each application in isolation. Clarke concurs that these knowledge artifacts require contextual processing before they can be deemed actionable knowledge but that each use builds on previous uses. Each part of the total knowledge base must be researched and combined with others, absorbed in the context of the decision to be made, and applied to the problem before a process of reflecting and sharing an abstraction of the artifact. This facilitates future novel applications based upon wisdom gained through previous iterations of that artifact. As discussed earlier, there is often little interaction between applications of knowledge artifacts and too frequently little reflection on the process or identification of quality improvement measures for successive iterations. For the next decision, the cycle starts again, thereby promoting a circular two-dimensional approach to knowledge application. There is therefore a need for a broader KM perspective in which the knowledge for decisions is held or applied not in isolation but in a broader government-wide knowledge environment where knowledge is valued and fully integrated into all agency processes as an interface to and between all intra- and interagency operations. Knowledge is essentially acquired in response to a decision point rather than in response to an agency function, making KM a reactive rather than proactive process. It is fragmented and isolated rather than integrated and assimilated. While Clarke's continuum represents the cognitive process involved in the development of higher-order information capacity, Figure 17.1 provides an adapted representation of knowledge acquisition and beyond that can serve as a template for KM from a government-wide perspective and demonstrates the responsibility domain for each process. Each civil servant should be responsible for identifying and capturing knowledge; a whole-of-government approach should be taken to define how knowledge is organized and to provide a single point of storage; and selecting, collating, applying, refining, and incorporating knowledge into everyday practice should occur at the agency level.

Knowledge Organization

For knowledge to be available, it must be accessible and available when, where, and how it is needed for a specific purpose. It needs to be easily assimilated into agency practices and amalgamated or isolated as required. Provision of data structures to facilitate this level of complexity is nontrivial and requires careful architecture. It requires the ability to store each artifice as an individual object but to provide a virtual data web with meta-analysis across all objects. Knowledge artifacts should be stored at a whole-of-government rather than decision level, except for classified information, and each artifact should be stored with reference to the time and date on which it was used, and the application for which it was used and related by reference so that the complete set of evidence for any decision can be retrieved for audit at any time. It must, of course, be realized that KM can truly be effective only in an electronic form. Hard-copy information can be isolated and invisible and is usually categorized in a subjectively limiting manner, resulting in its inability to be contextualized, accessed, or even realized. Use of ontologies and keyword coding can facilitate the process of electronic information organization, but again there is often a subjective aspect to this that can result in inconsistencies or imprecise coding, and the evolution of ontologies to accommodate changing agency foci is again nontrivial. These issues are the focus of current research in the fields of computer science and linguistics but are yet without demonstrated applied solutions in the public domain (DeVries and Roddick 2004; Shim and Shim 2006).

Most discussion on this point centers on the need to have a centralized store of information that can be accessed and searched by all with sufficient privileges. This

Figure 17.1   **Public Management Knowledge Domains**

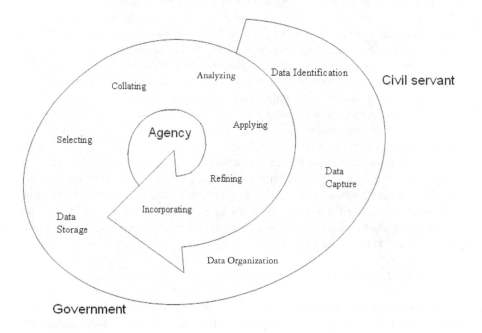

is a crucial step toward KM, but few have actually succeeded in this, and hence creation of an organized environment is a necessary first step before many of the issues identified previously can be overcome.

Knowledge Sharing and Distribution

Simply knowing what information is held by an agency and then storing it according to a universal structure does not in itself provide concrete benefit in terms of KM outcomes. The benefits of KM are realized only when the information is shared and applied.

Knowledge sharing is concerned with creating an awareness of the knowledge that an agency holds and ensuring that the knowledge is available to all agency members or external parties. The Internet has been a great facilitator of information sharing and provides an immense public repository for information. Intranets are also increasingly becoming vehicles of communication, and it has been suggested that information provision through e-mail is one of the greatest advances in government communications and collaborative facilitation (Al-Hawamdeh 2002). E-mails can be used either to notify of the existence of knowledge or to collect knowledge. They can also conversely form a repository of hidden knowledge accessible and understood only by the sender and the recipient and hence should be managed with careful consideration.

While information distribution is an intuitive step and the benefits are well documented, there are many examples of world-scale disaster resulting from a lack of knowledge sharing, as described in the following statement made on the floor of the House of Representatives by Lee H. Hamilton on November 8, 2005: "Poor information sharing was the single greatest failure of our government in the lead-up to the 9/11 attacks. The failure to share information adequately, within and across federal agencies, and from federal agencies to state and local authorities, was a significant contributing factor to our government's missteps in understanding and responding to the growing threat of al Qaeda in the years before the 9/11 attacks. There were several missed opportunities to disrupt the 9/11 plot. Most of them involved the failure to share information."

Even though allegedly the U.S. government held knowledge regarding potential terrorist activities, this knowledge was not shared and the results were disastrous by any measure. The impact of a lack of knowledge sharing is not always so hard-hitting, but there is a significant impact nonetheless at a localized level. Unless the knowledge is shared with all stakeholders and made available in a transparent form, it may as well not be held at all, as it is only when knowledge is available, understood, and applied that its power can be realized. An important factor in knowledge sharing identified in the Hamilton statement was the need not only to have a KM process defined and promoted but also to have a significant change of culture within government as a whole. Government decisions and knowledge are too often made at the agency level, leading to a propagation of the silo effect and the continued inability to make fully informed interagency decisions without a human knowledge carrier.

Metcalfe's law states that "the asset value of a computer network increases exponentially as each new node (individual user) is added to it" (Clarke 2004). This is of direct consequence to KM from various perspectives, as it provides a mechanism through which the capture, organization, and distribution of information can be facilitated and encouraged. It also suggests that the more nodes that are connected to the KM initiative, the greater potential for success in collecting and disseminating knowledge, as the sphere of influence will be greater. It also adds weight to the argument for KM implementation at a governmental level, as the effect would be greater than the sum of the effects at each individual agency level.

Knowledge Application

The application of knowledge can occur only if the preceding three processes have been achieved. The success of KM overall, however, is realized only when the resulting knowledge is applied to a task and is gauged by the somewhat subjective measures of effectiveness and usefulness (Clark 2004). The long-used term *garbage in, garbage out* certainly holds true here, and if the knowledge captured is of poor quality, then the knowledge applied and the resulting deliverable will also be of poor quality. Users must be educated in the need to provide quality inputs to ensure that the knowledge can truly be used as evidence—a reliable source of knowledge that can provide proof or otherwise of a concept. It is also important to facilitate this process by providing tools that genuinely facilitate KM and mimic the current KM processes of the users (Pfeffer and Sutton 2006). Change is not an easy concept to employ or manage, but if users' intuitive processes are leveraged, there is less likely to be antagonism toward the process and tools. Users must understand how, why, and where to place knowledge; why and how they must organize the knowledge; why and how they must make the knowledge available to others; and finally how to source and apply the knowledge that is available to them. Most important is the need to engage technologists that truly understand KM, government processes, and human psychology; this itself is not an easy task.

Application of knowledge to government processes is already occurring at the human level, so there is no question about the viability of applying the knowledge once it is made available. The difficulty is in removing the human repository of knowledge, and this is considered somewhere between very difficult and impossible and requires not only a process change and new technology but a complete culture change (Hurley and Green 2005). The question is, What evidence do we have for how governments have previously changed their knowledge culture and broadened their knowledge boundaries?

Application of Knowledge Management in Government

There are a number of documented roadmaps for KM. Few are roadmaps for success, as there is little to suggest that government has achieved any real success in this regard.

These initiatives describe KM as "critically important" and claim that not embracing the principles of KM will "undermine our success as a group by failing to fully share and collaborate" (NASA Team Collaboration 2009). KM is also considered critical to meeting "goals in the area of governance, economic development, protection of the environment, poverty alleviation and health and for the betterment of society as a whole" (UN Economic and Social Council 2002). These are not inconsequential statements from two influential organizations, but in the same publications it is also recognized that achieving maturity in KM will require considerable work and the achievement of "a number of substantive goals, policies, processes, actors, activities and structures" (UN Economic and Social Council 2002) that are developed collaboratively by government, academia, the private sector, and all citizens and result in improved e-literacy and connectivity for all stakeholders. On a global scale, the statistics on implementation of KM "add up to a fairly gloomy picture," with only thirty-seven countries having the capability to success and drive initiatives (UN Economic and Social Council 2002). Governments support and encourage innovation in science and technology, including KM, but lag behind in applying the results of these initiatives.

There are a number of fundamental impediments to success, and to overcome them the following issues and points of conjecture must be resolved (Gold, Malhotra, and Segars 2001).

The government must be seen as a leader in knowledge sharing and must make available its own knowledge in an organized, accessible form. There is much information in the public domain, but it is fragmented rather than centralized, and isolated at an agency level rather than integrated at a government level.

Diversity and integration of knowledge sources must be promoted as part of government culture to ensure completeness and integrity. This allows the knowledge provided to be verified and enhanced by a variety of input sources. Knowledge thus becomes a social, political, and corporate motivator through provision of a two-way flow of information.

A KM capacity must be developed and promoted within both government and the private sector. This capacity relies on an understanding of the cultural factors affecting knowledge sharing and absorption and the potential for incentives and rewards for engagement to facilitate the realization that power is gained through knowledge sharing rather than knowledge hoarding. Given that many of these "negative" cultural practices are endemic in the private sector and society in general, it is difficult to expect immediate success with these initiatives in government as a lone entity.

Education is required to promote KM objectives. Some suggest that this should commence within the public education system so that graduates and future leaders are equipped with an understanding of the principles and technologies required to implement a knowledge-centered management perspective in the future.

Cultural change is a factor in successful KM implementation. The need is for specialized change agents and the development of a supportive environment to drive the required cultural reorientation forward, and this must occur at a government rather than agency level or the pressure to slip backward will be too great and the perception of inequality will be the cause of further barriers. Fitting in is a basic psychological need within the human species, and such instinctive needs must be considered before any major change that could result in division is undertaken. If the current incumbents are entrenched in existing cultural practices, then change may be unfeasible; it may require a complete change of human resources to effect any real KM change. This of course requires that newly employed civil servants do not become indoctrinated before there is sufficient momentum to enforce change—again, not an easy commitment.

Financial burdens can be considerable in achieving these goals and in developing or procuring the necessary technological tools to implement effective KM. Due to the difficulty in performing a cost-benefit analysis for this, it is not easy to demonstrate that the required investment will be returned, and hence there will naturally be a reluctance to spend, especially in a financially constrained environment.

While there is a clear understanding of the benefits of KM and its potential to facilitate evidence-based public management, the final word is often that this is a difficult problem and more work needs to be done to determine if it is in fact feasible. The issues defined here are significant barriers to the implementation of KM in governments around the world, and there is quite simply no documented successful implementation of KM at the broad public management level and no standard framework to apply, although there is much research being done toward this goal. Unfortunately, until these issues have been resolved, no KM framework will deliver progress.

Success Criteria

Although we have yet to see what success looks like, there are success criteria available that agree upon the core requirements for a successful KM implementation (Gold, Malhotra, and Segars 2001), including the following:

- Prepare a knowledge environment. Educate the entire civil service on the benefits of KM and the advantages to themselves and to the process of government of sharing knowledge. Also, civil servants must understand that the knowledge they hold is essentially owned by the agency, not them.
- Understand the knowledge that is currently held within government through auditing knowledge resources. This requires consideration of the following questions:

  - What knowledge is currently held?
  - Where is it held?
  - Who owns the knowledge?
  - What format is it held in?
  - What are the common or disparate uses and users of each knowledge item?
  - What are the security risks and classification for each item?
  - What are the issues with use of each item?

Once this is known, a knowledge network model can be created and metrics can be developed to quantify the value of each item. This will provide a comprehensive view of what knowledge each agency holds and is responsible for organizing, disseminating, and applying.

The next step is to define what knowledge is used and determine how closely this aligns with the knowledge that is already held. This can be achieved by analyzing documentation on decisions, information requests, client questions, policy formulation, and so forth, and again developing a network model of what knowledge is used, where it originates, and where its use terminates. It is also important to speak with users to understand what knowledge is important to each person, role, or agency and what the generic or germane issues are with knowledge use, including what knowledge is not available but would add value to knowledge-based processes.

Not until these steps have been completed can the process of developing or implementing a government KM framework begin.

Conclusion

Too often it seems governments focus on the end result of KM and are unable to focus on the intermediate steps required to reach that endpoint—hence the over-arching statement that it is all too hard. With this as the prevailing message, it is no surprise that KM in public management is little more than a pipe dream and hence evidence-based practices are untenable for the foreseeable future. Rather than aiming for a complete KM solution and an almost overnight migration to evidence-based practices, the target should first be to simply understand all current knowledge assets and evidence uses within each government agency. Only then can government begin to look for technologies and frameworks to guide the management of that knowledge and thus the integration of evidence in their particular scenario. Robert Sutton states that companies have already wasted hundreds of millions on worthless KM systems with little or no measurable benefit, and we do not yet have documented evidence-based public management foundations, although again, many resources have already been consumed toward this goal, so there needs to be a change in methodology (Pearlman 2006). Much current research focuses on developing working frameworks and maturity models, but until we know what we are to manage, how can we possibly develop an effective management strategy for maturity or decide which framework to apply or which KM system will best suit our evidence needs? Clearly there is a need for further collaborative work among agencies, the government as a whole, and academia before evidence-based public management facilitated by effective KM can be realized with any measure of success.

References

Al-Hawamdeh, Suliman. 2002. "Knowledge Management: Re-thinking Information Management and Facing the Challenge of Managing Tacit Knowledge." *Information Research* 8 (1). http://InformationR.net/ir/8–1/paper143.html (accessed July 22, 2009).

BEI Consulting. 2003. "Estimating Return on Investment (ROI) for Knowledge Management (KM) Initiatives." www.bei-consulting.com/papera.pdf (accessed September 9, 2009).

Clark, Donald. 2004. "Knowledge Management." Big Dog and Little Dog's Performance Juxtaposition. www.nwlink.com/~donclark/knowledge/km.html (accessed September 24, 2009).

de Vries, Denise, and John Roddick. 2004. "Facilitating Database Attribute Domain Evolution Using Mesodata." In *Conceptual Modeling for Advanced Application Domains*. Lecture Notes in Computer Science 3289, 429–440. Berlin: Springer.

Free Dictionary. 2009. "Evidence." www.thefreedictionary.com/evidence (accessed June 16, 2009).

Gold, Andrew, Arvind Malhotra, and Albert Segars. 2001. "Knowledge Management: An Organisational Capabilities Perspective." *Journal of Management Information Systems* 18 (1): 185–214.

Hawker, Sara, and Julia Elliott. 2005. *Pocket Oxford English Dictionary.* 10th ed. Oxford: Oxford University Press.

Hurley, Tracy A., and Carolyn W. Green. 2005. "Creating a Knowledge Management Culture: The Role of Task, Structure, Technology and People in Encouraging Knowledge Creation and Transfer." http://cobacourses.creighton.edu/MAM/2005/papers/HurleyGreen%20 revision.doc (accessed October 19, 2009).

NASA Team Collaboration. 2009. Federal Knowledge Management Initiative. http://wiki. nasa.gov/cm/wiki/?id=6251 (accessed October 13, 2009).

Pearlman, Ellen. 2006. "Robert I. Sutton: Making a Case for Evidence-Based Management." *CIO Insight,* February 6 (interview). www.cioinsight.com/c/a/Expert-Voices/Robert-I-Sutton-Making-a-Case-for-EvidenceBased-Management/ (accessed May 21, 2009).

Pfeffer, Jeffrey, and Robert I. Sutton. (2006). *Hard Facts, Dangerous Half Truths, and Total Nonsense: Profiting from Evidence Based Management.* Cambridge, MA: Harvard Business School Press.

PowerKnow. 2009. "Knowledge Retention." www.powerknow.com/com/knowledge-retention-knowledge-preservation.htm (accessed September 9, 2009).

Sarbanes-Oxley Act. 2002. www.soxlaw.com/ (accessed 19 October 2008).

Shim, Junho, and Simon S.Y. Shim. 2006. "Ontology-based e-Catalog in e-Commerce." *Electronic Commerce Research and Applications* 5 (1) (special section).

UN Economic and Social Council. 2002. "Capacity of the Public Sector to Support the Creation and Application of Knowledge, Innovation and Technology for Development." Report of the Secretariat, May 10.

University of Technology Sydney. 2009. "About Information and Knowledge Management." Sydney University, New South Wales. http://www.communication.uts.edu. au/information_knowledge _management/about_information_knowledge_mgmt.html (accessed September 9, 2009).

Wikipedia. 2009. "List of Operating Systems." http://en.wikipedia.org/wiki/List_of_operating_systems (accessed September 9, 2009).

Yelden, Eugene, and James A. Albers. 2004. "The Business Case for Knowledge Management." *Journal of Knowledge Management Practice* 5 (August). www.tlainc.com/artic169.htm (accessed October 13, 2009).

About the Editors and Contributors

Editors

Anna Shillabeer is lecturer in information systems management at the Heinz College, Carnegie Mellon University, in Adelaide, Australia. She has worked as a Web developer and a fraud and behavioral analyst for the WorkCover Corporation in South Australia. She has also taught both undergraduate and postgraduate information technology courses for eight years in the areas of software engineering, project management, and database management. Her research focuses on medical informatics and the provision of automated tools to meet the unique needs of medical data analysis, with a particular focus on data-mining technologies.

Terry F. Buss, PhD, is distinguished professor of public policy at the Heinz College of Public Policy and Management, Carnegie Mellon University, in Adelaide, South Australia. He earned his doctorate in political science and mathematics from Ohio State University. He is one of a handful of people ever to be awarded two separate Fulbright Scholarships. He has published ten books and more than 350 journal articles, book chapters, edited books and journal symposia, and reports for national organizations. He is currently working on a book, *Performance Management for Developing Countries: Lessons without Borders* (London: Taylor and Francis).

Denise M. Rousseau, PhD, is the H.J. Heinz II University Professor of Organizational Behavior and Public Policy at Carnegie Mellon University's H. John Heinz III College and the Tepper School of Business. She is the faculty director of the Institute for Social Enterprise and Innovation and chair of the Health Care Policy and Management program. She was the 2004–2005 president of the Academy of Management and the 1998–2007 editor-in-chief of the *Journal of Organizational Behavior.* Rousseau received her AB, MA, and PhD from the University of California at Berkeley with degrees in psychology and anthropology. She has served on panels for the Institute of Medicine, National Science Foundation, and the National Institute for Education. Currently she serves on the editorial boards of five scholarly journals. She was previously on the faculty of Northwestern University's Kellogg School of Management, the University of Michigan's Department of Psychology and Institute for Social Research, and the Naval Postgraduate School at Monterey.

Contributors

Don Blohowiak is a certified executive coach and doctoral student at Fielding Graduate University.

Nathaniel J. Buss is in the doctoral program in public administration at the Center for Public Affairs and Policy, School of Public and International Affairs, Virginia Tech University.

David E. Cavazos, PhD, is assistant professor of management in the Department of Management, College of Business, at James Madison University in Harrisonburg, Virginia.

Roberto J. Cavazos, PhD, is a consultant in Washington, DC.

Denise de Vries, PhD, is a lecturer in the School of Computer Science, Engineering and Mathematics, at Flinders University, Adelaide, Australia.

Nancy Donovan is senior analyst in Applied Research and Methods at the U.S. Government Accountability Office in Washington, DC.

Judith A. Droitcour, PhD, is assistant director in Applied Research and Methods at the U.S. Government Accountability Office in Washington, DC.

Joshua Earl is on the staff of Thebarton Senior College in Adelaide, Australia.

Jeremy L. Hall, PhD, is assistant professor of public affairs, Graduate Programs of Public Affairs, University of Texas at Dallas.

Robert Hanson is principal risk adviser, Office of the Chief Information Officer, South Australian Government.

Evan Hill is senior policy officer, Division of Processes and Innovation, Department of Trade and Economic Development, in the South Australian Government.

Edward T. Jennings, Jr., PhD, is professor at the Martin School of Public Policy and Administration, University of Kentucky, Lexington.

John M. Kamensky is senior fellow and associate partner, IBM Center for the Business of Government, in Washington, DC.

Paul Kearns is director of Personnel Works Limited in Bristol, UK.

Nancy J. Kingsbury, PhD, is managing director of Applied Research and Methods at the U.S. Government Accountability Office in Washington, DC.

Alan Lyles, ScD, MPH, is Henry A. Rosenberg Professor of Public, Private and Nonprofit Partnerships, Health Systems Management, at the University of Baltimore's Yale Gordon College of Liberal Arts School of Public Affairs.

Kenneth J. Meier, PhD, is Charles H. Gregory Chair in the Department of Political Science at Texas A&M University, College Station, Texas.

Geoff Mulgan has been director of the Young Foundation in London since 2004.

Kathryn E. Newcomer, PhD, is director of the Trachtenberg School of Public Policy and Public Administration Program and codirector of the Midge Smith Center for Evaluation Effectiveness at George Washington University in Washington, DC.

Laurence J. O'Toole Jr., PhD, is the Margaret Hughes and Robert T. Golembiewski Professor of Public Administration in the Department of Public Administration and Policy, School of Public and International Affairs, at the University of Georgia.

Aaron Osterby is manager of systems solutions, Department for Family and Communities, in the South Australian Government.

F. Stevens Redburn, PhD, is study director, National Academy of Sciences, Washington, DC.

Stephanie L. Shipman, PhD, is assistant director of Applied Research and Methods at the U.S. Government Accountability Office in Washington, DC.

Ruth T. Zaplin, DPA, is assistant director of Key Executive Education Programs at American University in Washington, DC, president of the Zaplin Group, LLC, and a certified executive coach.

Index

CPSIA information can be obtained
at www.ICGtesting.com
Printed in the USA
LVHW081411081019
633555LV00017B/160/P